HOME GUARD LIST 1941

Northern Command

HOME GUARD LIST 1941

Northern Command

County Durham
Derbyshire
Leicestershire
Lincolnshire
Northamptonshire
Northumberland
Nottinghamshire
Rutland
Yorkshire

Published from original material held by the Imperial War Museum Department of Printed Books

Published by Savannah Publications, 90 Dartmouth Road, Forest Hill, London SE23 3HZ
Tel: +44 (0) 208 244 4350 Email: savpub@dircon.co.uk
Website: www.savannah-publications.com

British Library Cataloguing in Publication Data:
A CIP catalogue record is available from the British Library

ISBN: 9781902366241

Printed in the UK by Print Solutions Partnership

Cover design by Reggie Freeman

Cover photograph of the Home Guard was probably taken in the West Midlands (from the collection of Jon Mills)

TABLE OF CONTENTS

TABLE OF CONTENTS - contd.

TABLE OF CONTENTS - contd.

INTRODUCTION

Jon Mills

Created in May 1940 when a German invasion seemed imminent, the Local Defence Volunteers (LDV) were by July - and at Winston Churchill's insistence - renamed the Home Guard (HG). In the early days there were no ranks in the force and no officers. There was a system of appointments and some of these were clearly perceived as officers, but the War Office refused to grant military status to civilians and, with it, associated powers over regular troops.

It was not until February 1941 that the Home Guard was entitled to military ranks. Following the practice of the Army List, all HG officers were listed in the Home Guard List, of which this is the first edition. A separate list was published for each of the Military Commands into which the United Kingdom was divided. Subsequent editions were published at intervals until a final 'stand down' edition, dated October 1944, but actually published in August 1945.

These are some of the most rare documents of the Second World War. The size of the Commands dictated the number of copies printed and this was usually between 300 and 500 copies per Command. With the disbandment of the Home Guard, most seem to have been destroyed. Their republication provides an opportunity to study those who formed the Home Guard and laid the basis for the efficient defence force that it became. Many of those listed had already served their country during the First World War and the frequency with which the initials DSO, MC, DCM and MM appear after the officers' names indicates many brave and experienced soldiers serving as Home Guard officers. It is also interesting to find some who had already, by the time this list was published, been rewarded for services in the Second World War. More than one holder of the George Medal, not instituted until 1940, appears in the pages of these lists.

Each list has the same format. A dated title page is followed by a listing of the units within the publication. Corresponding to the HG's operational and administrative structure, this proceeds down the chain of command from Areas, to Zones, Groups and Battalions. Battalions are numbered within the counties in the Command, with any subsidiary title indicating a town, area or sometimes public utility where the battalion is based (e.g. 35th City of London (Hackney) Bn, 52nd County of London (Wandsworth) Gas Company Bn). Railway Company and General Post Office Battalions, together with some small independent units are also listed. At the end of each list is an alphabetical index showing on which page individuals can be found. A small section lists officers who have recently died and been removed from the List.

Within battalions, officers are listed by rank from the Commanding Officer downwards. Decorations to which they were entitled are indicated by post-nominal letters. In some cases former service is shown (for example, Major, late Rhodesia R, 2nd Lt Late E. Lanc. R.). HG battalions often varied in size and hence by number of officers. The 7th Cheshire (Crewe) Battalion has, including the regular Quartermaster (QM) and the Medical Officer, 98 officers in its ranks (including one retired Lieutenant Colonel serving as a 2nd Lieutenant). A few pages away the 11th Cheshire (Middlewich) Battalion has 38 officers (and no regular QM). The final entry for each officer gives his seniority date in the List. In the case of this List, an academic point, as they all have the date 1st February 1941, that at which HG officers were granted military rank.

These Lists will prove invaluable for medal collectors who can trace HG service and Defence Medal entitlement for many decorated officers, for local historians researching local personalities and for family historians now able, for the first time, to track down the commissioned service of their relatives who served with this unique force.

Northern Command

Covering the counties of Northumberland, Durham, Yorkshire, Derbyshire, Nottinghamshire, Lincolnshire, Leicestershire, Rutland and Northamptonshire this was the most rural of the Commands, with many wide open spaces used later in the war for training areas. Two unusual battalions could be found here, the 12th Leicestershire (Motor Recce) Battalion and the Trent River Patrol, whose members paraded in battledress with blue yachting caps.

Many of these counties were favoured retreats for retired officers and this is reflected in some of the battalion lists. Unlike some of the Commands, this List contains much information on the previous service of officers. Thus we can see that in the 2nd Northumberland (Alnwick) Battalion, of its 56 officers, 34 had previous military service. This ranged from the embryo RAF, through the RNVR and the Life Guards to the Army Cyclist Corps and from former Second Lieutenants to a former Indian Army Major General and ADC to the King. Other battalions in the Command drew their officers from the Canadian and Indian Armies, the Grenadier Guards, Machine Gun Corps, Tank Corps and 5th Dragoon Guards. Many similar stories may be discovered in this List.

Jon Mills

ARMY COUNCIL

CAPTAIN the Right Honourable H. DAVID R. MARGESSON, M.C., M.P., ret.

SECRETARY OF STATE FOR WAR
(President of the Army Council.)

BRIGADIER-GENERAL the Lord CROFT, C.M.G., T.D., ret. T.A.

PARLIAMENTARY UNDER-SECRETARY OF STATE FOR WAR
(Vice President of the Army Council.)

GENERAL Sir JOHN G. DILL, K.C.B., C.M.G., D.S.O., Col. E. Lan. R., i.d.c., p.s.c.† A.D.C.

CHIEF OF THE IMPERIAL GENERAL STAFF (First Military Member.)

LIEUTENANT-GENERAL Sir RONALD F. ADAM, Bt., C.B., D.S.O., O.B.E., Col. Comdt. R.A. and A.E.C., i.d.c., p.s.c.†

ADJUTANT-GENERAL TO THE FORCES (Second Military Member.)

GENERAL Sir WALTER K. VENNING, K.C.B., C.M.G., C.B.E., M.C., Col. D.C.L.I., p.s.c.†

QUARTER-MASTER-GENERAL TO THE FORCES (Third Military Member.)

LIEUTENANT-GENERAL (temp.) Sir HENRY R. POWNALL, K.B.E., C.B., D.S.O., M.C., i.d.c., p.s.c.†

VICE-CHIEF OF THE IMPERIAL GENERAL STAFF (Fourth Military Member.)

LIEUTENANT-COLONEL Sir EDWARD W. M. GRIGG, K.C.M.G., K.C.V.O., D.S.O., M.C., M.P., ret.

PARLIAMENTARY UNDER-SECRETARY OF STATE FOR WAR (Civil Member.)

CAPTAIN E. D. SANDYS, M.P., R.A. (T.A.)

FINANCIAL SECRETARY OF THE WAR OFFICE (Finance Member.)

Sir ROBERT J. SINCLAIR, K.B.E.

DIRECTOR-GENERAL OF ARMY REQUIREMENTS.

Sir JAMES GRIGG, K.C.B., K.C.S.I.

PERMANENT UNDER-SECRETARY OF STATE FOR WAR
(Secretary of the Army Council.)

56455-6(5)

HOME GUARD DIRECTORATE

Director-General	Maj.-Gen. (actg. 3/6/41) the Visct. Bridgeman, D.S.O., M.C., ret. pay (Res. of Off.) p.s.c.† (L)	3/ 6/41
Military Assistant	Capt. (actg. 4/3/41) L. A. Impey, Gen. List	3/ 6/41
Deputy Director	Lt.-Col. (temp. 18/11/40) K. Bayley, O.B.E., Oxf. & Bucks. L.I., p.s.c.†	-
Inspector of Administration	Lt.-Col. (actg. 7/5/41) P. C. Vellacott, D.S.O., Gen. List	7/ 5/41
Dep. Asst. Directors	Maj. (temp. 27/6/41) U. O. V. Verney, ret. pay (Res. of Off.)	27/ 3/41
	Capt. A. M Lindsay-Thomson, Res. of Off.	-
Staff Captains	Capt. (temp. 1/3/41) E. H. Ryley, Gen. List	30/11/40
	Capt. (temp. 26/2/40) C. E. Hodgson, M.B.E., R. War. R.	3/12/40
	Capt. R. T. Burton, O.B.E., Res. of Off.	-
	Capt. T. R. Wilbraham, Rifle Bde.	21/ 5/41

TERRITORIAL ARMY

Director-General	Maj.-Gen. (actg. 3/6/41) the Visct. Bridgeman, D.S.O., M.C. ret. pay (Res. of Off.) p.s.c.† (L)	-
Deputy Director-General	Lt.-Col. J. A. Longmore, M.B.E., T.D., Herts. R. (T.A.) t.a.	-

SPECIAL APPOINTMENTS

POST OFFICE GROUP

Commander	Reid, Col. F., M.C., T.D. (Lt. Col. ret. T.A.)	1/ 2/41
Second in command	Edwards, Lt.-Col. L. J.	1/ 2/41

LONDON MIDLAND AND SCOTTISH RAILWAY GROUP

Commander	Hussey, Col. G.S., M.C. (Capt. late R.E.)	1/ 2/41

SOUTHERN RAILWAY GROUP

Commander	Wymer, Col. F. J. (Capt. late R.G.A.)	1/ 2/41
Staff Officers	Ellson, Lt.-Col. K. R. (Lt. T.A.Res.)	1/ 2/41
	Layton, Lt.-Col. H. F., M.C. (Capt. late Rifle Bde.)	1/ 2/41
Staff Officer (A)	Mathews, Maj. H. S.	1/ 2/41
Assistant Staff Officer (A)	Cooper, Capt. C. J.	1/ 2/41
Assistant Staff Officer (G)	Reynolds, Lt. C. H.	1/ 2/41
Signals Officer	Hall, Maj. G. L.	1/ 2/41
Transport Officer	Potter, Maj. A. B.	1/ 8/41

NORTHERN COMMAND

General Staff Officer, 1st grade	Whatton, Lt.-Col. (actg. 22/3/41) S. M. de H., D.S.O., O.B.E., M.C., ret pay (Res. of off.)	22/ 3/41
General Staff Officer, 3rd grade	Collis, Capt. (actg. 28/3/41) H. J. G., Worc. R. (T.A.)	28/ 3/41

NORTHUMBERLAND DIVISION

General Staff Officer, 1st grade	Allen, Lt.-Col. R., ret. pay	-

NORTHUMBERLAND ZONE

Commander	Allendale, Col. The Visct., M.C., (Bt. Col. ret. T.A.)	1/ 2/41
Assistant to Commander	Gordon, Maj. E. B., C.M.G., D.S.O. (Lt.-Col. ret. pay)	1/ 2/41

Territorial Army Association administering	The Northumberland T.A. Association, Bowmer Bank, Morpeth.

No.1 GROUP

Commander	Bridgeman, Col. Hon. H. C. O., D.S.O., M.C. (Lt.-Col. late R.F.A.)	1/ 2/41

NORTHUMBERLAND DIVISION - contd.

NORTHUMBERLAND ZONE - contd.

No. 1 GROUP - contd.

1st NORTHUMBERLAND (BERWICK) BATTALION

Lt.-Colonel

Lambton, Hon. C., D.S.O. (Capt. late T.A.) 1/ 2/41

Majors

Joicey, The Lord, D.S.O. (Lt.-Col. ret. pay) 1/ 2/41
Mitchell, C., D.S.O., O.B.E., (Maj. late Gren. G'ds.) 1/ 2/41
Gilchrist, W. H. (Capt. late Foresters) 1/ 2/41
Goodson, Sir Alfred L. Bt. (Capt. late City of London Yeo.) 1/ 2/41

Captains

Milburn, A. W. (late North'd. H.) 1/ 2/41
Smail, H. R., T.D. (Maj. late R. North'd. Fus.) 1/ 2/41
Barber, A. H. (Lt. late R. North'd. Fus.) 1/ 2/41

Lieutenants

Watson, W. D.S.O. (Maj. ret. pay) 1/ 2/41
Heyder, J. G., M.C. (Capt. ret. pay) 1/ 2/41
Mackay, E. D. (Capt. late R. North'd. Fus.) 1/ 2/41
Atkinson, A., M.C. (Lt. late Middx. R.) 1/ 2/41
Taylor, C. E. (Capt. late Westmorland & Cumberland Yeo.) 1/ 2/41
Douglas, T. E. (Lt. late R.F.A.) 1/ 2/41
Robinson, R. 1/ 2/41
Scott, J. 1/ 2/41

Lieutenants - contd.

Durham, The Earl of (Capt. late North'd. Fus.) 1/ 2/41
Curry, F. S. 1/ 2/41
Hall, W. 1/ 2/41
Crow, F. S. C. 1/ 2/41
Davidson, W. 1/ 2/41
Miller, W. (Lt. late North'd. Fus.) 1/ 2/41
Watson, W. 7/ 5/41
Craster, G., C.B.E., D.S.O. (Col. late Ind. Army) 7/ 5/41
Haddon, W. G. 7/ 5/41
Grey, C. B. (Capt. late R.G.A.) 25/ 6/41
Patterson, J. 25/ 6/41

2nd Lieutenants

Rogers, J. L., M.C. (Lt. late M.G. Corps.) 1/ 2/41
Stawart, T. 1/ 2/41
Wardale, H. (Lt. late R.F.A.) 1/ 2/41
Lambert, G. G. 1/ 2/41
Dewhurst, L. 1/ 2/41
Hall, T. H. 1/ 2/41
Carmichael, J. W. L. 1/ 2/41
Macdonald, D. J. (Lt. late R.G.A.) 1/ 2/41
Reddihough, E. H. 7/ 5/41
Logan, J. J. 31/ 7/41

Adjutant & Quarter-Master

Blake, Capt. (actg. 9/5/41) Sir Francis E. C., Bt. T.A. Res. 9/ 5/41

Medical Officer

Sadler, Maj. J. T. 27/ 5/41

NORTHUMBERLAND DIVISION - contd.

NORTHUMBERLAND ZONE - contd.

No. 1 GROUP - contd.

2nd NORTHUMBERLAND (ALNWICK) BATTALION

Lt.-Colonel

Name	Date
Milvain, H. R. (Lt.-Col. late T.A.)	1/ 2/41

Majors

Name	Date
Beresford-Peirce, A.C.P. de la P., M.B.E. (Capt. late T.A. Res.)	1/ 2/41
Milward, Sir Clement A., K.C.I.E., C.B., C.B.E., D.S.O. (Maj.-Gen. ret. Ind. Army)	1/ 2/41
Straker, A. C. (Lt. late The Kings H.)	1/ 2/41
Fenwick, L. (Capt. late North'd. Fus.)	1/ 2/41
Carr-Ellison, C. F. C. (Capt. late T.A.)	1/ 2/41
McNay, G. Y. (Lt. late K.O.S.B.)	1/ 2/41

Captains

Name	Date
Mansfield J. H., M.M. (Lt. late Durham L. I.)	1/ 2/41
Donkin, T. O. (Capt. late R. North'd. Fus.)	1/ 2/41
Casey, W. J., M.M. (Lt. (Qr. Mr.) ret. H.L.I.)	1/ 2/41
Robson, J. E. (Capt. late R.S. Fus.)	1/ 2/41
Macdonald, W. (Capt. late Black Watch)	1/ 2/41

Lieutenants

Name	Date
Miller, W. R. (Lt. late Kings Own R.)	1/ 2/41
Milburn, Sir Leonard J., Bt. (Lt. late L. G.)	1/ 2/41
White, H., M.C. (Lt. late R. North'd. Fus.)	1/ 2/41
Shutt, C. S. (Capt. late A. Cyclist Corps)	1/ 2/41
Hardy, A. (Capt. late Foresters)	1/ 2/41
Jackson, D. P.	1/ 2/41
Scrowther, J.	1/ 2/41
Jackson, N. W.	1/ 2/41
Charleton, J. (Lt. late Gordons)	1/ 2/41
Patterson, C.	1/ 2/41
Goldie, R. M.	1/ 2/41
Howey, J. R.	1/ 2/41
Chrisp, J. F. H. (2/Lt. late North'd. H.)	1/ 2/41

Lieutenants - contd.

Name	Date
Hicks, F. W.	1/ 2/41
Hodgson, D.	1/ 2/41
Bound, C. G. (Lt. late Gloster R.)	1/ 2/41
Gibson, T.	1/ 2/41
Forster, C. M., O.B.E., T.D. (Maj. late R.E.)	1/ 2/41
Carr-Ellison, J. C. (Maj. late T.A.)	1/ 2/41
Frater, J. W. (2/Lt. late R.A.)	1/ 6/41
Grey, The Earl (Maj. late R. North'd. Fus.)	1/ 6/41
Phillips, J., D.C.M. (2/Lt. late Lan. Fus.)	1/ 6/41
Cushing, W. E. W. (Lt. late R.A.F.)	3/ 7/41

2nd Lieutenants

Name	Date
Lorimer, J. F., M.B.E.	1/ 2/41
Lynn, J., D.C.M., M.M.	1/ 2/41
Smetham, G. S.	1/ 2/41
Sinclair, R., M.C., M.M. (Capt. late D.W.R.)	1/ 2/41
Hemsley, F. J.	1/ 2/41
Ord. R., M.M.	1/ 2/41
Rutherford, H. I. F.	1/ 2/41
Bell, W. (2/Lt. late D.W.R.)	1/ 2/41
Sanderson, T. P. H.	1/ 2/41
Tully, A.	1/ 2/41
Smith, R. W. (Lt. late A.S.C.)	1/ 2/41
Gissing, A.	1/ 2/41
Kerr, W. (Lt. late M.G. Corps)	1/ 2/41
Sanderson, J. H. (Sub.-Lt. late R.N.V.R.)	1/ 2/41
Taylor, L.	1/ 2/41
Bland, W. J.	1/ 2/41
Nicoll, R.	1/ 2/41
Greenley, J. C.	1/ 2/41
Shell, M. B.	1/ 2/41
Archbold, J. C.	1/ 2/41
Hutchinson, J. I.	4/ 4/41

Adjutant & Quarter-Master

Medical Officer

Name	Date
Macleod, Maj. J. A. (Capt. late R.A.M.C.)	24/ 5/41

NORTHUMBERLAND DIVISION - contd.

NORTHUMBERLAND ZONE - contd.

No.2 GROUP

Commander — Straker, Col. R., O.B.E., M.C., T.D. (Lt.-Col. T.A.) 1/ 2/41

3rd NORTHUMBERLAND (MORPETH) BATTALION

Lt.-Colonel

Name	Date
Cruddas, B., D.S.O. (Bt. Col. ret. T.A.)	1/ 2/41

Majors

Name	Date
Sample, T. N. (Capt. late R.F.A.)	1/ 2/41
Abercrombie, J., M.B.E., M.M.	1/ 2/41
Swanston, C. B. (Capt. late R.A.F.)	1/ 2/41
Rutherford, G. L. (Flying Offr. late R.F.C.)	1/ 2/41
Pumphrey, C. E., M.C. (Capt. late Durham L.I.)	1/ 2/41
Flint, J. A. (Capt. late R. North'd. Fus.)	1/ 2/41
Craigs, W. N., M.C. (Lt. late R. North'd. Fus.)	1/ 2/41
Richards, A. S. E. (Capt. T.A. Res.)	1/ 2/41

Captains

Name	Date
Cowan, T. (2/Lt. late R. North'd. Fus.)	1/ 2/41
Fail, G. W.	1/ 2/41
Catcheside, G. A. (Capt. late A. Cyclists Corps.)	1/ 2/41
Dobson, S. G. M. (Lt. late R.G.A.)	1/ 2/41
Howell, G. F. (Lt. late The Buffs.)	1/ 2/41
Carmichael, N., M.M. (Lt. late R.T.C.)	1/ 2/41
Gibson, W.	1/ 2/41
Taylor, M. H. (Lt. late R.E.)	24/ 6/41

Lieutenants

Name	Date
Wilkinson, F. W. (Capt. late North'd. Fus.)	1/ 2/41
Barrow, H. G.	1/ 2/41
Harmer, T., M.M.	1/ 2/41
Robinson, W. G.	1/ 2/41
Scott, H. W., M.M.	1/ 2/41
Wilson, H. P.	1/ 2/41
Stanton, H. D.	1/ 2/41
Rogers, C. R.	1/ 2/41
Turner, W. E.	1/ 2/41
Armstrong, M. P. S. C.	1/ 2/41
Hully, M., M.C. (Lt. late Welch R.)	1/ 2/41
Miller, J. G.	1/ 2/41
Trevelyan, J. T.	1/ 2/41
Smith, J. E. (Lt. late North'd. H.)	1/ 2/41
Henderson, G. J.	1/ 2/41
Hall, W., M.C. (Lt. late North'd. Fus.)	1/ 2/41
Whitfield, W.	1/ 2/41
Atkin, R.	1/ 2/41
Welch, W. L.	1/ 2/41
Henderson, S. J., M.C. (Lt. late M.G. Corps.)	1/ 2/41
Fail, E. E. (2/Lt. late Scottish Horse)	1/ 2/41
Brian, R.	1/ 2/41
Ball, W. (Sub.-Lt. late R.N.V.R.)	1/ 2/41
Moscrop, T.	1/ 2/41
Amos, J. C.	1/ 2/41
Boutland, T.	1/ 2/41
Furness, J. J. (Lt. Res. of Off.)	1/ 2/41
Proctor, G. H.	1/ 2/41
Shepherd, J. D.	1/ 2/41
Downie, J. L.	1/ 2/41
Cannell, G. M.	1/ 2/41
Cummings, T.	23/ 7/41

NORTHUMBERLAND DIVISION - contd.

NORTHUMBERLAND ZONE - contd.

No. 2 GROUP - contd.

3rd Northumberland (Morpeth) Battalion - contd.

2nd Lieutenants

Name	Date
Harmer, R. H.	1/ 2/41
Smith, J. T.	1/ 2/41
Shaw, J. H.	1/ 2/41
Hindmarsh, T. L.	1/ 2/41
Barnes, H.	1/ 2/41
Howey, A., M.M.	1/ 2/41
Curley, W.	1/ 2/41
Hine, J. R. A.	1/ 2/41
Elliott, A. E. (Lt. late R. North'd. Fus.)	1/ 2/41
Ferguson, W. C.	1/ 2/41
Burnett, G. A. (Lt. late A.S.C.)	1/ 2/41
Dowson, R.	1/ 2/41
Nicholson, C., (Capt. late R.A.V.C.)	1/ 2/41
Middlemiss, G. A. (Capt. late R. North'd. Fus.)	1/ 2/41
Kennedy, G.	1/ 2/41
Suthren, D. P.	1/ 2/41
Mitchell, N.	1/ 2/41
Allison, H. H.	1/ 2/41
Lane, H.	1/ 2/41
Marriott-Statham, J. R.	1/ 2/41
Lawson, R. (2nd Lt. T.A. Res.)	1/ 2/41
Smailes, T. G.	1/ 2/41

Adjutant & Quarter Master

Medical Officer

Name	Date
Brown, Maj. H. S., M.D. (Capt. late R.A.M.C.)	17/ 6/41

14th NORTHUMBERLAND (BEDLINGTON) BATTALION

NORTHUMBERLAND DIVISION - contd.

NORTHUMBERLAND ZONE - contd.

NO. 3 GROUP

Commander — Greene, Col. J., D.S.O. (Hon. Brig. Gen. ret. pay) 1/ 2/41

5th NORTHUMBERLAND (GOSFORTH) BATTALION

Lt.-Colonel

Stevenson, W. E., T.D. (Maj. ret. T.A.) 1/ 2/41

Majors

Barrett, R. S. (Capt. late R.E.) 1/ 2/41
Irwin, H. (Lt.-Col. ret. R.F.A.) 1/ 2/41
Sweet, F., D.S.O. (Maj. late R.W. Fus.) 1/ 2/41
Pratt, R. S., M.C. (Lt.-Col. late Notts. & Derby R.) 1/ 2/41
Graham, C. W. (Lt. late R.A.) 1/ 2/41
Lennard, W. E., M.C. (2/Lt. late Durham L.I.) 1/ 2/41
Vart, V. (Capt. late Labour Corps) 21/ 4/41

Captains

Watson, W., M.C. (Maj. late T.A.) 1/ 2/41
Coates, J. M. S., O.B.E. (Capt. late M.G. Corps) 1/ 2/41
Edwards, J. T. 1/ 2/41
Lough, J. W. (Capt. late North'd. Fus.) 21/ 4/41

Lieutenants

Rayment, F., M.B.E., D.C.M. (Lt. Res. of Off.) 1/ 2/41
Robson, L. C. (Lt. late R.F.A.) 1/ 2/41
Mawson, G. S. (2/Lt. late M.G. Corps) 1/ 2/41
Cargill, D. R. (2/Lt. late R.E.) 1/ 2/41
Donaldson, W. A. 1/ 2/41
Graham, J., M.M. 1/ 2/41
Beaney, N. 1/ 2/41
Knox, J. 1/ 2/41
McSparron, S. 1/ 2/41
Watts, E. M. (Lt. ret. pay) 1/ 2/41
Cockburn, J. W. (Lt. late North'd. Fus.) 1/ 2/41
Milburn, R. 1/ 2/41
Whittingham, G. G. (Lt. late North'd. Fus.) 1/ 2/41
Welton, R. G. 1/ 2/41
Scott, T. M. (2/Lt. late R. North'd. Fus.) 1/ 2/41
Baxter, W. (Lt. late Durham L.I.) 1/ 2/41

Lieutenants - contd.

Clarke, W. H. (Lt. late Durham L.I.) 1/ 2/41
Wood, F. C. 1/ 2/41
Dendle, T. A. 1/ 2/41
Morley, S. 21/ 4/41
Child, F. A. 8/ 5/41
Stephenson, J. S. 5/ 7/41

2nd Lieutenants

Hutt, F. (Lt. late Durham L.I.) 1/ 2/41
Calvert, J. P. 1/ 2/41
Johnston, M. 1/ 2/41
Brass, A. M. 1/ 2/41
Proud, G. 1/ 2/41
Gregg, J. 1/ 2/41
Ridsdale, J. E. 1/ 2/41
Elliott, D. 1/ 2/41
Slater, J. R. 1/ 2/41
Cademy, H. 1/ 2/41
Hall, A. S. 1/ 2/41
Flanagan, P. 1/ 2/41
Charlton, P. A. 1/ 2/41
Howitt, V. H. (Lt. late North'd. Fus.) 1/ 2/41
Hedley, J. 1/ 2/41
Rae, R. A. E. 1/ 2/41
Armstrong, F. G. (2/Lt. late North'd. Fus.) 1/ 2/41
Hood, G. F. 1/ 2/41
Ballardie, I. S. 1/ 2/41
Fenwick, F. C. A. 1/ 2/41
Laidlaw, R. B. 1/ 2/41

Adjutant & Quarter-Master

Stabell, Capt. (actg. 26/4/41) A., Gen. List Inf. 26/ 4/41

Medical Officer

Picton, Maj. G. B., M.B. 29/ 7/41

56455-6 (13)

NORTHUMBERLAND DIVISION - contd.

NORTHUMBERLAND ZONE - contd.

NO. 3 GROUP - contd.

6th NORTHUMBERLAND (BLYTH) BATTALION

Lt.-Colonel

Watson, E. H., T.D. (Maj. ret. T.A.)	1/ 2/41

Majors

Williams, A. J. (Capt. late Welch R.)	1/ 2/41
Laird, A., M.C. (Capt. late Gloster R.)	1/ 2/41
Parry, N. O. (Lt. late R.W. Fus.)	1/ 2/41
Metcalf, J. A. (Lt. late R.E.)	1/ 2/41
Walton-Brown, S. (Capt. late R.A.S.C.)	1/ 2/41
Carson, J. S. (Lt. late R.E.)	1/ 2/41
Wintersgill, C. (Lt. late R.A.)	1/ 2/41
Gibson, J. A.	1/ 2/41
New, D. G. C.	19/ 6/41
Armstrong, G. C.	19/ 6/41
Ellis, G. L.	6/ 7/41

Captains

Thompson, W. H. (Maj. late R. Ir. Rif.)	1/ 2/41
Grenfell, H.	1/ 2/41
Porter, C. A. H.	1/ 2/41
Greig, A.	1/ 2/41
Amey, E. J.	1/ 2/41
Cullum, J. E.	19/ 6/41
Blunt, A. V. (Lt. late R.A.F.)	6/ 7/41
Welch, T. W.	8/ 7/41
Myers, R. C., M.M. (2/Lt. late R. North'd Fus.)	31/ 7/41

Lieutenants

Burrows, S.	1/ 2/41
Williams, T. J., M.M.	1/ 2/41
Foy, G. (2/Lt. late Durham L. I.)	1/ 2/41
Maddison, W.	1/ 2/41
Watson, A. H., M.C. (2/Lt. late R.E.)	1/ 2/41

Lieutenants - contd.

Wilson, T.	1/ 2/41
Agnew, W. E.	1/ 2/41
Aitchison, G.	1/ 2/41
Cogbill, A. J.	1/ 2/41
Oliver, R. J.	1/ 2/41
Sharp, R. M.	1/ 2/41
Croudace, C. T.	1/ 2/41
Thomson, C. J. (2/Lt. Lan. Fus.)	1/ 2/41
Hateley, T. S.	1/ 2/41
Armitage, G.	1/ 2/41
Sutherland, J. E.	1/ 2/41
Campbell, H. A. (Lt. late R.E.)	1/ 2/41
Barnes, W.	1/ 2/41
Wilson, G.	1/ 2/41
Trewick, M.	1/ 2/41
Pullan, S.	1/ 2/41
Minnikin, J.	1/ 2/41
Levy, F. (Lt. late Somerset L. I.)	1/ 2/41
Waugh, W. T.	1/ 2/41
Ward, J. J.	1/ 2/41
Reed, G. T.	1/ 2/41
Gilbertson, H. C.	1/ 2/41
Innerd, J. T.	1/ 2/41
Jackson, H.	1/ 2/41
Robson, T. W. (Capt. late North'd Fus.)	1/ 2/41
Dolan, J.	1/ 2/41
Seddon, W. M.	1/ 2/41
Robinson, C.	1/ 2/41
Smith, G.	1/ 2/41
Garrett, G.	1/ 2/41
Barlow, J. T.	1/ 2/41
Dalby, T. N.	1/ 2/41
Lamb, E. (Lt. late M.G. Corps)	1/ 2/41
Sanderson, G. (Lt. late R.G.A.)	19/ 6/41
Bullock, W. E.	6/ 7/41
Ashforth, F.	8/ 7/41
Crooks, C.	8/ 7/41
Bell, J. H., M.C. (Lt. late Foresters.)	1/ 8/41

56455-6(14)

NORTHUMBERLAND DIVISION - contd.

NORTHUMBERLAND ZONE - contd

NO. 3 GROUP - contd.

6th Northumberland (Blyth) Battalion - contd.

2nd Lieutenants

Name	Date
Carss, G. W.	1/ 2/41
McAlpine, D. D.	1/ 2/41
Venner, J.	1/ 2/41
Scott, J. H., M.M.	1/ 2/41
Mitchinson, W.	1/ 2/41
Grierson, J. J.	1/ 2/41
Lister, C. M.	1/ 2/41
Beaton, J. H.	1/ 2/41
Barrett, J. T.	1/ 2/41
Christmas, W. H., M.M.	1/ 2/41
Simpson, W.	1/ 2/41
Driffield, L. H.	1/ 2/41
Hymers, F.	1/ 2/41
Gleghorn, J. A.	1/ 2/41
Baron, D.	1/ 2/41
Gordon, T.	1/ 2/41
Laws, H. J.	1/ 2/41
Holmes, S. (Capt. late Durham, L. I.)	1/ 2/41
Murphy, T.	1/ 2/41
Reed, F.	1/ 2/41
Taylor, R.	1/ 2/41
Sharp, G. B.	1/ 2/41
Smeaton, J. J.	1/ 2/41
Dilks, F.	1/ 2/41
Wallett, J.	1/ 2/41
Whitfield, J. W., D.C.M.	1/ 2/41
Telford, W.	1/ 2/41
Davis, A. W.	1/ 2/41
Clayton, J. O.	1/ 2/41
Dixon, J. W.	1/ 2/41
Emmerson, G.	1/ 2/41
Fraser, W.	1/ 2/41
Henderson, G. W.	1/ 2/41
Dawson, T.	1/ 2/41
Warrener, S.	1/ 2/41
Little, J. P.	25/ 6/41
Robinson, C. N. B.	25/ 6/41
Taggart, J. W.	25/ 6/41
Taylor, R. T.	25/ 6/41
Lee, A.	18/ 7/41
Lee, G. W.	30/ 7/41

Adjutant & Quarter-Master

Name	Date
Burke, Capt. (actg. 1/5/41) E., Gen. List Inf.	1/ 5/41

Medical Officer

Name	Date
Eddleston, Maj. N. A., M.D.	18/ 6/41

NORTHUMBERLAND DIVISION - contd.

NORTHUMBERLAND ZONE - contd.

NO. 3 GROUP - contd.

7th NORTHUMBERLAND (TYNEMOUTH) BATTALION

Lt.-Colonel

Holmes, S. 1/ 2/41

Majors

Graham, H. (2/Lt. late R. Scots.) 1/ 2/41
Baume, F. H. (Capt. late D.W.R.) 1/ 2/41
Randell, J. W. (Lt. late Ind. Army) 1/ 2/41
Coulson, T. E., M.C. (Maj. late Durham L.I.) 1/ 2/41

Captains

Harvey, W. H. (Lt. late D.W.R.) 1/ 2/41
Blakey, J. F., M.C. (Lt. late Durham L.I.) 1/ 2/41
Langton, A. E. 1/ 2/41

Lieutenants

Wallace, J. R. (Capt. late Durham L.I.) 1/ 2/41
Sopwith, G., M.C. (Maj. late Durham L.I.) 1/ 2/41
Mouat, G. H. (Lt. late North'd. Fus.) 1/ 2/41
Darling, H. A. (Lt. late M.G.Corps) 1/ 2/41
Morpeth, R. 1/ 2/41
Veitch, L. D. 20/ 5/41
Cook, F. 20/ 5/41
Forsyth, C. H. 20/ 5/41
Craig, C. S., M.M. 20/ 5/41
Harrison, L. H. 20/ 5/41
Turner, J. R. 20/ 5/41
Patterson, J. A. 20/ 5/41
Jolley, W. 20/ 5/41
Brown, W., D.C.M., M.M. 20/ 5/41
Galilee, W. 20/ 5/41
Freeth, O. (Lt. late R.N.) 22/ 5/41
Watson, G. A. (Lt. late North'd. Fus.) 22/ 5/41
Stephenson, H. (2/Lt. late R.A.F.) 12/ 6/41

2nd Lieutenants

Carne, W. A. (Lt. late R.A.) 1/ 2/41
Harrison, L. H. (2/Lt. late N.Stafford R.) 1/ 2/41
Steedman, G. R. (2/Lt. late W. York. R.) 1/ 2/41
Hemsley, H. S. (2/Lt. late R.F.A.) 1/ 2/41
Trayhurn, G. (Lt. late North'd. Fus.) 1/ 2/41
Cheyne, J. P. 10/ 5/41
de Leeuw, R. H. 10/ 5/41
Ellis, J. W. 10/ 5/41
McMillan, P. H. 10/ 5/41
Munro, F. S. 10/ 5/41

2nd Lieutenants - contd.

Murray, T. B. 10/ 5/41
Ponton, H. 10/ 5/41
Rhoades, J. R. 10/ 5/41
Straughan, J. 10/ 5/41
Walker, J. M. 26/ 6/41
Johnson, M. 18/ 7/41

Adjutant & Quarter-Master

Meadows, Capt. (actg. 21/4/41) R. S., Gen. List Inf. 21/ 4/41

Medical Officer

Ogilvie, Maj. L. A., M.B. 10/ 5/41

15th NORTHUMBERLAND (FOREST HALL) BATTALION

Lt.-Colonel

Majors

Brass, H. W. (Capt. late R.E.) 9/ 6/41 1/ 2/41
Hamilton, M. C. (Capt. late S. Stafford R.) 9/ 6/41 1/ 2/41
Keating, J. W., M.C. (Capt. ret. R.A.) 9/ 6/41 1/ 2/41

Captains

Holdstock, H. T., M.C. (Capt. late R.A.F.) 9/ 6/41 1/ 2/41
Northern, A., C.B.E., D.S.O. (Lt.-Col. ret. pay) 30/ 6/41

Lieutenants

Keel, S. S. 9/ 6/41 1/ 2/41
Murray, D. C. 15/ 6/41
Christison, N. C. 1/ 7/41 1/ 2/41
Hall, J. L. 1/ 7/41 1/ 2/41

2nd Lieutenants

Philipson, L. 20/ 6/41
Smith, A. W. 30/ 6/41

Adjutant & Quarter-Master

Medical Officer

Craig, Maj. R. T. G. 9/ 6/41 1/ 2/41

56455-6 (16)

NORTHUMBERLAND DIVISION - contd.

NORTHUMBERLAND ZONE - contd.

NO. 4 GROUP

Commander	Bell, Col. G. F., T.D. (Bt. Col. ret. pay)	1/ 2/41
Second in Command	Sopwith, Maj. T. (Capt. late R. North'd. Fus.)	7/ 3/41
Assistant to Commander	Bird, Capt. W. G.	8/ 3/41

8th NORTHUMBERLAND (WALLSEND) BATTALION

Lt.-Colonel

Hall, J. J. W.	1/ 2/41

Majors

Walker, A.	1/ 2/41
Grice, J. J.	1/ 2/41
Lamble, J. M. S. (Lt. T.A. Res.)	1/ 2/41
Tweedy, I. M. (Maj. late T.A.)	1/ 2/41
Wilson, R.	1/ 2/41
Lithgow, H.	1/ 2/41
Redshaw, F. W., M.C., M.M. (Lt. late Y. & L.R.)	16/ 5/41
Crofton, H. B.	16/ 5/41
Nunn, G. (Lt. late Ind. Army)	16/ 5/41
Askew, J.	16/ 5/41
Maller, H. C. (2/Lt. late R.A.F.)	16/ 5/41

Captains

Campbell, H., M.C. D.C.M. (Lt. late R.E.)	1/ 2/41
O'Hanlon, J. M.	1/ 2/41
Embleton, G. W.	1/ 2/41
Halliburton, R.	1/ 2/41
Hayes, J. E. (2/Lt. late T.A.)	16/ 5/41
Christie, P. D. (Lt. R.N.V.R.)	16/ 5/41
Lightfoot, G.	16/ 5/41
Wilson, R. D.	16/ 5/41
Peak, T. T.	16/ 5/41
Wilkin, T. T.	16/ 5/41
O'Hara, J.	9/ 7/41

Lieutenants

Taylor, H. (2/Lt. late R.E.)	1/ 2/41
Ness, R.	1/ 2/41
Martin, G. W. S.	1/ 2/41
Cooper, T. K. (Capt. late K.O.Y.L.I.)	1/ 2/41
Leftwich, J. (2/Lt. late R.A.F.)	1/ 2/41
Boiston, C. W.	1/ 2/41
Mitchell, W.	1/ 2/41
Moderate, J. S.	1/ 2/41
Stapylton, T.	1/ 2/41
Guthrie, T.	1/ 2/41
Pringle, E. N.	1/ 2/41
Laws, W. G.	1/ 2/41
Rhoades, J. A. (Lt. late Can. Mil. Forces)	16/ 5/41
King, J. S.	16/ 5/41

Lieutenants - contd.

Smith, S.	16/ 5/41
Craggs, K. F.	16/ 5/41
Heywood, J. K.	16/ 5/41
Waller, M. A.	16/ 5/41
Wedderburn, H.	16/ 5/41
Tynan, J.	16/ 5/41
Wade, S. J.	16/ 5/41
Yeoman, E.	16/ 5/41
Turnbull, C. F.	16/ 5/41
Jopling, D.	16/ 5/41
Burn, J. H.	16/ 5/41
Paul, J. C.	16/ 5/41
Lennox, E. C.	16/ 5/41
McColm, T. C.	16/ 5/41
Anderson, G. E.	16/ 5/41
Banks, W. V.	16/ 5/41
Bell, R. H.	16/ 5/41
Legg, R. S.	16/ 5/41
Mackie, G. A. O.	16/ 5/41
Petrie, E. R. F.	16/ 5/41
Gospel, J. W.	30/ 6/41
Laws, J. W.	9/ 7/41

2nd Lieutenants

Veitch, A. E. (Lt. late R. North'd. Fus.)	1/ 2/41
Harley, W. S.	1/ 2/41
Hopkins, H.	1/ 2/41
Spencer, W. G.	1/ 2/41
Smith, F.	1/ 2/41
Taylor, J.	1/ 2/41
Bolt, P. T.	16/ 5/41
Dodsworth, H.	16/ 5/41
Smith, J. E.	16/ 5/41
Whyte, W.	16/ 5/41
Wood, J. L.	16/ 5/41
Greenshields, J.	8/ 6/41

Adjutant & Quarter-Master

Medical Officer

Mackenzie, Maj. A. W. R.	16/ 5/41

56455-6 (17)

NORTHUMBERLAND DIVISION - contd.

NORTHUMBERLAND ZONE - contd.

NO. 4 GROUP - contd.

9th NORTHUMBERLAND (CENTRAL NEWCASTLE) BATTALION

Lt.-Colonel

Parmeter, T. P. (Capt. ret. T.A.)	1/ 2/41

Majors

Falconer, K. J. (Lt. late Gordons)	1/ 2/41
Hartley, N. H.	1/ 2/41
Nesbit, F., M.M. (Lt. late North'd. Fus.)	1/ 2/41
Coyle, J. E. (Lt. late North'd. Fus.)	1/ 2/41
Andrews, W. F. (Capt. late The King's R.)	1/ 2/41
Gibson, A. (2/Lt. late Durham L.I.)	1/ 2/41
Cashman, J. D. (2/Lt. late D.W.R.)	7/ 7/41

Captains

Howey, T. W., M.C. (Capt. late Durham L.I.)	1/ 2/41
Richardson, W.	1/ 2/41
Seddon, E. B. (2/Lt. late R.F.A.)	1/ 2/41
Peters, N. (Lt. late R.F.C.)	1/ 2/41
Trail, A. J. F.	1/ 2/41
Donaldson, B. (2/Lt. late Durham L.I.)	1/ 2/41
Foreman, W. W.	1/ 2/41
Richardson, H. (2/Lt. late D.W.R.)	1/ 2/41
Harbottle, G., M.C. (2/Lt. late M.G.Corps)	1/ 2/41
Cross, A.	27/ 6/41

Lieutenants

Burgoyne-Johnson, G. H. (Lt. late R.A.F.)	1/ 2/41
Clapham, E. W. (Lt. late A. Cyclist Corps)	1/ 2/41
Coates, J. P.	1/ 2/41
Dix, C. W.	1/ 2/41
Fisher, W. L.	1/ 2/41
Gray, G. S.	1/ 2/41
Gunn, W. E. (Lt. late Welch R.)	1/ 2/41
Harvey, F. W.	1/ 2/41
Ker, G.	1/ 2/41
McAndrew, T. D.	1/ 2/41
McNeil, D. (Lt. late K.R.R.C.)	1/ 2/41
Malthouse, G. (2/Lt. late M.G.Corps)	1/ 2/41
Marks, H. V., M.C. (2/Lt. late North'd. Fus.)	1/ 2/41
Middleton, A. (Lt. late W. Yorks R.)	1/ 2/41

Lieutenants - contd.

Morrison, S. (Capt. T.A. Res.)	1/ 2/41
Pink, F.	1/ 2/41
Proctor, L. S.	1/ 2/41
Read, K. B. (Lt. late Ind. Army)	1/ 2/41
Ridley, H. C.	1/ 2/41
Thistle, A. G. (Flying Offr. late R.A.F.)	1/ 2/41
Thompson, J. C. (Lt. late North'd. Fus.)	1/ 2/41
Turton, P. (2/Lt. late The King's R.)	1/ 2/41
Walker, A. J.	1/ 2/41
Winter, R.	1/ 2/41
Winter, W.	1/ 2/41
Watson, G. H.	1/ 2/41
Forster, T.	2/ 5/41
Wood, J. H.	2/ 5/41
Booth, M. V.	7/ 7/41

2nd Lieutenants

Harwood, J. C.	2/ 6/41
Hindle, W. V. (Pilot Offr. late R.A.F.)	2/ 6/41
Smith, S. C. D. (2/Lt. late R. Fus.)	2/ 6/41
Bell, T. R. A.	18/ 6/41
Bustard, E. E. (Lt. late R.A.S.C.)	27/ 6/41
Ferguson, J. E.	27/ 6/41
Veitch, T.	27/ 6/41
Carter, W. C.	4/ 7/41
Curtice, R. W. (Lt. late Beds. & Herts. R.)	4/ 7/41
Plunkett, J.	4/ 7/41
Mawer, R. S.	1/ 8/41
Wheeler, H.	1/ 8/41

Adjutant & Quarter-Master

Medical Officer

Harrison, Maj. W. J., (Maj. late R.A.M.C.)	16/ 5/41

NORTHUMBERLAND DIVISION - contd.

NORTHUMBERLAND ZONE - contd.

NO. 4 GROUP - contd.

11th NORTHUMBERLAND (WEST NEWCASTLE) BATTALION

Lt.-Colonel

Rogers, A. D. S., T.D. (Bt. Col. T.A. Res.) 1/ 2/41

Majors

Wright, G. W., M.M., T.D. (Bt. Lt.-Col. ret. R.A.M.C.) 1/ 2/41
Blake, J. (Lt. late R. Norfolk R.) 1/ 2/41
Blackburn, J. W. K. (Capt. late Loyal R.) 1/ 2/41
Johnston, W. (Sqn./Ldr. late R.A.F.) 1/ 2/41
Smith, E. G. (Lt. late R. North'd. Fus.) 1/ 2/41
Clifford, E. K. (Flying Offr. late R.A.F.) 22/ 4/41
McQueen, G. (Capt. late R. North'd. Fus.) 22/ 4/41

Captains

Rose, F., A.F.C. (Capt. late R.F.C.) 1/ 2/41
Barnett, E. P. (Lt. late Durham L.I.) 1/ 2/41
Farina, T. G. (Capt. late North'd. Fus.) 1/ 2/41
Turner, W. H. (Lt. late R.T.C.) 1/ 2/41
Dixon, J. G. H. (Lt. late Green Howards) 1/ 2/41
MacLennan, R. R. F. 1/ 2/41
Dixon, J. E. (Capt. late Durham L.I.) 1/ 2/41
Scott, H. B. 1/ 2/41
Hendin, J. R. 22/ 4/41
Robson, E. S. 22/ 4/41
Davison, R. (Lt. late E. Lan. R.) 1/ 6/41
Crawford, J., M.M. 1/ 6/41
Carr, W. (Lt. late R. North'd. Fus.) 7/ 6/41

Lieutenants

Turnbull, S. (Lt. late T.A. Res.) 1/ 2/41
Cockerell, P. C., M.C. (2/Lt. late North'd. Fus.) 1/ 2/41
Telfer, J. (Capt. late R.F.A.) 1/ 2/41
Wallis, C. H. 1/ 2/41
Wallace, B. J. 1/ 2/41
Garvey, F. S. 1/ 2/41
Cotton, J. P. (2/Lt. late Durham L.I.) 1/ 2/41
Charlton, R. W. (Flight Lt. late R.A.F.) 1/ 2/41
Brown, T. W. (Lt. late Border R.) 1/ 2/41

Lieutenants - contd.

Langstaff, S. 1/ 2/41
Douglas, G. 1/ 2/41
Crawford, T. H. 1/ 2/41
Langstaff, G. W. 1/ 2/41
Jacob, G. H., M.M. (2/Lt. late Durham L.I.) 1/ 2/41
Chisholm, C. 1/ 2/41
Lattimer, R. P. (2/Lt. late Durham L.I.) 1/ 2/41
Gibb, N. 1/ 2/41
Allinson, J. A. 1/ 2/41
Gibson, W. (2/Lt. late North'd. Fus.) 1/ 2/41
Middlemas, T. F., M.M. 1/ 2/41
Henson, E. W. (2/Lt. late R.A.S.C.) 1/ 2/41
Hardie, E. R. (2/Lt. late A. & S.H.) 1/ 2/41
Rutter, F. W. (Lt. late Durham L.I.) 15/ 4/41
Adams, W. (Lt. late R.G.A.) 1/ 6/41
Wright, M. 1/ 6/41
Watson, S. C. 1/ 6/41
Nesbit, A. (2/Lt. late North'd. Fus.) 1/ 6/41
Bamber, T., M.M. 7/ 6/41
Wightman, W. 7/ 6/41
Sutherland, J. 13/ 6/41
Anderson, G. 15/ 7/41
Charlton, J. A. 15/ 7/41
Bell, A. H. 28/ 7/41

2nd Lieutenants

Dunne, C. 1/ 2/41
Heron, A. T. 1/ 2/41
Turner, C., M.M. 1/ 2/41
Rowley, W. A. 1/ 2/41
Browell, G. 1/ 2/41
Shield, T. 1/ 2/41
Hutchinson, J. 1/ 2/41
Kerr, R. 1/ 2/41
Chester, F. A. 1/ 5/41
Mawer, G. W. (2/Lt. late Black Watch) 20/ 6/41
Pickard, F. W., M.M. 20/ 6/41
Smith, C. C. 20/ 6/41

Adjutant & Quarter-Master

Medical Officer

Stephenson, Maj. G. E., M.C., M.D. (Capt. late R.A.M.C.) 15/ 4/41

12th NORTHUMBERLAND (EAST NEWCASTLE) BATTALION

Lt.-Colonel

Macdonald, J., M.C. (Maj. late T.A.) 1/ 2/41

Majors

Robinson, E. N. (Capt. late Green Howards) 1/ 2/41
Mennie, J. B., M.C. (Lt. late Cheshire R.) 1/ 2/41
Patterson, H. (Lt. late R.E.) 1/ 2/41
Murton, H. A. (Lt. late M.G. Corps) 1/ 2/41
Bell, F. V. (Maj. late R.A.F.) 1/ 2/41
Adam, G., M.C. (Capt. late R.E.) 1/ 2/41
Ingham, C. B. (Lt. late R.F.A.) 1/ 2/41
Potter, H. C. 1/ 2/41

Captains

Keenlyside, T. H. (Capt. late R. Sussex R.) 1/ 2/41
Wright, R. W., M.C. (Capt. late North'd Fus.) 1/ 2/41
Pickavance, J. 1/ 2/41
Walton, D. P. (Lt. late R.E.) 1/ 2/41
Wilkens, F. J. M. (2/Lt. late Camerons) 1/ 2/41
Storey, A., M.M. 1/ 2/41
Mole, J. L. 1/ 2/41
Buchan, H. R. 1/ 2/41

Lieutenants

Smith, M. D. 1/ 2/41
Turner, R. (Capt. late R.A.F.) 1/ 2/41
Golightly, W. 1/ 2/41
Paulin, W. S. 1/ 2/41
d'Assis Fonesca, H. J. M. 1/ 2/41
Brown, E. D., M.C. (Lt. late North'd Fus.) 1/ 2/41
Berkley, M. C. 1/ 2/41
Armstrong, H. J. (Capt. late R. North'd Fus.) 1/ 2/41
Barnett, G. J. (Lt. late W. Yorks R.) 18/ 6/41

2nd Lieutenants

Baker, G. M. 1/ 2/41
Browne, C. 1/ 2/41

2nd Lieutenants - contd.

Clark, T. 1/ 2/41
Craggs, W. J. 1/ 2/41
Cushing, T. 1/ 2/41
Davidson, V. S. 1/ 2/41
Duff, N. B. 1/ 2/41
Erikson, E. 1/ 2/41
Field, W. H. 1/ 2/41
Goss, J. R. 1/ 2/41
Jowett, E. (Lt. late R.W.K.) 1/ 2/41
Lewis, E. L. 1/ 2/41
McDowell, T. P., M.C., D.C.M., (Lt. late Rifle Bde.) 1/ 2/41
McQuillen, H. J. 1/ 2/41
Murdoch, S. S. 1/ 2/41
Richmond, I. A. 1/ 2/41
Robson, S. 1/ 2/41
Sawyers, S. M. 1/ 2/41
Sisson, G. M. 1/ 2/41
Storey, W. 1/ 2/41
Taylor, G. 1/ 2/41
Torry, F. W. 1/ 2/41
Stokes, A. E., M.M. 1/ 2/41
Barton, G. J. 1/ 2/41
Moorhead, F. 1/ 2/41
Thompson, V. 10/ 4/41
Caughey, J. A. 5/ 6/41
Davidson, F. A. 18/ 6/41
Duncan, W. S. 18/ 6/41
Hindmarsh, W. J. 18/ 6/41
Lucas, G. F. 18/ 6/41
Ritchie, W. A. 4/ 7/41
Goodwin, R. 9/ 7/41
Grainger, R. 9/ 7/41
Thirlwell, J. M. 26/ 7/41

Adjutant & Quarter-Master

Medical Officer

Shanley, Maj. G. H. (Lt. late North'd Fus.) 18/ 6/41

NORTHUMBERLAND DIVISION - contd.

NORTHUMBERLAND ZONE - contd.

NO. 5 GROUP

Commander	Jebb, Lt.-Col. G. D., C.B., C.M.G., C.B.E., D.S.O. (Hon. Brig.-Gen. ret. pay)	1/ 6/41

4th NORTHUMBERLAND (HEXHAM) BATTALION

Lt.-Colonel

Robb, J. R.	1/ 2/41

Majors

Trobridge, F. G., D.S.O. (Maj. late Gen. List)	1/ 2/41
Tulby, H. (Capt. late R. Mar.)	1/ 2/41
Renwick, W. L. (Capt. late Cameronians)	1/ 2/41
Grover, E. E. (Capt. late North'd. Fus.)	1/ 2/41
Straker, J. A. (Maj. late 9th L.)	1/ 2/41
Smith, D. (Capt. late Border R.)	1/ 2/41
Daysh, G. H. J.	1/ 2/41
Gent, C. R. (Maj. late M.G. Corps)	25/ 4/41

Captains

Patterson, W.	1/ 2/41
Clark, B. W.	1/ 2/41
Steenberg, F. S. (Lt. late M.G. Corps)	1/ 2/41
Keith, A. M. (Capt. late Derby Yeo.)	1/ 2/41
Lakeman, R. M. (Capt. late North'd. Fus.)	1/ 2/41
Renwick, G. F. (Lt. late E. Yorks R.)	1/ 2/41
Meyrick, R. (Lt. late Wilts R.)	1/ 2/41
Kewley, H.	1/ 2/41
Robson, G.	31/ 5/41
Rawson, R. R., M.C. (Capt. late R.E.)	18/ 6/41

Lieutenants

Faulkner, N.	1/ 2/41
Patterson, J.	1/ 2/41
Watson, H. R. (Capt. late North'd. Fus.)	1/ 2/41
Worters, N. K. (Lt. late North'd. Fus.)	1/ 2/41
Lay, S. D.	1/ 2/41
Murton, D. O.	1/ 2/41
Lundi, G. E. (Lt. late R.A.)	1/ 2/41
Bryson, V. H.	1/ 2/41
Higgins, T. D. V.	1/ 2/41
Finlay, J. M.	1/ 2/41
Newcomb, J.	1/ 2/41
Watson, E.	1/ 2/41
Robson, F.	1/ 2/41
Dix, W. L. (2/Lt. late Gloster R.)	1/ 2/41

Lieutenants - contd.

Hodgson, K. W. D. (Lt. late T.A.)	1/ 2/41
Clark, W., D.C.M., M.M.	1/ 2/41
Phillips, P. P. (Maj. late R. North'd. Fus.)	1/ 2/41
Blackett-Ord, J. R. (Maj. late North'd. Fus.)	1/ 2/41
Simpson, W. R.	1/ 2/41
Alexander, G. (Capt. late Durham L.I.)	1/ 2/41
Charlton, R. B.	1/ 2/41
Harrison, E.	1/ 2/41
Whitfield, F. G. (Lt. late K.R.R.C.)	1/ 2/41
Waugh, G. B.	1/ 2/41
Adamson, H.	1/ 2/41
Cordner, P.	1/ 2/41
Manderson, A. J.	1/ 2/41
Longridge, J.	1/ 2/41
Swinburne, K. M.	1/ 2/41
Hedley, W. P.	1/ 2/41
Beadle, L. C.	1/ 2/41
Blayney, O. G., M.C. (Maj. late R. North'd. Fus.)	1/ 2/41
Hutchinson, H.	1/ 2/41
Parkinson, V. H.	16/ 5/41
Graham, R. S.	5/ 6/41
Holloway, F. W., M.C. (Capt. late M.G.Corps)	5/ 6/41
Walker, H.	13/ 6/41
Wardle, G. R.	12/ 7/41
Blumberg, F. T., O.B.E. (Capt. late R. Mar.)	22/ 7/41
Taylor, R.	24/ 7/41

2nd Lieutenants

Cookson, R. A.	16/ 5/41
Waite, E.	16/ 5/41
Dodd, J. R. (Lt. late Ind. Army)	22/ 5/41
Henderson, A.	22/ 5/41
Parker, J. M.	22/ 5/41
Crombie, J.	7/ 7/41
Dean, J.	7/ 7/41
Winder, T.	7/ 7/41
Herdman, W. C.	17/ 7/41
Emerson, G. S.	22/ 7/41

Adjutant & Quarter-Master

Medical Officer

Bell, Maj. R., M.C. (Lt. late Border R.)	22/ 5/41

56455-6(21)

NORTHUMBERLAND DIVISION - contd.

NORTHUMBERLAND ZONE - contd.

No.5 GROUP - contd.

10th NORTHUMBERLAND (OTTERBURN) BATTALION

Lt.-Colonel

White, Sir Archibald W., Bt., T.D. (Capt T.A Res.) 1/ 2/41

Majors

Bell, H. S., C.M.G., D.S.O., T.D. (Lt.-Col. late R.A.) 1/ 2/41
Charlton, W. H. (Capt. late North'd. Fus.) 1/ 2/41
Anderson, G. D. (Maj. late R.F.A.) 17/ 6/41

Captains

Ridley, A. H. (Lt. late North'd. Hrs.) 1/ 2/41
Telfer, A. 1/ 2/41
Haggie, A. K. (Capt. late Worc. H.) 23/ 6/41

Lieutenants

Taylor, T. G., D.S.O. (Lt.-Col. late Gordons) 1/ 2/41
Robson, T., M.C. (Lt. late North'd H.) 1/ 2/41
Love, R. M. (Capt. late Ind. Army) 1/ 2/41
Wilson, R. W. (Capt. late T.A.) 1/ 2/41
Robson, J. (2/Lt. late North'd. Fus.) 1/ 2/41
Robson, G. (2/Lt. late North'd. Fus.) 1/ 2/41
Roberts, J. 28/ 6/41

2nd Lieutenants

Fraser, J. K. (Capt. late North'd. Fus.) 1/ [illegible]1
Hall, W. J. (Lt. Can. Mil. Forces) 1/ 2/41
Glass, T. H. 1/ 2/41
Watson, R. S. (Lt. late R. North'd. Fus.) 1/ 2/41
Waddell, G. 1/ 2/41
Civil, W. 1/ 2/41
Anderson, J. R. 1/ 2/41
Taylor, W. R. 1/ 2/41
Robson, J. (Lt. late Green Howards) 1/ 2/41
Tench, C. A. 1/ 2/41
Dickerson, J. 1/ 2/41
Robson, J. W. 1/ 2/41

Adjutant & Quarter-Master

Medical Officer

Carr, Maj. R. J., M.B. (Surgeon-Lt. late R.N.V.R.) 21/ 5/41

56455-6(22)

NORTHUMBERLAND DIVISION - contd.

NORTHUMBERLAND ZONE - contd.

No.5 GROUP - contd.

13th NORTHUMBERLAND (POST OFFICE) BATTALION

Lt.-Colonel

Johnston, F.	1/ 2/41

Majors

Cuthbert, L.	1/ 2/41
Anderson, J. B., D.C.M.	1/ 2/41
Hawitt, J., M.B.E.	1/ 2/41
Bentlett, W. J.	1/ 2/41
Atkinson, R. W.	1/ 2/41

Captains

McGregor, J. K. (Flying Offr. late R.A.F.)	1/ 2/41
Chapman, H. W.	1/ 2/41
Croney, J. B.	1/ 2/41
Hayes, S. F., M.M.	1/ 2/41
Seed, W. W.	1/ 2/41

Lieutenants

Walton, J. G. (2/Lt. late North'd. Fus.)	1/ 2/41
Beadsmoore, A. E.	1/ 2/41
Crow, R. W., M.M.	1/ 2/41
McArdle, T. A. D., M.M.	1/ 2/41
Wright, J., M.M.	1/ 2/41
Donaldson, C. H., M.M.	1/ 2/41
Ingram, C.	1/ 2/41
Moore, W. P.	1/ 2/41
Grant, C.	1/ 2/41
Bowen, R. F. R.	1/ 2/41
Thompson, J. G.	1/ 2/41
Elliott, W.	1/ 2/41
Brown, E. A.	1/ 2/41
Scrafton, C. D.	1/ 2/41

Lieutenants - contd.

Brown, J. W.	1/ 2/41
Johnson, H., D.C.M.	1/ 2/41
Collard, J. W.	1/ 2/41
Smith, C. J.	1/ 2/41
McDonald, A. T., M.M.	1/ 2/41
Dunbar, J. W.	27/ 5/41
Rogers, J.	27/ 5/41

2nd Lieutenants

Clay, R. H., M.C. (Capt. late Lincoln R.)	1/ 2/41
Eden, G. B.	1/ 2/41
Collins, J. R.	1/ 2/41
Firth, T.	1/ 2/41
Rowell, G. R.	1/ 2/41
Thomson, W.	1/ 2/41
Walker, A.	1/ 2/41
Blyth, T.	1/ 2/41
Stoddart, W.	1/ 2/41
Leece, W.	1/ 2/41
Lang, R. H.	1/ 2/41
Skelly, J. E.	1/ 2/41
Taylor, T. G.	1/ 2/41
Stewart, D. H.	19/ 4/41
Cooper, H. P.	1/ 7/41
Twizell, W.	17/ 7/41

Adjutant & Quarter-Master

Snowdon, Capt. (actg. 1/2/41) B., Gen. List Inf.	1/ 2/41

Medical Officer

DURHAM and NORTH RIDING DIVISION

General Staff Officer 1st Grade	Yeo, Lt.-Col. F. C., M.B.E. M.M., p.s.c †., ret. pay	1/10/41

DURHAM ZONE

Commander	Barnard, Col. The Lord, C.M.G., M.C., T.D. (Bt. Col. ret. T.A.)	1/ 2/41
Assistant to Commander	Elwes, Maj. R. C.	1/ 2/41
Territorial Army Association administering	The Durham T.A. & A.F. Association, 53, Old Elvet, Durham.	

NO. 1 GROUP

Commander	Shiel, Col. F. R. A., D.S.O., T.D. (Bt. Lt.-Col. T.A. Res.)	1/ 2/41
Second in Command	Browell, Lt.-Col. J. C., M.C. (Capt. T.A. Res.)	1/ 2/41

1st DURHAM (BLAYDON) BATTALION

Lt.-Colonel

Daniell, H. E. B. (Capt. ret. T.A.)	1/ 2/41

Majors

Ismay, A. N. (Capt. late Durham L.I.)	1/ 2/41
Scott, G. V. (Capt. late R.E.)	1/ 2/41
Oxley, E., M.C. (Lt. late Border R.)	1/ 2/41
Spencer, R. P. (Lt. late R.N.V.R.)	1/ 2/41
Emmerson, R., M.C. (2/Lt. late Durham L.I.)	1/ 2/41
Hamilton, J. (2nd Lt. Late R.E.)	1/ 2/41

Captains

Simpson, B. R. J. (Lt. late Durham L.I.)	1/ 2/41
Rock, D. I. B. (Flight Lt. late R.A.F.)	1/ 2/41
Flowers, H. R.	1/ 2/41
MacGregor, J. F.	1/ 2/41

Lieutenants

Pinkney, M. R., D.C.M. (2/Lt. late Durham L.I.)	1/ 2/41
Moore, T.	1/ 2/41
Graham, C. P., M.C. (Lt. late W. York R.)	1/ 2/41
Marshall, J. (2/Lt. late Labour Corps)	1/ 2/41
Smith, N.	1/ 2/41
Rowell, W. (Lt. late Green Howards)	1/ 2/41
Anderson, G. (2/Lt. late Black Watch)	1/ 2/41
Smillie, J. M. (2/Lt. late R.E.)	1/ 2/41
Willis, G. C. (2/Lt. late R. North'd. Fus.)	1/ 2/41

Lieutenants - contd.

Greener, J. N. F.	1/ 2/41
McCusker, T.	1/ 2/41
Lee, H. A.	1/ 2/41
Wigham, J. S.	1/ 2/41
Siddle, J. H. R.	1/ 2/41
Armstrong, J.	1/ 2/41
Winskill, T.	1/ 2/41
Cherry, J. W.	1/ 2/41
Bowerbank, A.	1/ 2/41
Winfield, F. C.	10/ 6/41

2nd Lieutenants

Craig, J. W., D.C.M., M.M. (Lt. late Durham L.I.)	1/ 2/41
Todd, J. C. (2/Lt. late R.E.)	1/ 2/41
Potts, J. J., M.M.	1/ 2/41
Little, J. S. (Lt. late R.T.C.)	1/ 2/41
Thomas, W. A. W.	1/ 2/41
Cumberledge, J.	1/ 2/41
Silcock, H. C. G.	1/ 2/41
Holmes, S.	1/ 2/41
Twizell, S.	1/ 2/41
Hudspith, E. H.	1/ 2/41
Dent, H.	1/ 2/41
Glasper, T. W.	1/ 2/41
Moralee, A.	1/ 2/41
Jackson, J.	1/ 2/41
Wood, R. W. L.	1/ 2/41
Kitchen, F.	1/ 2/41
Watkin, J. R.	7/ 7/41

Adjutant & Quarter-Master

Medical Officer

DURHAM and NORTH RIDING DIVISION - contd.

DURHAM ZONE - contd.

No.1 GROUP - contd.

2nd DURHAM (CHESTER-LE-STREET) BATTALION

Lt.-Colonel

Usher, L. (Capt. late Can. Mil. Forces)	1/ 2/41

Majors

Ayton, G. R. (Lt. late Durham L.I.)	1/ 2/41
Dixon, H. (Lt. late R. North'd. Fus.)	1/ 2/41
Rudd, R.	1/ 2/41
Rose, A.	1/ 2/41
Dawson, N. (Lt. late M.G. Corps.)	14/ 7/41

Captains

Blythe, J. C.	1/ 2/41
Walker, W., M.M.	1/ 2/41
Gascoigne, P.	1/ 2/41
Lowes, G. W. (Lt. late Ind. Army)	14/ 7/41
Kirkup, J. G., M.C. (Capt. late R. North'd. Fus.)	17/ 7/41

Lieutenants

Minto, W. (2/Lt. late R. North'd. Fus.)	1/ 2/41
Gibson, J. F.	1/ 2/41
Bland, G. J. (2/Lt. late R.A.F.)	1/ 2/41
Bamborough, J. G., M.M.	1/ 2/41
Snowdon, W.	1/ 2/41
Madden, R., D.C.M.	1/ 2/41
Pentland, W. H.	1/ 2/41
Widdas, C. G.	1/ 2/41
Tunney, J. (Lt. late Lincoln R.)	1/ 2/41
Williams, R. (2/Lt. late R.E.)	1/ 2/41
Thompson, J. T., M.C.	1/ 2/41
Barron, W.	1/ 2/41
Wilson, F.	1/ 2/41
Leach, H. N.	1/ 2/41
Donnelly, C. F. C.	1/ 2/41
Hunter, J. W. F.	1/ 2/41
Sandell, A.	26/ 5/41
Read, C. S.	14/ 7/41
Winn, H. W. (Lt. late R.G.A.)	14/ 7/41
Joyce, C. W. D.	14/ 7/41

Lieutenants - contd.

Watson, C. B.	14/ 7/41
Dodds, H.	14/ 7/41
Timothy, R., M.M.	14/ 7/41
Hobson, G. H., D.F.C. (Lt. late R.A.F.)	17/ 7/41

2nd Lieutenants

Laybourn, T.	1/ 2/41
Price, F.	1/ 2/41
Marshall, S.	1/ 2/41
Bell, E., D.C.M.	1/ 2/41
Woodman, W. J.	1/ 2/41
Kellett, G.	1/ 2/41
Robson, W.	1/ 2/41
Holmes, J. L.	1/ 2/41
Codling, C. T.	1/ 2/41
Watson, J. R.	1/ 2/41
Hair, F.	1/ 2/41
Redpath, W. S.	1/ 2/41
Witherspoon, J. V.	1/ 2/41
Gardiner, M. B.	1/ 2/41
Engleby, W.	1/ 2/41
Hope, W. T.	1/ 2/41
Dyson, H.	1/ 2/41
Walton, J.	1/ 2/41
Lowery, W.	1/ 2/41
Callaghan, W.	1/ 2/41
Hopkins, T.	1/ 2/41
Todd, T.	1/ 2/41
Cramond, R.	1/ 2/41
Brown, L. J. W.	1/ 2/41
Nuttall, J. R.	26/ 5/41
Burningham, A. C. J.	17/ 7/41
Tindle, R. H.	17/ 7/41

Adjutant & Quarter-Master

Medical Officer

Glynn, Maj. J.	10/ 6/41

DURHAM and NORTH RIDING DIVISION - contd.

DURHAM ZONE - contd.

NO. 1 GROUP - contd.

3rd DURHAM (LANCHESTER) BATTALION

Lt.-Colonel

Ritson, C. W., O.B.E. (Lt.-Col. ret. pay)	1/ 2/41

Majors

Anderson, A. G. I.	1/ 2/41
Penny, J.	1/ 2/41
Robson, J. J.	1/ 2/41
Welsh, W.	1/ 2/41
Wallace, J. J.	1/ 2/41
Wood, W.	1/ 2/41
Oliver, G. M. G.	1/ 2/41

Captains

Milner, M. H.	1/ 2/41
Rutter, H.	1/ 2/41
Brennan, J.	1/ 2/41
Metcalfe, J. W.	1/ 2/41
Wale, E. H., M.C. (Capt. late R.E.)	23/ 6/41
Palmer, J. T.	10/ 7/41

Lieutenants

Bertram, A. W. J.	1/ 2/41
Parker, B., M.M.	1/ 2/41
Coulthard, J. W.	1/ 2/41
Miller, G. A.	1/ 2/41
Jackson, G.	1/ 2/41
Million, J. H.	1/ 2/41
Walker, K. D.	1/ 2/41
Devenish, A., D.C.M.	1/ 2/41
Maycock, J.	1/ 2/41
Maddison, R.	1/ 2/41
Naisbitt, R. G.	1/ 2/41
Hughes, F.	1/ 2/41
Woods, J.	1/ 2/41
Holmes, N.	29/ 5/41

2nd Lieutenants

Dunn, J.	1/ 2/41
Hovvels, J.	1/ 2/41
Stubbs, T.	1/ 2/41
Herdman, A. L.	1/ 2/41
Hunter, G. C.	1/ 7/41
Walton, L. H.	16/ 7/41
Disberry, J. E.	18/ 7/41
Raine, J. G.	18/ 7/41

Adjutant & Quarter-Master

Rooney, Capt. (actg. 12/5/41) A. T., M.C., T.A. Res.	12/ 5/41

Medical Officer

Fenwick, Maj. C. (Lt. late E. York R.)	29/ 5/41

DURHAM and NORTH RIDING DIVISION - contd.

DURHAM ZONE - contd.

No.1 GROUP - contd.

4th DURHAM (CONSETT) BATTALION

Lt.-Colonel

George, F. B. (Lt. late T.A.)	1/ 2/41

Majors

Barrow, J. (Capt. late Durham L.I.)	1/ 2/41
Westthorp, R. S. (2/Lt. late Green Howards)	1/ 2/41
Henderson, A. G. (2/Lt. late Durham L.I.)	1/ 2/41
White, R., M.M. (Lt. late Durham L.I.)	1/ 2/41
Johnson, D. (Lt. late R. North'd. Fus.)	1/ 2/41

Captains

Jackson, E. (2/Lt. late Durham L.I.)	1/ 2/41
Evans, E.	1/ 2/41
McCree, G.	1/ 2/41

Lieutenants

Elliott, A.	1/ 2/41
Barker, E. (Flight-Lt. late R.A.F.)	1/ 2/41
Draffan, D. P.	1/ 2/41
Malpass, E.	1/ 2/41
Brodie, E.	1/ 2/41
Johnson, W.	1/ 2/41
Siddle, N. A. S.	1/ 2/41
Bowes, E.	1/ 2/41
Middleton, J. T., M.M.	1/ 2/41
Smith, E. H.	1/ 2/41
Wildsmith, A. E.	1/ 2/41
Moore, H., M.M.	1/ 2/41
Robinson, J. N.	1/ 2/41
Brittle, J. W.	1/ 2/41
Robertson, R. (2/Lt. late M.G. Corps.)	1/ 2/41
Bryden, F. D.	1/ 2/41
Small, J. R.	1/ 2/41
Barrow, T. E.	27/ 5/41

2nd Lieutenants

Grant, H.	1/ 2/41
Elliott, J. E.	1/ 2/41
Richardson, M.	1/ 2/41
Davis, C. J. S.	1/ 2/41
Hall, T.	1/ 2/41
Pinkney, J. S.	1/ 2/41
Marsh, W.	1/ 2/41
Muir, D. C.	1/ 2/41
Heslop, F. S.	1/ 2/41
Lose, F.	1/ 2/41
Hinken, W. G.	1/ 2/41
Oliver, J.	1/ 2/41
Turnbull, T.	1/ 2/41
Fowler, E.	1/ 2/41
Smith, G. F.	21/ 5/41
Richards, P. H.	28/ 5/41
Guy, G.	2/ 7/41

Adjutant & Quarter-Master

Medical Officer

Mackenzie, Maj. M. D. (Capt. late R.A.M.C.)	9/ 6/41

DURHAM and NORTH RIDING DIVISION - contd.

DURHAM ZONE - contd.

No.1 GROUP - contd.

5th DURHAM (HAMSTERLEY) BATTALION

Lt.-Colonel

Vereker, Hon. S. R., M.C. (Lt. late T.A.) 1/ 2/41

Majors

Braidford, F. G. (Lt. late Durham L.I.) 1/ 2/41
Ashworth, H. H., M.C. (Lt. late E. Lan. R.) 1/ 2/41
Alexander, W. F. 1/ 2/41
Robinson, G. 1/ 2/41
Ellison, R. W. 1/ 2/41
Ross, P. A. (Lt. late M.G. Corps) 1/ 2/41
Harper, G. O. (Lt. late R.A.) 1/ 2/41

Captains

Smith, J. 1/ 2/41
Pace, R. 1/ 2/41
Peel, R. 1/ 2/41
Taylor, F. 1/ 2/41
Smith, S. W., M.M. 1/ 2/41
Bentham, W. T., M.M. 1/ 2/41
Malpass, C., M.M. 1/ 2/41
Cowey, F. 13/ 6/41

Lieutenants

Smith, H. V. 1/ 2/41
Maude, R. 1/ 2/41
Sproat, E. C. 1/ 2/41
Stephenson, G. A., M.M. 1/ 2/41
English, J. 1/ 2/41
Welsh, T. 1/ 2/41
Elcoat, J. 1/ 2/41
Davis, W. (Capt. late R.E.) 1/ 2/41
Tuck, E. 1/ 2/41
Goldsmith, J. W. 1/ 2/41
Talbot, E. 1/ 2/41
Briggs, F. 1/ 2/41
Telford, W., M.M. 1/ 2/41
Armstrong, G. 1/ 2/41
Dyson, A. B. 1/ 2/41
Coxon, L. E. 1/ 2/41

Lieutenants - contd.

Wilson, C. W. 1/ 2/41
Robson, G. E. 1/ 2/41
Pearson, A. 1/ 2/41
Makepeace, J. 1/ 2/41
Harper, J. R. 1/ 2/41
Marr, J. H. 1/ 2/41
Coney, F. 13/ 6/41

2nd Lieutenants

Milburn, E. 1/ 2/41
Gray, A. E. 1/ 2/41
Lawson, L. F. 1/ 2/41
Jewson, A. M. 1/ 2/41
Kirkup, W. 1/ 2/41
Cross, F. 1/ 2/41
Sellar, C. 1/ 2/41
Mitchell, W. 1/ 2/41
Kerridge, F. 1/ 2/41
Sanderson, G. 1/ 2/41
Dorling, T. 1/ 2/41
Davison, J. E. (2/Lt. late R.G.A.) 1/ 2/41
Ritson, J. H. (2/Lt. late R. North'd. Fus.) 1/ 2/41
Bell, R. B. 1/ 2/41
Milburn, J. W. 1/ 2/41
Whitwood, W. 1/ 2/41
Fawcett, T. H. 1/ 2/41
Newby, R. 1/ 2/41
Forster, G. 1/ 2/41
Cook, J. 1/ 2/41
Dodds, G. 27/ 6/41
Twitchett, F. 18/ 7/41

Adjutant & Quarter-Master

Medical Officer

Roberts, Maj. A. 1/ 6/41

DURHAM and NORTH RIDING DIVISION - contd.

DURHAM ZONE - contd.

NO. 1 GROUP - contd.

6th DURHAM (STANLEY) BATTALION

Lt.-Colonel

Green, R., M.C. (Capt late T.A.) 1/ 2/41

Majors

Wilson, O. 1/ 2/41
Boggon, H. H. (Lt. late R.A.F.) 1/ 2/41
Smart, H. (2/Lt. late Durham L.I.) 1/ 2/41
Kuhlman, J. R. 1/ 2/41
Foreman, H. M. 1/ 2/41
Fox, C. J. B. (Lt. late R.A.F.) 27/ 5/41

Captains

Drummond, J. J. 1/ 2/41
Eagle, W. (2/Lt. late R. North'd Fus.) 1/ 2/41
Logan, J. 1/ 2/41
Walton, G. M. 1/ 2/41

Lieutenants

Soulsby, J. A. 1/ 2/41
Patterson, R. W. 1/ 2/41
Lawton, J. E. 1/ 2/41
Blackett, H. E. 1/ 2/41
Davison, T. W. 1/ 2/41
Rutherford, J. L. 1/ 2/41
Daglish, R., M.M. 1/ 2/41
Jobson, W. R. 1/ 2/41
Bellerby, N. H. 1/ 2/41
Bulman, G. S. 1/ 2/41
Painter, H. N. 1/ 2/41
Pears, J. 1/ 2/41

Lieutenants - contd.

Daglish, F. S. 1/ 2/41
Carlyon, H. 1/ 2/41
Pallas, C. S. 1/ 2/41
Bellis, J. E. 1/ 2/41

2nd Lieutenants

Elliott, W. W. 1/ 2/41
Lowes, J. W. 1/ 2/41
Iveson, J. 1/ 2/41
Curry, J. W. 1/ 2/41
Eagle, E. 1/ 2/41
Coxon, W. 1/ 2/41
Robertson, W. 1/ 2/41
Peel, R. 1/ 2/41
Lawson, T. W. 1/ 2/41
Wright, M. W. 1/ 2/41
Grenfell, W. H. 1/ 2/41
Richardson, F. 1/ 2/41
Gerry, T. J. 1/ 2/41
Brown, H. E. 1/ 2/41
Baird, J. 1/ 2/41
Bellis, T. J., M.M. 1/ 2/41

Adjutant & Quarter-Master

Medical Officer

Fox, Lt. C. J. B. 27/ 5/41

DURHAM and NORTH RIDING DIVISION - contd.

DURHAM ZONE - contd.

NO. 2 GROUP

Commander	Dawson, Col. F., M.C., T.D., (Lt.-Col. T.A.)	1/ 2/41
Second in Command	Dickinson, Lt.-Col. A. H. (Capt. late T.A.)	1/ 2/41
Assistant to Commander	McLellan, Capt. A. G.	1/ 2/41

7th DURHAM (JARROW) BATTALION

Lt.-Colonel

Chalmers, J.	1/ 2/41

Majors

Milburn, F. A.	1/ 2/41
Boulton, W. P. (Capt. late R.A.S.C.)	1/ 2/41
Wood, G. E. (Lt. Res. of Off.)	1/ 2/41
Ranken, C. T., M.C. (Capt. late R.F.A.)	1/ 2/41
Dodd, W. M., M.C. (Lt. late Y. & L.R.)	1/ 2/41
Rust, E. C. (2/Lt. late K.O.Y.L.I.)	1/ 2/41
Ritchie, P. D.	1/ 2/41
Stephenson, C., M.C. (Capt. late North'd. Fus.)	1/ 2/41

Captains

Tate, G. H.	1/ 2/41
Walker, G. (Lt. late K.O.Y.L.I.)	1/ 2/41
King, J.	1/ 2/41
Wright, G. E.	1/ 2/41
Thompson, J. A., D.C.M. (Lt. late R.E.)	1/ 2/41
Middleton, H. G. D.	1/ 2/41
Clarke, J.	1/ 2/41
Batey, J. L. (Lt. T.A. Res.)	1/ 2/41

Lieutenants

Birch, F. J. (Lt. late Cheshire R.)	1/ 2/41
Evans, L. W.	1/ 2/41
Mills, R. B., M.M.	1/ 2/41
Norman, W.	1/ 2/41
Hindmarsh, E.	1/ 2/41
Alderson, W.	1/ 2/41
Wishart, J.	1/ 2/41
Robinson, F. A.	1/ 2/41
McDonald, J. L.	1/ 2/41
Bateson, P.	1/ 2/41
Wilson, J. M.	1/ 2/41
Murrell, W. C.	1/ 2/41
Nixon, T. S.	1/ 2/41

Lieutenants - contd.

McCabe, J. J.	1/ 2/41
Sivell, J. R. W.	1/ 2/41
Lashford, W.	1/ 2/41
Cowell, J. H.	1/ 2/41
Gale, H. M.	1/ 2/41
Fellows, A.	1/ 2/41
Potts, M. H.	1/ 2/41
Hall, T. M.	1/ 2/41
Williams, J.	1/ 2/41
Singleton, R. (Lt. late A.S.C.)	1/ 2/41
Coats, J. W.	1/ 2/41
Hughson, S. (Lt. late R.A.M.C.)	23/ 6/41
Sinclair, J. W.	23/ 6/41
Tate, E.	23/ 6/41
Taylorson, J. D. (Capt. late R.A.)	23/ 6/41

2nd Lieutenants

Cliffe, H.	1/ 2/41
Evans, C. W.	1/ 2/41
Fairbairn, H.	1/ 2/41
Dowson, T.	1/ 2/41
Simpson, G. E.	1/ 2/41
Graham, A.	1/ 2/41
Crawford, L.	1/ 2/41
Boal, W.	1/ 2/41
Dunning, J. W.	1/ 2/41
Bradshaw, D.	23/ 6/41
Eddleston, R.	23/ 6/41

Adjutant & Quarter-Master

Medical Officer

Cort, Maj. F., M.B.	23/ 6/41

DURHAM and NORTH RIDING DIVISION - contd.

DURHAM ZONE - contd.

NO. 2 GROUP - contd.

8th DURHAM (S. SHIELDS) BATTALION

Lt.-Colonel

Gray, G. S. (Capt. late M. G. Corps.)	1/ 2/41

Majors

Spraggon, A. E.	1/ 2/41
Robinson, R. S. (Lt. late North'd Fus.)	1/ 2/41
Edgar, W. G. (Lt. late R. North'd Fus.)	1/ 2/41
Chipcase, R. S. (Capt. late R.E.)	1/ 2/41

Captains

Scott, W., M.C. (Lt. late M. G. Corps.)	1/ 2/41
Carr, E., (Lt. late North'd Fus.)	1/ 2/41
Burton, R. C.	1/ 2/41
McLean, D.	1/ 2/41
Jameson, J.	1/ 2/41
Hair, J. W.	1/ 2/41
Gray, G.	1/ 2/41
Muir, R. D.	1/ 2/41

Lieutenants

Hall, H.	1/ 2/41
Kieffer, A. C.	1/ 2/41
Hymers, C.	1/ 2/41
Trewhitt, R.	1/ 2/41
Park, J. O.	1/ 2/41
Thompson, M. W.	1/ 2/41
Sharp, S. M.	1/ 2/41
Buchanan, G. R.	1/ 2/41
Dinning, J., M.M. (Lt. late R.E.)	1/ 2/41
Walsh, E. C., M.M.	1/ 2/41
Smith, A.	1/ 2/41
Horn, G.	1/ 2/41
Dryden, J. W.	1/ 2/41
Mitchell, E. W.	1/ 2/41

Lieutenants - contd.

Blakey, G. C.	1/ 2/41
Lugton, W. J.	1/ 2/41
Holt, T. W. C.	1/ 2/41
Patterson, G. A.	1/ 2/41
Armstrong, T. C.	1/ 2/41
Charles, D. M.	1/ 2/41
Campbell, G. T. R.	1/ 2/41
Ward, J. R.	1/ 2/41
Goudie, T.	1/ 2/41
Little, T. R.	1/ 2/41
Kettlewell, J. H.	1/ 2/41
Berkley, T.	1/ 2/41
Gibson, J. W.	1/ 2/41
Young, C. D.	1/ 2/41
Edmenson, R. R.	1/ 2/41

2nd Lieutenants

Muir, W. J.	1/ 2/41
Rainey, G.	1/ 2/41
Winspear, T.	1/ 2/41
Brown, A. H.	1/ 2/41
Murray, H.	1/ 2/41
Newman, A. L.	1/ 2/41
Pearson, M. S.	1/ 2/41
Cross, J. B.	1/ 2/41
Wilkinson, N.	1/ 2/41
Wilkinson, C. H.	1/ 2/41
Turnbull, J. H.	1/ 2/41
Barnes, R.	1/ 2/41

Adjutant & Quarter-Master

Medical Officer

Ord, Maj. H. D., M.B.	12/ 6/41

DURHAM and NORTH RIDING DIVISION - contd.

DURHAM ZONE - contd.

NO. 2 GROUP - contd.

9th DURHAM (SUNDERLAND) BATTALION

Lt.-Colonel

Laing, L., T.D. (Bt. Col. ret. T.A.) 1/ 2/41

Majors

Wilson, H., O.B.E., T.D. (Bt. Col. late T.A. Res.) (Hon. Col. R.A. (T.A.)) 1/ 2/41
Patterson, A. C. 1/ 2/41
Brydon, G. (Capt. late Loyal R.) 1/ 2/41
Kelso, S., M.M. (2/Lt. late Foresters) 1/ 2/41
Kayll, J. P. (Maj. late Durham L.I.) 1/ 2/41
Marr, A. J. 1/ 2/41
Snowball, H. W. 1/ 2/41
Lewis, J. E. 1/ 2/41
Martin, W. S. (Maj. late R.A.) 1/ 2/41
Whillis, B. P., M.C. (Maj. late M.G. Corps) 1/ 2/41
Tripp, W. H. S., M.C. 1/ 2/41

Captains

Potts, C. W. M., M.C. (Capt. late R.E.) 1/ 2/41
Hedley, R. F. H. 1/ 2/41
Thompson, R. C. 1/ 2/41
Walker, W. P., M.C. (Lt. late R.F.A.) 1/ 2/41
Cunningham, T. W. (Capt. late North'd Fus.) 1/ 2/41
Thompson, J. V. 1/ 2/41

Captains - contd.

Pointer, H. 1/ 2/41
McCrum, J. 1/ 2/41
Gundy, T. 1/ 2/41
Alder, H. 1/ 2/41
Temple, A. 1/ 2/41
Mawson, J. H., M.C. (Maj. late R.E.) 1/ 2/41
Bellerby, N. 1/ 2/41
McMillan, W. F. (Lt. late R.E.) 1/ 2/41
Berry, A. J. (Lt.-Comdr. late R.N.) 1/ 2/41

Lieutenants

Eggleston, P. N., M.C. 1/ 2/41
Heptinstall, P. M., M.C. (Lt. late R.E.) 1/ 2/41
Stevens, W. F., M.M. 1/ 2/41
Fazey, J. W. 1/ 2/41
Cotton, G. A. (Lt. late Green Howards) 1/ 2/41
Iley, R. W., M.M. 1/ 2/41
Catenby, J. R. (2/Lt. T.A. Res.) 1/ 2/41
Martin, J. S. 1/ 2/41
Wood, W. 1/ 2/41
Crabbe, D. (Lt. late R.N.R.) 1/ 2/41
Cook, T. J., 1/ 2/41
Ramsay, C. (Lt. late Durham L.I.) 1/ 2/41
Williams, A. G. 1/ 2/41
Gray, W. (Lt. late Ind. Army) 1/ 2/41
Knott, F. 1/ 2/41
Marr, A. L. 1/ 2/41
Hodson, F. G. 1/ 2/41
Robins, H. T. G. 1/ 2/41
Randle, E. N. 1/ 2/41
May, D. F. 1/ 2/41
Robson, J. T. 1/ 2/41

DURHAM and NORTH RIDING DIVISION - contd.

DURHAM ZONE - contd.

NO. 2 GROUP - contd.

9th Durham (Sunderland) Battalion - contd.

Lieutenants - contd.

Heckels, S.	1/ 2/41
Howey, G. C.	1/ 2/41
Cunningham, C. R.	1/ 2/41
Smith, A. H.	1/ 2/41
Paul, W.	1/ 2/41
Chrishop, W. E.	1/ 2/41
Johnston, D. H.	1/ 2/41
Wake, M. H.	1/ 2/41
Potts, J.	1/ 2/41
Carroll, T.	3/ 7/41

2nd Lieutenants

Clark, C. R.	1/ 2/41
Ainslie, G. H.	1/ 2/41
Smith, A. W., M.M.	1/ 2/41
Johnson, B. J.	1/ 2/41
Parkinson, M. D.	1/ 2/41
Parker, W.	1/ 2/41
Oakley, H.	1/ 2/41
Hogg, R. H.	1/ 2/41
Stonock, R. B. B.	1/ 2/41
Cook, E.	1/ 2/41
Miller, A.	1/ 2/41
Rackstraw, R. B.	1/ 2/41
Richardson, W.	1/ 2/41
Sopp, J. A.	1/ 2/41
Rogers, A.	1/ 2/41
Munn, A.	1/ 2/41
Thompson, G.	1/ 2/41
Bainbridge, V. B.	1/ 2/41
Hudson, J. R.	1/ 2/41
Watson, T. H.	1/ 2/41
Redpath, J.	1/ 2/41
Henderson, G.	1/ 2/41

2nd Lieutenants - contd.

Metcalf, J.	1/ 2/41
Cawthorn, E. O.	4/ 6/41
Weatherley, R.	24/ 6/41
Harvey, C. W.	2/ 7/41
Hunter, C.	2/ 7/41
Pallas, T. M.	2/ 7/41
Allan, W. B. (Maj. late R.A.)	3/ 7/41
Steel, J.	3/ 7/41
Laws, D. (Lt. late R.E.)	14/ 7/41

Adjutant & Quarter-Master

Medical Officer

Mair, Maj. R.	1/ 2/41

56455-6(33)

DURHAM and NORTH RIDING DIVISION - contd.

DURHAM ZONE - contd

NO. 3 GROUP

Commander — Scott-Owen, Col. A. L., (Lt. late R.E.) 1/ 2/41

11th DURHAM (DURHAM) BATTALION

Lt.-Colonel

Majors

Macfarlane-Grieve, A. A., M.C., T.D. (Maj. (Bt. Lt.-Col.) late Seaforth) 1/ 2/41
Saint, T. A. (Lt. late Durham L.I.) 1/ 2/41
Burchnall, J. L., M.C. (Capt. late R.G.A.) 1/ 2/41
Winterbottom, H. A. (2/Lt. late R.E.) 1/ 2/41
Watson, G. S., (2/Lt. late The Queen's R.) 1/ 2/41
Howe, C. H. A. 1/ 2/41
Gibson, J. 1/ 2/41
Dinning, W. (Lt. late North'd Fus.) 1/ 7/41

Captains

Hope, E. W. 1/ 2/41
Logan, C., M.C. (Capt. late E. Lan. R.) 1/ 2/41
Hateley, J. 1/ 2/41
Murray, R. R. 1/ 2/41
Missing, C. M. S. (2/Lt. late Dorset R.) 1/ 2/41
Walton, R. 1/ 2/41

Lieutenants

Standen, H. P. R. (Lt. late E. Lan. R.) 1/ 2/41
Johnson, W. R. 1/ 2/41
Davis, C. E. 1/ 2/41
Morris, J. 1/ 2/41
Pearson, P. H. 1/ 2/41
Nixon, W. 1/ 2/41
Buxton, M. (Lt. late R.A.S.C.) 1/ 2/41
Bell, V. 1/ 2/41
Nesbit, G. W. I. 1/ 2/41

Lieutenants - contd.

Watkin, W. (2/Lt. late Durham L.I.) 1/ 2/41
Cottle, W. H. 1/ 2/41
Holmes, O. W. 1/ 2/41
Hutton, W. S. 1/ 2/41
Brown, D. McL. 1/ 2/41
Bradshaw, F. A. 1/ 2/41
Flower, W., D.C.M. 1/ 2/41
Willatt, J. F. (Maj. R.S. Fus. T.A.) 1/ 2/41
Briggs, A. M. (Lt. late H.L.I.) 1/ 2/41
Aberdeen, S., D.C.M., T.D. (Capt. late Durham L.I.) 1/ 2/41
Cockburn, W. H. 1/ 2/41
Longstaff, G. R., D.C.M., M.M. 1/ 2/41
Green, W. F. 1/ 2/41
Lawson, J. B. 1/ 2/41
Cook, A. (Lt. late Durham L.I.) 1/ 2/41
Boyle, W. 1/ 2/41
Prowse, W. A. (Capt. Gen. List) 10/ 7/41
McIntyre, J. D. 21/ 7/41
Skilbeck, J. A. 21/ 7/41

2nd Lieutenants

Smith, R. S. 1/ 2/41
Urwin, L. 1/ 2/41
Lewis, A. 1/ 2/41
Jones, J. R. 1/ 2/41
Young, H. (2/Lt. late E. York R.) 1/ 2/41
Walton, C. 1/ 2/41
Scott, G. 1/ 2/41
Hunter, W. 1/ 2/41
Mullin, R. 25/ 6/41
Hopkins, W. (2/Lt. ret.) 10/ 7/41

Adjutant & Quarter-Master

Medical Officer

DURHAM and NORTH RIDING DIVISION - contd.

DURHAM ZONE - contd.

NO. 3 GROUP - contd.

12th DURHAM (CASTLE EDEN) BATTALION

Lt.-Colonel

Tate, R. S. (Lt. late Durham L.I.)	1/ 2/41

Majors

Larby, W. G.	1 2/41
Fawcett, T. C. (Capt. late K.O.Y.L.I.)	1/ 2/41
Johnson, R. P. B., M.C. (Lt. late R.F.A.)	1/ 2/41
Best, E., M.C. (Capt. late R.E.)	1/ 2/41
Liddell, W. L. (Lt. late R.E.)	1/ 2/41

Captains

Ingram, J.	1/ 2/41
Hutchinson, H.	1/ 2/41
Forrester, T.	1/ 2/41
Mitchell, J. R. (Lt. late R.A.)	1/ 2/41
Hardy, S.	1/ 2/41

Lieutenants

Booth, W. H.	1/ 2/41
Knaggs, C. R.	1/ 2/41
Dixon, C. (Lt. late W. York R.)	1/ 2/41
Welsh, R. W. (2/Lt. late North'd Fus.)	1/ 2/41
Alderson, W. H. R. (Lt. late R.A.)	1/ 2/41
Tulip, A. W. P.	1/ 2/41
Heckle, E. W. (Lt. late Green Howards)	1/ 2/41
Walton, T. H. (Lt. late Durham L.I.)	1/ 2/41
Naisbitt, E. W.	1/ 2/41
Whitfield, O.	1/ 2/41
Martindale, A.	1/ 2/41
Bradford, P. S. (Capt. late R.G.A.)	1/ 2/41
Lee, B.	1/ 2/41

Lieutenants - contd.

Williams, F. (2/Lt. late Durham L.I.)	1/ 2/41
Sneddon, T. N.	1/ 2/41
Perry, W. B.	1/ 2/41
Morris, E.	1/ 2/41
McCarroll, F.	1/ 2/41
Douglas, G.	1/ 2/41
Hewitt, J.	1/ 2/41
Wealands, P.	1/ 2/41

2nd Lieutenants

Lonie, A.	1/ 2/41
Oswald, J. T.	1/ 2/41
Storey, W. N.	1/ 2/41
Jackson, G., M.M. (2/Lt. late North'd Fus.)	1/ 2/41
Thomson, D. H.	1/ 2/41
Armstrong, M. (2/Lt. late Durham L.I.)	1/ 2/41
Nicholson, W. D., D.C.M.	1/ 2/41
Scott, J. R.	1/ 2/41
Nicholson, G. C., M.M.	1/ 2/41
Welsh, A.	1/ 2/41
Brown, J. N.	1/ 2/41
Murray, J. D. H.	1/ 2/41
Pearce, I.	1/ 2/41
Simpson, F.	1/ 2/41

Adjutant & Quarter-Master

Medical Officer

56455-6(35)

DURHAM and NORTH RIDING DIVISION - contd.

DURHAM ZONE - contd.

NO. 3 GROUP - contd.

13th DURHAM (SEAHAM) BATTALION

Lt.-Colonel

Allan, A. (Capt. late Ind. Army)	1/ 2/41

Majors

Mackey, T. A.	1/ 2/41
Douglass, J. R. (2/Lt. late R.F.A.)	1/ 2/41
Taylor, H. L. (Capt. late R.A.F.)	1/ 2/41
Dickinson, R. (Lt. late M.G. Corps.)	1/ 2/41
Henderson, R., M.M. (Lt. late Somerset L.I.)	1/ 2/41
Coxon, T. (2/Lt. late Labour Corps)	1/ 2/41
Charlton, R. H.	1/ 2/41

Captains

Wigham, J. T. (Lt. late R.A.S.C.)	1/ 2/41
Tuffs, A. A., M.C. (2/Lt. late Durham L.I.)	1/ 2/41
Ward, J. H.	1/ 2/41
Hunter, R., D.C.M.	1/ 2/41
Morgan, H. E.	1/ 5/41

Lieutenants

Brown, D. S., M.M.	1/ 2/41
Milburn, A.	1/ 2/41
Barkel, W.	1/ 2/41
Norris, F. F., M.M.	1/ 2/41
Thompson, W. S.	1/ 2/41
Boyd, C.	1/ 2/41
Harrison, N.	1/ 2/41
Douglas, S.	1/ 2/41
Knowles, R. H.	1/ 2/41
Wilson, T. G. (Lt. late Green Howards)	1/ 2/41
Pearson, J. W.	1/ 2/41

Lieutenants - contd.

Watt, W. H., M.M. (Lt. late R.F.A.)	1/ 2/41
Brown, A. E.	1/ 2/41
Harrison, J.	1/ 2/41
Hutton, W. (2/Lt. late North'd Fus.)	1/ 2/41
Colvin, W. B.	1/ 2/41
Ingram, W. J.	1/ 2/41
Gray, W.	1/ 2/41
Long, G. H. A. (Lt. late W. York R.)	1/ 2/41
Brewster, J. H.	1/ 5/41
Smart, R. G. (Lt. late R.G.A.)	17/ 6/41

2nd Lieutenants

Armbrister, E. R.	1/ 2/41
Barry, R. W. (Lt. late R.A.)	1/ 2/41
Miller, A. N.	1/ 2/41
Elliott, J. S.	1/ 2/41
Tulley, G. R., M.M.	1/ 2/41
Openshaw, J. W. S.	1/ 2/41
Baines, J.	1/ 2/41
Beattie, W. S.	1/ 2/41
Brown, C.	1/ 2/41
Greenshields, E. W.	1/ 2/41
Beamson, C. H.	1/ 2/41
Defty, F.	1/ 2/41
Adams, G. H.	1/ 2/41
Bainbridge, J. G.	1/ 2/41
Watson, J. R.	17/ 6/41

Adjutant & Quarter-Master

Medical Officer

Neilan, Maj. J. A.,	1/ 2/41

DURHAM and NORTH RIDING DIVISION - contd.

DURHAM ZONE - contd.

NO. 3 GROUP - contd.

14th DURHAM (HOUGHTON-LE-SPRING) BATTALION

Lt.-Colonel

Rogers, J. N. O. (Capt. ret. T.A.)	1/ 2/41

Majors

Carr, G. A., M.C. (Capt. late K.R.R.C.)	1/ 2/41
McLaren, J. W., M.B.E. (Capt. late R.A.S.C.)	1/ 2/41
Oliver, J. P. (Capt. late Loyal R.)	1/ 2/41
King, T. A. (Lt. late Ind. Army)	1/ 2/41
Sharp, A. W., M.M.	1/ 2/41
Elliott, W. C.	1/ 2/41
Atkinson, W. H. (Lt. late North'd. Fus.)	1/ 2/41
Loadman, L. W. (Lt. late North'd. Fus.)	1/ 2/41

Captains

Whittaker, J. E. H.	1/ 2/41
Martin, E. M.	1/ 2/41
Sanderson, R. H.	1/ 2/41
Tumelty, J. C.	1/ 2/41
Wilkinson, J. W. (Lt. late Lan. Fus.)	1/ 2/41
McLaren, D. I.	1/ 2/41
McLaren, R. M.	1/ 2/41
Kirkup, A. (Jun.) (2/Lt. late R.A.)	1/ 2/41
Bell, J. W.	1/ 2/41

Lieutenants

Gill, F. J.	1/ 2/41
Willis, J. M.	1/ 2/41
Jackson, J. W. (Lt. late Durham L.I.)	1/ 2/41
Bell, G. T., D.C.M.	1/ 2/41
Crosthwaite, R.	1/ 2/41
Nurse, J. O.	1/ 2/41
Swann, F. W. S.	1/ 2/41
Lambton, J.	1/ 2/41
Watson, J. F., M.M.	1/ 2/41
Johnson, J.	1/ 2/41
Battensby, A. A.	1/ 2/41
Hodgson, J. T.	1/ 2/41
Thwaite, H.	1/ 2/41
Adamson, T. B.	1/ 2/41
VC McNally, W., M.M.	1/ 2/41
Farrelly, G., M.M.	1/ 2/41
Gott, J. L. (2/Lt. late Durham L.I.)	1/ 2/41
Thompson, G. W.	1/ 2/41
Jenkins, W. H.	1/ 2/41
France, W., D.C.M., M.M.	1/ 2/41

Lieutenants - contd.

Pattison, P.	1/ 2/41
Adamson, W. H.	1/ 2/41
Bailey, H. M. L.	1/ 2/41
Fawcett, H. W.	1/ 2/41
Anderson, J. R., M.M.	1/ 2/41
Thompson, R. M.	1/ 2/41
Thompson, A.	1/ 2/41
Brown, R.	1/ 2/41
Metcalfe, W. O.	1/ 2/41
Atkinson, G. R.	31/ 5/41

2nd Lieutenants

Priddin, E. A. B.	1/ 2/41
Little, B.	1/ 2/41
Brereton, G. H.	1/ 2/41
Siddell, G. W.	1/ 2/41
Bunker, W.	1/ 2/41
Mairns, T. W.	1/ 2/41
Hudson, J.	1/ 2/41
Davison, T. W.	1/ 2/41
Cambell, F. W.	1/ 2/41
Curry, T.	1/ 2/41
Noble, S.	1/ 2/41
Forster, C.	1/ 2/41
Ball, T.	1/ 2/41
Williams, W.	1/ 2/41
Cook, W. F.	1/ 2/41
Bailey, J.	1/ 2/41
Quinn, J.	1/ 2/41
Anderson, F.	1/ 2/41
Scott, P. D.	23/ 6/41

Adjutant & Quarter-Master

Medical Officer

Boyd, Maj. F. J., M.B.	23/ 5/41

22nd DURHAM (WHEATLEY HILL) BATTALION

Lt.-Colonel

Simpson, J. A. (2/Lt. late R.E.)	1/ 2/41

Lieutenants

Temple, A. D.	19/ 7/41

2nd Lieutenants

McBriar, D.	24/ 7/41
Wilson, G.	24/ 7/41

Adjutant & Quarter-Master

Medical Officer

DURHAM and NORTH RIDING DIVISION - contd.

DURHAM ZONE - contd.

NO. 4 GROUP

Commander	Rogerson, Col. J. C. (Capt. ret. (15th/19th H.)	1/ 2/41

18th DURHAM (WEST HARTLEPOOL) BATTALION

Lt.-Colonel

Graham, J. B. (Maj. late T.A.)	1/ 2/41

Majors

Moor, J. M.C. (Lt. late W. York R.)	1/ 2/41
Downey, J. A. L., D.S.O. (Maj. late Durham L.I.)	1/ 2/41
Forslina, C. V., M.C. (Lt. late M.G. Corps.)	1/ 2/41
Cameron, J. W. (2/Lt. late R.G.A.)	1/ 2/41
Gray, Sir William, Bt. (Capt. late York R.)	1/ 2/41
Philipson, S.	1/ 2/41
Metcalfe, J.	1/ 2/41
Swallow, M. G. S. (Capt. late Durham L.I.)	1/ 2/41
Gray, G. B.	1/ 2/41
Ward, J. M. (Lt. late R.W.K.)	16/ 5/41

Captains

Hall, F. J. R.	1/ 2/41
Willis, C. M.	1/ 2/41
Simmonds, O. W.	1/ 2/41
Pailor, T.	1/ 2/41
Cooper, T.	1/ 2/41
Barstow, H. H. A. (Lt. late Lan. Fus.)	1/ 2/41
Broadbent, F. G.	1/ 2/41
Battye, R. N. (Lt. late York R.)	1/ 2/41
Mitchell, G.	1/ 2/41

Lieutenants

Searle, A.	1/ 2/41
Robinson, G. R.	1/ 2/41
Rogers, V. F. (Pilot Offr. late R.A.F.)	1/ 2/41
Watson, J. S.	1/ 2/41
Purdon, A. S.	1/ 2/41
Dobbie, R.	1/ 2/41
Wootton, G.	1/ 2/41
Stone, T. W. (Lt. late H.L.I.)	1/ 2/41
Parker, J.	1/ 2/41
Dobson, H.	1/ 2/41
Bartlett, T.	1/ 2/41
West, F., M.M.	1/ 2/41
Allison, H. C.	1/ 2/41
Davidson, A. W.	1/ 2/41
Forster, G. R.	1/ 2/41

56455-6(38)

DURHAM and NORTH RIDING DIVISION - contd.

DURHAM ZONE - contd.

NO. 4 GROUP - contd.

18th Durham (West Hartlepool) Battalion - contd.

Lieutenants - contd.

Ayre, F.	1/ 2/41
Wynn, S. H.	1/ 2/41
Brown, J. T. T.	1/ 2/41
Mitchell, E. E.	1/ 2/41
Reynard, J. J.	1/ 2/41
Wenn, E.	1/ 2/41
Siddell, W. C.	1/ 2/41
Parker, J.	1/ 2/41
White, A. P., M.M.	1/ 2/41
Gordon, S.	1/ 2/41
Whales, R. W.	1/ 2/41
Wright, N.	1/ 2/41
Meynell, G. H.	1/ 2/41
Sweeney, J. R.	1/ 2/41
Humphries, J.	1/ 2/41
Brown, J. E.	24/ 6/41
Salmon, H. P.	24/ 6/41
Lund, J. K.	7/ 7/41

2nd Lieutenants

D'Evelin, C. W. H.	1/ 2/41
Clark, W. S.	1/ 2/41
Wood, R.	1/ 2/41
Stockill, J. W.	1/ 2/41
Johnston, W.	1/ 2/41
Woodhead, F. A.	1/ 2/41
Brooks, E. J.	1/ 2/41
Pearson, R. A.	1/ 2/41
Harvey, J. B.	1/ 2/41
Dodds, J. B.	1/ 2/41
Perryman, F. S.	1/ 2/41
Lawson, T.	1/ 2/41
Sanderson. S.	1/ 2/41
Metcalfe, S.	1/ 2/41
Ward, R.	1/ 2/41

2nd Lieutenants - contd.

Tucker, C. A. E.	1/ 2/41
Guttridge, B.	1/ 2/41
McElhone, J. F.	1/ 2/41
Pounder, R.	1/ 2/41
Arrowsmith, J. R.	1/ 2/41
Reed, J. W.	1/ 2/41
Welch, F.	1/ 2/41
Naisbitt, R. H.	1/ 2/41
Barker, E. D.	1/ 2/41
Barker, J. J.	7/ 7/41
Edmundson, F.	7/ 7/41
Greenwell, T.	7/ 7/41
Marshall, G.	7/ 7/41
Taylor, C. A.	7/ 7/41

Adjutant & Quarter-Master

Stott, Capt. (actg. 10/5/41) H. J., Gen. List Inf.	10/ 5/41

Medical Officer

Lithgow, Maj. J., M.B. (Lt. late R.G.A.)	1/ 2/41

DURHAM and NORTH RIDING DIVISION - contd.

DURHAM ZONE - contd.

NO. 4 GROUP - contd.

19th DURHAM (STOCKTON) BATTALION

Majors

Stopford, C. J. 1/ 2/41
Alton, H. 1/ 2/41
Andrew, G. B. (Lt. late Durham L.I.) 1/ 2/41
Ropner, J. R. (Lt. late T.A.) 1/ 2/41
Cross, J. H. (Capt. late R.F.C.) 1/ 2/41
Braham, J. E. (Capt. late R.A.) 1/ 2/41
Minter, B. T. 1/ 2/41
Graham, E. (2/Lt. late R.A.F.) 1/ 2/41

Captains

Castle, H. (Lt. late R.A.F.) 1/ 2/41
Jones, W. H. 1/ 2/41
Tremholme, P. J. (Capt. late R.T.C.) 1/ 2/41
Allan, H. (2/Lt. late York R.) 1/ 2/41
Hunton, J. A. 1/ 2/41
Williams, H. (2/Lt. late R.A.) 1/ 2/41
Candler, A. B. (Lt. late R.E.) 1/ 2/41
Ainsworth, W. M. 21/ 5/41

Lieutenants

Corner, W. H. J. 1/ 2/41
Abbott, W. (Lt. late Midd'x R.) 1/ 2/41
Robson, T. H. 1/ 2/41
Dixon, J. R., M.M. 1/ 2/41
Lonie, L. C. (2/Lt. late Durham L.I.) 1/ 2/41

Lieutenants - contd.

Atkinson, G. B. (Lt. late R.G.A.) 1/ 2/41
Marwood, W. E. (Lt. late Durham L.I.) 1/ 2/41
Ware, W. 1/ 2/41
Hutton-Wilson, M. J. C. 1/ 2/41
Metcalfe, J. 1/ 2/41
Coulson, H. J. L. 1/ 2/41
Spark, G. W. 1/ 2/41
Brownlee, T. H. (Lt. late R.F.A.) 1/ 2/41
Coop, F. E. 1/ 2/41
Wright, W. 1/ 2/41
Corfield, J. 1/ 2/41
Ring, A. V. 1/ 2/41
Wilson, P. (Flying Offr. late R.F.C.) 1/ 2/41
Cockerline, G. A. 1/ 2/41
O'Neill, H. (2/Lt. late R. North'd Fus.) 1/ 2/41
Robinson, A. S. 1/ 2/41
Sladden, A. (Lt. late Durham, L.I.) 1/ 2/41
Campbell, W. McI. (Capt. late R.A.S.C.) 1/ 2/41
Reay, J. L. (Lt. late Durham, L.I.) 1/ 2/41
Bosanquet, C. H. (Capt. late R.E.) 1/ 2/41
Skillings, A. G. (2/Lt. late R.A.S.C.) 1/ 2/41
Kay, W. E. 1/ 2/41
Sykes, P. H. 1/ 2/41
Leetch, S., M.C. (Lt. late M.G. Corps.) 1/ 2/41
Leng, J. R. 1/ 2/41
Coleby, M. V. 1/ 2/41
Telford, T. (Lt. late The King's R.) 1/ 2/41
Naden, J. G., M.M. 1/ 2/41
Brookfield, G. A. 1/ 2/41
Baker, H. J. G., M.M. 1/ 2/41
Woods, R. (Lt. late Inniskilling Fus.) 1/ 2/41

DURHAM and NORTH RIDING DIVISION - contd.

DURHAM ZONE - contd.

NO. 4 GROUP - contd.

19th Durham (Stockton) Battalion - contd.

Lieutenants - contd.

Jackson, T. A. (2/Lt. late R.A.F.)	1/ 5/41
Arkless, M. G., M.M.	21/ 5/41
Eastall, H.	5/ 7/41

2nd Lieutenants

Hall, W.	1/ 2/41
Jammeson, F. D.	1/ 2/41
Hall, J. S.	1/ 2/41
Wood, W. F.	1/ 2/41
Alderson, N. H.	1/ 2/41
Knaggs, W.	1/ 2/41
Dukes, F.	1/ 2/41
Fail, C. H.	1/ 2/41
Cooper, G. E. (2/Lt. late R. War R.)	1/ 2/41
Pakenham, G. R. M. (Lt. late Rifle Bde.)	1/ 2/41
Buttriss, J.	1/ 2/41
Wright, E. B.	1/ 2/41
Smith, R. H.	1/ 2/41
Whitfield, E. (2/Lt. late R.A.F.)	1/ 2/41
Painter, H. F.	1/ 2/41
Foulkes, R. A.	1/ 2/41
Dufton, H.	1/ 2/41
Prince, W. A.	1/ 2/41
Burn, P. T.	1/ 2/41
Bowen, R. S.	19/ 6/41
Jones, T.	19/ 6/41
Lander, C. E.	19/ 6/41
Milne, P. J.	19/ 6/41
Murray, W. E.	19/ 6/41

2nd Lieutenants - contd.

Taylor, G. B. (Lt. late R.A.)	19/ 6/41
Wice, H. G.	19/ 6/41
Aitchison, R.	22/ 7/41
Brodie, H. T.	22/ 7/41
Chave, F. C. G.	22/ 7/41
Fairbrother, J.	22/ 7/41
Herbert, S. R.	22/ 7/41
McKean, J.	19/ 6/41
Parkinson, A.	22/ 7/41
Whitehead, S. C.	22/ 7/41

Adjutant & Quarter-Master

Medical Officer

Harkness, Maj. R., M.B.	1/ 2/41

56455-6(41)

20th DURHAM (DARLINGTON) BATTALION

Lt.-Colonel

Lord, S. R. (Capt. late Gren. G'ds.) 1/ 2/41

Majors

Leake, A. B., M.C. (Capt. late R. North'd. Fus.) 1/ 2/41
Baister, S. L. (Maj. late R.E.) 1/ 2/41
Smith, H. W. (Flying Offr. late R.A.F.) 1/ 2/41
Smeddle, R. A. (2/Lt. late R.F.A.) 1/ 2/41
Ropner, R. D. (Lt. T.A. Res.) 1/ 2/41
Crozier, R. N. 1/ 2/41
Brown, T. F. W. (Capt. late R.G.A.) 1/ 2/41

Captains

Pearce, R. C. (Lt. late Durham L.I.) 1/ 2/41
Golightly, L. (Capt. late Green Howards) 1/ 2/41
Haggie, D. A. (Capt. late Scottish Horse) 1/ 2/41
Reeves, L. 1/ 2/41
Stobbs, H. 1/ 2/41
Wood, P., D.S.O. (Capt. late Durham L.I.) 1/ 2/41

Lieutenants

Challands, R. S. (Capt. late Gren. G'ds.) 1/ 2/41
Burrell, H. (Capt. late Durham L.I.) 1/ 2/41
Scrope, R. H. 1/ 2/41
Harris, W. G. (Lt. late R.F.A.) 1/ 2/41
Gill, E. W., O.B.E. (Lt.-Col. late R.E.) 1/ 2/41
Robertson, T. (Lt. late R. Fus.) 1/ 2/41
Spielman, C. M., M.C. (Maj. late R.E.) 1/ 2/41
Huss, J. W., M.B.E. 1/ 2/41
Pugh, W. D. 1/ 2/41
Hall, W. A. 1/ 2/41
Miller, W. 1/ 2/41
Wain, G. T., T.D. 1/ 2/41
Lax, N. 1/ 2/41
Burlinson, F. J. 1/ 2/41
Foster, C. W., M.C. 1/ 2/41
Taylor, J. (Lt. late R.A.F.) 1/ 2/41
Marsden, H. 1/ 2/41
Tarn, J. 1/ 2/41
Heslop, T. 1/ 2/41
Duncan, N. MacI. R. (Lt. late R.E.) 1/ 2/41
Kenyon, F. 1/ 2/41
Frith, R. 1/ 2/41
Harrison, D. R. 1/ 2/41
Whent, H. 1/ 2/41
Morgan, J. C. 1/ 2/41
Wallace, C. R. 1/ 2/41
Webster, J. A. (Lt. late Black Watch) 1/ 2/41

Lieutenants - contd.

Oliver, G. R. (Lt. late Durham L.I.) 1/ 2/41
Dunne, W. F. (Capt. late Durham L.I.) 1/ 2/41
Francombe, K. W. (Capt. late T.A.) 1/ 2/41
Welek, E. F. 1/ 2/41
Owen, A. J. (2/Lt. late The King's R.) 17/ 7/41

2nd Lieutenants

Haylett, R., M.C. (Capt. late Durham L.I.) 1/ 2/41
Burnip, C. W. (Lt. late Durham L.I.) 1/ 2/41
Lupton, F., M.M. 1/ 2/41
Robinson, W. 1/ 2/41
Smart, W. J. 1/ 2/41
Carter, W. N. (Capt. late London R.) 1/ 2/41
Winn, R. 1/ 2/41
Snowdon, R. 1/ 2/41
Waters, F. 1/ 2/41
Routledge, H. (2/Lt. late R. North'd. Fus.) 1/ 2/41
Brownless, F. O. 1/ 2/41
Davenport, J. W. 1/ 2/41
Henderson, W. 1/ 2/41
Gibson, T. 1/ 2/41
Moody, J. B. 1/ 2/41
Nowlin, S. J. 1/ 2/41
Proud, W. 1/ 2/41
Vickerton, W. R. 1/ 2/41
Moffatt, T. E. 1/ 2/41
Smith, P. C. S. (Lt. late R.S. Fus.) 1/ 2/41
Knowles, F. H. 1/ 2/41
Davie, B. 1/ 2/41
Scott, J. 1/ 2/41
Stafford, H. C. (Lt. late Ind. Army) 1/ 2/41
Walker, F. T. 1/ 2/41
Raeburn, R. B. 1/ 2/41
Appleby, A. 1/ 2/41

Adjutant & Quarter-Master

Medical Officer

Tindall, Maj. R., M.C. (Maj. late R.A.M.C.) 1/ 2/41

DURHAM and NORTH RIDING DIVISION - contd.

DURHAM ZONE - contd.

NO. 5 GROUP

Commander — Walton, Col. F., M.C. (Lt.-Col. late Durham L.I.) 1/ 2/41

15th DURHAM (BISHOP AUCKLAND) BATTALION

Lt.- Colonel

Dewhurst, N., O.B.E. (Maj. late R.A.S.C.)	1/ 2/41

Majors

Steel, J. R. (Lt. T.A. Res.)	1/ 2/41
Spanton, G.	1/ 2/41
Guthrie, K. M., M.C. (Capt. T.A. Res.)	1/ 2/41
Myers, E. M.	1/ 2/41
Dixon, R. H. (Lt. late Durham L.I.)	1/ 2/41
Salkeld, G. L. (Lt. late R.E.)	1/ 2/41
Brown, J. C. (Capt. late R.E.)	1/ 2/41
Thorpe, S. D., M.C. (Maj. late Durham L.I.)	1/ 2/41

Captains

Farra, R. E., M.B.E. (Lt. late R.E.)	1/ 2/41
Ware, C. R.	1/ 2/41
Ferens, A. (Capt. late R.A.S.C.)	1/ 2/41
Knox, S. (Lt. late R.T.C.)	1/ 2/41
Rickinson, P. W. T. (Lt. late Durham L.I.)	1/ 2/41
Flesher, H., M.C. (Capt. late R.E.)	1/ 2/41
Stitt, W. E.	1/ 2/41
Ramsay, W. M., M.C. (Capt. late North'd Fus.)	1/ 2/41
Richardson, F. S. (Lt. late Durham L.I.)	1/ 2/41

Lieutenants

Bradley, G.	1/ 2/41
Huntley, O. (2/Lt. late R.A.S.C.)	1/ 2/41
Drummond, J.G.L. (Lt. late R.A.S.C.)	1/ 2/41
Usherwood, E. E.	1/ 2/41
Pletts, H. (2/Lt. late Suffolk R.)	1/ 2/41
Selkirk, A.	1/ 2/41
Chambers, T.	1/ 2/41
Wyllie, D. G.	1/ 2/41
Greer, R.	1/ 2/41
Rogers, W.	1/ 2/41
Morgan, E.	1/ 2/41
Stephenson, R. B.	1/ 2/41
Greenwood, J.	1/ 2/41
Gittins, W.	1/ 2/41
Pattison, C. F. A.	1/ 2/41
Morgan, R. W.	1/ 2/41
Joyce, W.	1/ 2/41
Reavley, R. B.	1/ 2/41
Chapman, J. W., M.M., D.S.M.	1/ 2/41
Adams, T. H. F. (Capt. late M.G. Corps.)	1/ 2/41
Waddell, C. L.	1/ 2/41
Woodfine, S.	1/ 2/41
Childs, W. J.	1/ 2/41
Elland, W. K.	1/ 6/41
Watkins, R. S.	13/ 6/41
Beilby, R. D.	20/ 6/41
Hodgson, E. S. (2/Lt. late R.T.C.)	23/ 6/41

DURHAM and NORTH RIDING DIVISION - contd.

DURHAM ZONE - contd.

NO. 5 GROUP - contd.

15th Durham (Bishop Auckland) Battalion - contd.

2nd Lieutenants

Baber, C. H. (Lt. late E. York R.)	1/ 2/41
Elliott, J. G.	1/ 2/41
Lodge, G.	1/ 2/41
Hemsley, W.	1/ 2/41
Robinson, G. L.	1/ 2/41
Miller, J.	1/ 2/41
Pope, S.	1/ 2/41
Burdess, G.	1/ 2/41
Paterson, W.	1/ 2/41
Murray, J. M., M.M.	1/ 2/41
Ellis, E.	1/ 2/41
Wailes, H.	1/ 2/41
Harrison, J.	1/ 2/41
Gardiner, W. J.	1/ 2/41
Craggs, E. W.	1/ 2/41
Johnson, T.	1/ 2/41
Snaith, A. F.	1/ 2/41
Brown, A.	1/ 2/41
Ridley, H.	1/ 2/41

Adjutant & Quarter-Master

Rudd, Capt. (actg. 7/5/41) J., Gen. List Inf.	7/ 5/41

Medical Officer

16th DURHAM (WEARDALE) BATTALION

Lt.-Colonel

Sprot, H. (Lt.-Col. ret. pay)	1/ 2/41

Majors

Hildyard, E. J. W.	1/ 2/41
Angus, G. R., M.C. (Capt. late Durham L.I.)	1/ 2/41
Pattison, J. (Lt. late Durham L.I.)	1/ 2/41

Captains

Gowdy, E. H. (Lt. late R. North'd Fus.)	1/ 2/41
Turnbull, F., M.M.	1/ 2/41
Dunham, K. C.	1/ 2/41
Hobson, B., M.M.	1/ 2/41
Cundle, R. B., M.C. (Capt. late K.O.S.B.)	1/ 2/41

Lieutenants

Dickinson, G. W.	1/ 2/41
Cowen, G. A.	1/ 2/41
Bainbridge, J. T.	1/ 2/41
Phillipson, W. H.	1/ 2/41
White, W. H.	1/ 2/41
Graham, C., D.C.M.	1/ 2/41
Mews, T.	1/ 2/41
Johnson, R. E.	1/ 2/41
Vickers, J. J.	1/ 2/41
Tanner, G. W.	1/ 2/41
Thompson, J.	1/ 2/41
Ridley, J.	1/ 2/41
Cain, N.	1/ 2/41
Gill, F.	1/ 2/41

2nd Lieutenants

Riseborough, L.	1/ 2/41
Newton, G. W.	1/ 2/41
Pattinson, C. K.	24/ 4/41

Adjutant & Quarter-Master

Medical Officer

DURHAM and NORTH RIDING DIVISION - contd.

DURHAM ZONE - contd.

NO. 5 GROUP - contd.

17th DURHAM (BARNARD CASTLE) BATTALION

Lt.-Colonel

Darling, C. C. (Lt. late T.A.)	1/ 2/41

Majors

Clark, E. P. (Lt. late W. York R.)	1/ 2/41
Peat, W., M.M. (2/Lt. late R. North'd Fus.)	1/ 2/41
Phillips, S. R. E., T.D. (Lt. late Hereford R.)	1/ 2/41
Holmes, E. R. H. (Capt. late Durham L.I.)	1/ 2/41

Captains

Beetham, B.	1/ 2/41
Russell, A. (Lt. late W. York R.)	1/ 2/41
Pease, C. E. (Lt. late Green Howards)	1/ 2/41
Cruickshank, G. A.	12/ 7/41

Lieutenants

Walton, H.	1/ 2/41
Shortridge, R.	1/ 2/41
Beadle, J. R.	1/ 2/41

Lieutenants - contd.

Williams, P. C.	1/ 2/41
Walton, S.	1/ 2/41
Simpson, G.	1/ 2/41
Bousfield, W.	1/ 2/41
Hunter, C.	1/ 2/41
Forster, A.	1/ 2/41
Steel, J. F.	1/ 2/41

2nd Lieutenants

Peacock, T. C., M.M.	1/ 2/41
Alderson, W. G.	1/ 2/41
Harris, A. S.	1/ 2/41
Birkbeck, H. E.	1/ 2/41
Place, E. A. (Lt. late R.E.)	26/ 6/41

Adjutant & Quarter-Master

Medical Officer

Campbell, Maj. A., M.C., M.B. (Capt. late R.A.M.C.	1/ 2/41

DURHAM and NORTH RIDING DIVISION - contd.

DURHAM ZONE - contd.

NO. 6 GROUP

Commander	Kirkup, Col. E. H. (Maj. ret. T. A.)	1/ 2/41
Second in Command	Haswell, Lt.-Col. J.	1/ 2/41
Assistant to Commander	Taylor, Capt. J. (2/Lt. late R. F. C.)	1/ 2/41

10th DURHAM (GATESHEAD) BATTALION

Colonel

Lambert, D., M.M.	1/ 2/41

Majors

Mossman, T.	1/ 2/41
Carr, W. D.	1/ 2/41
Stout, N.	1/ 2/41
Campbell, A. A. (Lt. late M. G. Corps)	1/ 2/41
Bradley, G. L., T.D., (Maj. late R. North'd. Fus.)	1/ 2/41
Irvine, W.	1/ 2/41

Captains

Booth, H. A. (Lt. late R. G. A.)	1/ 2/41
Jordan, W. S.	1/ 2/41
Balmain, D.	1/ 2/41
Hinchcliffe, A.	1/ 2/41

Lieutenants

McGranaghan, G. R.	1/ 2/41
Parkin, S.	1/ 2/41
Taylor, R.	1/ 2/41
Robinson, E. C.	1/ 2/41
Heal, O. W.	1/ 2/41
Earnshaw, H. D. W.	1/ 2/41
Day, R. F.	1/ 2/41
Dinning, J. L.	1/ 2/41
Dowdeswell, T. R. (Maj. late Welch. R.)	1/ 2/41
Venables, T. V.	1/ 2/41
Macintyre, G. R.	1/ 2/41
Peacock, W. T.	1/ 2/41
Stobbs, A. G.	1/ 2/41
Scarth, F. L.	1/ 2/41
Thompson, A.	1/ 2/41
Jones, S. G. (Lt. late R. E.)	1/ 2/41
Richardson, W.	1/ 2/41
Gunter, S.	1/ 2/41
Humble, R.	1/ 2/41
Bryden, D. G. (2/Lt. late R. G. A.)	1/ 2/41
Statters, A. W.	1/ 2/41
Hall, T. R.	1/ 2/41

Lieutenants - contd.

Fisher, J. N.	16/ 5/41
Duddin, A. (Lt. late M. G. Corps.)	30/ 5/41

2nd Lieutenants

Macdonald, J.	1/ 2/41
Guest, C.	1/ 2/41
Read, A. E.	1/ 2/41
Woodman, A. L.	1/ 2/41
Fender, H.	1/ 2/41
Richardson, W.	1/ 2/41
Wilkinson-Cox, D. G.	1/ 2/41
Brown, D. G.	1/ 2/41
Hogg, R. (2/Lt. late Ind. Army)	1/ 2/41
Bridge, E. W.	1/ 2/41
Richardson, L. (2/Lt. late North'd. Fus.)	1/ 2/41
Swan, R. H.	1/ 2/41
Ryle, P. J. (2/Lt. late R.G.A.)	1/ 2/41
Pedersen, G.	1/ 2/41
Oades, W. (Sub-Lt. late R. N. V. R.)	1/ 2/41
McManus, J. E.	1/ 2/41
Johnson, E. R.	1/ 2/41
Rose, L.	6/ 6/41
Lauder, W. G.	6/ 6/41
Simon, G. W. L.	7/ 6/41
Rutherford, J.	20/ 6/41
Bainbridge, F.	11/ 7/41
Gibson, E. B.	11/ 7/41
Seed, T. G.	11/ 7/41
Stephenson, C., M.C. (Capt. late Durham L. I.	11/ 7/41
Allan, R. G.	11/ 7/41
Sharp, J. S.	11/ 7/41
Cooper, C. R.	11/ 7/41

Adjutant & Quarter-Master

Medical Officer

Hall, Maj. J. C.	20/ 6/41

56455-6(46)

DURHAM and NORTH RIDING DIVISION - contd.

DURHAM ZONE - contd.

NO. 6 GROUP - contd.

21st DURHAM (GATESHEAD) BATTALION

Lt.-Colonel

Topping, J. W. 1/ 2/41

Majors

Sisterson, R. S. (Lt. late Res. Dragoons) 1/ 2/41
Brown, A. (Lt. late Durham L.I.) 1/ 2/41
Foster, E. (2/Lt. late R. North'd Fus.) 1/ 2/41
Mole, D. A. 1/ 2/41
Baldock, L. W. J. 1/ 2/41

Captains

Chamberlain, R. F. O. M. (2/Lt. late R.A.F.) 1/ 2/41
Bland, R. (2/Lt. late Bedfs. & Herts. R.) 1/ 2/41
Williamson, D. 1/ 2/41
Woodeson, G. A. 1/ 2/41

Lieutenants

McAughtry, L., M.M. 1/ 2/41
Gibson, R. 1/ 2/41
Clouston, J. H. 1/ 2/41
Cousin, J. W. (2/Lt. late Durham L.I.) 1/ 2/41
Foster, T. 1/ 2/41
Cowey, T. 1/ 2/41
Spark, C. 1/ 2/41
Juan, C. (2/Lt. late R.E.) 1/ 2/41
Lawton, G. K. (2/Lt. late R. North'd Fus.) 1/ 2/41

Lieutenants - contd.

Stephenson, N., M.M. 1/ 2/41
Cockburn, P. R. 1/ 2/41
Harris, E. 1/ 2/41
Millar, W. H. (2/Lt. late Cameronians) 1/ 2/41
Carruthers, J. B. 1/ 2/41
Cairns, M. 1/ 2/41

2nd Lieutenants

Wilson, D. 1/ 2/41
Conway, T. 1/ 2/41
Wilson, S. F. 1/ 2/41
Johnson, S. H. D. 1/ 2/41
Robson, R. O. 1/ 2/41
Appleby, W. 1/ 2/41
Mossman, A. (2/Lt. late Durham L.I.) 1/ 2/41
Broderick, W. S. 1/ 2/41
Dickson, J. H., M.M. 1/ 2/41
Smith, G. 1/ 2/41

Adjutant & Quarter-Master

Medical Officer

DURHAM and NORTH RIDING DIVISION - contd.

NORTH RIDING ZONE (County of Yorkshire)

Commander	Wilkinson, Col. W. T., D.S.O. (Lt.-Col. ret. T.A.)	1/ 2/41
Territorial Army Association administering	The Yorkshire (North Riding) T.A. & A.F. Association, Thirsk Road, Northallerton.	

NO.1 GROUP

Commander	McCurdie, Col. J. R., M.C. (Maj. late R.A.M.C.)	1/ 2/41
Assistant to Commander	Usher, Capt. W. T.	1/ 2/41

8th NORTH RIDING (MIDDLESBROUGH) BATTALION

Lt.-Colonel

Garbutt, H. C., M.C. (Lt. late R.E.)	1/ 2/41

Majors

Pickering, J. H. (Lt. late Lan. Fus.)	1/ 2/41
Telfer, W. E.	1/ 2/41
Jackson, F., M.M.	1/ 2/41
Southern J. H.	11/ 7/41
Stewart, P. C.	11/ 7/41

Captains

Charlton, J. C., D.C.M.	1/ 2/41
Cox, F.	1/ 2/41
Bromwich, B. A.	11/ 7/41
Taylor, J. B. (Lt. late A. & S.H.)	11/ 7/41
Burton, C.	21/ 7/41

Lieutenants

Brooks, G.	1/ 2/41
Tindale, J. J.	1/ 2/41
Gilligan J.	1/ 2/41
Robson, G. W.	1/ 2/41
Gregory, G. W. F.	1/ 2/41
Williamson, W. J.	1/ 2/41
Huddlestone, S. A. (2/Lt. late R.A.F.)	1/ 2/41
Rudd, J. P.	1/ 2/41
Brodie, B.	11/ 7/41
Capes, R. S. H. (Lt. late Lond. R.)	11/ 7/41
Corkish, R. W.	11/ 7/41
Dawson, H. S.	11/ 7/41
Fletcher, W. L.	11/ 7/41
Heslop, A. W. (Lt. late R.E.)	11/ 7/41
Metcalfe, N.	11/ 7/41
Murphy, R. S., M.M.	11/ 7/41
Pringle, G. W.	11/ 7/41
Toms, J. W. (Lt. late R.N.R.)	11/ 7/41
Walker, H. L.	11/ 7/41
Parker, H.	11/ 7/41

Lieutenants - contd.

Foxall, J. W.	21/ 7/41
Brown, H.	21/ 7/41

2nd Lieutenants

McCormack, H. MacD.	1/ 2/41
Aaronricks, W. T. (2/Lt. late N. Stafford R.)	1/ 2/41
Lambert, E. J.	1/ 2/41
McLauchlan, T. W.	1/ 2/41
Jones, J. G.	1/ 2/41
Davison, I.	1/ 2/41
Boyd, R. O'C. D.	11/ 7/41
Burdon, M. F.	11/ 7/41
Byers, J. W., M.M.	11/ 7/41
Carter, D. W. L.	11/ 7/41
Dobson, R.	11/ 7/41
Galilee, R.	11/ 7/41
Griffiths, H. R.	11/ 7/41
Jones, J. T., M.M.	11/ 7/41
Popple, W.	11/ 7/41
Sykes, W.	11/ 7/41
Zipfell, J. B. (Lt. late K.R.R.C.)	11/ 7/41
Fysh, G., M.M.	12/ 7/41
Gales, W. C.	12/ 7/41
Watson, C. D. G.	12/ 7/41

Adjutant & Quarter-Master

Battalion Medical Officer

Murphy, Maj. R. W., O.B.E., M.D. (Maj. late R.A.M.C.)	1/ 5/41

DURHAM and NORTH RIDING DIVISION - contd.

NORTH RIDING ZONE (County of Yorkshire) - contd.

No.1 GROUP - contd.

9th NORTH RIDING (MIDDLESBROUGH) BATTALION

Lt.-Colonel

Grabham, S. (Capt. late T.A. Res.)	1/ 2/41

Majors

Smith, C. B. (2/Lt. late R.A.S.C.)	1/ 2/41
Proudlock, J. H.	1/ 2/41
Cooper, L. B. (Maj. late T.A.)	1/ 2/41
Ellis, W. T. (Lt. late Green Howards)	1/ 2/41

Captains

Harrison, A. (Lt. late R.F.A.)	1/ 2/41
Lynn, C.	1/ 2/41
Malcolm, I. C.	1/ 2/41
Mellanby, F. A.	13/ 6/41

Lieutenants

Watson, H.	1/ 2/41
Sargeant, J. H.	1/ 2/41
McCreton, J. B.	1/ 2/41
Clayton, E. J.	1/ 2/41
Metcalfe, A. I.	1/ 2/41
Hart, J. H.	1/ 2/41
Underwood, J. K.	1/ 2/41
Young, J. H. (Lt. late K.O.S.B.)	1/ 2/41
North, W. S. (Lt. late Monmouth R.)	1/ 2/41
Pledger, S.	1/ 2/41
Trees, W. W. M. (2/Lt. late R. Mar.)	1/ 2/41

Lieutenants - contd.

Brown, J. A.	1/ 2/41
Tomlinson, A.	1/ 2/41
Crosby, A. T.	16/ 5/41
Wycherley, T.	30/ 5/41
Metcalfe, J.	13/ 6/41

2nd Lieutenants

Rushford, E.	1/ 2/41
Beckwith, G. A.	1/ 2/41
Barker, W.	1/ 2/41
Burnell, R.	1/ 2/41
Hughes, W.	1/ 2/41
Bowley, T. H.	1/ 2/41
Bernard, J. W.	1/ 2/41
Imeson, C. C. (Lt. late R.T.C.)	1/ 2/41
Patterson, N. A.	1/ 2/41
Roe, T. N.	1/ 2/41
Cunnlett, T. E.	9/ 6/41
Bell, C.	9/ 7/41

Adjutant & Quarter-Master

Medical Officer

Hubbersty, Maj. F. C.	19/ 5/41

DURHAM and NORTH RIDING DIVISION - contd.

NORTH RIDING ZONE (County of Yorkshire) - contd.

No.2 GROUP

Commander	Kitching, Col. H. E., M.B.E. (Bt. Col. T.A. Res.) (Hon. Col. T.A.)	1/ 2/41
Assistant to Commander	Savage, Capt. H. L.	1/ 7/41

3rd NORTH RIDING (THORNABY) BATTALION

Lt.-Colonel

Faber, H. G., T.D. (Col. T.A.)	1/ 2/41

Majors

Sowerby, G. L., M.C. (Capt. late Durham L.I.)	1/ 2/41
Robinson, J. R., M.B.E., T.D. (Maj. late Durham L.I.)	1/ 2/41
Palmer, A. L. (Capt. late R.A.F.)	1/ 2/41
Cundey, J. W. L.	1/ 2/41

Captains

Papworth, W. (Lt. late R.G.A.)	1/ 2/41
VC Cooper, E. (Lt. late K.R.R.C.)	1/ 2/41

Lieutenants

Norminton, E.	1/.2/41
Pain, J. F., M.C. (2/Lt. late Hampshire R.)	1/ 2/41
Barthram, J.	1/ 2/41
Macfarlane, W. C. (Lt. late W. York R.)	1/ 2/41
Pattinson, J. L.	1/ 2/41
Brooke, T. B.	1/ 2/41
Bradley, R.	1/ 2/41
Briggs, W. F. (Lt. late Green Howards)	1/ 2/41

Lieutenants - contd.

Clarke, J. H.	1/ 2/41
Thurston, D.	1/ 2/41

2nd Lieutenants

Bond, N. R.	1/ 2/41
Twiddy, H. C.	1/ 2/41
Heaton, H.	1/ 2/41
Priddle, A.	1/ 2/41
Clayton, J. R.	1/ 2/41
Johnson, A. E.	25/ 3/41
Brudenell, J.	15/ 7/41
Bell, W. H. B.	30/ 7/41

Adjutant & Quarter-Master

Keyworth, Capt. (actg. 7/5/41) H. S., Green Howards (T.A.)	7/ 5/41

Medical Officer

Waldie, Capt. J. T.	24/ 5/41

DURHAM and NORTH RIDING DIVISION - contd.

NORTH RIDING ZONE (County of Yorkshire) - contd.

No.2 GROUP - contd.

4th NORTH RIDING (GUISBOROUGH) BATTALION

Lt.-Colonel

Fitton, C. V., M.C. (Capt. late Ind. Army)	1/ 2/41

Majors

Tate, J. H. (Capt. late R.T.C.)	1/ 2/41
Emsley, H., M.C. (Lt. late Manch. R.)	1/ 2/41
Simmonds, J. H. (Lt. late North'd. Fus.)	1/ 2/41
Wilken, A. G. (Hon. Maj. late Can. Mil. Forces)	1/ 2/41
Forty, H. J., M.C. (Capt. late D.W.R.)	8/ 7/41

Captains

Hutton, F. P.	1/ 2/41
Teasdale, E. W. (2/Lt. late Green Howards)	1/ 2/41
Ogden, S. R. (Lt. late R.N.)	1/ 2/41
Walker, S., M.C. (Capt. late Y. & L.R.)	1/ 2/41
Gibb, W. H.	1/ 2/41
Sanderson, A. H.	1/ 2/41
Atterton, R.	1/ 2/41

Lieutenants

Gaudie, R.	1/ 2/41
Heslop, G. C., M.C. (Capt. late Durham L.I.)	1/ 2/41
Spence, V.	1/ 2/41
Thomas, I.	1/ 2/41
Turley, W.	1/ 2/41
Roberts, S. A.	1/ 2/41
Barker, J.	1/ 2/41
Barker, P.	1/ 2/41
Jellicoe, J. A. (Capt. late Ind. Army)	1/ 2/41
Reed, S., M.M. (2/Lt. late Royal R.)	1/ 2/41
Groves, A. E., D.C.M.	1/ 2/41
Wedgewood, J.	1/ 2/41
Boardman, G.	1/ 2/41
Kingston, T.	1/ 2/41
Tubbs, W. H. (Lt. late R.F.A.)	1/ 2/41

Lieutenants - contd.

Dorman, R. B. (Capt. late M.G. Corps	1/ 2/41
Dixon, T. B.	1/ 2/41
Pilgrim, F. (Lt. late R.M.)	1/ 2/41
King, H.	1/ 2/41
Scott, F.	1/ 2/41
Lawsen, W. B.	1/ 2/41
Taylor, J.	1/ 2/41
Blackett, J.	1/ 2/41
White, A. H.	1/ 2/41
Wright, E. W.	1/ 2/41
Kerr, R.	1/ 2/41
Chaplin, A. W.	1/ 2/41
Ford, J. E.	1/ 2/41
Dixon, E. R.	20/ 5/41
Sillars, D. O.	2/ 6/41
Moore, E. C.	19/ 6/41
Crooks, F. W.	21/ 6/41

2nd Lieutenants

Franklin, F. S.	1/ 2/41
Hotten, F.	1/ 2/41
Porton, J.	1/ 2/41
Birch, Le R. G.	1/ 2/41
Stockburn, R. G.	1/ 2/41
Flatters, E. V.	1/ 2/41
Munroe, G. E.	1/ 2/41
Yorke, F. R.	1/ 2/41
Wicks, T.	1/ 2/41
Thompson, G. W.	1/ 2/41
Richardson, J., M.M.	1/ 2/41
Thompson, G. A.	1/ 2/41
Richardson, N.	19/ 6/41
Heselton, S.	25/ 6/41
Green, E.	5/ 8/41
Wright, J. H.	5/ 8/41
Woodcock, F.	5/ 8/41

Adjutant & Quarter-Master

Bolton, Capt. (actg. 26/4/41) J. H., Gen. List Inf.	26/ 4/41

Medical Officer

DURHAM and NORTH RIDING DIVISION - contd.

NORTH RIDING ZONE (County of Yorkshire) - contd.

NO. 2 GROUP - contd.

5th NORTH RIDING (SOUTH BANK) BATTALION

Lt.-Colonel

Barnley, G. W. W., T.D. (Maj. late T.A.) 1/ 2/41

Majors

Hutton, A. J. (Capt. late R.A.S.C.) 1/ 2/41
Kinnell, D. R. (2/Lt. late T.A.) 1/ 2/41
Thompson, P. H. 1/ 2/41
Baker, J. H. (Capt. late K.O.Y.L.I.) 1/ 2/41
Wood, A. 1/ 2/41
Armitage, J. (Lt. late W. York R.) 1/ 2/41

Captains

Linton, W. 1/ 2/41
Robson, P. 1/ 2/41
Allen, F. V. 1/ 2/41
Turnbull, J. T., D.C.M. 1/ 2/41
Cooke, W. 1/ 2/41
Connor, B. 1/ 2/41
Watson, R. B. 1/ 2/41
Geary, W. (2/Lt. late R.A.F.) 1/ 2/41
Moody C. (2/Lt. late R.A.F.) 1/ 2/41
Atkinson, T. E. 1/ 2/41
Fisher, E. 1/ 2/41
Forsyth, S. H., M.M. 1/ 2/41
Trees, R. 1/ 2/41
Winney, A. B. 15/ 5/41
Odell, C. F. 1/ 6/41
Sherwood, F. W. 1/ 6/41
Huthwaite, J. 21/ 6/41

Lieutenants

Bennington, T. H. 1/ 2/41
Plomor, S. W. 1/ 2/41
Turner, E. B. 1/ 2/41
Stoddart, T. E. 1/ 2/41
Mynott, P. 1/ 2/41
Stubbs, H. M. 1/ 2/41
Darke, P. E. 1/ 2/41
Fairbrass, W. 1/ 2/41
Buxton, S. 1/ 2/41
Thomas, E., M.M. 1/ 2/41
Payne, H. E. 1/ 2/41
Williams, G. H. 1/ 2/41
Ingram, W. W. 1/ 2/41
Warrior, F. G. 1/ 2/41
Whyte, J. 1/ 2/41
Blissendon, A. 1/ 2/41
Gilbraith, R. W. 1/ 2/41
Hopwood, E. E. 1/ 2/41
Grover, W. H. (2/Lt. late R.G.A.) 1/ 2/41
Hodgson, F. 1/ 2/41
Marshall, J. H. (Lt. late D.W.R.) 1/ 2/41
McGinn, J. 1/ 2/41
Alcock, H. A. 1/ 2/41

Lieutenants - contd.

Bell, P. 1/ 2/41
Parker, S., M.M. 1/ 2/41
Walton, J. 1/ 2/41
Larum, G., D.C.M., M.M. 1/ 2/41
Harris, J. W. 1/ 2/41
Overton, A. E. 1/ 2/41
Curtis, P. 1/ 2/41
Tye, J. G. 1/ 2/41
Owen, W. 1/ 2/41
Best, H. 1/ 2/41
Bringlow, J. H. 1/ 2/41
Duffy, J. J. 1/ 2/41
Empson, A. 1/ 2/41
Gibson, A. M. 1/ 2/41
Morley, A. 1/ 2/41
Griggs, P. R. 1/ 2/41
Duff, W. G. 1/ 2/41
Harris, A. H. 1/ 2/41
Scott, A. D. (Capt. late Green Howards) 1/ 2/41
Dickie, W. S., O.B.E. (Maj. late R.A.M.C.) 1/ 2/41
Hurst, T. W. 1/ 2/41
Williams, A. 1/ 2/41
King, E. C. L. 1/ 2/41
Cate, F. W. 1/ 2/41
Goodwill, J. W. 22/ 5/41
Wiles, W. S. 1/ 6/41
Kirton, E. D. 1/ 6/41
Odell, C. F. 1/ 6/41
Bean, S. 21/ 6/41
Addison, J. T. 21/ 6/41
Arnett, W. H. 19/ 7/41
Parsons, T., M.M. 19/ 7/41

2nd Lieutenants

Mackintosh, I. 1/ 2/41
Pilgrim, F. 1/ 2/41
Newhouse, J. C. 1/ 2/41
Whyman, W. E. 1/ 2/41
Page, M. 1/ 2/41
Hanson, W. 1/ 2/41
Smith, J. F. 1/ 2/41
Appleby, H. R. 1/ 2/41
Leng, W. 1/ 2/41
Fellows, T. 1/ 2/41
Lagan, W. 1/ 2/41

Adjutant & Quarter-Master

Medical Officer

Marshall, Maj. R. M., F.R.C.S. 26/ 5/41

DURHAM and NORTH RIDING DIVISION - contd.

NORTH RIDING ZONE (County of Yorkshire) - contd.

NO. 3 GROUP

Commander — Fairfax, Col. B. C., C.M.G. (Col. ret. pay) 1/ 2/41

1st NORTH RIDING (NORTHALLERTON) BATTALION

Lt.-Colonel

Gardner-Waterman, A. (Lt.-Col. ret. pay) 1/ 2/41

Majors

Pearson, G. T., C.B.E. (Lt.-Col. late R.F.A.) 1/ 2/41
Constantine, W. W., M.C., T.D. (Lt.-Col. late Green Howards) 1/ 2/41
Prior-Wandesforde, F. C. R., D.S.O. (Capt. late R.F.A.) 1/ 2/41
Green, H., M.C. (Capt. late Durham L. I.) 1/ 2/41
Ellis, F. C. 1/ 2/41

Captains

Coates, J. C. (Maj. S.U.L. Ind. Army) 1/ 2/41
Patterson, J., D.S.O. (Maj. ret. pay R.A.) 1/ 2/41
Powell, T. F. (Lt. late C.G'ds.) 1/ 2/41

Lieutenants

Parrington, W. F., M.C. (Capt. late R.F.A.) 1/ 2/41
Wombwell, B. M. (Capt. late S. G'ds.) 1/ 2/41
Hunter, J. W., D.S.O. (Capt. late North'd Fus.) 1/ 2/41
Green, D., M.C. (Capt. late W. York R.) 1/ 2/41
MacGregor, M. 1/ 2/41

Lieutenants - contd.

Porter, H.A., M.C. (Lt. late S. Stafford R.) 1/ 2/41
Heslop, J. C. (Lt. late Durham L.I.) 1/ 2/41
English, T. 1/ 2/41
Armstrong, A. E. 1/ 2/41
Robinson, H. 1/ 2/41
Gibson, L. (2/Lt. late Lan. Fus.) 1/ 2/41
Trechman, C. 1/ 2/41
Pollard, A. 1/ 2/41
Hutchinson, F. 1/ 2/41
Sigsworth, W. T. 1/ 2/41
Richards, E. J. 1/ 2/41
Buffy, F. G. (2/Lt. late E. York R.) 1/ 2/41
Patterson, L. M. 1/ 2/41

2nd Lieutenant

Bradley, J. 1/ 2/41

Adjutant & Quarter-Master

Medical Officer

McKim. Lt. W. 18/ 5/41

DURHAM and NORTH RIDING DIVISION - contd.

NORTH RIDING ZONE (County of Yorkshire) - contd.

NO. 3 GROUP - contd.

6th NORTH RIDING (HEWORTH) BATTALION

Lt.-Colonel

Crawford, J. (Capt. late K.O.S.B.) 1/ 2/41

Majors

Deakin, F. F., D.S.O. (Lt.-Col. ret.) 1/ 2/41
Scott, R. W. R., O.B.E., T.D. (Maj. Bt. Lt.-Col. T.A. Res.) 1/ 2/41
Stainer, P. (Flt.-Lt. late R.A.F.) 1/ 2/41
Bannister, H. 1/ 2/41
Kidd, C. H. 1/ 2/41

Captains

Thompson, W. 1/ 2/41
Widdicombe, F. R. 1/ 2/41
Dawson, B., M.M. 1/ 2/41
Curtis, W. (Lt. late R.G.A.) 1/ 2/41
Beevers, J. W. 1/ 2/41
Rider, B. 1/ 2/41
Ward, G., (2/Lt. late D.W.R.). 1/ 2/41
Whiteley, R. (Lt. late Manch. R.) 18/ 6/41
Wood, J. O. (Pilot Offr. late R.A.F.) 18/ 6/41

Lieutenants

Lloyd-Jones, T. (late Chaplain to the Forces (4th class)) 1/ 2/41
Smedley, A., D.C.M. (Capt. ret. pay) 1/ 2/41
Hetherton, J. (Lt. late W. York R.) 1/ 2/41
Abbey, T. E., M.M. (Lt. late Green Howards) 1/ 2/41

Lieutenants - contd.

King, G. (Lt. late R.A.F.) 1/ 2/41
Cobham, J. H. A. 1/ 2/41
Cowling, T. 1/ 2/41
Watson, J. A. (Lt. late R.G.A.) 1/ 2/41
Lumsden, T. D. 1/ 2/41
Peat, W. 1/ 2/41
McKinney, S. 1/ 2/41
Dunstan, J. E. 1/ 2/41
Walburn, J. S. H. 1/ 2/41
Bullen, J. N. 1/ 2/41
Cliff, A. D. 1/ 2/41
Pulleyn, T. J. 1/ 2/41
Hawking, T. A 1/ 2/41
Dunn, H. 1/ 2/41
Broadley, A. C. 1/ 2/41
Wood, L. E. 17/ 6/41
Booth, N. L. 17/ 6/41
Chadwick, C. A. 19/ 6/41
Pamley, T. R. 23/ 6/41
Kewport, H. (Late Chaplain to the Forces (4th class)) 25/ 6/41

2nd Lieutenants

Dennis, G. V. 1/ 2/41
Copley. A E. 1/ 2/41
Roe, S 13/ 6/41

Adjutant & Quarter-Master

Comb, Capt. (actg. 19/6/41) W., Gen. List Inf. 19/ 6/41

Medical Officer

Bullen, Capt. C E. S. 27/ 5/41

56455-6(54)

DURHAM and NORTH RIDING DIVISION - contd.

NORTH RIDING ZONE (County of Yorkshire) - contd.

NO. 3 GROUP - contd.

7th NORTH RIDING (MALTON) BATTALION

Lt.-Colonel

Holt, V. H., M.C. (Capt. late R.A.)	1/ 2/41

Majors

Kennedy, C. F. (Col. ret. pay)	1/ 2/41
Smith, P. G., T.D. (Maj. late T.A.)	1/ 2/41
Dawnay, E. G. (Capt. late 20th H.)	1/ 2/41
Whitehead, J. L. (Capt. late Green Howards)	1/ 2/41

Captains

Pearson, R. T., M.C. (Capt. late R.A.F.)	1/ 2/41
Bielby, H.	1/ 2/41
Smith, G.	1/ 2/41
Warren, E. C.	9/ 7/41

Lieutenants

Fife, R. D'A., C.M.G., D.S.O. (Lt.-Col. ret. pay)	1/ 2/41
Nobbs, C. H. H. (Flying Offr. late R.A.F.)	1/ 2/41
Pearson, H. W. (Maj. late M.G. Corps.)	1/ 2/41
Dicker, A. C.	1/ 2/41
Gordon, A., D.C.M., M.M.	1/ 2/41
Ward, C. T.	1/ 2/41
MacGregor, C.	1/ 2/41
Steel, T. M.M.	1/ 2/41
Nicholson, E. B.	1/ 2/41

Lieutenants - contd.

Beauvais, C. (2/Lt. late North'd H.)	1/ 2/41
Edwards, T. W. (Chaplain to the Forces (4th Class T.A. Res.)	1/ 2/41
Frost, J. C. M.	1/ 2/41
Moore, J.	1/ 2/41
Fenwick, J.	1/ 2/41
Nelson, G. H. (Capt. late M.G. Corps)	1/ 2/41
Coates, G. A.	1/ 2/41
Lee. H.	1/ 2/41
Smith, R. K.	25/ 4/41
Oliphant, L. R.	8/ 7/41

2nd Lieutenants

Brooke, T. (Maj. late K.R.R.C.)	1/ 2/41
Shaw, J. E. D., T.D. (Maj. late T.A.)	1/ 2/41
Longworth, S.	1/ 2/41
Hill, G. F. G. (Lt. Late The Queen's R.)	1/ 2/41

Adjutant & Quarter-Master

Comb, Capt. (actg. 19/6/41) W., Gen. List Inf.	19/ 6/41

Medical Officer

Murray, Capt. D. A.	17/ 6/41

DURHAM and NORTH RIDING DIVISION - contd.

NORTH RIDING ZONE (County of Yorkshire) - contd.

NO. 4 GROUP

Commander
Wilson, Col. A. E. J., D.S.O. 1/ 2/41

2nd NORTH RIDING (WHITBY) BATTALION

Lt.-Colonel

Gladstone, R. M. (M[illegible] late York R.)	1/ 2/41

Majors

Mass[illegible], [illegible] E., M.C. (C[illegible] late R.A.S.C.)	1/ 2/41
Smal[illegible], [illegible] W., T.D. (Capt. [illegible] R.F.A.)	1/ 2/41
Gallowa[illegible], [illegible] (Lt. [illegible] R.F.A.)	1/ 2/41

Captains

Sherratt, W. N.	1/ 2/41
Smales, L., M.C. (Maj. late R.A.S.C.)	1/ 2/41
Turnbull, T. M. (Capt. late A.S.C.)	1/ 2/41
Byass, A., M.C. (Capt. late R.A.S.C.)	1/ 2/41
Armstrong, P. B.	1/ 2/41

Lieutenants

Puckrin, G. M. (Lt. late W. York R.)	1/ 2/41
Overfield, F. W.	1/ 2/41
Ainsley, A. E. (2/Lt. late Green Howards)	1/ 2/41
Walker, W. M.	1/ 2/41
Taylor, T. A.	1/ 2/41
Richardson, J. P. A., D.S.C. (Lt. Cmdr. late R.N.R.)	1/ 2/41

Lieutenants - contd.

Hay, C.	1/ 2/41
Williamson, W. E.	1/ 2/41
Hodgson, J. W.	1/ 2/41
Grayson, W.	1/ 2/41
Harrison, G., M.M.	1/ 2/41
Cutforth, J. E.	1/ 2/41
Kenyon, G.	1/ 2/41
Wray, J. C.	1/ 2/41
Winspear, H.	1/ 2/41
Featherstone, A. P.	1/ 2/41
Wilson, J. W.	3/ 5/41
O'Donnell, J. W.	12/ 6/41

2nd Lieutenants

Hay, P. H.	1/ 2/41
Rosher, W. D.	1/ 2/41
Rutland, P. C.	1/ 2/41
Thompson, H. G.	1/ 2/41
Tames-Locking, S. T.	23/ 5/41
Marlow, F. H.	12/ 6/41

Adjutant & Quarter-Master

Medical Officer

Clarkson, Maj. F.	23/ 5/41

DURHAM and NORTH RIDING DIVISION - contd.

NORTH RIDING ZONE (County of Yorkshire) - contd.

NO. 4 GROUP - contd.

10th NORTH RIDING (SCARBOROUGH) BATTALION

Lt.-Colonel

Kitching, J. P. S. (Capt. late 5th Innis D.G.) 1/ 2/41

Majors

Heseltone, C. P. (Capt. late R.F.A.) 1/ 2/41
Moore, G. E., M.C. (Lt. late R.A.F.) 1/ 2/41
Hawksby, F. C. 1/ 2/41
Bielby, J. W. 1/ 2/41
Twiddy, G. W. 1/ 2/41
Longbottom, G. 1/ 2/41
Smith, A. B. (2/Lt. late K.R.R.C.) 1/ 2/41

Captains

Ellis, J. G., D.C.M. 1/ 2/41
Smith, F. G. 1/ 2/41
Coulson, E. T. 1/ 2/41
Scriven, C. N. 1/ 2/41
Greenwood, W. (2/Lt. late R.A.F.) 1/ 2/41
Thompson, A. 1/ 2/41

Lieutenants

Holmes, G. C. 1/ 2/41
Thornton, A. H. 1/ 2/41
Middlebrook, N. (Lt. late R.F.C.) 1/ 2/41
Davison, S. 1/ 2/41
Brown, A. 1/ 2/41
Young, J. P. M. 1/ 2/41
Dent, W. M. 1/ 2/41

Lieutenants - contd.

Dowty, A. G., (2/Lt. late S. Stafford R.) 1/ 2/41
Newton, J. 1/ 2/41
King, N. L. 1/ 2/41
Cooper, J. 1/ 2/41
Hazell, G. S. 1/ 2/41
Pearson, W. L. 1/ 2/41
Woodhouse, M. T. 1/ 2/41
Teale, W. J. 1/ 2/41
Coulson, C. S. 1/ 2/41
Herman, C. W., M.M. 1/ 2/41
Grimwood, C. H. W., (Capt. late Essex R.) 1/ 2/41
Wright, G. W., D.C.M., (Lt. late R. Signals) 1/ 2/41
Swift, H. 1/ 2/41
Urwin, F. D. 1/ 2/41
Fish, A. S. 1/ 2/41
Allan, J. R. 1/ 2/41
Robinson, A. J. 1/ 2/41
Molyneux, W. 6/ 5/41
Miles, W. 8/ 5/41

2nd Lieutenants

Adjutant & Quarter-Master

Medical Officer

Stalker, Maj. W. F., M.B. 13/ 5/41

DURHAM and NORTH RIDING DIVISION - contd.

CATTERICK GARRISON

Territorial Army Association administering	The Yorkshire (North Riding) T.A. & A.F. Association, Thirsk Road, Northallerton.

CATTERICK GARRISON GROUP

Commander	Vaux, Col. C., M.C., T.D., (Lt.-Col. T.A.)	1/ 2/41

11th NORTH RIDING (HANG) BATTALION

Lt.-Colonel

Heymann, F. A., O.B.E. (Col. ret. pay) (Res. of Off.)	15/ 4/41

Majors

Hill, G. N., D.S.O. (Lt.-Col. ret. pay R.A.)	1/ 2/41
Whitehead, R. H. (Capt. late Y. & L.R.)	1/ 2/41
Rendell, C. B. (Capt. late Ind. Army)	1/ 2/41
Wright, C. O. (Lt. late King's Own R.)	1/ 2/41
Watkinson, T., M.M.	1/ 2/41

Captains

Ord, A. F. T. (Lt. late W. York R.)	1/ 2/41
Bradford, J. P.	1/ 2/41
Mallinson, A. W. (Capt. late R.A.S.C.)	1/ 6/41

Lieutenants

Robinson, F., M.M.	1/ 2/41
Stubbs, G. B.	1/ 2/41
Meggison, E. T.	1/ 2/41
Foster, G. L. L. (Capt. late 8th H.)	1/ 2/41
Heseltine, R.	1/ 2/41
Pybus, F.	1/ 2/41
Edmonds, J. V.	1/ 2/41
Moore, E.	1/ 2/41
Harrison, W.	1/ 2/41
Muir, G. B. F.	1/ 2/41
Airey, J. W.	1/ 2/41
Bedford, S. W. N.	1/ 2/41
Dinsdale, G.	1/ 2/41
Peacock, M. H.	1/ 2/41
Wood, J.	1/ 2/41

56455-6(58)

Lieutenants - contd.

Armstrong, G. R. (2/Lt. late 5th L.)	1/ 2/41
Beswick, J. W.	1/ 2/41
Maughan, R. F.	1/ 2/41
Hutchinson, R. N.	1/ 2/41

2nd Lieutenants

Dand, R. (Lt. late Innis. D. G.)	1/ 2/41
Watts, A. W.	1/ 2/41
Webster, H. M.	1/ 2/41
Skidmore, J. (2/Lt. late R.A.F.)	1/ 2/41
Tucker, C. E. (Lt. late R. War R.)	1/ 2/41
Scaife, T.	1/ 2/41
Peel, H. (2/Lt. late R.E.)	27/ 6/41
Robson, S. T.	1/ 7/41
Dinsdale, C. J.	3/ 7/41
Lambert, R. A.	29/ 7/41

Adjutant & Quarter-Master

Medical Officer

DURHAM and NORTH RIDING DIVISION - contd.
CATTERICK GARRISON - contd.
CATTERICK GARRISON GROUP - contd.

12th NORTH RIDING (GILLING) BATTALION

Lt.-Colonel

Sherston, G. W., M.C. (Capt. late Rifle Bde.)	1/ 2/41

Majors

Pease, Sir Richard A., Bt. (Capt. late North'd. H.)	1/ 2/41
Bigge, H. J. (Capt. late 19th H.)	1/ 2/41
Peat, C. U. (Maj. late Durham L. I.)	1/ 2/41
Thornton, H. E., M.C. (Capt. late Ind. Army)	1/ 2/41
Arnett, L. W.	1/ 2/41
Pearson, G. M.	1/ 2/41
Porter, T. E.	1/ 2/41
Hart, P. E.	1/ 2/41

Captains

Benson, R. C., M.C. (Capt. late R.A.)	1/ 2/41
Best, C. E. (Capt. late R.A.S.C.)	1/ 2/41
Bigge, W. E. (Capt. late North'd. H.)	1/ 2/41
Schofield, S. (2/Lt. Res. of Off.)	1/ 2/41
Wagstaff, J. S.	1/ 2/41
Nevison, F. J.	1/ 2/41
Wright, R. G. (Maj. late R.E.)	1/ 2/41
Burghes, C. M.	5/ 6/41

Lieutenants

Wilkinson, M. (2/Lt. late Green Howards)	1/ 2/41
Stoddart, B.	1/ 2/41
Peacock, H. D.	1/ 2/41
Sinclair, R., M.M.	1/ 2/41
Applegarth, G. (2/Lt. late The King's R.)	1/ 2/41
Radcliffe, C. H.	1/ 2/41
Shaw, E., M.M.	1/ 2/41
Jones, J. J. (Lt. late North'n. R.)	1/ 2/41
Singleton, R. G.	1/ 2/41
Lawson, H. B. (2/Lt. late The King's R.)	1/ 2/41
Peat, G. C.	1/ 2/41
Barkes, R. D.	1/ 2/41
Barkes, J. M.	1/ 2/41
Steedman, J.	1/ 2/41
Lambert, M. B.	1/ 2/41
Beattie, H. M.	1/ 2/41
Harrison, T. F. P.	1/ 2/41
Hanson, G. R.	1/ 2/41
Hutchinson, W. M.	1/ 2/41

Lieutenants - contd.

Lowe, A.	1/ 2/41
Addison, J. R.	1/ 2/41
Gill, R.	1/ 2/41
Young, G. W.	1/ 2/41
Bourke, U. J. D., C.M.G. (Grp. Capt. late R.A.F.)	5/ 6/41

Adjutant & Quarter-Master

Medical Officer

13th NORTH RIDING (WORSALL) BATTALION

Lt.-Colonel

Evans, H. K. D., M.C. (Maj. late 4th H.)	1/ 2/41

Major

Serginson, E. W.	1/ 2/41

Lieutenant

Dickinson, H.	1/ 2/41

2nd Lieutenants

Thornton, J. C. P.	1/ 2/41
Bell, J.	1/ 2/41
Shaw, S. C.	1/ 2/41

Adjutant & Quarter-Master

Medical Officer

YORKSHIRE DIVISION

EAST RIDING ZONE

Commander	Clitherow, Col. T. C., D.S.O. (Lt.-Col. ret. pay)	1/ 2/41
Second in Command	Godsal, Lt.-Col. P., M.C. (Maj. late Mila)	1/ 2/41
Territorial Army Association administering	The Yorkshire (East Riding) T.A. & A.F. Association, Mail Buildings, Jameson St., Hull	

NO. 1 GROUP

1st EAST RIDING (HULL) BATTALION

Lt.-Colonel

Wilson, Hon. G. G., C.M.G., D.S.O., T.D. (Col. ret. T.A.)	1/ 2/41

Majors

Morrill, T. J., T.D. (Lt.-Col. T.A. Res.) (Hon. Col. T.A.)	1/ 2/41
Lawrence, G. E. (Maj. late E. York R.)	1/ 2/41
Cole, A. J. (Capt. ret. pay E. York R.)	1/ 2/41
MacIlwaine, G. W. (Lt. late 12th R.L.)	1/ 2/41
Bellamy, D.	1/ 2/41
Boulton, E. S.	1/ 2/41

Captains

Corke, J., M.C. (Capt. T.A. Res.)	1/ 2/41
Green, F., M.C., D.C.M. (Capt. late Cheshire R)	1/ 2/41
Mitchell, G. W. (Lt. late E. York R.)	1/ 2/41
Prince, F. G. (2/Lt. late K.R.R.C.)	1/ 2/41
Gilliam, H.	1/ 2/41
Richardson, G., M.C. (2/Lt. late Green Howards)	1/ 2/41
Readman, T. A.	1/ 2/41
Williamson, S. J. (2/Lt. late Durham L.I.)	1/ 2/41
Brown, W. G.	1/ 2/41
Kidd, F.	26/ 7/41

Lieutenants

Bacon, A. T. (Lt. late Aust. Imp. Forces)	1/ 2/41
Redfern, J. G., D.S.O. (Capt. late E. York R.)	1/ 2/41
Hirst, J., M.C. (Capt. late E. York R.)	1/ 2/41
Grant, E.	1/ 2/41
Cranswick, W. (Capt. late Ind. Army)	1/ 2/41
Warne, A. C. (Lt. late E. York R.)	1/ 2/41
Vollans, C. H., D.C.M.	1/ 2/41
Fairgrieve, D. E.	1/ 2/41
Casterson, J.	1/ 2/41
Havelock, H.	1/ 2/41
McArthur, J. H.	1/ 2/41

Lieutenants - contd.

Franks, H. B. S.	1/ 2/41
Friend, D. R., M.M.	1/ 2/41
Dargavel, J. S.	1/ 2/41
Dunkley, W. H.	1/ 2/41
Oates, C. S.	1/ 2/41
Pearson, H.	1/ 2/41
Moss, A.	1/ 2/41
Heesom, J. R.	1/ 2/41
Snowdon, J.	1/ 2/41
Evered, H. F. G. (Lt. late R.N.)	1/ 2/41
Clark, W. H. (Lt. late W. York R.)	1/ 2/41
Phimister, J.	1/ 2/41
Ebrey, R. T. (Capt. late S. Lan. R.)	1/ 2/41
Bonner, L.	1/ 2/41
Bell, F., D.C.M.	1/ 2/41
Dalton, J.	1/ 2/41
Cookson, E.	1/ 2/41
Hill, T. A.	26/ 7/41

2nd Lieutenants

Williamson, J. H., D.C.M. (2/Lt. late R.A.)	1/ 2/41
Bareham, W. G.	1/ 2/41
Green, N.	1/ 2/41
Nixon, J. T.	1/ 2/41
Jevons, T. A.	1/ 2/41
Smith, A. E.	1/ 2/41
Spencer, A.	1/ 2/41
Morrell, S.	1/ 2/41
Fowler, H.	1/ 2/41
Trumble, R. H.	1/ 2/41
Stark, F.	1/ 2/41
Harbottle, W.	1/ 2/41
Dent, W. G.	1/ 2/41
Everett, F. J.	1/ 2/41
Ripley, E.	1/ 2/41

Adjutant & Quarter-Master

Daniel, Capt. (actg. 1/5/41) R. H., Gen. List Inf.	1/ 5/41

Medical Officer

Scott, Maj. P. M., M.B.	1/ 2/41

YORKSHIRE DIVISION - contd.

EAST RIDING ZONE - contd.

NO. 1 GROUP - contd.

2nd EAST RIDING (BROUGH) BATTALION

Lt.-Colonel

Cooper, C. H. S., T.D. (Bt. Col. T.A. Res.) 1/ 2/41

Majors

Slack, C. M., M.C. (Capt. late E. York R.) (T.A. Res.) 1/ 2/41
Carmichael, J. W. (Capt. late K.O.Y.L.I.) 1/ 2/41
Cargill, E. (Capt. late E. York R.) 1/ 2/41
McGough, J. V. 1/ 2/41

Captains

Coombe, J. G. (Capt. late R.A.F.) 1/ 2/41
Gregory, T. (Capt. late Ind. Army) 1/ 2/41
Fenner, J H., M.C. (Maj. late R.G.A.) 1/ 2/41
Oughtred, J. A., M.C. (Capt. late E. York R.) 1/ 2/41
Hobson, G., M.C., M.M. (Lt.-Col. ret. Can. Mil. Forces) 1/ 2/41
Golding, W. V. 1/ 2/41
Hutchinson, A. S. (Lt. R.A.C. Supp'y. Res.) 1/ 2/41
Saltmarsne, P. (Capt. late K.R.R.C.) 1/ 2/41
Buchanan, R. B., M.C. (Maj. late M.G. Corps) 1/ 2/41

Lieutenants

Bilton, H. C. (Capt. late E. York R.) 1/ 2/41
Judge, L. F. (Lt. late E. York R.) 1/ 2/41
Gate, D. W. (Lt. late Black Watch) 1/ 2/41
Rae, A. G. 1/ 2/41
Dorning, E. S. (Capt. late The King's R.) 1/ 2/41
Scholfield, E. P. (Capt. late R.G.A.) 1/ 2/41
Tiplady, G. 1/ 2/41
Nuttall, J. T., M.C. (Capt. late Bedfs. & Herts. R.) 1/ 2/41
Shield, J. W. (Lt. late Durham L.I.) 1/ 2/41
Mountifield, R. H. 1/ 2/41
Howdle, H. (Lt. late E. York R.) 1/ 2/41
Mooney, A. G. (2/Lt. late T.A. Res.) 1/ 2/41
Darby, H. J. 1/ 2/41
Maclemann, K., M.C. (Capt. late R.A.M.C.) 1/ 2/41

2nd Lieutenants

Stewart, N. A. (Lt. late The King's R.) 1/ 2/41
Davison, T. 1/ 2/41
Hirschfeld, M.M., M.C. 1/ 2/41
Graham, S. H. (Lt. late R.A.) 1/ 2/41
Whitehead, G. O. 1/ 2/41
Calvert, W. E. 1/ 2/41
Ford, E. 1/ 2/41
Martin, A. S. 1/ 2/41
Holdroyd, F. V. (Lt. late K.O.Y.L.I.) 1/ 2/41
Jameson, P. O., M.M. 1/ 2/41
Holliday, F., D.C.M. (Lt. late R.G.A.) 1/ 2/41
Bettesworth, F. C. 1/ 2/41
Mowforth, C. B. 1/ 2/41
Hayes, W. (2/Lt. late Lincoln R.) 1/ 2/41
Dixon, H. 1/ 2/41
Atkinson, G. H. 1/ 2/41
Butcher, N. A. 1/ 2/41
Brooks, A. V. (Lt. late R.F.A.) 1/ 2/41
Pickard, J. 1/ 2/41
Hardy, C. L. (2/Lt. late M.G. Corps) 1/ 2/41
Locke, A. E. 1/ 2/41
Beck, H., M.M. 1/ 2/41
Robinson, R. L. 1/ 2/41
Rix, R. K. 1/ 2/41
Roche, Hon. J. F. A. 1/ 2/41
Powell, J. (Flight-Lt. late R.A.F.) 1/ 2/41

Adjutant & Quarter-Master

Dawson, Capt. (actg. 1/2/41) C., Gen. List Inf. 1/ 2/41

Medical Officer

YORKSHIRE DIVISION - contd.

EAST RIDING ZONE - contd.

NO. 1 GROUP - contd.

3rd EAST RIDING (BEVERLEY) BATTALION

Lt.-Colonel

Majors

Wellsted, C. G., T.D. (Lt.-Col. late T.A.)	1/ 2/41
Macdonald, J. R., O.B.E. (Maj. late London R.)	1/ 2/41
Holtby, E., M.C. (Maj. late E. York R.)	1/ 2/41
Stephenson, T. S. C. (Capt. late T.A.)	1/ 2/41
Cardwell, N. (Lt. late K.O.Y.L.I.)	1/ 2/41

Captains

Plimpton, A. A. (Capt. late E. York R.)	1/ 2/41
Barr, W. N. L.	1/ 2/41
Walgate, A. I.	1/ 2/41
Johnson, N. H.	1/ 2/41

Lieutenants

Walkinton, J. J. G. (Capt. late Lincoln R.)	1/ 2/41
Smith, G. A., D.C.M.	1/ 2/41
Robinson, R.	1/ 2/41
Shepherd, J. W., M.B.E.	1/ 2/41
Odey, G. W.	1/ 2/41
Dixon, G. C.	1/ 2/41

Lieutenants - contd.

Medforth, A.	1/ 2/41
Staveley, C. H. (late Chaplain to the Forces) (4th class))	1/ 2/41
Hutchinson, D. W.	1/ 2/41
Berry, H.	1/ 2/41
Kirk, A. J.	1/ 2/41
Whalley, B. E.	1/ 2/41
Dearing, R. W.	1/ 2/41
Catterick, C. H.	1/ 2/41

2nd Lieutenants

Wileman, H.	1/ 2/41
Shaw, A. A.	30/ 7/41
Shuttleworth, F. (Lt. late Ind. Army)	30/ 7/41

Adjutant & Quarter-Master

Medical Officer

Peterkin, Maj. J. H. S., M.C. (Lt. late M.G. Corps)	7/ 8/41

NO.2 GROUP

4th EAST RIDING (POCKLINGTON) BATTALION

Lt.-Colonel

Palmes, E. W. E., M.C. (Capt. ret. pay)	1/ 2/41

Majors

Adam, C. G. F., C.S.I. (Lt. late Ind. Army)	1/ 2/41
Mackay, A. H. (Capt. late Midd'x. R.)	1/ 2/41
Palmes, G. B., D.S.O. (Cmdr. late R.N.)	1/ 2/41
Stephenson, E. V., M.C. (Capt. late R.A.)	1/ 2/41
Coulson, A. T. (2/Lt. late 3rd H.)	1/ 2/41
Denny, V. E. G.	1/ 2/41
Sugden, G. C., M.C. (Lt. late D.W.R.)	21/ 5/41

Captains

Smith, J. E.	1/ 2/41
Stephenson, R. S. (Capt. late T.A.)	1/ 2/41
Walker, T. W.	1/ 2/41
Sampson, L.	1/ 2/41
Bains, T. H.	21/ 5/41
Whitelock, J. (Lt. late E. York. R.)	1/ 8/41

Lieutenants

Weston, P.. D.	1/ 2/41
Ludman, C. J., M.C. (Capt. late R. Berks. R.)	1/ 2/41
Campbell, R. H.	1/ 2/41
Place, R.	1/ 2/41
Munby, E. W.	1/ 2/41
Ross, W.	1/ 2/41
Oates, C. W. A.	1/ 2/41
Dale, W. T.	1/ 2/41
Storey, G. S.	1/ 2/41
Fridlington, J. L.	1/ 2/41
Blacker, T. A.	1/ 2/41
Megginson, W. B.	1/ 2/41

2nd Lieutenants

Nicholls, W. A.	1/ 2/41
Burton, A. H.	1/ 2/41
Stark, E. P.	1/ 2/41

Adjutant & Quarter-Master

Medical Officer

YORKSHIRE DIVISION - contd.

EAST RIDING ZONE - contd.

NO. 2 GROUP - contd.

5th EAST RIDING (BRIDLINGTON) BATTALION

Lt.-Colonel

Lambert, A. S., M.C. (Lt. late T.A.) 1/ 2/41

Majors

Walker, J. W., M.C. (Capt. late Green Howards) 1/ 2/41
Spark, T. E. (Lt. late M.G. Corps) 1/ 2/41
Herman, H. C. 1/ 2/41
Fisher, M. E. 1/ 2/41
Rowell, H. T. (Lt. late M.G. Corps) 1/ 2/41

Captains

Austin, S A. 1/ 2/41
Hart, J. 1/ 2/41
Newton, W. B. A. 1/ 2/41
Milner, A. H. 1/ 2/41
Simpson, R. L. 1/ 2/41

Lieutenants

Bucknell, L. A. 1/ 2/41
Stride, W. 1/ 2/41
Ralph, W. (Lt. late R.F.A.) 1/ 2/41
Ridley, J. T. 1/ 2/41
Large, E. T. 1/ 2/41
Watson, J. B. 1/ 2/41
Sinclair, W. V. 1/ 2/41
Orton, W. H. 1/ 2/41
North, C. G. 1/ 2/41
Wilkinson, A. E. 1/ 2/41
Bufton, G. E. 1/ 2/41
Warrack, A. N. 1/ 2/41
Boyd, R. 1/ 2/41
Hall, W. B. 1/ 2/41
Gambles, S. G. 1/ 2/41
Trenery, H. L. 1/ 2/41
Popple, G. 1/ 2/41
Endley, W. L. 1/ 2/41
Saltmer, W. 1/ 2/41
Rodda, J. W. 1/ 2/41
Littlewood, J. F. 1/ 2/41

2nd Lieutenants

Nellist, B., D.C.M. 1/ 2/41
Wise, R. W. 1/ 2/41
Thompson, M. 1/ 2/41
Byass, J. K. 1/ 2/41

Adjutant & Quarter-Master

Saltonstall, Capt. (actg. 28/2/41) E. R., Gen. List Inf. 28/ 2/41

Medical Officer

Taylor, Maj. C. R., O.B.E., M.D. (Capt. late R.A.M.C.) 30/ 4/41

6th EAST RIDING (DRIFFIELD) BATTALION

Lt.-Colonel

Gibson, T. G. (Capt. late 6th Innis. D.G.) 1/ 2/41

Majors

Wormald, W. F. (Maj. late York H.) 1/ 2/41
Russell, K. G. 1/ 2/41
Ullyott, R. D. (Lt. late E. Riding Yeo.) 1/ 2/4
Jackson, C. 1/ 2/41
Little, R. W. 1/ 2/41
Potter, G. C. 1/ 2/41
Dawnay, C. H., M.C. (Capt. late Green Howards) 1/ 2/4

Captains

Smith, J. L. (Maj. late E. Riding Yeo.) 1/ 2/4
Sykes, F. B. (Capt. late R.A.S.C.) 1/ 2/4
Eagle-Clark, F. 19/ 5/4
Wardle, H. M. (Capt. late Durham L.I.) 19/ 5/4

Lieutenants

Raw, A. C. H. 1/ 2/4
Robson, H. T. (Lt. late Green Howards) 1/ 2/4
Naylor, J. A., M.C. (Lt. late J. & L.R.) 1/ 2/4
Bryant, S. R. 1/ 2/4
Wilson, H. 1/ 2/4
Otley, E. J. 1/ 2/4
Robinson, J. D., M.C. (Lt. late E. Riding Yeo.) 1/ 2/4
Robinson, T. L. 1/ 2/4
Cooper, R. S. 1/ 2/4
Yates, R. 1/ 2/4
Weatherill, H. F. (2/Lt. late Green Howards) 1/ 2/4
Hodgson, C. W. 1/ 2/4
Bradshaw, J. C. 1/ 2/4
Barton, C. G. B. 1/ 2/4
Howe, D. E. 1/ 2/4
Wilson, W. H. 1/ 2/4
Davison, N. 1/ 2/4
Hardy, W. H. 1/ 2/4
Ward, E. (2/Lt. late R.A.F.) 1/ 2/4

Adjutant & Quarter-Master

Medical Officer

YORKSHIRE DIVISION - contd.

EAST RIDING ZONE - contd.

NO. 2 GROUP - contd.

7th EAST RIDING (WITHERNSEA) BATTALION

Lt.-Colonel

Angus, A. M. (Lt. late Gordons)	1/ 2/41

Majors

Moore, H.	1/ 2/41
Andrews, T. W.	1/ 2/41
Grainger, J.	1/ 2/41
North, S. W.	1/ 2/41
Camp, J. W.	1/ 2/41

Captains

Nicholson, L. B.	1/ 2/41
Rhodes, C.	1/ 2/41
Dixon, H. N.	1/ 2/41
Quarmby, W. E.	1/ 2/41
Hoy, E. (2/Lt. late R.A.F.)	1/ 2/41

Lieutenants

Peacock, T. D.	1/ 2/41
Patterson, G. W.	1/ 2/41
Lear, F. F.	1/ 2/41
Middleton, R. W.	1/ 2/41
Vidler, W.	1/ 2/41
Storey, J. W.	1/ 2/41
Faill, C. R.	1/ 2/41
Durrant, W. S.	1/ 2/41
Newsam, H.	1/ 2/41

Lieutenants - contd.

Benson, H.	1/ 2/41
Frankland, J.	1/ 2/41
Smith, H. R.	1/ 2/41
Thornton, G.	1/ 2/41
Knapton, C. L.	10/ 6/41
Wilde, W. H.	10/ 6/41
Miles, C. S.	14/ 6/41
Wilkinson, A. S. A.	27/ 7/41

2nd Lieutenants

Sewards, G. W.	1/ 2/41
Gait, A. J.	1/ 2/41
Gwilliam, D. F. A.	2/ 6/41
Lane, W. F.	2/ 6/41

Adjutant & Quarter-Master

Medical Officer

Young, Maj. D. J., M.B.	1/ 2/41

YORKSHIRE AREA

General Staff Officer, 1st grade	Hughes, Col. A. C., T.D., T.A., t.a.	24/ 3/41

WEST RIDING ZONE

Commander	Walker, Col. J., D.S.O., T.D. (Col. ret. T.A.)	1/ 2/41
Second in Command	Armytage, Sir George A. Bt., C.M.G., D.S.O. (Hon. Brig.-Gen. ret. pay)	1/ 2/41
Assistants to Commander	Knights-Trench, Maj. J. Womersley, Capt. E. (Capt. late R. Signals)	1/ 2/41
Territorial Army Association administering	The Yorkshire (West Riding) T.A. Association, 9, St. Leonards, York.	

SKIPTON GROUP

Commander	Harrison, Col. G. B. (Lt. late Worc. R.)	1/ 2/41
Second in Command	Tempest, Lt.-Col. R. S., C.M.G., D.S.O. (Bt. Col. late S. G'ds.)	1/ 2/41
Assistant to Commander	Rogers, Capt. E.	1/ 2/41

32nd WEST RIDING (SKIPTON) BATTALION

Lt.-Colonel

Carruthers, D. (Lt. late Tank Corps) 1/ 2/41

Majors

Humphries, E. B. (Capt. late R.A.F.) 1/ 2/41
Dennis, W. E. 1/ 2/41
Garnett, T. A. 1/ 2/41
Summers, J. N. (Lt. late London R.) 1/ 2/41

Captains

Conchar, J. (Capt. late W. York R.) 1/ 2/41
Anderson, F. R. (2/Lt. late R.F.A.) 1/ 2/41

Lieutenants

Robb, J. (Lt. late Gordons) 1/ 2/41
Long, O. A. (2/Lt. late Border R.) 1/ 2/41
Sharples, T. C. (Lt. late D.W.R.) 1/ 2/41
Wilman, T. (Lt. late R.F.A.) 1/ 2/41
Hesledene, J. R. (Capt. late Foresters) 1/ 2/41
Gunby, E. H. 1/ 2/41
Vaulkhard, N. G. 1/ 2/41
Brundrit, R. G. 1/ 2/41
Collingwood, C. D. 1/ 2/41
Watson, J. K. 1/ 2/41
Sherlock, D. R. 1/ 2/41
Shaw, H. 1/ 2/41

Lieutenants – contd.

Lawson, W. 1/ 2/41
Roberts, W. D. 1/ 2/41
Scales, F. H. 1/ 2/41
Henderson, W. B. 1/ 2/41
Lee, N. N. 1/ 2/41
Cutmore, E. J. 1/ 2/41
Wynn, R. 1/ 2/41
Robinson, G. E. G. (2/Lt. late Labour Corps) 26/ 5/41

2nd Lieutenants

Rogers, H. C. 1/ 2/41
Tyrer, F., M.M. 1/ 2/41
Standeven, D. W. 1/ 2/41
Aldersley, A. 1/ 2/41
Andrews, W. 1/ 2/41
Armitage, T. 16/ 6/41

Adjutant & Quarter-Master

Medical Officer

Fisher, Maj. G. A., M.C. (Maj. late R.A.M.C. (T.A.)) 19/ 7/41

YORKSHIRE AREA - contd.

WEST RIDING ZONE - contd.

SKIPTON GROUP - contd.

33rd WEST RIDING (SKIPTON) BATTALION

Lt.-Colonel

Driver, A., D.S.O., M.C. (Maj. late T.A.)	1/ 2/41

Majors

Barr, A. (Maj. late R.A.M.C.)	1/ 2/41
Clegg, A. H. (Capt. late D.W.R.)	1/ 2/41
Gibbon, A. M. (Lt. late King's Own R.)	1/ 2/41
Humphreys, A.	1/ 2/41
Winstanley, J. H.	1/ 2/41

Captains

Gaunt, W. E. (2/Lt. late London R.)	1/ 2/41
Pollard, A.	1/ 7/41
Simpson, W.	1/ 7/41
Turnbull, W. (2/Lt. late D.W.R.)	1/ 7/41

Lieutenants

Wilkinson, C. H. (Lt. late D.W.R.)	1/ 2/41
Kemp, A.D. (Pilot Offr. late R.A.F.)	1/ 2/41
Crowther, J. B.	1/ 2/41
Atkinson, R. H., M.M.	1/ 2/41

Lieutenants - contd.

Clough, S. B.	1/ 2/41
Bancroft, W.	1/ 2/41
Wilson, K.	1/ 2/41
Gadney, B. C.	1/ 2/41
Bentley, J.	1/ 2/41
Carter, N. D.	1/ 2/41
Harrison, J.	1/ 2/41
Barratt, F., M.M.	1/ 2/41
Peacock, D.	1/ 2/41
Shorrock, T. W.	1/ 2/41
Nevison, D.	1/ 2/41
Barratt, B. R.	1/ 2/41

2nd Lieutenants

Crabtree, W. P.	18/ 6/41
Coe, E. (Lt. late R.F.A.)	7/ 7/41
Pavey, C. M. (Pilot Offr. late R.A.F.)	7/ 7/41

Adjutant & Quarter-Master

Medical Officer

Rankin, Capt. J. D.	7/ 7/41

YORKSHIRE AREA - contd.

WEST RIDING ZONE - contd.

SETTLE GROUP

Commander — Clay, Col. H. C. H. (Lt. late R.E.) — 1/ 2/41

31st WEST RIDING (SETTLE) BATTALION

Colonel

Clay, H. C. H. (Lt. late R.E.) 1/ 2/41

Majors

Roberts, W. (Capt. late Loyal R.) 1/ 2/41
Farrer, J. O., M.C. (Capt. late K.S.L.I.) 1/ 2/41
Ainsworth, T. H. 1/ 2/41
Parker, H. J. (Lt. late E. Lan. R.) 1/ 2/41
Mountain, H. D. (Capt. late Lincoln R.) 1/ 2/41
Cooper, L. (Maj. K.O.Y.L.I., T.A.) 1/ 2/41

Captains

Fell, R. G. (Capt. T.A. Res.) 1/ 2/41
Hewetson, T. S. (Lt. late S. Stafford R.) 1/ 2/41
Ashbee, G. C. 1/ 2/41
Edwards, L. (Capt. late The King's R.) 1/ 2/41
Sharples, J. 23/ 6/41

Lieutenants

Farrer, S. J. (Lt. late R. Sussex R.) 1/ 2/41
Walter, H. E. 1/ 2/41
Druce, A. N. 1/ 2/41
Dunnicliffe, W. (Maj. late R.E.) 1/ 2/41
Pedder, J. L., M.M. 1/ 2/41
Downhill, W. 1/ 2/41
Poole, H. 1/ 2/41
Sloman, T. W. 1/ 2/41
Tubby, W. 1/ 2/41
Ellis, A. N. 1/ 2/41
Harding, T. 1/ 2/41
Tattersall, J. A. 1/ 2/41
Shuttleworth, J. W. W. 1/ 2/41
Cottam, H. 1/ 2/41
Glover, J. R. H. 1/ 2/41
Barlow, J. MacD. 1/ 2/41

Lieutenants - contd.

Tomlinson, R. M. 1/ 2/41
Wiseman, J. 1/ 2/41
Close, F. 1/ 2/41
Gilchrist, J. H. (Lt. late M.G. Corps.) 1/ 2/41
Perfect, W. M. 1/ 2/41
Partridge, E. H. 1/ 2/41
Rostron, J. 1/ 2/41
Haggas, J. (2/Lt. late R.F.A.) 1/ 2/41
Archer, C. J. 1/ 2/41
Redhead, C. H. 6/ 6/41

2nd Lieutenants

Richardson, J. L. 1/ 2/41
Burrow, G., D.C.M., M.M. 1/ 2/41
Monk, C. W. 1/ 2/41
Braithwaite, G. 1/ 2/41
Windle, W. W. 1/ 2/41
Lund, R. W. 1/ 2/41
Robinson, E. 1/ 2/41
Dutton, L. P. 1/ 2/41
Sharples, W. 1/ 2/41
Bleazard, I. 1/ 2/41
Duckworth, A. R. 1/ 2/41
Robinson, L. 1/ 2/41
Miles-Sharp, M. C. 1/ 2/41
Clay, J. 1/ 2/41
Bland, H. H. (2/Lt. late R.A.F.) 1/ 2/41
Evans, J. 1/ 2/41
Bibby, J., D.C.M. 21/ 5/41
Stevens, J. H. (2/Lt. late Green Howards) 6/ 6/41

Adjutant & Quarter-Master

Medical Officer

YORKSHIRE AREA - contd.

WEST RIDING ZONE - contd.

OTLEY GROUP

Commander	Petrie, Col. P. C., D.S.O., M.C. (Maj. late T.A.)	1/ 2/41
Second in Command	White, Lt.-Col. F. W., M.C. (Maj. T.A. Res.)	1/ 2/41

29th WEST RIDING (OTLEY) BATTALION

Lt.-Colonel

Duncan, H. S., M.C., T.D. (Bt. Col. T.A. Res.)	1/ 2/41

Majors

McQueen, N., D.S.O. (Maj. late A. & S.H.)	1/ 2/41
Fawcett, R. A., M.C. (Maj. late W. York R.)	1/ 2/41
Ryott, H. A. (Bt. Maj. late North'd. Fus.)	1/ 2/41
Walker, P. H., M.C. (Capt. late R.F.A.)	1/ 2/41
Bulay-Watson, D., A.F.C. (Capt. late E. York R.)	1/ 2/41
Dean, W. H., M.C. (Maj. late R.F.A.)	1/ 2/41

Captains

Burt, A. E., D.S.O. (Maj. late Oxf. & Bucks. L.I.)	1/ 2/41
Early, W. W. (Capt. late R.F.A.)	1/ 2/41
Warburton, J. W. (Capt. late K.O.Y.L.I.)	1/ 2/41
White, H. J. (Lt. late The King's R.)	1/ 2/41
Skinner, H. F., M.B.E. (Lt. late R. Sussex R.)	1/ 2/41
Banks, C.	1/ 2/41
Norton, G. P., D.S.O., T.D. (Bt. Col. ret. D.W.R.)	1/ 2/41

Lieutenants

Horton-Fawkes, Le G. G. W. (Maj. ret. pay)	1/ 2/41
Sowden, A. (Maj. late W. York R.)	1/ 2/41
Hannam, C. D., M.C. (Capt. W. York R.)	1/ 2/41
Tankard, L. (Lt. late Y. & L.R.)	1/ 2/41
Tolson, R. H. (Lt. late Green Howards)	1/ 2/41
Seager, J. O. (Lt. late Midd'x. R.)	1/ 2/41
Wilkinson, C., M.M.	1/ 2/41
Sharpe, G. L., D.S.O. (Maj. T.A., Res.)	1/ 2/41

Lieutenants - contd.

Dawson, W. S. (Capt. late W. York R.)	1/ 2/41
Harland, G. E. (2/Lt. late R.T.C.)	1/ 2/41
Coggill, H. M. (Capt. late Foresters)	1/ 2/41
Frost, G. R. (2/Lt. late D.W.R.)	1/ 2/41
Mudd, T. (2/Lt. late D.W.R.)	1/ 2/41
Nixon, N. P.	1/ 2/41
Whaley, R. J. (Lt. late R.T.C.)	1/ 2/41
Knowles, A. W. (Capt. late Y. & L.R.)	1/ 2/41
Dawson, A. (Lt. late W. York R.)	1/ 2/41
West, T.	1/ 2/41
Butterfield, A. J.	1/ 2/41
Hall, A.	1/ 2/41
Spence, H. T.	1/ 2/41
Bird, W. L. (Lt. late The King's R.)	1/ 2/41
Beverley, F., M.C. (Capt. late R.A.)	1/ 2/41
Rhodes, J. R., D.C.M. (2/Lt. late R.F.A.)	1/ 2/41
Walker, A. C. C. (Maj. late R.A.S.C.)	1/ 2/41
Runton, S. R. (Lt. late T.A.)	1/ 2/41
Lethbridge, L. S. (Lt. late R. Sussex R.)	1/ 2/41
Windeler, B. C., A.F.C. (Maj. late R.A.F.)	1/ 2/41
Platts, J. E. A. (Lt. late R.F.A.)	12/ 5/41
Sinclair, C. M.	1/ 6/41
Milner, G. H. (Lt. late D.W.R.)	1/ 6/41
Booth, T. (Lt. late D.W.R.)	1/ 6/41
Barber, C.	21/ 7/41

YORKSHIRE AREA - contd.

WEST RIDING ZONE - contd.

OTLEY GROUP - contd.

29th West Riding (Otley) Battalion - contd.

2nd Lieutenants

Kitson, W. F. C., O.B.E. (Maj. late R.A.S.C.)	1/ 2/41
Furness, H. H. (2/Lt. late D.W.R.)	1/ 2/41
Stewart, W.	1/ 2/41
Holbrook, L. E.	1/ 2/41
Pickering, A. D.	1/ 2/41
Northrop, R. (Capt. late R. Mar.)	1/ 2/41
Adkins, T. C.	1/ 2/41
Stewart, M.	1/ 2/41
Chary, E. W.	1/ 2/41
Dalton, P., D.C.M.	1/ 2/41
(2/Lt. late R.F.A.)	1/ 2/41
Smith, A. J. K.	1/ 2/41
Rhodes, A. W. (Capt. late D.W.R.)	1/ 2/41
Walter, G. C.	1/ 2/41
Clough, F. V. (Lt. late W. York R.)	1/ 2/41
Fenwick, J. (Lt. late A. & S.H.)	1/ 2/41
Whitaker, J. S. D.	1/ 2/41
Hastings, G. G. W. (Lt. late K.O.S.B.)	1/ 2/41
Price, W. J. (Capt. late R.F.A.)	1/ 2/41
Knapton, J. C. L.	1/ 2/41
Thompson, F.	1/ 2/41
Ingham, J. E.	1/ 2/41
Pope, A., M.M.	1/ 2/41
Hale, G. B.	1/ 2/41
Clegg, R. V.	1/ 2/41
Willoughby, J. V. B.	1/ 2/41
Barnes, P. R., M.C. (Lt. late W. York R.)	1/ 2/41
Payne, R. G.	1/ 2/41
Tankard, C. G.	1/ 2/41
Tuckett, H. E., M.M.	1/ 2/41
Barrett, R. B.	1/ 2/41
Scott, J. C. (Capt. late R.A.)	1/ 2/41
Holmes, W. G.	1/ 2/41
Boden, J. B., M.C. (Lt. late R.A.)	1/ 2/41
Arthur, F. S.	1/ 2/41

2nd Lieutenants - contd.

Walker, G. F. D. (Lt. late W. York R.)	1/ 2/41
Brayshaw, L.	1/ 2/41
Ralphs, F. G. (Lt. late Ind. Army)	26/ 4/41
Allison, I. H.	9/ 5/41
Ackernely, A. K. (Lt. late W. York R.)	11/ 6/41
Peel, H. F., D.C.M.	11/ 6/41

Adjutant & Quarter-Master

Medical Officer

YORKSHIRE AREA - contd.

WEST RIDING ZONE - contd.

OTLEY GROUP - contd.

30th WEST RIDING (OTLEY) BATTALION

Lt.-Colonel

Grimshaw, R. (Capt. late R.A.)	1/ 2/41

Majors

Rogers, T. P. W., M.C. (Capt. late W. York R.)	1/ 2/41
Nunns, C. B.	1/ 2/41
Kerr, W. V. (Lt. late N. Stafford R.)	1/ 2/41
Swift, H. (Lt. late Tank Corps.)	1/ 2/41
Chambers, J. G.	1/ 2/41
Gray, A. E.	1/ 2/41
Pilley, H. C. (2/Lt. late R.E.)	1/ 2/41
Carr, S.	1/ 6/41

Captains

Winn, A., D.C.M.	1/ 2/41
Gee, H.	1/ 2/41
Driver, J. H. (Lt. late Loyal R.)	1/ 2/41
Atkinson, J.	1/ 2/41
Wilson, A. N.	1/ 2/41
Hunter, T.	1/ 2/41
Horner, F. M. (Capt. late W. York R.)	1/ 2/41
Bracegirdle, P. H.	1/ 2/41
Sanderson, G. H.	5/ 6/41

Lieutenants

Garnett, F. W.	1/ 2/41
Brown, F., M.M.	1/ 2/41
Lupton, A. W. (Maj. late W. York R.)	1/ 2/41
Marshall, A., M.C. (Capt. late Black Watch)	1/ 2/41
Black, A.	1/ 2/41
Milnes, J. H.	1/ 2/41
Ramsden, J. (Lt. late D.W.R.)	1/ 2/41
Palmer, H. G.	1/ 2/41
Cooper, H.	1/ 2/41
Hebron, B.	1/ 2/41
Massheder, A.	1/ 2/41
Bradley, F. (Lt. late Manch. R.)	1/ 2/41

Lieutenants - contd.

Kershaw, B.	1/ 2/41
Johnson, W.	1/ 2/41
Catton, F. J. (2/Lt. late R. North'd Fus.)	1/ 2/41
Hooper, W. H.	19/ 4/41
Kellond, C. F.	22/ 5/41
Helstrip, F.	22/ 5/41

2nd Lieutenants

Williamson, R.	1/ 2/41
Blackburn, D.	1/ 2/41
Knapton, J.	1/ 2/41
Clapham, E.	1/ 2/41
Smithies, G.	1/ 2/41
Musgrave, G. E. S.	1/ 2/41
Shipley, G. H.	1/ 2/41
Gallant, H. H.	1/ 2/41
Cowperthwaite, T. S. (Flying Offr. late R.A.F.)	1/ 2/41
Knowles, M. S.	1/ 2/41
Spence, A.	1/ 2/41
Brook, R.	1/ 2/41
Child, W. R.	1/ 2/41
Mason, F.	1/ 2/41
Chippindale, A. (Capt. late D.W.R.)	1/ 2/41
Barr, A. C.	1/ 2/41
Ayrey, W. G.	1/ 2/41
Robinson, C.	1/ 2/41
Hinds, G. D. (Lt. late W. York R.)	1/ 2/41
Brunton, H. W. I.	1/ 2/41
Barker, B. R. (2/Lt. late K.R.R.C.)	1/ 2/41
Westcott, W. U.	1/ 2/41
West N. C.	1/ 2/41
Fisher, D. S.	1/ 2/41
Coates, H.	19/ 7/41

Adjutant & Quarter-Master

Medical Officer

Hutchinson, Maj. R., M.B.	19/ 6/41

YORKSHIRE AREA - contd.

WEST RIDING ZONE - contd.

KEIGHLEY GROUP

Commander	Horsfall, Col. Sir John D. Bt. (Capt. late T.A.)	1/ 2/41
Second in Command	Moore, Lt.-Col. F. W., D.S.O., M.C. (Maj. late R.E.)	1/ 2/41

27th WEST RIDING (KEIGHLEY) BATTALION

Lt.-Colonel

Bateman, C. M., D.S.O., T.D. (Bt. Col. ret. T.A.)	1/ 2/41

Majors

Tillotson, J. E., D.S.O., M.C. (Lt. late W. York R.)	1/ 2/41
Stocks, J., M.C. (Lt. late D.W.R.)	1/ 2/41

Captains

Feather, N., M.C. (Capt. late W. York R.)	1/ 2/41
Hardwicke, H. P.	1/ 2/41
Snowden, F. A.	1/ 2/41
Seddon, S.	1/ 2/41

Lieutenants

Hick, G.	1/ 2/41
Sykes, J. M. S. (Lt. T.A. Res.)	1/ 2/41
Allison, W. C., M.M. (2/Lt. late R.E.)	1/ 2/41
Hudson, D. C., M.M.	1/ 2/41
Baldwin, S. (Lt. late D.W.R.)	1/ 2/41
Taylor, S. (2/Lt. late D.W.R.)	1/ 2/41
Baxandall, W.	1/ 2/41
Flanagan, J.	1/ 2/41
Whalley, E.	1/ 2/41
Newsholme, D. W.	1/ 2/41
Sugden, W. S.	1/ 2/41
Enright, G. L. (Lt. late Tank Corps.)	1/ 2/41
Richards, P.	1/ 2/41
Hill, J. E.	1/ 2/41
Caswell, E. P.	1/ 2/41
Tosney, H. W.	1/ 2/41
Ferrand, V. W.	1/ 2/41

2nd Lieutenants

Wrigglesworth, E.	1/ 2/41
Lund, P. (Lt. late Durham L.I.)	1/ 2/41
Nelson, T. J.	1/ 2/41
Sunderland, W.	1/ 2/41
Leighton, F.	1/ 2/41
Morgan, P. J.	1/ 2/41
Wilkinson, A.	1/ 2/41
Dalton, H.	1/ 2/41
Berry, C.	1/ 2/41
Waller, C.	1/ 2/41
Reynolds, H. S.	1/ 2/41
Hackman, F. T.	1/ 2/41
Binns, F.	1/ 2/41
Harrison, G. H.	1/ 2/41
Denton, W.	1/ 2/41

Adjutant & Quarter-Master

Medical Officer

Gardiner, Maj. A. W., M.B.	30/ 6/41

YORKSHIRE AREA - contd.

WEST RIDING ZONE - contd.

KEIGHLEY GROUP - contd.

28th WEST RIDING (KEIGHLEY) BATTALION

Lt.-Colonel

Dixon, H. (Maj. ret. T.A.) 1/ 2/41

Majors

Wright, T. K., M.B.E. (Maj. late D.W.R.) 1/ 2/41
Delves, F. W. (Lt. late E. Riding T.A. Yeo.) 1/ 2/41
Pawson, C. E. (Capt. late Res.) 1/ 2/41
Holdsworth, H. (Lt. late W. York R.) 1/ 2/41

Captains

Shaw, J H. 1/ 2/41
Rushworth, N. (Lt. late W. York R.) 1/ 2/41
Williams, D. G. (Capt. late Manch. R.) 1/ 2/41
Ambler, T. 28/ 6/41

Lieutenants

Bateman, S. 1/ 2/41
White, W. F. C., M.M. 1/ 2/41
Green, H. 1/ 2/41
Penn, W. H. 1/ 2/41
Hopewell, A. J. 1/ 2/41
Minnikin, J. W. 1/ 2/41
Leighton, J. W. 1/ 2/41
Binns, C. 1/ 2/41
Johns, N. 1/ 2/41
Fieldhouse, G. 1/ 2/41
Morrison, W H. 1/ 2/41
Goldstraw, A N. 1/ 2/41

Lieutenants - contd.

Smith, A. (2/Lt. late Y. & L.R.) 1/ 2/41
Craven, J. (Lt. late W. York R.) 1/ 2/41
Awty, H. 1/ 2/41
Bracewell, R. A. 1/ 2/41

2nd Lieutenants

Crossley, L. 1/ 2/41
Spratt, F. D. 1/ 2/41
Sharp, W. 1/ 2/41
Smith, F. G. 1/ 2/41
Peacock, G. W. 1/ 2/41
Horn, H. 1/ 2/41
Raistrick, J. 1/ 2/41
Milner, W. 1/ 2/41
Pattinson, S. 1/ 2/41
Glover, S. 1/ 2/41
Gledhill, F. 1/ 2/41
de Rome, E. R. 1/ 2/41
Hoult, H. 10/ 5/41
Firth, P., M.M. 19/ 5/41

Adjutant & Quarter-Master

Medical Officer

Baird, Maj. J. E., M.B. 23/ 6/41

56455-6(73)

YORKSHIRE AREA - contd.

WEST RIDING ZONE - contd.

LEEDS GROUP

Commander	Bousfield, Col. H. D., C.M.G., D.S.O., T.D. (Col. ret. T.A.)	1/ 2/41
Second-in-Command	McLaren, Lt.-Col. H., D.S.O., M.C., T.D.	1/ 2/41
Assistant to Commander	Dickins, Capt. B. (2nd Lt. late Hampshire R.)	1/ 2/41

7th WEST RIDING (LEEDS) BATTALION

Lt.-Colonel

Glazebrook, A. R., M.C., T.D. (Bt. Col. T.A. Res.)	1/ 2/41

Majors

Hollis, A. (Lt. late Hampshire R.)	1/ 2/41
Butler, A. (Capt. late K.O.Y.L.I.)	1/ 2/41
Read, W., M.C. (Capt. late K.O.Y.L.I.)	1/ 2/41
Wallace, M. (Capt. late T.A.)	1/ 2/41
Hague, H. H.	1/ 2/41

Captains

Cameron, J. W., M.C. (Capt. ret.)	1/ 2/41
Scarr, A. C. (2/Lt. late R.A.F.)	1/ 2/41
Alvin, A. R. (Lt. late Y. & L.R.)	1/ 2/41
Hall, F. L., M.C. (Capt. late Scottish Horse)	1/ 2/41
Martin, N. (Capt. late Foresters)	1/ 2/41
Eggleton, R. T.	1/ 2/41
de Lacy, P. (Lt. late W. York R.)	1/ 2/41
Birch, J. S.	1/ 2/41
Holdsworth, A.	1/ 2/41
Lumb, H. (Lt. late K.O.Y.L.I.)	1/ 2/41

Lieutenants

Smee, L. V.	1/ 2/41
Harris, L. E. (Lt. late M.G. Corps)	1/ 2/41
Hellier, J. H.	1/ 2/41

Lieutenants - contd.

Mason, T. E. (2nd Lt. late R.G.A.)	1/ 2/41
Simpson, T. B.	1/ 2/41
Musgrave, R. (Lt. late R.A.F.)	1/ 2/41
Johnson, A.	1/ 2/41
Akeroyd, F.	1/ 2/41
Lee, P. L., T.D. (Capt. late W. York R.)	1/ 2/41
Gavins, W. (2/Lt. late W. York R.)	1/ 2/41
Scott, S. (2/Lt. late R.A.F.)	1/ 2/41
Jackson, J.	1/ 2/41
Theile, A. H.	1/ 2/41
Hullah, F. (Lt. Late Gen. List)	1/ 2/41
Wiles, H., M.M. (Capt. late D.W.R.)	1/ 2/41
Scruton, F.	1/ 2/41
de Ritter, J. R., M.C. (Capt. late R. Fus.)	1/ 2/41
Skinner, W. R. T. (Lt. late Middx. R.)	1/ 2/41
Ranger, C. S. D.	1/ 2/41
Harper, H. N.	1/ 2/41
Frazer, H. M. (Lt. late M.G. Corps)	1/ 2/41
Howells, I. R.	1/ 2/41
Adamson, H.	1/ 2/41
Nutt, D. L. (Capt. late R.A.F.)	1/ 2/41
Crick, W.	1/ 2/41
Bourn, J. W., D.C.M.	1/ 2/41
Hillier, C. C.	1/ 2/41
Mackenzie, W. A. (Capt. late A.S.C.)	1/ 2/41
McDavid, F. H. S.	1/ 2/41
Day, F. T.	31/ 5/41

YORKSHIRE AREA - contd.

WEST RIDING ZONE - contd.

LEEDS GROUP - contd.

7th West Riding (Leeds) Battalion - contd.

2nd Lieutenants

Vodden, Rev. A C. (Chaplain to the Forces 4th Class T.A. Res.)	1/ 2/41
Smith, H H. (Lt. late Devon R.)	1/ 2/41
Armitage, S. L. (Lt. late M.G. Corps)	1/ 2/41
Wolstenholme, F.	1/ 2/41
Alder, C. V. (Lt. late North'd Fus.)	1/ 2/41
Paley, G.	1/ 2/41
Davies, G. J.	1/ 2/41
Linscott, W. E.	1/ 2/41
Walton, F. M.	1/ 2/41
Polley, T. D.	1/ 2/41
Evans, E. T.	1/ 2/41
Martin, E. J.	1/ 2/41
Hare, H.	1/ 2/41
Parker, H. J. (Lt. late M.G. Corps)	1/ 2/41
McKean, J. B. B.	1/ 2/41
Baldwin, E.	1/ 2/41
Broadbent, E. W. (2/Lt. late R.G.A.)	1/ 2/41
Binge, G. H.	1/ 2/41
North, E. R. (Capt. late R.F.A.)	1/ 2/41
Farrow, J. A.	1/ 2/41
Gall, C. W.	1/ 2/41
Evans, W. A. (2/Lt. late R.A.F.)	1/ 2/41
Brook, F.	1/ 2/41
Farley, C. A. (Lt. late R.G.A.)	1/ 2/41
Gledhill, H.	1/ 2/41
Camidge, C. F.	1/ 2/41
Percival, J., D.C.M., M.M.	1/ 2/41
Warburton, R.	1/ 2/41
Byrne, J. F.	1/ 2/41
Huffer, W. A.	1/ 2/41
Brand, J. E.	29/ 4/41
Walker, J. (2/Lt. late E. York R.)	16/ 5/41
Bean, W. H.	31/ 5/41
Ripley, J. H.	31/ 5/41

2nd Lieutenants - contd.

Pickersgill, G. L.	7/ 6/41
Gorrie, H. R. H. (Lt. late A. & S.H.)	9/ 6/41
Brown, C. N.	20/ 6/41
Jackson, R. F.	20/ 6/41
Dunn, H. R.	17/ 7/41
Armitage, J. A.	22/ 7/41
Lenygon, F. N.	22/ 7/41

Adjutant & Quarter-Master

Medical Officer

Stewart, Maj. B.	21/ 5/41

56455-6(75)

8th WEST RIDING (LEEDS) BATTALION

Lt.-Colonel

Name	Date
Moncrieff, A., M.C. (Maj. late R.E.)	1/ 2/41

Majors

Name	Date
McLaren, H., D.S.O., M.C., T.D. (Bt. Col. T.A. Res.)	1/ 2/41
Brooke, H. W. (Capt. late W. York R.)	1/ 2/41
Phillips, R. S. (Capt. late Ind. Army)	1/ 2/41
Abbott, T. H. E., M.C. (Lt.-Col. ret. Gordons)	1/ 2/41
Leach, C. (Lt. late T. & L.R.)	1/ 2/41
Sanders, A. F. (2/Lt. late R.G.A.)	1/ 2/41
Kitson, G. L., T.D. (Maj. T.A. Res.)	1/ 2/41
Morland, W. V. (Capt. late R.E.)	1/ 2/41
Wilde, A. (Flying Offr.) late R.A.F.)	1/ 2/41
VC Sanders, G., M.C. (Capt. late W. York R.)	1/ 2/41
Butler, P. M.	1/ 2/41
Mitchell, J. R. D.	1/ 2/41

Captains

Name	Date
Huggan, J. R.	1/ 2/41
Freeman, W. H., M.C. (Capt. T.A. Res.)	1/ 2/41
Walker, F., O.B.E. (Capt. late W. York R.)	1/ 2/41
Mitchell, A. J. (Capt. late Res. of Off.)	1/ 2/41
Knowles, J. (Capt. late Y. & L.R.)	1/ 2/41
Mustill, C. W.	1/ 2/41
Cook, W.	1/ 2/41
Harvey, G. B. (Maj. late Ind. Army)	1/ 2/41
Thickbroom, C. H.	1/ 2/41
Skyrme, R. H.	1/ 2/41
Taylor, H. M.	1/ 2/41
Huddleston, G. R. G. (Maj. late Ind. Army)	1/ 2/41
Blakey, C. G.	1/ 2/41
Forbes, C. L.	1/ 2/41
Hamilton, J. S., D.S.O. (Capt. late W. York R.)	1/ 2/41
Gill, J. B.	1/ 2/41
Clucas, A. H., M.B.E. (Capt. late W. York R.)	1/ 2/41

Lieutenants

Name	Date
urkin, W. J.	1/ 2/41
alton, E. E.	1/ 2/41

Lieutenants - contd.

Name	Date
Town, H. (Fl. Lt. late R.A.F.)	1/ 2/41
McColl, J. S. (Lt. late Ind. Army)	1/ 2/41
Hull, A. V.	1/ 2/41
Carlin, T. P.	1/ 2/41
Cockcroft, R.	1/ 2/41
Clark, J. H.	1/ 2/41
Beanland, H. H.	1/ 2/41
Thornton, M.	1/ 2/41
Battle, J. P.	1/ 2/41
Dunn, J., M.C. (Lt. late R.W. Fus.)	1/ 2/41
Thomas, A. H.	1/ 2/41
Thornton, E.	1/ 2/41
Abbott, G. (2/Lt. late R.F.A.)	1/ 2/41
Wilson, C. A.	1/ 2/41
Hustler, J.	1/ 2/41
Spofforth, J. R.	1/ 2/41
Ormerod, S. H.	1/ 2/41
Marshall, F. (Capt. late R.E.)	1/ 2/41
Brewer, C. D.	1/ 2/41
Briggs, R.	1/ 2/41
Smith, D., M.M.	1/ 2/41
Pearson, E. R.	1/ 2/41
Mathers, W. R.	1/ 2/41
Elgar, A. W. (Lt. late R.A.)	1/ 2/41
Moss, W.	1/ 2/41
Burbridge, J.	1/ 2/41
Daggett, A. A. (Lt. late Midd'x. R.)	1/ 2/41
Gilbertson, L. (2/Lt. late Green Howards)	1/ 2/41
Rosindale, H. G., D.C.M.	1/ 2/41
Blenkhorn, E.	1/ 2/41
Whincup, J. H.	1/ 2/41
Holdsworth, T. C.	1/ 2/41
Hartley, W.	1/ 2/41
Kershaw, R. L.	1/ 2/41
Newham, C. A.(2/Lt. late R.A.F.)	1/ 2/41
Aspinall, J.	1/ 2/41
Hubbard, W. S.	1/ 2/41
Stead, A.	1/ 2/41
Stammers, G. M.	1/ 2/41
Tomlinson, J. G.	1/ 2/41
Beecroft, J. W.	1/ 2/41
Maleham, A.	1/ 2/41
Rushworth, P. (2/Lt. late R.A.F.)	1/ 2/41
Field, M. E.	1/ 2/41
Cooper, W. H., D.C.M. (Lt. late M.G. Corps)	1/ 2/41
Downes, L.	1/ 2/41
Dawson, E.	1/ 2/41
Woods, C. V.	1/ 2/41
Joseph, H.	1/ 2/41
Hinde, N.	1/ 2/41
Lee, H., M.M.	22/ 5/41
Wood, H.	22/ 5/41
Davison, A.	1/ 6/41

YORKSHIRE AREA - contd.

WEST RIDING ZONE - contd.

LEEDS GROUP - contd.

8th West Riding (Leeds) Battalion - contd.

2nd Lieutenants

Bergman, S.	1/ 2/41
Pemberton, E. C.	1/ 2/41
Allen, W. E. H. (Lt. ret.)	1/ 2/41
Martin, M. N.	1/ 2/41
Dale, W.	1/ 2/41
Greehy, M.	1/ 2/41
Walker, R. W.	1/ 2/41
Marshall, A. P.	1/ 2/41
Manning, C. H.	1/ 2/41
Byard, S. (2/Lt. late Foresters)	1/ 2/41
Robertson, G. E.	1/ 2/41
Wilks, A. G.	1/ 2/41
Robinson, J. E.	1/ 2/41
Whitworth, C.	1/ 2/41
Inchbold, W. H.	1/ 2/41
Wetton, G.	1/ 2/41
Coley, D.	1/ 2/41
Robinson, O. O.	1/ 2/41
Niekirk, P. B.	1/ 2/41
Skinner, C. R.	1/ 2/41
Shaw, J.	1/ 2/41
Bull, A. C. P.	1/ 2/41
Yates, W. E.	1/ 2/41
Hutley, A. W. R. (Capt. late Lan. Fus.)	1/ 2/41
Nixon, F.	1/ 2/41
Smith, T. N. F.	1/ 2/41
Gough, T. C.	1/ 2/41
Salkeld, F.	1/ 2/41
Cunningham, W. M.	1/ 2/41
McMillan, D.	1/ 2/41
Ure, R. J.	1/ 2/41
Widdas, H. R.	1/ 2/41
Motley, H.	1/ 2/41
Talbot, C.	1/ 2/41
Hare, J.	1/ 2/41
Pullan, A. E.	1/ 2/41
Barker, T. E.	1/ 2/41
McLusky, W. B., M.C. (Capt. late W. York R.)	1/ 2/41
Ballantyne, T. H. N.	21/ 4/41
Lawson, R.	21/ 4/41
Orford, S. F.	22/ 4/41
Wilson, H. E.	29/ 4/41

2nd Lieutenants - contd.

Anderson, O. H.	18/ 5/41
Lee, W. H.	18/ 5/41
Thornton, F.	18/ 5/41
Whitham, H.	18/ 5/41
Pryor, H. E.	23/ 5/41
Barwick, J. C.	24/ 5/41
Pullan, E. (2/Lt. late R.E.)	3/ 6/41
Warnes, S. H.	4/ 7/41
Hood, S. A. (2/Lt. late W. York R.)	21/ 7/41

Adjutant & Quarter-Master

Medical Officer

Stalker, Maj. A., M.B.	20/ 5/41

YORKSHIRE AREA - contd.
WEST RIDING ZONE - contd.
LEEDS GROUP - contd.

9th WEST RIDING (LEEDS) BATTALION

Lt.-Colonel

Bray, G., M.C., T.D. (Bt. Col. T.A. Res. of Off.) 1/ 2/41

Majors

Boyle, H. K., D.S.O. (Maj. late T.A. Res.) 1/ 2/41
Dawson, H. B., M.C. (Lt. late R.F.A.) 1/ 2/41
Lister, E. I. 1/ 2/41
Lupton, A. W., M.C. (Lt. T.A. Res.) 1/ 2/41
Butler, B. H. (Maj. late R.F.A.) 1/ 2/41

Captains

Lewis, O. W. H., M.B.E. (Capt. late R.G.A.) 1/ 2/41
Ward, J. H. (Capt. late D.W.R.) 1/ 2/41
Goodall, C. M., M.C. (Capt. late North'd. Fus.) 1/ 2/41
Wright, W. L. (Lt. late Res. of Off.) 1/ 2/41
Whiteker, G. B., O.B.E. (Maj. late R.E.) 1/ 2/41
Cowell, F. R. 1/ 2/41
Rimmel, A. G. H. (2/Lt. late R.A.S.C.) 20/ 5/41

Lieutenants

Turberville, A. S., M.C. (Capt. late K.R.R.C.) 1/ 2/41
Glover, A. F. 1/ 2/41
Brown, E. J. (Lt. late Naval Div. Arty.) 1/ 2/41
Whyte, G. N. D. (Capt. late W. York R.) 1/ 2/41
Knowles, V. (Lt. late R.G.A.) 1/ 2/41
Westlake, H. L., M.C. (Capt. late Wilts R.) 1/ 2/41
Jessop, J. C. 1/ 2/41
Walker, F. H. (Lt. late R.A.S.C.) 1/ 2/41
Holmes, E. E. 1/ 2/41
Little, B. L. 1/ 2/41
Dawson, W. F. (Lt. late R.E.) 1/ 2/41
Hobson, H. N. (Lt. late Loyal R.) 1/ 2/41
Hartley, C., D.C.M. (Lt. late R.F.A.) 1/ 2/41
Kenworthy, C. T. (Lt. late Labour Corps) 1/ 2/41
Williamson, M. 1/ 2/41
Hollings-Smith, W. (Lt. late E. York R.) 1/ 2/41
Cotton, J. C. (Lt. ret.) 1/ 2/41

Lieutenants - contd.

Hetherington, W. (2/Lt. late R.A.) 1/ 2/41
Lister, B. S. (Lt. late R.F.C.) 1/ 2/41
Nicholson, K. B., M.C. (Maj. late R.F.A.) 1/ 2/41
Butler, R. F. (2/Lt. late R.F.A.) 1/ 2/41
Haig, T. H. 1/ 2/41
Johnson, B. 1/ 2/41
Rowe, F. M. 9/ 5/41
Gross, L. F. (Lt. late R.A.F.) 21/ 5/41
Pickles, H. M., M.M. 9/ 7/41

2nd Lieutenants

Shute, N. 1/ 2/41
Haggen, G. L. (Capt. late Oxf. & Bucks., L.I.) 1/ 2/41
Hendry, J. (Lt. late Gordons) 1/ 2/41
Green, A. E. (Lt. late Wilts. R.) 1/ 2/41
Hughes, F. (Lt. late Res. of Off.) 1/ 2/41
Armitage, W. A. (Lt. late W. York R.) 1/ 2/41
Duffy, J. F. (2/Lt. late W. York R.) 1/ 2/41
Boston, W. R. (2/Lt. late R.H.A.) 1/ 2/41
Fletcher, J. 1/ 2/41
Saville, H. 1/ 2/41
Kent, H. F., M.C. (Late T.A. Res.) 1/ 2/41
Tomalin, H., M.C. (Lt. late K.O.Y.L.I.) 1/ 2/41
Demaine, J. (Capt. late T.A.) 1/ 2/41
Smith, A. (2/Lt. late E. York R.) 1/ 2/41
Fortune, G. E. (Lt. late Y. & L.R.) 1/ 2/41
Wood, H. C. 1/ 2/41
Knight, H., M.M. 1/ 2/41
Briggs, J. 1/ 2/41
Staincliffe, W. E. 1/ 2/41
MacKenzie, W. (Lt. late K.O.Y.L.I.) 1/ 2/41
Castle, E. R. M. (Capt. late R.A.S.C.) 1/ 2/41
Parker, H. E. 1/ 2/41
Metcalfe, C. P. (Lt. late Durham L.I.) 1/ 2/41
Hobbs, T. H. C., M.M. (Lt. late R. Fus.) 1/ 2/41
Prince, J. 1/ 2/41
Bennett, C. E. (Lt. late R. Signals) 1/ 2/41
Overton, C. 1/ 2/41
Muirhead, A. D. H. (Lt. late T.A.) 1/ 2/41
Brewin, S., M.C. (Lt. late North'd. Fus.) 1/ 2/41
Lee, A. (Lt. late Lan. Fus.) 1/ 2/41
Thacker, L. (Maj. late Ind. Army) 1/ 2/41
Bargh, J. (Lt. late R.F.A.) 1/ 2/41
Robinson, J. 1/ 2/41
Bedford, L. L. 1/ 2/41
Fox, G. P. (Lt. late R.F.A.) 1/ 2/41

YORKSHIRE AREA - contd.

WEST RIDING ZONE - contd.

LEEDS GROUP - contd.

9th West Riding (Leeds) Battalion - contd.

2nd Lieutenants - contd.

Biddle, H. W. (Lt. late R. Signals)	1/ 2/41
Suckling, J. H. (2/Lt. late R.N.V.R.)	1/ 2/41
Kean, T. V. (Capt. late London R.)	1/ 2/41
Morley, W.	1/ 2/41
Dubery, R. F.	1/ 2/41
Palmer, L. W. (Lt. late S. Wales Bord.)	1/ 2/41
Bellingham, G. W. (Lt. late S. Stafford R.)	1/ 2/41
Arnold, I. D. O. (Lt. late R.W. Fus.)	1/ 2/41
Cartwright, R. P.	1/ 2/41
Bain, W. A.	1/ 2/41
Anderson, R. N. (Capt. late 9th H.)	1/ 2/41
Hudson, A. O.	1/ 2/41
Franklyn, A. G. (2/Lt. late R.A.S.C.)	1/ 2/41
Alderson, J. E. W., M.M.	1/ 2/41
Farrar, A. E.	1/ 2/41
Woosnam, R. L. (Lt. late W. York R.)	1/ 2/41
Crowther, N. J. V. (Lt. late R.G.A.)	15/ 5/41
Durward, A.	15/ 5/41
Geen, G. A. (2/Lt. late K.R.R.C.)	15/ 5/41
Greaves, E.	15/ 5/41
Gilliat, E. V. (Lt. late R.A.F.)	23/ 5/41
Hunt, A.	23/ 5/41
Ayres, E. (Lt. late M.G. Corps)	26/ 5/41
Padley, H. (Lt. late Durham L.I.)	24/ 7/41

Adjutant & Quarter-Master

Medical Officer

Muir, Maj. R. C. (Capt. late R.A.M.C.)	21/ 5/41

AIRE & CALDER NAVIGATION COMPANY

Major

Emley, H. B., C.M.G. (Capt. late R.E.)	1/ 2/41

Captain

Nottingham, A., D.C.M. (2/Lt. late D.W.R.)	1/ 2/41

Lieutenants

Spink, D. C. (Lt. late R.G.A.)	1/ 2/41
Mountford, C. W. J.	1/ 2/41
Bradshaw, W. J. (2/Lt. late R.A.F.)	1/ 2/41

YORKSHIRE AREA - contd.

WEST RIDING ZONE - contd.

BRADFORD GROUP

Commander	Fenton, Col. W. C., M.C. (Maj. ret. T.A.)	1/ 2/41
Second in Command	Dallas, Lt.-Col. T. L. (Capt. ret.)	1/ 2/41

1st WEST RIDING (BRADFORD) BATTALION

Lt.-Colonel

Hodgson, D. V. (Lt. late R.A.F.) 1/ 2/41

Majors

Parker, T. G. (Lt. late W. York R.) 1/ 2/41
Hutton, A. N., M.C. (Capt. late R.T.C.) 1/ 2/41
Wood, G. (2/Lt. late R.E.) 1/ 2/41
Yeadon, N. J. 1/ 2/41
Mountain, G. (Capt. late W. York R.) 1/ 2/41
Hickson, S. H. V. (Capt. late W. York R.) 7/ 4/41

Captains

Higginbotham, J. C. (Capt. late R.A.) 1/ 2/41
Spencer, F. B., M.M. 1/ 2/41
Harrisson, R. (2/Lt. late Green Howards) 1/ 2/41
Tempest, E. V., D.S.O., M.C. (Capt. late W. York R.) 1/ 2/41
Woodhead, R. (Lt. late W. York R.) 1/ 2/41
Mason, R. S. (Capt. late R.A.M.C.) 7/ 4/41

Lieutenants

Wilson, F. M. 1/ 2/41
Jennison, H., M.C. (Lt. late Inniskilling Fus.) 1/ 2/41
Woodgate, F. G. (Lt. late R.E.) 1/ 2/41
Walde, E. H., M.M. (Lt. late R.A.) 1/ 2/41
Chappell, S. S. (Capt. late K.O.Y.L.I.) 1/ 2/41
Reilly, C. O. C., M.B.E. (Capt. late R.E.) 1/ 2/41
Smith, J. F. 1/ 2/41
Parker, F. 1/ 2/41
Stevenson, A. W., D.F.C. (Lt. late R.F.C.) 1/ 2/41
Taylor, C. S. 1/ 2/41
Laycock, F. H. 1/ 2/41
Pratt, F. S. 1/ 2/41
Wilson, H. S. (2/Lt. late H.L.I.) 1/ 2/41
Lyddon, J. (Lt. late R.A.) 1/ 2/41
Coutts, J. G. 1/ 2/41
Greenhalgh, W. 1/ 2/41
Head, V. G. (2/Lt. late R.T.C.) 1/ 2/41
Parsey, J. L., D.C.M. (Capt. late W. York R.) 1/ 2/41
Newby, G. L., M.M. 1/ 2/41
Allum, C. E., M.C. (Lt. late Cheshire R.) 1/ 2/41
Duncan, A. V. 1/ 2/41
Wheeldon, J. W., M.M. 1/ 2/41
Hindle, D. P. 1/ 2/41

Lieutenants - contd.

Milner, W. 1/ 2/41
Keighley, A. 1/ 2/41
Laycock, H. 1/ 2/41
Smith, C. (2/Lt. late R.T.C.) 1/ 2/41

2nd Lieutenants

Currie, W. M. 1/ 2/41
Smith, E. (Lt. late W. York R.) 1/ 2/41
Binks, A. 1/ 2/41
Booth, R. 1/ 2/41
Dixon, F. (2/Lt. late W. York R.) 1/ 2/41
Swaine, G. V. 1/ 2/41
Kemp, R. J. A. (2/Lt. late R.A.F.) 1/ 2/41
Larkins, H. A. 1/ 2/41
Rayner, H. 1/ 2/41
Benfield, W., D.C.M. 1/ 2/41
Prevett, H. 1/ 2/41
Varley, W. J. 1/ 2/41
Cowgill, A. 1/ 2/41
Barnes, W. L. 1/ 2/41
Hanson, E. 1/ 2/41
Hopwood, W. L. 1/ 2/41
Woodhead, H. 1/ 2/41
Lee, M. 1/ 2/41
Haines, W. D. 1/ 2/41
Binns, J. M. 1/ 2/41
Maxfield, L. 1/ 2/41
Rockliff, G. A. 1/ 2/41
Sunderland, J. L. (2/Lt. late W. York R.) 1/ 2/41
Hartley, R. W. H. (Lt. late W. York R.) 1/ 2/41
Brown, G. H. 1/ 2/41
Wishart, K. F. 1/ 2/41
Dobson, J. 1/ 2/41
Broadbent, C. 1/ 2/41
Lennon, C. B. 1/ 2/41
Creyke, F. (2/Lt. late R.A.S.C.) 1/ 2/41
Souster, S. 1/ 2/41
Baxter, J. H. 1/ 2/41
Overend, F. L. 1/ 2/41
Biggs, J. N. 1/ 2/41
Hammond, I. P., M.M. 1/ 2/41
Walker, S. 1/ 2/41

Adjutant & Quarter-Master

Medical Officer

Sewrey, Maj. W. C. S. B. 21/ 4/41

YORKSHIRE AREA - contd.

WEST RIDING ZONE - contd.

BRADFORD GROUP - contd.

2nd WEST RIDING (BRADFORD) BATTALION

Lt.-Colonel

Frost, R., M.C., T.D. (Bt. Col. ret. T.A.)	1/ 2/41

Majors

Pearson, W., M.C. (Lt. late R. Irish R.)	1/ 2/41
Walker, H. (2/Lt. late D.W.R.)	1/ 2/41
Scriven, F. A. (Maj. late W. York R.)	1/ 2/41
Atkins, C. A. (Flying Offr. late R.A.F.)	1/ 2/41

Captains

Smith, H., M.C. (Maj. late D.W.R.)	1/ 2/41
Tannam, G. R.	1/ 2/41
Bowler, W.	1/ 2/41
Shorrock, J. V.	1/ 2/41
Pickles, J.	1/ 2/41
Shaw, F.	22/ 4/41

Lieutenants

Read, W., D.C.M., M.M.	1/ 2/41
Sugden, A. J.	1/ 2/41
Graham, N. (Lt. late M.G. Corps)	1/ 2/41
Neal, F. T. (2/Lt. late Gordons)	1/ 2/41
Bacon, T. K.	1/ 2/41
Dumville, H.	1/ 2/41
Hirst, G. H.	1/ 2/41
Greenwood, G. W.	1/ 2/41
Stead, C. (Lt. late R.G.A.)	1/ 2/41
Sutcliffe, H. (2/Lt. ret.)	1/ 2/41
Webster, E.	1/ 2/41
Robson, M. (Capt. late R. North'd. Fus.)	1/ 2/41
Rotheray, F.	1/ 2/41
Wood, W. P.	1/ 2/41
Fearn, A. C.	1/ 2/41
Smith, W.	1/ 2/41
Barraclough, A.	1/ 2/41
Latham T. B.	1/ 2/41
Pratt, S. L.	1/ 2/41
Bray, H.	1/ 2/41
Sisman, E. W.	1/ 2/41
Lambert, D.	21/ 5/41
Middlemass, A. B.	5/ 6/41

2nd Lieutenants

Taylor, J. H.	1/ 2/41
Mortimer, R. A.	1/ 2/41

2nd Lieutenants - contd.

Bastow, J. W. (Lt. late M.G. Corps)	1/ 2/41
Whitworth, J. W.	1/ 2/41
Wilkinson, M. H.	1/ 2/41
Stansfield, G. G. (Lt. late K.A. Rif.)	1/ 2/41
Thorpe, B. C.	1/ 2/41
Kettlewell, A. W.	1/ 2/41
Senior, A.	1/ 2/41
Sharp, M., M.C. (Lt. late R.F.A.)	1/ 2/41
Greenwood, B.	1/ 2/41
Stevenson, E. G. F. (2/Lt. late Foresters)	1/ 2/41
Dover, G.	1/ 2/41
Robbins, F.	1/ 2/41
Cooper, A. N.	1/ 2/41
Kitchen, F.	1/ 2/41
Leonards, J.	1/ 2/41
Harrison, W. E.	1/ 2/41
Kitchen, G. F.	1/ 2/41
Stringer, A.	1/ 2/41
Wood, F.	1/ 2/41
Stubbs, R.	1/ 2/41
Anderson, H.	1/ 2/41
Booth, J.	1/ 2/41
Edmondson, T.	1/ 2/41
Slater, F.	1/ 2/41
Kerr, J. McE.	1/ 2/41

Adjutant & Quarter-Master

Medical Officer

Robinson, Maj. H. W., M.C. (Capt. late R.A.M.C.)	21/ 4/41

YORKSHIRE AREA - contd.

WEST RIDING ZONE - contd.

BRADFORD GROUP - contd.

3rd WEST RIDING (BRADFORD) BATTALION

Lt.-Colonel

Hodgson, C. H. (Lt. late T.A.) 1/ 2/41

Majors

Farnish, P. F. (Capt. late K.O.Y.L.I.) 1/ 2/41
Downs, W. (Lt. late N. Lancs. R.) 1/ 2/41
Behrens, J. H. (Lt. late W. York R.) 1/ 2/41
Brown, G. L. (Lt. late M.G. Corps.) 1/ 2/41

Captains

Stansfield, E. D., M.C. (Maj. late W. York R.) 1/ 2/41
Murray, S. A., M.C. (Capt. late Mon. R.) 1/ 2/41
Lumb, F. E., D.C.M. 1/ 2/41
Durrant, N. W. (Capt. late M.G. Corps.) 1/ 2/41
Palin, A. (2/Lt. late A. Cyclist Corps) 1/ 2/41
Lynn, A. C. 1/ 2/41
Yates, W., M.C. (Lt. late D.W.R.) 19/ 7/41

Lieutenants

Robinson, H. W. (Capt. late W. York R.) 1/ 2/41
Goodall, F. L. (2/Lt. late T.A.) 1/ 2/41
Dobson, R. (Lt. late D.W.R.) 1/ 2/41
Emmott, H. L. J. 1/ 2/41
Noble, H. 1/ 2/41
Brogden, J. H. (Lt. late E. Surrey R.) 1/ 2/41
Buffham, J. 1/ 2/41
Malby, J. J. 1/ 2/41
Burgess, J. (Lt. late Lond. R.) 1/ 2/41
Hill, J. S. (Lt. late Lincoln R.) 1/ 2/41
Bulmer, L. T. (Lt. late R.A.F.) 1/ 2/41
Marchmont, D. H. (Lt. late K.R.R.C.) 1/ 2/41
Parkinson, E., M.C. (Lt. late R.F.A.) 1/ 2/41
Jaques, H. 1/ 2/41
Brook, G. H., M.C. (Capt. late K.O.Y.L.I.) 1/ 2/41
Golden, W. 1/ 2/41
Quin, W. C. 1/ 2/41
Kenyon, F. W. 1/ 2/41
Crowther, F. 1/ 2/41
Speight, G. H., M.C. (Lt. late W. York R.) 1/ 2/41
Sharples, F. 10/ 6/41
Symons, H. W. 10/ 6/41
Nicholson, C. H. (Capt. late K.O.Y.L.I.) 10/ 6/41
Renton, G. F. (Lt. late R.E.) 10/ 6/41
Dawson, J. E. J. (Capt. late R.T.C.) 19/ 7/41

YORKSHIRE AREA - contd.

WEST RIDING ZONE - contd.

BRADFORD GROUP - contd.

3rd West Riding (Bradford) Battalion - contd.

2nd Lieutenants

Brigg, W. L. (Capt. late Ind. Army)	1/ 2/41
Naylor, F.	1/ 2/41
Lister, R.	1/ 2/41
Rigby, W. H. (Capt. late Leicester R.)	1/ 2/41
Bottomley, W. C. (Lt. late R.A.S.C.)	1/ 2/41
Smith, A. J. (2/Lt. late Y. & L.R.)	1/ 2/41
Smith, L. F. (2/Lt. late York R.)	1/ 2/41
Booth, H. H. (2/Lt. late K.O.Y.L.I.)	1/ 2/41
Pattison, A.	1/ 2/41
Purrier, A. A.	1/ 2/41
Barker, W. C.	1/ 2/41
Keirl, A. (Capt. late R.A.)	1/ 2/41
Brooke, J. H.	1/ 2/41
Howe, H.	1/ 2/41
Trusson, H. (Lt. late R.A.)	1/ 2/41
Smith, H.	1/ 2/41
Parkinson, H.	1/ 2/41
McNair, J. B. R. (Lt. late Cheshire R.)	1/ 2/41
Golden, H.	1/ 2/41
Wright, E.	1/ 2/41
Craven, W. E.	1/ 2/41
Whitaker, A., M.M.	1/ 2/41
Myers, E., M.C. (Capt. late W. York R.)	1/ 2/41
Clayton, F. R.	1/ 2/41
Knight, W. D.	1/ 2/41
Webster, G. W. (Capt. late W. York R.)	1/ 2/41
Tullie, C. S.	1/ 2/41
Finch, D.	1/ 2/41
Tuke, H. S.	1/ 2/41
Richardson, S. L. (Lt. late R.E.)	1/ 2/41
Sagar, B. H.	1/ 2/41
Naylor, A.	1/ 2/41
Naylor, F.	1/ 2/41
Barrett, L.	1/ 2/41

2nd Lieutenants - contd.

Brigham, W. W.	1/ 2/41
Parker, T. B.	1/ 2/41
Wakefield, L. E., M.C. (Lt. late Gloster R.)	1/ 2/41
Clay, H.	1/ 2/41
Gadie, E. A.	10/ 6/41
Sim, W. (Lt. late R.F.A.)	28/ 7/41

Adjutant & Quarter-Master

Medical Officer

Shackleton, Maj. H. P., O.B.E. (Capt. late R.A.M.C.)	24/ 4/41

YORKSHIRE AREA - contd.

WEST RIDING ZONE - contd.

BRADFORD GROUP - contd.

4th WEST RIDING (BRADFORD) BATTALION

Lt.-Colonel

Thornton, W. H., M.C., T.D. (Maj. ret. T.A.) (Hon. Col. T.A.)	1/ 2/41

Majors

Robertshaw, H. R. (2/Lt. late London R.)	1/ 2/41
Drake, R., M.M.	1/ 2/41
Houghton, F. W.	23/ 6/41

Captains

Macdonald, L. J.	1/ 2/41
Morley, E.	1/ 2/41
Thackery, E. A., M.C., (Lt. late W. York R.)	1/ 2/41
Horsman, S. L. (Lt. late R.F.C.)	1/ 2/41
Smith, L. J. H.	1/ 2/41
Rimington, J.	1/ 2/41

Lieutenants

Peel, H. H. (Flying Offr. late R.A.F.)	1/ 2/41
Sutherland, G. O. (Maj. late R. Scots.)	1/ 2/41
Bullus, T. G	1/ 2/41
Blenkin, E.	1/ 2/41
Hodgson, A.	1/ 2/41
Parker, S.	1/ 2/41
James, T. W.	1/ 2/41
Askham, H.	1/ 2/41
Farrand, H.	1/ 2/41
McGowan, J.	1/ 2/41
Sheldon, S.	1/ 2/41
Marsh, C.	1/ 2/41
Woolley, H. (2/Lt. late Loyal R.)	1/ 2/41
Roberts, W., M.M.	1/ 2/41
Ogden, L. V. (2/Lt. late M.G. Corps)	1/ 2/41
Crowther, J. A.	1/ 2/41
Harland, J. P.	1/ 2/41
Anderson, A. L.	1/ 2/41
Berry, F.	1/ 2/41
Linney, C. A.	1/ 2/41
Davis, C. E.	1/ 2/41
Smith, E. H.	1/ 2/41

56455-6(84)

Lieutenants - contd.

Nott, C.	1/ 2/41
Shaw, S. A.	1/ 2/41
Hand, A. C.	1/ 2/41
Hodgson, A. E.	1/ 2/41
Douglas, V. A.	22/ 5/41

2nd Lieutenants

Ingham, F.	1/ 2/41
Rasche, J. E.	1/ 2/41
Scott, T. L.	1/ 2/41
Lawrie, A.	1/ 2/41
Shaw, H. (Pilot Offr. late R.A.F.)	1/ 2/41
Fowle, C. (Lt. late D.W.R.)	1/ 2/41
Western, S.	1/ 2/41
Scott, L.	1/ 2/41
Tuson, T. W. G.	1/ 2/41
Barker, T. H., D.C.M., M.M.	1/ 2/41
Watmough, G.	1/ 2/41
Wilford, E.	1/ 2/41
Burlison, E.	1/ 2/41
Emmett, I.	1/ 2/41
Brearley, N. C.	1/ 2/41
Thrush, P.	1/ 2/41
Lawton, E. G.	1/ 2/41
Warburton, N.	1/ 2/41
Crapper, W.	1/ 2/41
Archer, S. T.	1/ 2/41
Marton, J. D. L.	1/ 2/41
Pratt, C. F.	1/ 2/41
Thomlinson, W.	1/ 2/41
Warwick, J. A.	1/ 2/41
Halstead, W. E.	1/ 2/41
Horsfall, S. F.	30/ 4/41
Hughes, J.	30/ 4/41
Strudwick, J. W.	22/ 5/41
Hunter, W. S.	30/ 5/41

Adjutant & Quarter-Master

Medical Officer

West-Watson, Maj. W. N. W. (Capt. late R.A.M.C.)	25/ 4/41

YORKSHIRE AREA - contd.

WEST RIDING ZONE - contd.

CALDER VALLEY GROUP

Commander	Shaw, Col. R. M., D.S.O., M.C. (Maj. late T.A.)	1/ 2/41
Assistant to Commander	Sayer, Capt. M. M. (Lt. late The Queen's R.)	1/ 2/41

21st WEST RIDING (CALDER VALLEY) BATTALION

Lt.-Colonel

Whitworth, R. B., M.C. (Capt. late T.A.)	1/ 2/41

Majors

Hoyle, J. C. (Capt. late Cheshire R.)	1/ 2/41
Mitchell, J., M.C., D.F.C. (Capt. late R.A.F.)	1/ 2/41
Robertshaw, G. F. (Capt. late D.W.R.)	1/ 2/41
Robinson, J. (Lt. late D.W.R.)	1/ 2/41

Captains

Barker, W. A. (2/Lt. late R.T.C.)	1/ 2/41
Walton, P. B. (Lt. late D.W.R.)	1/ 2/41
Yelland, V.	1/ 2/41

Lieutenants

Earnshaw, H.	1/ 2/41
Thain, C. M.	1/ 2/41
Oldfield, G. A. G.	1/ 2/41
Leeming, A., D.C.M.	1/ 2/41
Hollingrake, J. R.	1/ 2/41
Barker, W.	1/ 2/41
Hall, W. N. (Lt. late R.W.K.)	1/ 2/41
Ashworth, L. W. (2/Lt. late E. York R.)	1/ 2/41
Jackson, G.	1/ 2/41
Smith, H. C. (Lt. late R.T.C.)	1/ 2/41
Whiteley, J. S.	1/ 2/41
Killin, W., M.M.	1/ 2/41

Lieutenants - contd.

Sutcliffe, A. (Lt.-late D.W.R.)	1/ 2/41
Butterworth, R.	1/ 2/41
Longbottom, C.	17/ 6/41
Smith, J. M., M.M.	17/ 6/41

2nd Lieutenants

Clay, H.	1/ 2/41
Howarth, W.	1/ 2/41
Graham, J.	1/ 2/41
Widdup, R. A.	1/ 2/41
Lever, J.	1/ 2/41
Johnson, J. H.	1/ 2/41
Ashworth, T.	1/ 2/41
Dunn, J. H.	1/ 2/41
Jackson, W.	1/ 2/41
Crabtree, K.	1/ 2/41
Bottomley, A. G.	1/ 2/41
Macauley, D. A. R.	1/ 2/41
Boothman, A.	1/ 2/41
Peace, E. J.	1/ 2/41
Sunderland S.	17/ 6/41

Adjutant & Quarter-Master

Medical Officer

Bayley, Maj. J. C. P. (Capt. late R.A.M.C.)	1/ 2/41

YORKSHIRE AREA - contd.

WEST RIDING ZONE - contd.

CALDER VALLEY GROUP - contd.

22nd WEST RIDING (CALDER VALLEY) BATTALION

Lt.-Colonel

Blakey, E. V., M.C. (Capt. late T.A.)	1/ 2/41

Majors

Lumb, A., M.C. (Capt. late R.A.)	1/ 2/41
Warrington, J. (Capt. late Border R.)	1/ 2/41
Dunn, G. A. (Capt. late Camerons)	1/ 2/41
Binns, C. E. (Lt. late D.W.R.)	1/ 2/41
Cordingley, L., M.C. (Capt. late D.W.R.)	1/ 2/41

Captains

Lavers, R. W. D.	1/ 2/41
Williams, J. E. (2/Lt. late Leicester R.)	1/ 2/41
Cocker, F., M.C. (Lt. late K.O.Y.L.I.)	1/ 2/41
Shave, S. O. (Capt. late London R.)	1/ 2/41

Lieutenants

Gudgin, G. E. (2/Lt. late R.A.F.)	1/ 2/41
Wardrop, J. W. (Lt. late Can. Mil. Forces)	1/ 2/41
Little, J. J. (Pilot Offr. late R.F.C.)	1/ 2/41
Brook, A.	1/ 2/41
Taylor, G.	1/ 2/41
Pilling, H.	1/ 2/41
Evans, G.	1/ 2/41
Helliwell, W.	1/ 2/41
Cave, A. (Lt. late R.W.K.)	1/ 2/41
Prynne, A. L. (Lt. late D.W.R.)	1/ 2/41

Lieutenants - contd.

Blakeborough, J. B.	1/ 2/41
Mabbott, A.	1/ 2/41
Mills, W. S. (Maj. late Ind. Army)	1/ 2/41
Turner, J.	1/ 2/41
Spencer, A. K. N.	1/ 2/41
Wood, A. J.	24/ 7/41
Mason, G. R.	24/ 7/41

2nd Lieutenants

Webster, L. (Lt. late Labour Corps)	1/ 2/42
Bradley, G.	1/ 2/41
Crossley, G. H.	1/ 2/41
Haigh, H., D.C.M., M.M.	1/ 2/41
Hammond, W. S.	1/ 2/41
Beech, G. E. B.	1/ 2/41
Noble, H., M.M.	1/ 2/41
Wardingley, H.	1/ 2/41
Moore, F.	1/ 2/41
Parr, G. H.	1/ 2/41
Slade, H. J.	1/ 2/41
Stevens, A. R.	1/ 2/41
Carr, J. T.	1/ 2/41
Shoesmith, R. C. P.	1/ 2/41
Pell, J. F. M.M.	1/ 2/41
Chapman, A.	1/ 2/41
Walker, N.	1/ 2/41
Irwin, W.	1/ 2/41
Prynne, P. J.	24/ 7/41

Adjutant & Quarter-Master

Medical Officer

Smellie, Maj. R. MacD. (Lt. late Gordons)	1/ 2/41

YORKSHIRE AREA - contd.

WEST RIDING ZONE - contd.

HALIFAX GROUP

Commander	Huntriss, Col. E. M., M.C. (Lt.-Col. late Serv. Bn. D.W.R.)	1/ 2/41
Second in Command	Ainley, Lt.-Col. A.	1/ 2/41
Assistant to Commander	Bell, Capt. W. O.	1/ 2/41

23rd WEST RIDING (HALIFAX) BATTALION

Lt.-Colonel

Horsley, W. E. (Lt. late T.A.)	1/ 2/41

Majors

Shaw, J. T., D.S.O. (Capt. late Green Howards)	1/ 2/41
Mitchell, W. H., M.M	1/ 2/41
Bodger, E. (Lt. late R.F.A.)	1/ 2/41
Youngman, M.	1/ 2/41
Clark, F. C. C., M.C. (Maj. late R.G.A.)	1/ 2/41
Shaw, F. A. (2/Lt. late Tank Corps)	1/ 2/41

Captains

Hall, E.	1/ 2/41
Green, H. T.	1/ 2/41
Swale, J. F	1/ 2/41
Ostler, G. G.	1/ 2/41
Thompson, A.	1/ 2/41
Harding, H. G.	1/ 2/41
Field, A. R.	1/ 2/41
Webb, W.	4/ 7/41

Lieutenants

Harwood, H. (2/Lt. late D.W.R.)	1/ 2/41
Ashley, L. F. (Flying Offr. late R.A.F.)	1/ 2/41
Wolstanholme, H.	1/ 2/41
Swaine, V.	1/ 2/41
Sutcliffe, J. A.	1/ 2/41
Midgley, N. W.	1/ 2/41
Miller, E.	1/ 2/41
Gallop, F. C.	1/ 2/41
Slater, M. H.	1/ 2/41
Hawkes, A. R., M.M.	1/ 2/41
Habishaw, J.	1/ 2/41
Hardie, L.	1/ 2/41
Kershaw, D. R.	1/ 2/41
Walsh, J.	1/ 2/41
Holcroft, N. (Lt. late R.F.A.)	1/ 2/41
Holdsworth, H. R. (Capt. late D.W.R.)	1/ 2/41
Morgan, T. E.	1/ 2/41
Robinson, J. S.	1/ 2/41
Garfitt, W. (Lt. late W. York R.)	1/ 2/41

Lieutenants - contd.

Hirst, F. C.	1/ 2/41
Newsome, F. W.	1/ 2/41
Haigh, W. S.	1/ 2/41
Johnson, C. L.	1/ 2/41
Stuart, W. L.	1/ 2/41
Metcalfe, L., M.M.	4/ 7/41

2nd Lieutenants

Hodgson, R.	1/ 2/41
Hayes, B. B.	1/ 2/41
Wilkinson, R.	1/ 2/41
Mitchell, A.	1/ 2/41
Jamieson, W. S.	1/ 2/41
Buckley, H.	1/ 2/41
Hitch, R. A.	1/ 2/41
Halliday, W.	1/ 2/41
Feather, P. K.	1/ 2/41
Ryan, J. A.	1/ 2/41
Welburn, J., M.M.	1/ 2/41
Wurr, G.	1/ 2/41
Hoyle, F. C.	1/ 2/41
Grey, J. H.	1/ 2/41
Kay, S. A. A.	1/ 2/41
Hargreaves, F. N. (Lt. late R.F.A.)	1/ 2/41
Athea, H.	1/ 2/41
Knowles, T., M.M.	1/ 2/41
Alty, T. W.	1/ 2/41
Cullen, G.	1/ 2/41
Longbottom, J. B.	1/ 2/41
Wadsworth, E.	1/ 2/41
Wilkinson, W.	1/ 2/41
Lucas, C. H.	15/ 7/41
Brearley, A.	18/ 7/41

Adjutant & Quarter-Master

Medical Officer

Readdie, Maj. A. F., M.C. (Capt. late R.A.M.C.)	1/ 2/41

YORKSHIRE AREA - contd.

WEST RIDING ZONE - contd.

HALIFAX GROUP - contd.

24th WEST RIDING (HALIFAX) BATTALION

Lt.-Colonel

Beswick, N. S. (Lt. late T.A.) 1/ 2/41

Majors

Connell, A. G., M.M. 1/ 2/41
Robinson, D. 1/ 2/41
Ideson, A., M.C. (Maj. late R.A.) 1/ 2/41
McBain, J. (Lt. late R.E.) 1/ 2/41
Wright, P. A., M.C. (Maj. late R.A.S.C.) 23/ 5/41

Captains

Hanson, F., M.C. (Capt. late W. York R.) 1/ 2/41
Millward, H. L. 1/ 2/41
Wright, F. R. (Capt. late R.W.K.) 1/ 4/41
Rooke, W. E., M.M. (2/Lt. late K.R.R.C.) 23 5/41

Lieutenants

McKelvie, J. 1/ 2/41
Garside, H. H. (Lt. late W. York R.) 1/ 2/41
Shales, J. 1/ 2/41
Butterworth, H., M.M. (2/Lt. late K.R.R.C.) 1/ 2/41
Kershaw, C. 1/ 2/41
Bentley, F. 1/ 2/41
Jagger, C. 1/ 2/41
Wood, F. G. 1/ 2/41
Goodall, I. 1/ 2/41
Topley, H. 1/ 2/41
Sellers, H. 1/ 2/41

Lieutenants - contd.

Berry, W. 1/ 2/41
Roscoe, H. 1/ 2/41
Sykes, J. F. 1/ 4/41

2nd Lieutenants

Longbottom, E., M.M. 1/ 2/41
Sweeney, B., M.M. 1/ 2/41
Pullan, J. E., D.C.M. 1/ 2/41
Oates, H., M.M. 1/ 2/41
Bentley, C. H. 1/ 2/41
Fogg, A. (Lt. late M.G. Corps.) 1/ 2/41
Halliday, A. 1/ 2/41
Huddleston, O. C. (Lt. late R. Fus.) 1/ 2/41
Whitaker, A. 1/ 2/41
Wright, J. 1/ 2/41
Shackleton, F. D. 1/ 2/41
Wadsworth, J. 1/ 4/41

Adjutant & Quarter-Master

Medical Officer

Craig, Maj. W., M.B. (Lt. late Ind. Army) 1/ 2/41

YORKSHIRE AREA - contd.

WEST RIDING ZONE - contd.

DEWSBURY GROUP

Commander	Sproulle, Col. W. J. M., M.C. (Maj. late D.W.R.)	1/ 2/41
Assistant to Commander	Talbot, Capt. G. W. (2/Lt. late Suffolk R.)	1/ 2/41

40th WEST RIDING (DEWSBURY) BATTALION

Lt.-Colonel

Akeroyd, W. T. (Capt. late K.O.Y.L.I.)	1/ 2/41

Majors

Rennison, W., M.C. (Capt. late Manch. R.)	1/ 2/41
Buckley, H. G. (Lt. late R.A.F.)	1/ 2/41
Talbot, G. W.	1/ 2/41

Captains

Walker, H. (2/Lt. late K.O.Y.L.I.)	1/ 2/41
Wilson, J. R. (Lt. late K.O.Y.L.I.)	1/ 2/41
Allen, C. (Lt. late K.R.R.C.)	1/ 2/41
Pilgrim, H.	1/ 2/41
Harding, H. K. (Capt. late D.W.R.)	1/ 2/41

Lieutenants

Broadhead, A. R.	1/ 2/41
Clark, W.	1/ 2/41
Hodgson, G.	1/ 2/41
Hodgson, G. (Lt. late R.A.F.)	1/ 2/41
Cummins, J. N. C. (2/Lt. ret.)	1/ 2/41
Popplewell, W. M. (Lt. late W. York R.)	1/ 2/41
Walker, G. G.	1/ 2/41
Blackburn, O. B. (2/Lt. late Lan. Fus.)	1/ 2/41
Jenkinson, B. P. (2/Lt. late K.O.Y.L.I.)	1/ 2/41
Simpkin, S. F., M.C. (Lt. late R.A.)	1/ 2/41
Walker, H. (Flying Offr. late R.A.F.)	1/ 2/41
Ingram, F. E. (Capt. late Ind. Army)	1/ 2/41
Booth, C. G. (Lt. late W. York R.)	1/ 2/41

56455-6(89)

Lieutenants - contd.

Houston, R. L. (Lt. late R.E.)	1/ 2/41
Hunter, D., D.C.M.	1/ 2/41
Battye, W. W.	1/ 2/41
Benstead, A. S. (Lt. late Lincoln R.)	1/ 2/41
Walker, J. C.	1/ 6/41
Jackson, T.	1/ 6/41

2nd Lieutenants

Mitchell, C. W.	1/ 2/41
Glover, E. (2/Lt. late R.A.S.C.)	1/ 2/41
Harrison, G. C.	1/ 2/41
Wilson, B.	1/ 2/41
Gladhill, J. B.	1/ 2/41
Wingate, N.	1/ 2/41
Pickup, W.	1/ 2/41
Watson, J.	1/ 2/41
Page, H.	1/ 2/41
Hollyhurst, S.	1/ 2/41
Powell, C. C. R.	1/ 2/41
Lee, C. N.	1/ 2/41
Nelson, B.	1/ 2/41
Leathley, R.	1/ 2/41
Haigh, J. H.	6/ 6/41
Naylor, A.	7/ 6/41
Sykes, R. L.	23/ 6/41

Adjutant & Quarter-Master

Medical Officer

Maher, Maj. J. J.	1/ 5/41

YORKSHIRE AREA - contd.

WEST RIDING ZONE - contd.

DEWSBURY GROUP - contd.

41st WEST RIDING (DEWSBURY) BATTALION

Lt.-Colonel

Edwards, H. W., D.S.O., M.C. (Lt.-Col. T.A. Res.)	1/ 2/41

Majors

Lee, N., M.C. (Capt. late K.O.Y.L.I.)	1/ 2/41
Goodall, T., D.S.O., M.C. (Maj. late D.W.R.)	1/ 2/41
Pyrah, A. L. (Capt. late K.O.Y.L.I.)	1/ 2/41
Shepherd, H. C.	1/ 2/41

Captains

Thornton, J., M.M.	1/ 2/41
Balme, S. (Capt. late D.W.R.)	1/ 2/41
Horsfall, G. (Lt. late Green Howards)	1/ 2/41
Brewster, J. A. (Lt. late Ind. Army)	1/ 2/41
Firth, H.	1/ 2/41

Lieutenants

Oxley, F.	1/ 2/41
Fisher, H., M.C. (Capt. late K.O.Y.L.I.)	1/ 2/41
Williams, C. R.	1/ 2/41
Hanson, E. (Lt. late Green Howards)	1/ 2/41
Riley, H. H.	1/ 2/41
Allatt, N.	1/ 2/41
Thornton, R. (Lt. late D.W.R.)	1/ 2/41
Moodie, J. (Lt. late A. & S.H.)	1/ 2/41
Keith, G. L.	1/ 2/41
Bracewell, C. C., M.C., (2/Lt. late Lan. Fus.)	1/ 2/41
Lawrence, D. K.	1/ 2/41
Watson, P. S. O.	1/ 2/41
Jackson, F.	1/ 2/41
Shaw, A., M.C. (Lt. late K.O.Y.L.I.)	1/ 2/41
Bingley, A. L. (Lt. late K.O.Y.L.I.)	1/ 2/41
Critchley, L. (Capt. late R.F.A.)	1/ 2/41
Marsden, W. (Lt. late R.A.F.)	1/ 2/41

Lieutenants - contd.

Holdsworth, L.	1/ 2/41
Kettlewell, J. E.	1/ 2/41
Wilson, C. N.	1/ 2/41
Lowe, W. H. (Lt. late R.E.)	21/ 5/41

2nd Lieutenants

Fisher, L.	1/ 2/41
Lang, J. R.	1/ 2/41
Docton, H. M.	1/ 2/41
Howard, G.	1/ 2/41
Temp, J.	1/ 2/41
Thackrah, H.	1/ 2/41
Bailey, A. C.	1/ 2/41
Pearson, N. C.	1/ 2/41
Clarkson, J.	1/ 2/41
Farrow, T. (Lt. late Green Howards)	1/ 2/41
Wilman, A. B.	1/ 2/41
Beardsell, P.	1/ 2/41
Goddard, G. H.	1/ 2/41
Sheard, A.	1/ 2/41
Wood, A. E.	1/ 2/41
Marriott, J. F. W.	1/ 2/41
Barrowclough, G.	1/ 2/41
Hocknell, B. C.	1/ 2/41
Milner, H.	1/ 2/41
Pocklington, B. D.	1/ 2/41
Mitchell, T., M.M.	1/ 2/41
Hatton, R. C.	1/ 2/41
Bellman, D. S.	1/ 2/41
Armitage, T.	1/ 2/41
Crowther, H. M.	1/ 2/41
Freeman, J.	1/ 2/41
Micklethwaite, E.	1/ 2/41

Adjutant & Quarter-Master

Medical Officer

Laing, Capt. H. W.	31/ 5/41

56455-6(90)

YORKSHIRE AREA - contd.

WEST RIDING ZONE - contd.

WAKEFIELD GROUP

Commander	Burnyeat, Col. W. M. B., M.C. (Capt. late Mon. R.)	1/ 2/41
Second in Command	Aikman, Lt.-Col. J. A. S. S. (Capt. T.A. Res.)	1/ 2/41
Assistant to Commander	Proctor, Capt. H.	1/ 7/41

50th WEST RIDING (WAKEFIELD) BATTALION

Lt.-Colonel

Chadwick, T., M.C., T.D., (Lt.-Col. ret. T.A.)	1/ 2/41

Majors

Kingswell, W. H.	1/ 2/41
Leake, R. L. (Capt. late S. Lan. R.)	1/ 2/41
Firth, J. H., D.C.M., M.M.	1/ 2/41
Holdsworth, L. (Lt. late R.A.S.C.)	1/ 2/41
Cross, T. H.	1/ 5/41
Binns, A. L., M.C. (Capt. late Lincoln R.)	23/ 7/41

Captains

Finney, A. F. (Lt. late R.G.A.)	1/ 2/41
Smith, L. (Lt. late R.A.F.)	1/ 2/41
Brass, F. B.	1/ 5/41
Wilson, F.	24/ 6/41

Lieutenants

Wood, F.	1/ 2/41
Burdin, K.	1/ 2/41
Wilkinson, G. D.	1/ 2/41
Hall, D. M. W.	1/ 2/41
Kellett, F.	1/ 2/41
Finnigan, W.	1/ 2/41
Manley, E. R.	1/ 2/41
Bellwood, C. W.	1/ 2/41
Lockwood, F.	1/ 2/41
Cropper, J.	1/ 2/41
Hargrave, T.	1/ 2/41
Wood, N. C.	1/ 2/41

Lieutenants - contd.

Davis, J. H.	1/ 2/41
Ellison, H. (2/Lt. late R.F.C.)	1/ 2/41
Gibson, J. W. (Lt. late R.A.F.)	1/ 2/41
Chisholm, J.	1/ 2/41
Senior, O.	1/ 2/41
Gebhard, K.	1/ 2/41
Stephenson, W. E. (Lt. late K.O.Y.L.I.)	1/ 2/41
Packer, H.	9/ 5/41
Sweeting, R.	24/ 6/41
Warmington, G. E. D. (Capt. late Durham L.I.)	23/ 7/41

2nd Lieutenants

Waddington, D.	1/ 2/41
Mainstone, W. J.	1/ 2/41
Cunnington, A.	9/ 5/41
Fieldhouse, A., M.B.E.	9/ 5/41

Adjutant & Quarter-Master

Medical Officer

Osmaston, Maj. R. L.	3/ 5/41

56455-6(91)

YORKSHIRE AREA - contd.

WEST RIDING ZONE - contd.

WAKEFIELD GROUP

51st WEST RIDING (WAKEFIELD) BATTALION

Lt.-Colonel

Todd, G. L., M.C. (Lt. late T.A.)	1/ 2/41

Majors

Blair, G. N., M.C. (Lt. late M.G. Corps)	1/ 2/41
Lofthouse, W.	1/ 2/41
Bothwell, F., M.M.	1/ 2/41
Horner, E. M., D.C.M., M.M.	1/ 2/41
Boardman, A. J. (Lt. late Green Howards)	1/ 2/41

Captains

McDonald, J. R.	1/ 2/41
Linney, R. C.	1/ 2/41
Musgrave, E. I.	1/ 2/41
Hulse, W.	1/ 2/41

Lieutenants

Hudson, F. C.	1/ 2/41
Moss, F. W.	1/ 2/41
Taylor, B.	1/ 2/41
Baker, G.	1/ 2/41
Vernon, F. S. (Lt. late Green Howards)	1/ 2/41
Anderson, D. J.	1/ 2/41
Boon, I. G.	1/ 2/41
Laidlaw, J., M.M. (2/Lt. late London R.)	1/ 2/41
James, G.	1/ 2/41
Holmes, J.	1/ 2/41
Mills, R. A.	1/ 2/41
Clarke, E.	1/ 2/41
Caton, A. J. (Lt. late Lan. Fus.)	1/ 2/41
Manson, P.	1/ 2/41
Knox, R. E.	1/ 2/41
Brook, A. (Lt. late K.O.Y.L.I.)	1/ 2/41
Harnell, G. (Lt. late D.W.R.)	1/ 2/41
Shoesmith, S. W.	1/ 2/41
Hartley, H.	1/ 2/41
Townsend, H.	1/ 2/41
Ward, C. W.	1/ 2/41
Ainsworth, H.	1/ 2/41

2nd Lieutenants

Forster, J. P.	14/ 5/41
Borer, A. L.	20/ 5/41
Broomhead, A.	23/ 5/41
Cowan, W., M.C. (Capt. late R.E.)	11/ 6/41
Edwards, B., M.M.	21/ 7/41

Adjutant & Quarter-Master

Medical Officer

Downie, Maj. D.	19/ 5/41

52nd WEST RIDING (WAKEFIELD) BATTALION

Lt.-Colonel

Wright, F. E. (Maj. late T.A.)	1/ 2/41

Majors

James, W. G.	1/ 2/41
Twyman, P. W. H. (Capt. late R.A.F.)	1/ 2/41
Phillips, G. M. C. (Maj. late R.F.A.)	1/ 2/41
Wilson, G. G. (Capt. late R. War. R.)	1/ 2/41

Captains

Lenthall, T. A.	1/ 2/41
Dickinson, H. C.	1/ 2/41
Shaw, G., M.C. (2/Lt. late M.G. Corps)	1/ 2/41
Knott, S. A. A.	24/ 6/41

Lieutenants

Elliott, T. H.	1/ 2/41
Oddie, M. M.	1/ 2/41
Thirtle, J. L.	1/ 2/41
Firth, J. P. (Maj. late K.O.Y.L.I.)	1/ 2/41
Roberts, E. F. H.	1/ 2/41
Walker, E. H.	1/ 2/41
Middleton, F. W.	1/ 2/41
Billington, G.	1/ 2/41
Burton, J. R.	1/ 2/41
Haigh, J. V.	1/ 2/41
Pearson, H.	1/ 2/41
Twycross, A. E.	1/ 2/41
Fitton, J.	1/ 2/41
Morris, W. M.	1/ 2/41
Metcalfe, R.	1/ 2/41
Cussons, L. W.	1/ 2/41
Harrap, G.	1/ 2/41
Pulsford, L. M.	1/ 2/41
Colman, J. (Lt. late Durham L.I.)	1/ 2/41
Gubbins, R. P.	1/ 2/41
Hadfield, C. F. (Lt. late K.O.Y.L.I.)	1/ 2/41

2nd Lieutenants

Pearson, S. E. (Lt. late M.G. Corps)	1/ 2/41
Summerscales, R.	1/ 2/41
Midgley, H. B.	1/ 2/41
Turner, R.	1/ 7/41

Adjutant & Quarter-Master

Kay, Capt. (actg. 3/7/41) M.C., M.C., Gen. List Inf.	3/ 7/41

Medical Officer

Neil, Maj. G. L., O.B.E. (Capt. late R.A.M.C.)	24/ 7/41

YORKSHIRE AREA - contd.

WEST RIDING ZONE - contd.

HUDDERSFIELD GROUP

Commander	Broadbent, Col. J. T. C. (Lt.-Col. late Ind. Army)	1/ 2/41
Second in Command	Brierly, Lt.-Col. S. C., D.S.O., T.D. (Bt. Col. ret. R.A.)	1/ 2/41
Assistant to Commander	Eastwood, Capt. D. C. (Lt. late R.A.S.C.)	1/ 2/41

25th WEST RIDING (HUDDERSFIELD) BATTALION

Lt.-Colonel

Moxon, P., T.D. (Bt. Col. ret. T.A.)	1/ 2/41

Majors

Moxon, C. S., D.S.O. (Capt. late D.W.R.)	1/ 2/41
Pearson, R. H., M.C. (Capt. late R.A.)	1/ 2/41
White, W. A. (Capt. late K.O.Y.L.I.)	1/ 2/41
Brown, R. L. (Lt. late King's Own R.)	1/ 2/41
Woodhead, J., M.C. (Lt. late W. York R.)	1/ 2/41
Currie, F. J. W. (Capt. late Cheshire R.)	1/ 2/41

Captains

Sykes, A. T. K., M.C. (Capt. late D.W.R.)	1/ 2/41
Sewell, G., A.F.C. (Flt. Comdr. late R.A.F.)	1/ 2/41
Scott, A.	1/ 2/41
Goodwin, G. W. (Lt. late R.F.A.)	1/ 2/41
Sellers, W. L. (Maj. late Lincoln R.)	1/ 2/41
Arnold, T. F.	1/ 2/41
Hallas, G.	1/ 2/41
Allen, W. H. (Lt. late R.A.F.)	1/ 2/41
Beaumont, D.	1/ 2/41
Hawkyard, W. H.	1/ 2/41
Lodge, F.	1/ 2/41

Lieutenants

Ainley, E. E. (Capt. late R.E.)	1/ 2/41
Broadbent, B. L. (Lt. late R.E. Signals)	1/ 2/41
Grant, A. E.	1/ 2/41
Kettlewell, C.	1/ 2/41
Selby, E.	1/ 2/41
Sykes, F.	1/ 2/41

Lieutenants - contd.

Sheldrick, G. (Lt. R. North'd. Fus. Supp'y. Res.)	1/ 2/41
Berry, R. N.	1/ 2/41
Milner, P. (2/Lt. late R.T.C.)	1/ 2/41
Parson, D.	1/ 2/41
Coles, L. A.	1/ 2/41
Shaw, J.	1/ 2/41
Cunningham, W.	1/ 2/41
Taylor, H. (2/Lt. late R.F.A.)	1/ 2/41
Glendinning, H.	1/ 2/41
Barker, P. R.	1/ 2/41
Hopkinson, I. G. (Lt. (O.M.E. 4th Class) R.A.O.C., T.A.)	1/ 2/41
Davis, K. R.	1/ 2/41
Gowing, W. P.	1/ 2/41
Dyson, G. W.	1/ 2/41
Leece, H. (Lt. late D.W.R.)	1/ 2/41

2nd Lieutenants

Kemp, H.	1/ 2/41
Rhymes, H. S.	1/ 2/41
Smith, J. C.	1/ 2/41
Wilkinson, H.	1/ 2/41
Charters, W.	1/ 2/41
Jessop, G. L.	1/ 2/41
North, A. M.	1/ 2/41
Illingworth, E.	1/ 2/41
Howarth, H.	1/ 2/41
Matthews, C.	1/ 2/41
Bygott, E.	1/ 2/41
Chapman, L. M.	1/ 2/41
Simpson, F.	1/ 2/41
Darlington, F.	1/ 2/41

Adjutant & Quarter-Master

Medical Officer

Ogden, Maj. R. J.	7/ 4/41

YORKSHIRE AREA - contd.

WEST RIDING ZONE - contd.

HUDDERSFIELD GROUP - contd.

26th WEST RIDING (HUDDERSFIELD) BATTALION

Lt.-Colonel

Rippon, R., T.D. (Bt. Col. ret. T.A.) 1/ 2/41

Majors

Dawson, W. N., T.D. (Maj. late T.A.) 1/ 2/41
Beaumont, G. (Maj. late D.W.R.) 1/ 2/41
Barrett, F. P. (Capt. late Yorkshire D.) 1/ 2/41
Walker, J., M.B.E. (Capt. late Gen. List) 1/ 2/41
Taylor, N., M.C. (Capt. late R.E.) 1/ 2/41

Captains

Turner, G. (Capt. late W. York R.) 1/ 2/41
Willson, C. V. (Lt. late R.A. (T.A.)) 1/ 2/41
Simpson, H. L. 1/ 2/41
Holdsworth, A. (Lt. late R.A.) (T.A.) 1/ 2/41

Lieutenants

Potter, A. C., M.C. (Lt. late D.W.R.) 1/ 2/41
Wordley, S. S. (Lt. late I. Gds.) 1/ 2/41
Lumb, J. (Lt. late R.N.V.R.) 1/ 2/41
Chrispin, J. G. H., D.F.C. (Lt. late R.F.C.) 1/ 2/41
Backhouse, R. (Lt. late K.O.Y.L.I.) 1/ 2/41
Cunliffe, H. R., M.C. (2/Lt. late Durham L.I.) 1/ 2/41
Shires, F. (Lt. late R.T.C.) 1/ 2/41
Spratt, W., M.C. (Lt. late D.W.R.) 1/ 2/41
Dyson, F. K., M.C. (Lt. late Loyal R.) 1/ 2/41
Hanson, D. (Capt. late D.W.R.) 1/ 2/41
Walker, G. S. (Lt. T.A. Res.) 1/ 2/41
Middleton, F. 1/ 2/41
Wilson, H. D. 1/ 2/41
Lodge, W. 1/ 2/41

Lieutenants - contd.

Lockwood, T. W. (Lt. late Durham L.I.) 1/ 2/41
Fuller, H. C. 1/ 2/41

2nd Lieutenants

Millward, H. A. 1/ 2/41
Ward, L. 1/ 2/41
Wilkinson, G. 1/ 2/41
VC Coverdale, C. H., M.M. (2/Lt. late Manch. R.) 1/ 2/41
Hirst, J. A. 1/ 2/41
France, L., M.M. (2/Lt. late R.T.C.) 1/ 2/41
Shaw, D. G. (Lt. late D.W.R.) 1/ 2/41
Bradbury, H. 1/ 2/41
Gallaway, A. C. (2/Lt. late Lan. Fus.) 1/ 2/41
Mettrick, B. (2/Lt. late D.W.R.) 1/ 2/41
Waterhouse, C. N. (Lt. late R.A.F.) 1/ 2/41
Shaw, A. 1/ 2/41
Turner, T. 1/ 2/41
Kay, V. 1/ 2/41
Jordan, F. 1/ 2/41
Cardno, J. D. 1/ 2/41
Freebairn, J. B. 1/ 2/41
Barnes, C. C. 1/ 2/41
Kaye, W. 1/ 2/41
Smith, C. 1/ 2/41
Heather, H., M.M. 1/ 2/41
Davy, W. K. 1/ 2/41
Graham, G. A. 1/ 2/41
Cooper, G. E. 1/ 2/41
Oddy, J. V. 1/ 2/41
Beaumont, J. R. 1/ 2/41
Broadhead, F. 1/ 2/41
Utley, R. 1/ 2/41
Best, A. W. 1/ 2/41
Lunn, N. S. 1/ 2/41

Adjutant & Quarter-Master

Medical Officer

Tomlin, Maj. H., M.D. (Capt. late R.A.M.C.) 1/ 5/41

YORKSHIRE AREA - contd.

WEST RIDING ZONE - contd.

UPPER AGBRIGG GROUP

Commander	Sykes, Col. K., O.B.E., T.D. (Col. T.A.)	1/ 2/41
Second-in-Command	Haigh, Lt.-Col. W. (Flight Lt. late R.F.C.)	1/ 2/41
Assistant to Commander	Kaye, Capt. Sir Henry G., Bt. (Flight Comdr. late R.F.C.)	1/ 2/41

34th WEST RIDING (UPPER AGBRIGG) BATTALION

Lt.-Colonel

Barber, H. (Capt. late T.A.) 1/ 2/41

Majors

Tinker, B., T.D. (Maj. late T.A.) 1/ 2/41
Lawton, N. T. (Capt. late D.W.R.) 1/ 2/41
Reynolds, J. (2/Lt. late D.W.R.) 1/ 2/41

Captains

Gardner, R. L., M.B.E. (Capt. late Manch. R.) 1/ 2/41
Senior, N. (Capt. late D.W.R.) 1/ 2/41

Lieutenants

Floyd, C. S. (Lt. late D.W.R.) 1/ 2/41
Pott, M. (Lt. late A. & S.H.) 1/ 2/41
Black, T. 1/ 2/41
Mallinson, B. (Lt. late The King's R.) 1/ 2/41
Hallitt, W. (Lt. late R.F.C.) 1/ 2/41
Wood, F. S. 1/ 2/41
Woolger, C. (Lt. late S. Stafford R.) 1/ 2/41

Lieutenants - contd.

Butterworth, F. (2/Lt. late R.W. Fus.) 1/ 2/41
Openshaw, S. E. 1/ 2/41
Haigh, H. 1/ 2/41
Wilkinson, C. 1/ 2/41
Ingledew, B. S. 1/ 2/41

2nd Lieutenants

Armitage, J. B. (2/Lt. late North'd Fus.) 1/ 2/41
Roberts, L. H. 1/ 2/41
Lee, T. S. 1/ 2/41
Beardsell, H. G. (Lt. late D.W.R.) 1/ 2/41
Bennett, T. 1/ 2/41

Adjutant & Quarter-Master

Medical Officer

YORKSHIRE AREA - contd.

WEST RIDING ZONE - contd.

UPPER AGBRIGG GROUP

35th WEST RIDING (UPPER AGBRIGG) BATTALION

Lt.-Colonel

Lockwood, C. W., M.C. (Capt. late T.A.)	1/ 2/41

Majors

Aspinwall, G. R. (Capt. late D.W.R.)	1/ 2/41
Crabtree, N., M.C. (Capt. late D.W.R.)	1/ 2/41
Pogson, W. C. (Capt. late D.W.R.)	1/ 2/41
Brown, D. Mck. (Lt. late D.W.R.)	1/ 2/41

Captain

Whitwam, R. (Capt. late Ind. Army)	1/ 2/41

Lieutenants

McLintock, W. J., M.C. (Lt. late W. York R.)	1/ 2/41
Shaw, T. P.	1/ 2/41
Crowther, F., M.M.	1/ 2/41
Newsome, A. E., M.M.	1/ 2/41
Shrigley, N.	1/ 2/41
Bain, T.	1/ 2/41

2nd Lieutenants

Thornber, T. A.	1/ 2/41
Sykes, S. F.	1/ 2/41
Barker, L.	1/ 2/41
Ashby, F. W. (Lt. late R.T.C.)	1/ 2/41
Wood, H. E.	1/ 2/41
Shaw, F.	1/ 2/41
Bennett, W. E. (Pilot Offr. late R.A.F.)	1/ 2/41
Bateson, C. G. (Lt. late R.A.F.)	1/ 2/41

Adjutant & Quarter-Master

Medical Officer

36th WEST RIDING (UPPER AGBRIGG) BATTALION

Lt.-Colonel

Rhodes, H., D.F.C. (Lt. late R.A.F.)	1/ 2/41

Major

Byron, B. L.	1/ 2/41

Captains

Mallalieu, C. (Capt. late D.W.R.)	1/ 2/41
Marsland, H. W.	1/ 2/41
Mallalieu, F. B. du L.	1/ 2/41
Hopkinson, C. B.	1/ 2/41

Lieutenants

Greenehalgh, A. P. W.	1/ 2/41
Lawton, R.	1/ 2/41
Street, S.	1/ 2/41
Lee, A. E. (Maj. late T.A. Res.)	1/ 2/41
Peet, D. J.	1/ 2/41
Chadwick, H.	1/ 2/41
Buckley, R.	1/ 2/41
Levens, L.	1/ 2/41
Love, G. R.	1/ 2/41

2nd Lieutenant

Hill, W. R.	18/ 6/41

Adjutant & Quarter-Master

Medical Officer

YORKSHIRE AREA - contd.

POST OFFICE ZONE

Commander	Hill, Col. H. (Capt. late R. Signals)	1/ 2/41
Second in Command	Watts, Lt.-Col. S. G. (Lt. late R.E.)	1/ 2/41
Assistants to Commander	Mathie, Maj. P. D. (Capt. late E. Surrey R.)	1/ 2/41
	Faulks, Capt. L.	1/ 2/41
Territorial Army Association administering	The Yorkshire (West Riding) T.A. Association, 9, St. Leonards, York.	

15th WEST RIDING (POST OFFICE) BATTALION

Lt.-Colonel

Sifton, S. E. (Lt.-Col. late R.E.)	1/ 2/41

Majors

Magnall, J.	1/ 2/41
Roddis, E., M.B.E. (Lt. late R.E.)	1/ 2/41
Spillman, W. C.	1/ 2/41
Cownley, J. J., M.C. (Lt. late Green Howards)	1/ 2/41
White, A. H.	1/ 2/41
Beaumont, G. A.	28/ 6/41

Captains

Eagers, H.	1/ 2/41
Bentley, R. H.	1/ 2/41
Thomas, J. H.	1/ 2/41
Bedford, G.	28/ 6/41

Lieutenants

Hearn, L.	1/ 2/41
Downing, E.	1/ 2/41
Lamminan, C.	1/ 2/41
Powell, C. C.	1/ 2/41
Fairhurst, H., M.M.	1/ 2/41
Smethurst, T.	1/ 2/41
Roast, G.	1/ 2/41
Richardson, F. V.	1/ 2/41
Frizelle, G.	1/ 2/41
Hirst, G.	1/ 2/41
Shields, S.	1/ 2/41

Lieutenants - contd.

Cross, N. H.	1/ 2/41
Sparling, G. (Lt. late W. York R.)	1/ 2/41
Harris, A. G.	1/ 2/41
Rome, A. E., D.C.M.	20/ 5/41
Fryer, A. E.	15/ 7/41
Holmes, M. F.	15/ 7/41
Scholey, E. A.	15/ 7/41

2nd Lieutenants

Braiden, A. E.	1/ 2/41
Burnett, F. G. L.	1/ 2/41
Wetherbed, H.	1/ 2/41
Keys, J. G.	1/ 2/41
Blezard, E. R., D.C.M.	1/ 2/41
Spires, C. H., M.M.	1/ 2/41
Cowen, W., M.M.	20/ 5/41
Lister, J. D.	20/ 5/41
Boothman, F. R.	27/ 5/41
Goulding, J. H.	27/ 5/41

Adjutant & Quarter-Master

Medical Officer

YORKSHIRE AREA - contd.

POST OFFICE ZONE

16th WEST RIDING (POST OFFICE) BATTALION

Lt.-Colonel	
Shanahan, J. E. (Lt. late T.A.)	1/ 2/41
Majors	
McConnell, T. W. (Capt. late R.E.)	1/ 2/41
Hearn, G.	1/ 2/41
Peace, F.	1/ 2/41
Halsall, T. G. (Capt. late Res. of Off.)	1/ 2/41
Graham, R. B. (Lt. late R.E.)	1/ 2/41
Hopkin, F. M.	1/ 2/41
Captains	
Green, W. H.	1/ 2/41
Tootell, T. E.	1/ 2/41
Clark, F.	1/ 2/41
Wilshire, H.	1/ 2/41
Bulmer, P. C. L. H., M.M.	1/ 2/41
Ward, B.	1/ 2/41
Lieutenants	
Alderton, A. G.	1/ 2/41
Ellwood, J.	1/ 2/41
Leach, W.	1/ 2/41
Hey, P.	1/ 2/41
Furse, W. F. J.	1/ 2/41
Simcox, H.	1/ 2/41
Quinn, J.	1/ 2/41
Bryant, J. W.	1/ 2/41
Lancaster, A. E.	1/ 2/41
Broadbent, W. H., D.C.M.	1/ 2/41
Parry, T.	1/ 2/41
Woodhouse, E. E.	1/ 2/41
Allen, D.	1/ 2/41
Evans, J. J.	1/ 2/41
2nd Lieutenants	
Chadwick, G. G.	1/ 2/41
Kershaw, S.	1/ 2/41
Gower, E.	1/ 2/41
Ramsden, S.	1/ 2/41
Ilett, W. (Lt. late D.W.R.)	1/ 2/41
Spedding, W.	1/ 2/41
Nutter, E.	1/ 2/41
Booth, N.	1/ 2/41
James, J. K.	1/ 2/41
Law, T.	1/ 2/41
Parker, F. W.	1/ 2/41
Taylor, W. C.	1/ 2/41

Adjutant & Quarter-Master

Medical Officer

17th WEST RIDING (POST OFFICE) BATTALION

Lt.-Colonel	
Bayly, A. J.	1/ 2/41
Majors	
Gardiner, T. A.	1/ 2/41
Parsons, R. A. E.	1/ 2/41
Thompson, W. H., M.M.	1/ 2/41
Kenny, G. S.	1/ 2/41
Cook, G. H.	1/ 2/41
Captains	
Clark, F. P.	1/ 2/41
Hill, G.	1/ 2/41
Cumberland, W. B. (Lt. late R.E.)	1/ 2/41
Holdsworth, C., M.B.E.	1/ 2/41
Phillips, R. S.	1/ 2/41
Wright, G. L.	1/ 2/41
Lieutenants	
Brennan, J.	1/ 2/41
Connon, J.	1/ 2/41
Copley, T. E.	1/ 2/41
Major, A. S.	1/ 2/41
Nicholson, H. A.	1/ 2/41
Stewart, A. D.	1/ 2/41
Whiting, H. C.	1/ 2/41
Templeman, G. H., D.C.M.	1/ 2/41
Wherrit, T. A.	1/ 2/41
Guy, J. W., M.M.	1/ 2/41
McGowan, C. R. (Maj. late H.A.C.)	1/ 2/41
Merrin, J.	1/ 2/41
Taylor, H. A.	1/ 2/41
Atkinson, B. M.	1/ 2/41
Doran, J. J.	1/ 2/41
Martin, B. G.	1/ 2/41
Hawksley, J.	1/ 2/41

Adjutant & Quarter-Master

Medical Officer

YORKSHIRE AREA - contd.

HARROGATE ZONE

Commander	Greenwood, Col. V. J., M.C. (Col. ret. pay) (Res. of Off.)	1/ 5/41
Assistant to Commander	Bargh, Maj. M. T. (Maj. late R.F.A.)	17/ 4/41
Territorial Army Association administering	The Yorkshire (West Riding) T.A. Association, 9, St. Leonards, York.	

CLARO GROUP

Commander	Glynton, Col. G. M., D.S.O. (Col. ret. Ind. Army)	1/ 5/41

5th WEST RIDING (HARROGATE) BATTALION

Lt.-Colonel

Williamson, G. H., M.C. (Lt. late T.A.)	1/ 2/41

Majors

Quickfall, P. H. (Lt. late Durham L.I.)	1/ 2/41
Peck, L. (Capt. late K.O.Y.L.I.)	1/ 2/41
Briggs, A. S. (Lt. late R.F.A.)	1/ 2/41
Gardner, S. T. P., M.C. (Lt. late Gren G'ds.)	1/ 2/41
Tolley, G., D.C.M. (2/Lt. late R.T.C.)	1/ 2/41

Captains

Horner, B. (Lt. late North'd. Fus.)	1/ 2/41
Dawson, A. C.	1/ 2/41
Reeve, H. D. (Capt. late Y. & L.R.)	1/ 2/41
Hamilton, H. D. S. (Lt. Comdr. late R.N.)	1/ 2/41
Baines, E., D.C.M. (2/Lt. K.O.Y.L.I.)	1/ 2/41
Walker, C.	1/ 2/41
Aykroyd, C. W.	12/ 6/41

Lieutenants

Ogden, J. R. (2/Lt. late K.O.Y.L.I.)	1/ 2/41
Roberts, H. (Lt. late R.F.C.)	1/ 2/41
Porter, W. H. (Capt. late York R.)	1/ 2/41
Faber, E. W. (Lt. late Durham L.I.)	1/ 2/41
Cartmell, S. (Capt. late R.T.C.)	1/ 2/41
Leamon, R. W. (Capt. late Y. & L.R.)	1/ 2/41
Forbes, A. (Lt. late E. York R.)	1/ 2/41
Roberts, A. (Lt. late Oxf. & Bucks. L.I.)	1/ 2/41
McLintock, W. (Lt. late Cameronians)	1/ 2/41
Wilcox, H. (Sub-Lt. late R.N.)	1/ 2/41
Carlisle, G. C. (Lt. late W. York R.)	1/ 2/41

Lieutenants - contd.

Ward, R. W. (Lt. late W. York R.)	1/ 2/41
Worth, H. I. S. J. (2/Lt. late Essex R.)	1/ 2/41
Brown, B. C.	1/ 2/41
Bulmer, F. T.	1/ 2/41
Cleasby, N. D.	1/ 2/41
Clarke, W. J.	1/ 2/41
Carr, R. W.	1/ 2/41
Jones, C. S.	1/ 2/41
Hamlyn, W. T. (Capt. late Ind. Army)	1/ 2/41
Kendrew, J.	1/ 2/41
Rabbin, H. J.	1/ 2/41
Robinson, E.	1/ 2/41
Scott, H.	1/ 2/41
Cawdry, E. A. G.	1/ 2/41
Scott, E.	1/ 2/41
Clapham, H.	1/ 2/41
Gaunt, R. W.	1/ 2/41
Fawcett, P. T.	1/ 2/41
Morley, G. W. (2/Lt. late R.A.)	23/ 6/41
Cordingley, H.	21/ 7/41

Adjutant & Quarter-Master

Medical Officer

Foskett, Maj. S.	1/ 2/41

YORKSHIRE AREA - contd.

HARROGATE ZONE - contd.

CLARO GROUP - contd.

6th WEST RIDING (HARROGATE) BATTALION

Lt.-Colonel

Majors

Aykroyd, H. H., O.B.E., M.C., T.D. (Col. T.A.)	1/ 2/41
Collins, E. R., D.S.O. (Maj. late E. Lan. R.)	1/ 2/41
Holliday, L. B., O.B.E., T.D. (Maj. late D.W.R.)	1/ 2/41

Captains

Grainger, J. P.	1/ 2/41
Lodge, J. E. H., M.C. (Capt. late Inniskilling Fus.)	1/ 2/41
Stevenson, W. H. H. (Light-Comdr. R.N. ret.)	1/ 2/41
Lupton, H. (Lt. late W. York R.)	1/ 2/41

Lieutenants

Jackson, W. (Capt. late York Dns.)	1/ 2/41
Mostyn, J. E. H. (Capt. late R. Sussex R.)	1/ 2/41
Aked, H. L. C. (Lt. late W. York R.)	1/ 2/41
Appleyard, W. (Lt. late R.A.S.C.)	1/ 2/41
Johnson, E. R. (Lt. late The Buffs)	1/ 2/41
Pulleyn, J. (2/Lt. I. G'ds.)	1/ 2/41
Hey, D., M.C. (Col. late R. Signals)	1/ 2/41
Rhodes, F. E.	1/ 2/41
Mangin, E. B., M.C. (Maj. ret. Ind. Army)	1/ 2/41
Breare, L. D. (Lt. late D.W.R.)	1/ 2/41
Appleby, J. (Maj. late York R.)	1/ 2/41

Lieutenants - contd.

Pulford, N. E.	1/ 2/41
Fisher, E.	1/ 2/41
Hesselwood, H.	1/ 2/41
Bolton, A. G.	1/ 2/41
Kell, J. K.	1/ 2/41
Buchanan, R. W. (Lt. late W. York R.)	1/ 2/41
Lewin, H. A.	10/ 5/41
Lister, C. F.	24/ 7/41

2nd Lieutenants

Metcalfe, J. H. (Lt. late R.F.A.)	1/ 2/41
Burrows, H. B. (Sub.-Lt. late R.N.R.)	1/ 2/41
McMinn, J. A.	1/ 2/41
Frape, H. W.	1/ 2/41
Peckitt, W.	1/ 2/41
Richmond, E.	1/ 2/41
Burrill, H.	1/ 2/41
Wood, J. E. C.	17/ 7/41
Machin, W. B. R. D.	17/ 7/41
Stubbs, W. (2nd Lt. late Green Howards)	24/ 7/41

Adjutant & Quarter-Master

Medical Officer

Anning, Maj. R. M. H. (Lt. late R.A.)	1/ 2/41

YORKSHIRE AREA - contd.

HARROGATE ZONE - contd.

TADCASTER GROUP

Commander	Riley-Smith, Col. W. (Capt. ret. 13th H.)	1/ 2/41
Second in Command	Forbes-Sempill, Lt.-Col. Hon. A. L. O. (Rear Admiral ret.)	1/ 2/41

11th WEST RIDING (TADCASTER) BATTALION

Lt.-Colonel

Charlesworth, W. G., T.D. (Lt.-Col. ret. T.A.)	1/ 2/41

Majors

Foulds, C. E. (Maj. late W. York R.)	1/ 2/41
Colley, F., D.S.O. (Maj. late Y. & L.R.)	1/ 2/41
Aykroyd, A. H. (Maj. late R.F.A.)	1/ 2/41
Wheelwright, E. L., O.B.E. (Capt. late K.O.Y.L.I.)	1/ 2/41

Captains

Whaley, L. A. (Capt. late W. York R.)	1/ 2/41
Highmor, S. G., M.C. (Lt. late Durham L.I.)	1/ 2/41
Mason, H.	1/ 2/41

Lieutenants

Harewood, Earl of, K.G., G.C.V.O., D.S.O., T.D., (Maj. late Gren. G'ds.)	1/ 2/41
Lipscomb, W. T., T.D. (Maj. late York D'ns.)	1/ 2/41
Hudson, J. H., M.C. (Lt. late R.F.A.)	1/ 2/41
Sheldon, O. (Capt. late R.E.)	1/ 2/41
Goode, C. W. (Lt. late R.F.A.)	1/ 2/41
Moore, H. L., M.M.	1/ 2/41
Perkins, W. H. (Lt. late R.A.)	1/ 2/41
Saunders, W. E.	1/ 2/41
Ingham, J. L., T.D. (Maj. late Yorkshire D.)	1/ 2/41
Marshall, J. C.	1/ 2/41
Shiach, A. U.	1/ 2/41

Lieutenants - contd.

Dawson, B.	1/ 2/41
Quarton, H. W.	1/ 2/41
Hall, J. S.	1/ 2/41
Robson, W.	1/ 2/41
Stacey, H.	1/ 2/41
Wilkinson, F. P.	1/ 2/41

2nd Lieutenants

Gibbon, O. L. (Lt. late R.E.)	1/ 2/41
Hamilton, W.	1/ 2/41
Richardson, T.	1/ 2/41
Raspin, K. W.	1/ 2/41
Pyrah, N.	1/ 2/41
Watson, L. J. (Maj. late R.A.O.C.)	1/ 2/41
Atkinson, H.	1/ 2/41
Rich, C. S. S.	1/ 2/41
Parkinson, K. W.	1/ 2/41
Walters, L. R. (Lt. late R.F.A.)	1/ 2/41
Clark, G. E.	1/ 2/41
Leach, J. W.	3/ 6/41
Walker, T. R.	30/ 6/41

Adjutant & Quarter-Master

Medical Officer

YORKSHIRE AREA - contd.

HARROGATE ZONE - contd.

TADCASTER GROUP - contd.

12th WEST RIDING (TADCASTER) BATTALION

Lt-.Colonel

Passey, R. D., M.C. (Capt. late R.A.M.C.) 1/ 2/41

Majors

Massey, B., M.C. (2nd Lt. late R.G.A.) 1/ 2/41
Salisbury, W. L. (Lt. late R.F.A.) 1/ 2/41
Smith, S. S., M.C. (Maj. late E. York R.) 1/ 2/41
Thompson, A. (Capt. late W. York R.) 1/ 2/41
Jackson, J. E. (Lt. late R.F.A.) 1/ 2/41

Captains

Platts, H. 1/ 2/41
Curteis, H. C. (Capt. late R.A.S.C.) 1/ 2/41
Evans, R. G. 1/ 2/41
Emsley, C. H., T.D. (Bt. Col. late R.A.) 1/ 2/41

Lieutenants

Thompson, C. K. 1/ 2/41
Veitch, R. W. 1/ 2/41
Lister, E. B., M.C. (Capt. late R.F.A.) 1/ 2/41
Barker, J. S., M.C. (Capt. late Lan. Fus.) 1/ 2/41
Richardson, D. R. (2/Lt. late D.G.) 1/ 2/41
Furniss, H. B. 1/ 2/41

Lieutenants - contd.

Bretherick, G. T. E. 1/ 2/41
Jolley, R. A. 1/ 2/41
Terry, B. 1/ 2/41
Short, E. W. 1/ 2/41
Gordon, J. A. 1/ 2/41
Gould, C. (2/Lt. late W. York R.) 1/ 2/41
Longden, H. A. 1/ 2/41
Wilkinson, W. E. 1/ 2/41
Dunn, W. S. 1/ 2/41
Clarkson, G. E. 1/ 2/41
Bygate, R. H. 1/ 2/41
Cowie, J. McM. 6/ 6/41

2nd Lieutenants

Hervey, F. J. B. 1/ 2/41
Callaghan, J. 1/ 2/41
Toleman, J. S. 1/ 2/41
Johns, D. 1/ 2/41
Lax, L. 1/ 2/41
Boyce, E. G. 1/ 2/41
Squire, M. 1/ 2/41
Bramley, T. A. 1/ 2/41
Wilson, N. 1/ 2/41
Kershaw, J. L. 1/ 2/41
Hannant, J. E. 1/ 2/41

Adjutant & Quarter-Master

Medical Officer

YORKSHIRE AREA - contd.

HARROGATE ZONE - contd.

TADCASTER GROUP - contd.

13th WEST RIDING (TADCASTER) BATTALION

Lt.-Colonel

Wheler, G. B. H., M.C. (Maj. ret. pay)	1/ 2/41

Majors

Capel-Cure, R. C. (2/Lt. late R.A.F.)	1/ 2/41
Peacock, F. W., D.C.M.	1/ 2/41
Charlesworth, J. E.	1/ 2/41
Sherborne, H. F., M.C. (2/Lt. late R.E.)	15/ 5/41

Captains

Garlick, W.	1/ 2/41
Marsh, G. H.	1/ 2/41
Taylor, J. H.	1/ 2/41

Lieutenants

Butterick, F.	1/ 2/41
Palfreyman, J.	1/ 2/41
Tabb, R.	1/ 2/41
Wilson, P. L.	1/ 2/41
Connell, D.	1/ 2/41
Orwin, W.	1/ 2/41
Read, R. E.	1/ 2/41
Seville, R. H.	1/ 2/41
Rae, G. P.	1/ 2/41
Jackson, F.	1/ 2/41
Hills, E.	1/ 2/41

Lieutenants - contd.

Elstob, J. W. L.	15/ 5/41
Fothergill, H., M.M.	15/ 5/41
Haines, L. G., (Capt. late Lan. Fus.)	15/ 5/41
Mackintosh, D.	15/ 5/41
Maher, J. H.	15/ 5/41
Bullough, W.	30/ 5/41
Ormsby, W. B.	5/ 6/41
Adams, S.	9/ 6/41
Stables, H. A. D.	18/ 6/41

2nd Lieutenants

Phillips, W. H.	17/ 7/41

Adjutant & Quarter-Master

Medical Officer

Goldsborough, Maj. C. E.	1/ 2/41

YORKSHIRE AREA - contd.

HARROGATE ZONE - contd.

INDEPENDENT BATTALION

14th WEST RIDING (YORK) BATTALION

Lt.-Colonel

Kelly, P. J. V., C.M.G., D.S.O., (Hon. Brig.-Gen. ret. pay) (Res. of off.)	1/2/41

Majors

Crombie, D. L. (Lt. late Ind. Army)	1/2/41
Warner, R. E. (Capt. late Leinster R.)	1/2/41
Trollope, R. B. (Capt. late R.F.A.)	1/2/41
Weeks, M. (Capt. late R.E.)	1/2/41
Moorhouse, B. (Capt. late R.E.)	1/2/41
Jaques, R. A.	1/2/41
Stembridge, E., D.C.M.	1/2/41
Ferguson, S. V.	1/2/41
Richards, D. S.	1/2/41

Captains

Shearston, J. A. (Capt. late Lan. Fus.)	1/2/41
Garbutt, W. D. (Lt. late M.G. Corps.)	1/2/41
Scarr, S., M.C. (2/Lt. late K.O.Y.L.I.)	1/2/41
Jackson, S. B., (Lt. late W. York R.)	1/2/41
Watson, E.	1/2/41
Watson, L. S.	1/2/41
Pitfield, F. E.	1/2/41
Binns, H.	1/2/41
Burton, H. G. (2nd Lt. late 20th H.)	1/2/41

Lieutenants

Pawley, F. L., T.D., (Lt.-Col. late T.A. Res.)	1/2/41
Ditcham, V. R., (Maj. late A. E. Corps.)	1/2/41
Bell, F. (Lt. late M.G. Corps.)	1/2/41
Wheway, C. G., (Lt. late R.F.A.)	1/2/41
Danton de Rouffignac, C. (2/Lt. late King's R.)	1/2/41
Blackett, F. A., (Lt. late Durham L.I.)	1/2/41
Rook, A. S. (Lt. late R.F.A.)	1/2/41
Harman, R. M.	1/2/41
Davies, T. E. (Lt. late K.O.Y.L.I.)	1/2/41
Jackson, P. N. (Lt. late T.A.)	1/2/41
Jackson, G. F.	1/2/41
Oldham, M. A.	1/2/41
Darley, W. H.	1/2/41
Bennett, D. S.	1/2/41
Smith, A. N.	1/2/41
Coates, C. E.	1/2/41
Ledward, J. H.	1/2/41
Wilson, H.	1/2/41
Cooper, S.	1/2/41
Clitheroe, H.	1/2/41
Dunn, J. W.	1/2/41
Wrigglesworth, T.	1/2/41
Snowden, H.	1/2/41
Newby, J. C.	1/2/41
Chipper, S. A.	1/2/41
Newcombe, J.	1/2/41
Lund, T., M.M.	1/2/41
Dodd, E. R.	1/2/41
Cuthbert, C. L.	1/2/41
Hunt, E. H.	1/2/41
Barnes, F. W.	1/2/41
Dean, R. A.	1/2/41
Sims, C. E. F.	1/2/41
Stephens, A. G. (2/Lt. late K.R.R.C.)	6/5/41
Cotterill, R. T. (Lt. late Stafford R.)	1/2/41
Bull, J. N.	6/5/41

YORKSHIRE AREA - contd.

HARROGATE ZONE - contd.

INDEPENDENT BATTALION - contd.

14th West Riding (York) Battalion - contd.

2nd Lieutenants

Anderson, L. C. (Capt. late E. York R.)	1/ 2/41
Barton, F. L. (Lt. late R.H.A.)	1/ 2/41
Johnson, G. Y. (Lt. late R.E.)	1/ 2/41
Showler, L. (2/Lt. late R.A.F.)	1/ 2/41
Taylor, E. W. (Lt. late R.N.V.R.)	1/ 2/41
Harrison, G. W.	1/ 2/41
Helstrip, G.	1/ 2/41
Knight, C.	1/ 2/41
Richardson, N.	1/ 2/41
Steele, F. F.	1/ 2/41
Simpson, C.	1/ 2/41
Weatherley, L.	1/ 2/41
Patrick, S. E.	1/ 2/41
Garland, W., M.M.	1/ 2/41
Pattison, T. A.	1/ 2/41
Lund, R.	1/ 2/41
Douglas, F. R.	1/ 2/41
Wood, H. S.	1/ 2/41
Ormiston, H.	1/ 2/41
Hardcastle, H.	1/ 2/41
Peterkin, W. T.	1/ 2/41
Monkman, E.	1/ 2/41
Hinchcliffe, R.	1/ 2/41
Pygott, D.	1/ 2/41
Pratt, J.	1/ 2/41
Burley, W.	1/ 2/41
Potter, T.	22/ 4/41
Battle, D.	20/ 5/41
Rudkin, A. P.	5/ 6/41

Adjutant & Quarter-Master

Medical Officer

Dangerfield, Maj. A. (Lt. late R.A.M.C.)	13/ 5/41

YORKSHIRE AREA - contd.

DONCASTER ZONE

Commander	Warde-Aldam, Col. W. St. A., D.S.O. (Col. ret. pay) (Res. of Off.)	1/ 5/41
Second in Command	Warde-Aldam, Lt.-Col. J. R. P., T.D.	1/ 5/41
Territorial Army Association administering	The Yorkshire (West Riding) T.A. Association, 9, St. Leonards, York.	

PONTEFRACT GROUP

Commander	Hustler, Col. C. B. (Capt. late R.E.)	1/ 2/41
Assistant to Commander	Amies, Capt. F. A.	1/ 2/41

48th WEST RIDING (PONTEFRACT) BATTALION

Lt.-Colonel

Schofield, J. J. (Maj. late Dorset R.)	1/ 2/41

Majors

Elliott, J. W. (Lt. late T.A.)	1/ 2/41
Arnold, E. (Lt. late A.E.C.)	1/ 2/41
Taylor, C. D.	1/ 2/41
Prior, S. E.	1/ 2/41
Braim, A.	1/ 2/41

Captains

Robinson, D.	1/ 2/41
Pollitt, J. K. (Lt. late R.A.F.)	1/ 2/41
Hattan, H. (2/Lt. late K.O.Y.L.I.)	1/ 2/41
Newton, W. H. (Lt. late R.E.)	1/ 2/41
Pease, C. (Lt. late Loyal R.)	1/ 2/41
Powell, E., M.M. (2/Lt. late R. Ir. L.)	5/ 6/41
Smith, A. D., M.C. (Capt. late R.A.)	17/ 6/41
Andrew, L. H.	17/ 6/41

Lieutenants

Kershaw, J. L., M.C. (Lt. late R.F.A.)	1/ 2/41
Smith, W.	1/ 2/41
Brown, A.	1/ 2/41
Knowles, J. N.	1/ 2/41
Lodge, T. G.	1/ 2/41
Shepherd, G. W. (Lt. late R.A.)	1/ 2/41
Townend, H. B. (Lt. late W. York R.)	1/ 2/41
Coates, C. L.	1/ 2/41
Farrally, A. E.	1/ 2/41
Clarke, E. W.	1/ 2/41
Keyzer, C. E.	1/ 2/41
Hardcastle, J. S.	1/ 2/41
Mann, J.	1/ 2/41
Atkins, F., M.M. (Lt. late D.W.R.)	1/ 2/41

Lieutenants - contd.

Melvin, R.	1/ 2/41
Simpson, T. H.	1/ 2/41
Major, S. E.	1/ 2/41
Dean, E.	1/ 2/41
Kirkbride, A.	1/ 2/41
Billbrough, A. S.	1/ 2/41
Coward, J. W.	1/ 2/41
Donovan, H. L.	1/ 2/41
Ellis, W.	1/ 2/41
Hobbs, H. H.	1/ 2/41
Howdle, A. T.	1/ 2/41
Ward, H.	1/ 2/41
Wood, H.	1/ 2/41
Davies, H.	5/ 6/41
Hartley, J. W.	5/ 6/41
Nuttridge, J.	5/ 6/41
Forster, E.	5/ 6/41
Swaine, M. G	5/ 6/41

2nd Lieutenants

Watson, W. R.	1/ 2/41
Lancaster, H. J. (Lt. late Loyal R.)	1/ 2/41
Holt, A. E.	1/ 2/41
Balmer, J.	1/ 2/41
Bashforth, R.	1/ 2/41
Walker, J. H.	1/ 6/41

Adjutant & Quarter-Master

Medical Officer

Johnston, Maj. G. G. S. (Capt. late R.A.M.C.)	1/ 2/41

YORKSHIRE AREA - contd.

DONCASTER ZONE - contd.

PONTEFRACT GROUP - contd.

49th WEST RIDING (PONTEFRACT) BATTALION

Lt.-Colonel

Penlington, H. N. (Capt. late R.A.F.)	1/ 2/41

Majors

Seeley, H. W.	1/ 2/41
Clayton-Smith, G. V. H. (2/Lt. late K.O.Y.L.I.)	1/ 2/41
Dixon, G.	1/ 2/41
Fleming, W. H.	1/ 2/41
Aspinall, H.	1/ 2/41
Swales, H.	19/ 6/41

Captains

Rainforth, W. A. (Lt. late R.F.A.)	1/ 2/41
Batten, H.	1/ 2/41
Haigh, J. A.	1/ 2/41
Daley, W. H.	1/ 2/41
Turner, H.	13/ 6/41

Lieutenants

Veitch, A.	1/ 2/41
Cooke, P. B. (Lt. late R.A.F.)	1/ 2/41
Smith, W. C.	1/ 2/41
Archer, J. R.	1/ 2/41
Bradbury, J.	1/ 2/41
Holmes, S.	1/ 2/41
Hirst, A., M.M.	1/ 2/41
Berry, A., M.M.	1/ 2/41
Beaumont, N.	1/ 2/41

Lieutenants - contd.

Tate, W.	1/ 2/41
Smith, G. W.	1/ 2/41
Marsh, J.	1/ 2/41
Covell, W. E.	1/ 2/41
Bunting, J.	1/ 2/41
Davis, S.	1/ 2/41
Goodall, W.	1/ 2/41
Wilson, J.	1/ 2/41
Oxley, J.	1/ 2/41
Finn, C. P.	1/ 2/41
Bennett, E. R.	1/ 2/41
Guest, G.	1/ 2/41
Ford, C.	1/ 2/41
Sharpe, C.	1/ 2/41
Kenney, J. McN.	1/ 2/41
Cartwright, A. E.	1/ 2/41
Williams, R. F.	9/ 6/41
Cairns, J. W. (Maj. late R.A.M.C.)	13/ 6/41

2nd Lieutenants

Fishwick, H.	1/ 2/41
Scott, A. B.	1/ 2/41
Henger, F.	1/ 2/41
Dallas, W. G.	1/ 2/41

Medical Officer

Sullivan, Maj. F. W., M.D. (Capt. late R.A.M.C.)	19/ 6/41

YORKSHIRE AREA - contd.

DONCASTER ZONE - contd.

GOOLE GROUP

47th WEST RIDING (GOOLE) BATTALION

Lt.-Colonel

Richardson, H. W. (Capt. late T.A.)	1/ 2/41

Majors

Welham, H. (Lt. late R.F.A.)	1/ 2/41
Timm, C.	1/ 2/41
Hudson, R. P. (Lt. late E. York R.)	1/ 2/41
Coulman, R. H.	1/ 2/41
Adam, J. McI. P. (Flying Offr. late R.F.C.)	1/ 2/41
King, S. J.	1/ 2/41

Captains

Coggrave, C. H. (2/Lt. late K.O.Y.L.I.)	1/ 2/41
Thompson, E. L.	1/ 2/41
Dowdall, H., M.C. (Lt. late R.E.)	1/ 2/41
Poskitt, H.	1/ 2/41
Ganley, C.	1/ 2/41

Lieutenants

Northey, H. G. (Lt. late K.O.Y.L.I.)	1/ 2/41
Hart, J. A. E. (Capt. late R.T.C.)	1/ 2/41
Calder, W. (Capt. late Camerons)	1/ 2/41
Coxon, L. A. (2/Lt. late R.A.)	1/ 2/41
Hudson, V. B.	1/ 2/41
Taylor, G. A.	1/ 2/41
Tabiner, T.	1/ 2/41
Walker, J.	1/ 2/41
Freeman, D.	1/ 2/41
Schofield, A. S.	1/ 2/41
Spencer, S.	1/ 2/41
Sampson, E.	1/ 2/41
Fawbert, R.	1/ 2/41
Longden, J. E.	1/ 2/41
Beevers, J.	1/ 2/41
Brears, P. S.	1/ 2/41
Watson, K.	1/ 2/41
Fawcett, J. W.	1/ 2/41
Hedley, M. T.	1/ 2/41

Lieutenants - contd.

Henderson, H. H.	1/ 2/41
Lattimore, C. R.	1/ 2/41
Lancaster, T. W.	1/ 2/41
Stafford, V. K.	1/ 2/41
Cundall, W. S.	1/ 2/41
Clark, G. E.	1/ 2/41
Sidebottom, O.	1/ 2/41

2nd Lieutenants

Windle, H.	1/ 2/41
Jackson, J.	1/ 2/41
Frankland, J. H. (Lt. late R.G.A.)	1/ 2/41
Leason, S. B.	1/ 2/41
Pitts, J. S.	1/ 2/41
Law, C. H.	1/ 2/41
Nicholson, W. P.	1/ 2/41
Fletcher, H.	1/ 2/41
Broadbent, F.	1/ 2/41
Bassindale, T.	1/ 2/41
Chafer, F. B.	1/ 2/41
Cobbett, C. W.	1/ 2/41
Dixon, J.	1/ 2/41
Percival, J.	1/ 2/41
Alder, W.	1/ 2/41
Townson, C. K.	1/ 2/41
Barker, R. W.	1/ 2/41
Bateman, W. G.	1/ 2/41
Fawcett, C.	1/ 2/41
Windle, G. S.	1/ 2/41
Jessop, E.	1/ 2/41
Webster, C. E.	1/ 2/41
Jackson, H.	1/ 2/41
Hind, F. N.	1/ 2/41
Tall, R.	1/ 2/41
Roberts, F. L.	1/ 2/41
Sammon, E.	1/ 2/41
Fenton, J.	1/ 2/41
Margrave, O.	1/ 2/41
Pearson, A., M.M.	10/ 5/41

Adjutant & Quarter-Master

Medical Officer

McDiarmid, Maj. P. J.	3/ 6/41

YORKSHIRE AREA - contd.

DONCASTER ZONE - contd.

SELBY GROUP

Commander

10th WEST RIDING (SELBY) BATTALION

Lt.-Colonel

Baker, H. H. (Lt. late Tank Corps.) 1/ 2/41

Majors

Ward, A. (Flying Offr. late R.A.F.) 1/ 2/41
Higgins, J. S. R. (Lt. late K.O.S.B.) 1/ 2/41
Pickles, J. W. (2/Lt. late R. North'd. Fus.) 1/ 2/41
Gray, J. (2/Lt. late R. North'd. Fus.) 1/ 2/41
Swift, S. W. 1/ 2/41

Captains

Exelby, A. 1/ 2/41
Bulmer, D. 1/ 2/41
Wilson, H. 1/ 2/41
Parvin, S. 1/ 2/41
Hanley, B. 1/ 2/41

Lieutenants

Wood, G. W. (Lt. late Durham L.I.) 1/ 2/41
Bell, H. (Lt. late Y. & L.R.) 1/ 2/41

Lieutenants - contd.

Grant, D. P., M.C. (Capt. late Y. & L.R.) 1/ 2/41
Lobley, H. O. 1/ 2/41
Kirkland, E. W. 1/ 2/41
Thompson, J. H. 1/ 2/41
Stainburn, C. V. 1/ 2/41
Neville, W. 1/ 2/41
Pollard, H. A. 1/ 2/41
Meeze, E. H. 1/ 2/41
Dickinson, T. F. 1/ 2/41
Morley, A. 1/ 2/41
Dyson, C. H. 1/ 2/41
Schofield, J. B. 1/ 2/41
Dodgson, C. 1/ 2/41
Parker, G. C. 1/ 2/41
Clayton, A. 1/ 2/41
Baron, S. B. 1/ 2/41
Guttridge, H. 1/ 2/41
Gray, V. 1/ 2/41

Adjutant & Quarter-Master

Medical Officer

Hiley, Maj. C. R., M.B. 11/ 5/41

YORKSHIRE AREA - contd.

DONCASTER ZONE - contd.

DONCASTER GROUP

Commander	
Second in Command	Shearman, Lt.-Col. T., D.S.O., T.D. (Maj. ret. T.A.) 1/ 2/41
Assistant to Commander	Barber, Capt. N. E. (Lt.-Col. T.A. Res.) 10/ 5/41

44th WEST RIDING (DONCASTER) BATTALION

Lt.-Colonel

Grant-Dalton, C.	31/ 3/41

Majors

Nicklin, A.	1/ 2/41
Neelands, A. R., M.C. (Capt. late Can. Mil. Forces)	1/ 2/41
Wilson, A.	1/ 2/41
Wigglesworth, H. T., M.M.	1/ 2/41

Captains

Pickersgill, W. A.	1/ 2/41
Tomlinson, S.	1/ 2/41
Jameson, B. B-C. E. (Lt. Comdr. ret. R.N.)	1/ 2/41
Nicholson, H. N.	1/ 2/41

Lieutenants

Stevens, P. B.	1/ 2/41
Abbott, G., M.M. (Lt. late K.O.Y.L.I.)	1/ 2/41
Hobson, H. C.	1/ 2/41
Whiteley, J. F.	1/ 2/41
Thornhill, G.	1/ 2/41
Howe, W. G.	1/ 2/41
Shipman, H., M.M.	1/ 2/41
Simons, E. J.	1/ 2/41
Baker, W. L.	1/ 2/41
Hardy, P. L.	1/ 2/41
Haywood, A.	1/ 2/41

2nd Lieutenants

Ratcliffe, H.	1/ 2/41
Young, T. M.	1/ 2/41
Smith, R.	1/ 2/41
Medcalf, H. (Lt. late Manch. R.)	1/ 2/41
Clarke, L. A.	1/ 2/41
Pilling, A.	1/ 2/41
Marshall, H.	1/ 2/41
Dickson, A.	1/ 2/41

Adjutant & Quarter-Master

Medical Officer

Erskine, Maj. J. T.	4/ 5/41

45th WEST RIDING (DONCASTER) BATTALION

Lt.-Colonel

Le-Brun, M. P. D. (Lt. late R.G.A.)	1/ 2/41

Majors

Brown, C.	1/ 2/41
Stockdale, E. B.	1/ 2/41
Hirst, H. L.	1/ 2/41
Lewis, G. M., M.M.	22/ 7/41

Captains

Harrop, D. W.	1/ 2/41
Cutts, G. C.	1/ 2/41
Jenkinson, A. (Lt. late K.O.Y.L.I.)	1/ 2/41

Lieutenants

Clear, A. (Maj. late Manch. R.)	1/ 2/41
Storry, F. W. S. (Capt late R.A.S.C.)	1/ 2/41
Bedford, A. E. (Lt. late York R.)	1/ 2/41
Fenn, J.	1/ 2/41
Greig, J.	1/ 7/41

2nd Lieutenants

Farr, G. E.	1/ 2/41
Hobday, J. H.	1/ 2/41
Bulmer, J. T. (2/Lt. late Y. & L.R.)	1/ 2/41
Stables, G.	1/ 2/41
Hardcastle, A. F.	1/ 2/41
Bilton, G. H.	12/ 5/41
Kitchener, H.	12/ 5/41
Knowles, W. F.	12/ 5/41
Slater, W. J.	13/ 5/41
Wilson, H.	8/ 7/41
Devereux, H.	25/ 7/41

Adjutant & Quarter-Master

Medical Officer

McColm, Maj. J. L., M.B.	4/ 5/41

YORKSHIRE AREA - contd.

DONCASTER ZONE - contd.

DONCASTER GROUP - contd.

46th WEST RIDING (DONCASTER) BATTALION

Lt.-Colonel

Name	Date
Elwy-Jones, W. (Lt.-Col. Spec. Res.)	1/ 2/41

Majors

Name	Date
Muir, J. C. (Capt. late The King's R.)	1/ 2/41
Harrison, N. S. (Capt. late E. York R.)	1/ 2/41
Bland, J., M.C. (Capt. late Cheshire R.)	1/ 2/41
Stewart, G. (2/Lt. late D.W.R.)	1/ 2/41
Coats, H. M.	1/ 2/41
Reyner, S.	1/ 2/41
Holroyde, B. (Capt. T.A. Res.)	1/ 2/41
Taylor, W., M.M. (Lt. late Durham L.I.)	1/ 2/41

Captains

Name	Date
Eccelstone, A. (Lt. late S. Stafford R.)	1/ 2/41
Lewis, J. L. D.	1/ 2/41
Woodward, F. C. J.	1/ 2/41
Brown, G. A. (Lt. late W. York R.)	1/ 2/41
Cunningham, C. M. S. (Lt. late Manch. R.)	1/ 2/41
Lord, F. M. (Lt. late R.E.)	1/ 2/41
Uttley, H. R.	1/ 2/41
Smith, P. F.	1/ 2/41
Stott, S.	1/ 2/41
Wealthall, C. (Lt. late R.A.F.)	1/ 2/41
Day, F. D.	1/ 2/41
South, W.	1/ 2/41
Walden, W.	1/ 2/41
Williams, H. J. (Capt. late R.E.)	1/ 2/41
Hudson, E. (Lt. late Durham L.I.)	1/ 2/41
Peck, F. J.	1/ 2/41

Lieutenants

Name	Date
Anson, R. W. (Sub-Lt. late R.N.V.R.)	1/ 2/41
Hoare, J. G. (Capt. late Ind. Army)	1/ 2/41
Reasbeck, S. (Lt. late D.W.R.)	1/ 2/41
Garland, T. (Lt. late R.W.K.)	1/ 2/41
Brierley, B. (Lt. late R.A.S.C.)	1/ 2/41
Kitchen, N.	1/ 2/41
Gosling, C. T.	1/ 2/41
Amphlett, R. E. T.	1/ 2/41
Richards, L. R.	1/ 2/41
Dinn, G. H. K.	1/ 2/41

Lieutenants - contd.

Name	Date
Price, W. T.	1/ 2/41
Allen, J. S.	1/ 2/41
Sargent, P.	1/ 2/41
Tuxworth, H.	1/ 2/41
Piper, L.	1/ 2/41
Barlow, J.	1/ 2/41
Parker, W. J.	1/ 2/41
Haw, R. P.	1/ 2/41

2nd Lieutenants

Name	Date
Davies, R. C.	1/ 2/41
Cooper, C., D.C.M.	1/ 2/41
Clarke, E.	1/ 2/41
Abbott, C. E.	1/ 2/41
Haswell, E. J.	1/ 2/41
Jackson, R. V.	1/ 2/41
Lister, W.	1/ 2/41
Buckenham, F. G.	1/ 2/41
Huntington, L. H.	1/ 2/41
Brooke, J. S.	1/ 2/41
Dalby, W.	1/ 2/41
Fenton, W., M.M.	1/ 2/41
Vollands, H.	1/ 2/41
Higgens, C. C.	1/ 2/41
Williams, E., M.M.	1/ 2/41
Tulloch, J. S.	1/ 2/41
Jenkinson, A., M.M.	1/ 2/41
Jackson, T. R.	1/ 2/41
Miller, R. R.	1/ 2/41
Haslam, G. S.	1/ 2/41
Wilson, G. H. (2/Lt. late R.A.F.)	1/ 2/41
Hupple, H.	1/ 2/41
Claybourn, J. E.	1/ 2/41
Utting, D. L. K.	1/ 2/41
Mills, W. B.	1/ 2/41
Brookes, A.	1/ 2/41
White, E.	1/ 2/41
Allen, S. R.	1/ 2/41
Harman, P. E. T.	1/ 2/41
Anderson, T. A.	1/ 2/41
Cliff, H.	1/ 2/41
Pearce, T. H.	1/ 2/41
Wright, W.	1/ 2/41
Bamber, J. W., M.M.	1/ 2/41
Bird, C. H.	1/ 2/41
Mackinder, H. H.	1/ 2/41
Sailes, B. T.	1/ 2/41
Nicklin, S.	1/ 2/41
Rasberry, H.	1/ 2/41

Adjutant & Quarter-Master

Name	Date
Bridge, Capt. F. W., Res. of Off.	22/ 4/41

Medical Officer

Name	Date
Bury, Maj. H. S.	26/ 6/41

YORKSHIRE AREA - contd.

DONCASTER ZONE - contd.

HATFIELD GROUP

Commander — Fowler, Col. G. N., M.C., T.D. (Col. T.A.) 1/ 2/41

42nd WEST RIDING (HATFIELD) BATTALION

Lt.-Colonel

Whittaker, J. (Lt. late T.A.) 1/ 2/41

Majors

Walton, R. M. 1/ 2/41
Wain, R. C., M.C. (Capt. late R.E.) 1/ 2/41
Haslam, H. S. 1/ 2/41
Otter, E. (2/Lt. late Foresters) 1/ 2/41
Sharman, G. F. (Lt. late R.A.F.) 1/ 2/41
Uhthoff, R. K., M.C. (Lt. late R.E.) 1/ 2/41

Captains

Leach, S. T. 1/ 2/41
Crampton, S. (Lt. late R.T.C.) 1/ 2/41
Stacey, G. 15/ 6/41
Bailey, A. 24/ 6/41
Taylor, S. A. 24/ 6/41

Lieutenants

Robinson, B., M.M. 1/ 2/41
Woodcock, J. 1/ 2/41
Davidson, R. 1/ 2/41
Robinson, W. M. 1/ 2/41
Farr, G. K. 1/ 2/41

Lieutenants - contd.

Burland, L., O.B.E. (Capt. late K.S.L.I.) 1/ 2/41
Herrington, C. H. 1/ 2/41
Lindley, W. K. 1/ 2/41
Dowdall, F. O. 1/ 2/41
Clare, S., M.B.E. (Capt. late R.A.F.) 1/ 2/41
Richmond, F. A. (2/Lt. late R.E.) 1/ 2/41
Linford, H. J. (2/Lt. late North'd. Fus.) 1/ 2/41
Gover, C. 1/ 2/41
Bunting, S. (Lt. late K.O.Y.L.I.) 1/ 2/41
Aykroyd, T. (Lt. late K.O.Y.L.I.) 1/ 2/41
Beever, C. 1/ 2/41
Barraclough, B. 1/ 2/41
Haley, H. (Lt. late King's R.) 1/ 2/41
Severn, A. 30/ 5/41
Garthwaite, J. S. 16/ 7/41

Adjutant & Quarter-Master

Medical Officer

Hart, Maj. B., O.B.E. (Sub.-Lt. late R.N.V.R.) 1/ 2/41

YORKSHIRE AREA - contd.

DONCASTER ZONE - contd.

HATFIELD GROUP

43rd WEST RIDING (HATFIELD) BATTALION

Lt.-Colonel

Keates, J. B., M.C. (Maj. late M.G. Corps.)	1/ 2/41

Majors

Frost, T. (Capt. late E. York R.)	1/ 2/41
Walker, J. R. M. (Capt. late R.A.)	1/ 2/41
Hulley, N.	1/ 2/41
Brocklesby, P. (Lt. late Y. & L.R.)	1/ 2/41
Robinson, R. U., M.C. (2/Lt. late R.T.C.)	1/ 2/41
Munson, E. E. (Lt. late R.F.A.)	1/ 2/41
Dodds, K. D. N.	1/ 2/41
Vincent, J. E. (Lt. late R.E.)	1/ 2/41

Captains

Rushworth, J.	1/ 2/41
Pickett, C. J., M.C. (Sub-Lt. late R.N.)	1/ 2/41
Blackburn, R. D. (Lt. late R.N.)	1/ 2/41
Morris, J. H.	1/ 2/41
Blount, A. (Lt. late R.A.F.)	1/ 2/41
Thacker, W.	1/ 2/41
Durdy, F. G. (2/Lt. late R.F.A.)	1/ 2/41
Bailey, H.	17/ 7/41
Shelbourn, H. A.	1/ 2/41
Otley, H.	1/ 2/41
Wood, T. O.	1/ 2/41
Woad, H.	1/ 2/41
Langley, C. (Flg. Off. late R.A.F.)	1/ 2/41
Ross, R.	1/ 2/41
Wheeliker, J.	1/ 2/41
Wake, R., D.C.M., M.M.	1/ 2/41

Lieutenants - contd.

Roberts, A.	1/ 2/41
Ellis, H., D.C.M., M.M.	1/ 2/41
Bashforth, L.	1/ 2/41
McKie, H.	1/ 2/41
Jackson, E.	1/ 2/41
Oldfield, G., M.M.	1/ 2/41
Gater, A.	1/ 2/41
Lightfoot, R. W.	1/ 2/41
Fox, J. J.	1/ 2/41
Marriott, H.	1/ 2/41
May, A. E.	1/ 2/41
Hayes, T. E. S., M.M.	1/ 2/41
Dixon, J., M.M.	1/ 2/41
Watson, T. M., M.M.	1/ 2/41
Jones, L.	1/ 2/41
Winder, G. H.	1/ 2/41
Frank, W. G.	1/ 2/41
Smith, F. G.	1/ 2/41
Hume, H. B.	1/ 2/41
Cowley, A. J.	1/ 2/41
Fullwood, N. E.	1/ 2/41
Middleton, J.	16/ 4/41
Howitt, R.	24/ 7/41

2nd Lieutenants

Wagstaff, L.	1/ 2/41
Pope, E. V.	1/ 2/41

Adjutant & Quarter-Master

Medical Officer

YORKSHIRE AREA - contd.

HALLAMSHIRE ZONE

Commander	Neill, Col. F. A. (Col. T.A.)	1/ 2/41
Assistants to Commander	Platt, Maj. C. B. M., M.B.E. (Capt. late R. Signals)	1/ 2/41
	Broughton, Capt. C. D.	1/ 2/41
Territorial Army Association administering	The Yorkshire (West Riding) T.A. Association, 9, St. Leonards, York.	

BARNSLEY GROUP

Commander	Rideal, Col. J. G. E., D.S.O., T.D. (Maj. late M G. Corps)	1/ 2/41
Second in Command	Jubb, Lt.-Col. N. (Capt. late T.A.)	1/ 2/41
Assistant to Commander	Taylor, Capt. P. W. H.	1/ 2/41

56th WEST RIDING (BARNSLEY) BATTALION

Lt.-Colonel

Mallinson, A. N. (Maj. late T A.)	1/ 2/41

Majors

Pratt, C. M. (Lt. late E. York R.)	1/ 2/41
Beevers, T. W. (Capt. late W. York R.)	1/ 2/41
Smith, G. G. (Lt. late Ind. Army)	1/ 2/41
Charlesworth, C. E., M.B E.	1/ 2/41
Pickering, H.	1/ 2/41
Wilson, A. E.	1/ 2/41

Captains

Wilcock, R. B., M.C., M.M. (Lt. late R.F.A.)	1/ 2/41
Cameron, D.	1/ 2/41

Captains - contd.

Smith, A. (Capt. late Y. & L.R.)	1/ 2/41
Harrison, J. (Lt. late K.O.Y L.I.)	1/ 2/41
Cherry, E. (Lt. late R.A.F.)	1/ 2/41
Foweather, J. (2/Lt. late Y. & L.R.)	1/ 2/41
Rawson, D.	1/ 2/41
Finlay, A.	1/ 2/41
Saville, B. W.	1/ 2/41
Cartledge, J.	1/ 2/41

Lieutenants

Stirling, G. L.	1/ 2/41
Philbin, J. (Lt. late R.A.)	1/ 2/41
Harrison, G. (Lt. late Y. & L.R.)	1/ 2/41

56455-6(114)

YORKSHIRE AREA - contd.

HALLAMSHIRE ZONE - contd.

BARNSLEY GROUP - contd.

56th West Riding (Barnsley) Battalion - contd.

Lieutenants - contd.

Rawlings, W. A. H.	1/ 2/41
Davies, S. (Lt. late Seaforth)	1/ 2/41
Carrington, P. St. J. (Lt. late T.A.)	1/ 2/41
Gledhill, T. L.	1/ 2/41
Frankland, A. (2/Lt. late M.G. Corps.)	1/ 2@41
Stott, G. H. (2/Lt. late Y. & L.R.)	1/ 2/41
Strutt, T.	1/ 2/41
Bailey, F. J. H.	1/ 2/41
Hey, J. R., D.C.M., M.M.	1/ 2/41
Rollinson, J.	1/ 2/41
Litherland, C.	1/ 2/41
Swann, E.	1/ 2/41
Chapman, W., M.M.	1/ 2/41
Bradley, H.	1/ 2/41
Oxtaby, H., M.M.	1/ 2/41
Bramley, A.	1/ 2/41
Mitchell, J. T.	1/ 2/41
Fawley, A.	1/ 2/41
Heald, H.	1/ 2/41
Matthews, J.	1/ 2/41
Bower, C. W.	1/ 2/41
Pratt, F.	1/ 2/41
Sawyer, F. W.	1/ 2/41
Lund, T. D.	1/ 2/41
Shrigley, H. F. E.	1/ 2/41
Willoughby, J. W.	1/ 2/41
Howe, H.	1/ 2/41
Greenland, R. H.	1/ 2/41
Leigh, E.	1/ 2/41
Pigott, S.	1/ 2/41
Crow, F. B.	1/ 2/41
Moore, A. F.	1/ 2/41
Powell, G. B.	1/ 2/41
Reid, F. C. A.	1/ 2/41

2nd Lieutenants

Allum, E. W.	1/ 2/41
Halton, J. A., M.M.	1/ 2/41
Goodall, G.	1/ 2/41
Bussingham, P.	1/ 2/41
Park, J. W.	1/ 2/41
Allan, C.	1/ 2/41
Scott, J. W.	1/ 2/41
Beard, H. C.	1/ 2/41
Addey, A. R.	1/ 2/41
Hyde, H.	1/ 2/41
Williams, C.	1/ 2/41
Cooke, J.	1/ 2/41
Leatham, A.	1/ 2/41
Pierrepont, F.	1/ 2/41
Dunnington, H.	1/ 2/41
Squires, F.	1/ 2/41
Fletcher, A. E.	1/ 2/41
Taylor, A.	1/ 2/41
Carr, S.	1/ 2/41
Hanson, P.	1/ 2/41
Bradley, R.	1/ 2/41
Marshall, J. E. J.	1/ 2/41
Docker, H.	1/ 2/41
Brook, J.	1/ 2/41
Leay, W. H.	1/ 2/41
Dickinson, J. A.	1/ 2/41

Adjutant & Quarter-Master

Medical Officer

Slack, Maj. A. B., M.C., M.B. (Capt. late Lan. Fus.)	1/ 2/41

YORKSHIRE AREA - contd.

HALLAMSHIRE ZONE - contd.

BARNSLEY GROUP - contd.

57th WEST RIDING (BARNSLEY) BATTALION

Lt.-Colonel

Prest, S. O. (Capt. late T.A.)	1/ 2/41

Majors

Potter, H. (Capt. late Y. & L.R.)	1/ 2/41
Snowden, H. (Lt. late Y. & L. R.)	1/ 2/41
Lancaster, G. B. (Capt. late Green Howards)	1/ 2/41
Portman, B. W. L. (2/Lt. late S. Stafford R.)	1/ 2/41
Arden, C. A.	1/ 2/41

Captains

Benford, A.	1/ 2/41
Field, A.	1/ 2/41
Goodyear, G. R.	1/ 2/41
Green, F., D.C.M.	1/ 2/41
Sandiforth, E. S.	1/ 2/41
Clark, A. W.	1/ 2/41
Wilkinson, C. A. B. (Lt. late R.E.)	1/ 2/41
Stringfellow, J.	1/ 2/41
Appleyard, A. W.	1/ 2/41

Lieutenants

Rusling, W.	1/ 2/41
Harris, A. L.	1/ 2/41
Mansfield, W., M.M.	1/ 2/41
King, G. C.	1/ 2/41
McKenny, J. W., D.C.M.	1/ 2/41
Hayes, J.	1/ 2/41
Fodden, A., M.M.	1/ 2/41
Harston, J. C., M.M.	1/ 2/41
Bowers, C.	1/ 2/41
Davis, G.	1/ 2/41
Clapham, W. C.	1/ 2/41
Parker, H.	1/ 2/41
Killingbeck, J. T.	1/ 2/41
Ward, J. N.	1/ 2/41
Howe, A.	1/ 2/41
Fisher, G. G.	1/ 2/41
Bentley, J. G.	1/ 2/41

Lieutenants - contd.

Burgin, A. W.	1/ 2/41
Ward, W. H.	1/ 2/41
Armitage, B.	1/ 2/41
Ferguson, T. H.	1/ 2/41
Warburton, J.	1/ 2/41
Norris, R.	1/ 2/41
Lackin, J.	1/ 2/41
Hinds, W. O.	1/ 2/41
Darren, G.	1/ 2/41
Skilton, W. J.	1/ 2/41
Ogley, A.	1/ 2/41
Jones, J.	1/ 2/41
Berrisford, A. H.	1/ 2/41

2nd Lieutenants

Loe, J. J., M.M.	1/ 2/41
Perry, T.	1/ 2/41
Winkless, A.	1/ 2/41
Bright, O.	1/ 2/41
Cotton, T.	1/ 2/41
Parker, J. B.	1/ 2/41
Bennett, J.	1/ 2/41
Lunn, F.	1/ 2/41
Coldwell, A. I.	1/ 2/41
Totney, R.	1/ 2/41
Ramsden, J. E.	1/ 2/41
Copping, E. F.	1/ 2/41
Hoyle, H.	1/ 2/41
Gill, T.	1/ 2/41
Darnell, H. W.	1/ 2/41

Adjutant & Quarter-Master

Medical Officer

Pick, Maj. N., M.B. (Capt. late R.A.M.C.)	1/ 2/41

YORKSHIRE AREA - contd.

HALLAMSHIRE ZONE - contd.

STAINCROSS GROUP

Commander	Hallam, Col. L. (Lt. late T.A.)	1/ 2/41
Second in Command	Atter, Lt.-Col. H. F., O.B.E., (Capt. late T.A.)	1/ 2/41

70th WEST RIDING (STAINCROSS) BATTALION

Lt.-Colonel

Jackson, H. S., D.S.O. (Capt. late late T.A.)	1/ 2/41

Majors

Rigby, C. V., M.C., (Maj. late D.W.R.)	1/ 2/41
Pardoe, J. H. (Capt. late E. York R.)	1/ 2/41
MacLachlan, L. (Lt. late K.R.R.C.)	1/ 2/41

Captains

Hoyland, W. (Lt. late R.E.)	1/ 2/41
Sawtell, H. D. (Lt. late R.A.O.C.)	1/ 2/41
Andrew, F.	1/ 2/41
Durrans, P. H. (2/Lt. late R.A.)	1/ 2/41

Lieutenants

Jackson, R.A.	1/ 2/41
Booth, G.	1/ 2/41
Lockwood, H.	1/ 2/41
Booth, J. F.	1/ 2/41
Oxley, A.	1/ 2/41
Moxon, C. H.	1/ 2/41
Taylor, A. J. S. (2/Lt. late D.W.R.)	1/ 2/41

Lieutenants - contd.

Cowburn, D. (Lt. late R.E.)	1/ 2/41
Broomhall, H. H. (Lt. late Y. & L.R.)	1/ 2/41
Hurdman, W. L.	21/ 7/41
Millington, T.	21/ 7/41
Woolmore, J. W. R.	21/ 7/41

2nd Lieutenants

Kenyon, E. W.	1/ 2/41
Walker, D. J.	1/ 2/11
Taylor, W. J.	1/ 2/41
Sheardown, G.	1/ 2/41
Wharncliffe, The Earl of (Capt. late L.G.) (Res. of Off.)	1/ 2/41
Dalby, H. S. H. (Capt. late The King's R.)	1/ 2/41
Lello, H.	1/ 2/41

Adjutant & Quarter-Master

Medical Officer

Harris, Maj. L. B., M.B.,	7/ 5/41

71st WEST RIDING (STAINCROSS) BATTALION

Lt.-Colonel

Simmons, G. L. 1/ 2/41

Majors

Wilson, A. L. 1/ 2/41
Addy, R. (Capt. late R.F.C.) 1/ 2/41
Callinan, C. A. (Lt. late North'd Fus.) 1/ 2/41
Leich, D. J. 1/ 2/41
Fearn, W., M.M. 1/ 2/41
Hesketh, C. (2/Lt. late Y. & L.R.) 1/ 2/41
Cooper, A. R. 1/ 2/41
Hawke, F. A. 21/ 7/41

Captains

Baddeley, H., M.B.E., (Lt. late 21st L.) 1/ 2/41
Stott, L. 1/ 2/41
Shaw, J., D.C.M., M.M. 21/ 7/41
Dickinson, F. J. 21/ 7/41
Cowen, G. 21/ 7/41

Lieutenants

Taylor, W. T. 1/ 2/41
Stringer, R. 1/ 2/41
Mallinson, T. H. 1/ 2/41
Tolson, E. (Lt. late Worc. R.) 1/ 2/41
Littlewood, H. E. 1/ 2/41
Cowling, A. 1/ 2/41
Idle, P. W. D. 1/ 2/41
Clare, P. H. 1/ 2/41
May, D., M.M. 1/ 2/41
Jenkins, H. W. B. 1/ 2/41
Purslow, E. C. W. 1/ 2/41
Reece, J. W. 1/ 2/41
Armitage, W. 1/ 2/41

Lieutenants - contd.

Allen, F. 1/ 2/41
Brookes, G. A., D.C.M. 1/ 2/41
Turner, H. 1/ 2/41
Ledger, A. E. 1/ 2/41
Salt, C. 1/ 2/41
Sargesson, J. H. 1/ 2/41
Weaver, L. T. 1/ 2/41
Perry, C., D.C.M. 14/ 5/41
Williams, C. 14/ 5/41

2nd Lieutenants

Hayes, H. 1/ 2/41
Whiteley, S. 1/ 2/41
Thompson, G. 1/ 2/41
Payne, J. 1/ 2/41
Walker, J. A. 1/ 2/41
Green, H., M.M. 1/ 2/41
Williams, F. 1/ 2/41
Wiggins, C. 1/ 2/41
Wassell, J. 1/ 2/41
Mabbott, H. 1/ 2/41
Milton, H. 1/ 2/41
Robinson, C. E. 1/ 2/41
Spacey, W. 1/ 2/41
Hanson, A. 1/ 2/41
Sunderland, T. 1/ 2/41
Cater, W. W. 20/ 6/41

Adjutant & Quarter-Master

Medical Officer

Henderson, Maj. J., M.B. 7/ 5/41

YORKSHIRE AREA - contd.

HALLAMSHIRE ZONE - contd.

STAINCROSS GROUP - contd.

72nd WEST RIDING (STAINCROSS) BATTALION

Lt.-Colonel

Young, M. H. (Capt. late T.A.) 1/ 2/41

Majors

Ellwood, C. F. (Maj. late Y. & L.R.) 1/ 2/41
Hall, J. B. 1/ 2/41
Thompson, A. A. (2/Lt. late King's Own R.) 1/ 2/41
Worthington, J. 1/ 2/41
Cattell, S. B. (Lt. late M.G. Corps) 1/ 2/41
Bennett, D. F. 1/ 2/41
Brass, T. F. S. (Lt. late R.E., Supply Res.) 1/ 2/41
Smith, H. P. (Maj. late Y. & L.R.) 1/ 2/41

Captains

Barry, J. N. (Capt. late R. Dublin Fus.) 1/ 2/41
Taylor, R. H. H. 1/ 2/41
Hall, G. (2/Lt. late K.O.Y.L.I.) 1/ 2/41
Saville, J. E. 1/ 2/41
Brittain, S. 1/ 2/41
Dunn, S. H. 1/ 2/41

Lieutenants

Mackie, F. C. 1/ 2/41
Petch, R. G. 1/ 2/41
Pilkington, R. W. 1/ 2/41
Dickinson, C. 1/ 2/41
Moore, F. M. 1/ 2/41
Brown, L. (2/Lt. late K.O.Y.L.I.) 1/ 2/41
Walsh, W. H. R. 1/ 2/41
Surtees, D. 1/ 2/41
Hackett, W. M. 1/ 2/41
Wordley, C. 1/ 2/41
Walters, J. 1/ 2/41
Coe, F. 1/ 2/41
Maidment, G. A. 1/ 2/41
Lee, M. J. 1/ 2/41
Sutcliffe, A. 1/ 2/41
Moore, H. 1/ 2/41
Sanders, T. M. 1/ 2/41
Round, A. 1/ 2/41

Lieutenants - contd.

Gleadall, A. (Lt. late Can. Mil. Forces) 1/ 2/41
Hayes, V. 1/ 2/41
Bland, H. 1/ 2/41
Jones, A., M.M. 1/ 2/41
Baker, F. H. 1/ 2/41
Nash, D. E. 1/ 2/41
Garton, H. 1/ 2/41
Dunk, A. 1/ 2/41
Smith, A. (Lt. late K.O.Y.L.I.) 1/ 2/41
Guest, G. A. 1/ 2/41
Burton, C. E. (Lt. late A.C. Corps) 1/ 2/41
Ashmore, W. 1/ 2/41

2nd Lieutenants

Webster, H. 1/ 2/41
Bellamy, H. 1/ 2/41
Bellamy, S. 14/ 5/41
Bellis, J. E. 14/ 5/41
Briggs, J. W. 14/ 5/41
Cox, J. 14/ 5/41
Fairhurst, E. 14/ 5/41
Hargreaves, A. A. 14/ 5/41
Heyes, A. 14/ 5/41
Kay, E. 14/ 5/41
Mayhew, W. 14/ 5/41
Monkhouse, F. 14/ 5/41
Tart, H. 14/ 5/41
Taylor, A. E. 14/ 5/41
Taylor, C. H. 14/ 5/41
Venters, H. 14/ 5/41
Wadsworth, A. (Lt. late R.G.A.) 14/ 5/41
Wilkinson, S. 14/ 5/41
Damley, H. P. 14/ 5/41
Sharpe, C. 20/ 6/41

Adjutant & Quarter-Master

Medical Officer

Dickinson, Maj. W. R. (Capt. late R.A.M.C.) 7/ 5/41

YORKSHIRE AREA - contd.

HALLAMSHIRE ZONE - contd.

ROTHERHAM GROUP

Commander	Landon, Col. J. W. B., D.S.O., (Lt.-Col. late T.A.R.O.)	1/ 2/41
Second in Command	Martyn, Lt.-Col. M. C., D.S.O., M.C., (Lt.-Col. T.A. Res.)	1/ 2/41
Assistant to Commander	Robson, Capt. N. S. (Lt. late R.A.F.)	1/ 2/41

58th WEST RIDING (ROTHERHAM) BATTALION

Lt.-Colonel

Denham, W. G., D.C.M.	1/ 2/41

Majors

Dickinson, J. H. (2/Lt. late R.R. Dns.)	1/ 2/41
Spearing, G. T. (Capt. late R.F.A.)	1/ 2/41
Michael, A.	1/ 2/41
Ball, R. (Lt. late N.Stafford R.)	1/ 2/41
Longstaff, J. (2nd Lt. late Durham L.I.)	1/ 2/41

Captains

Milnes, C. (2nd Lt. late R.F.A.)	1/ 2/41
Perkins, H. C.	1/ 2/41
Birkett, D. L.	1/ 2/41
Silvester, L., D.C.M.	1/ 2/41

Lieutenants

Slack, T. R. (Lt. late E. York R.)	1/ 2/41
Ash, F. S. (Lt. late R.T.C.)	1/ 2/41
Allott, T. B.	1/ 2/41
Lewis, A. B.	1/ 2/41
Stonehouse, D., M.C. (Lt. late M.G.C.)	1/ 2/41
Meakin, A.	1/ 2/41
Goodall, W.	1/ 2/41
Rising, P. H.	1/ 2/41
Carr, C. W. (2nd Lt. late S. Lan. R.)	1/ 2/41
Taylor, C. A. (2nd Lt. late R.A.F.)	1/ 2/41
Williamson, W.	1/ 2/41
Tooms, D. E.	1/ 2/41
Beard, H. H.	1/ 2/41
Norburn, F.	1/ 2/41
Marsh, C. R.	1/ 2/41
Johnson, J.	1/ 2/41

Lieutenants - contd.

Dean, J.	1/ 2/41
Dean, H. J.	1/ 2/41
Ball, H.	1/ 2/41
Atkinson, G.	1/ 2/41
Bristowe, S.	1/ 2/41
Aubrey, R. G.	1/ 2/41

2nd Lieutenants

Maxwell, N.	1/ 2/41
Harvey, F.	1/ 2/41
Sellars, F.	1/ 2/41
Bingham, F.	1/ 2/41
Parkin, O.	1/ 2/41
Toone, A. R.	1/ 2/41
Chapman, G. W. (2/Lt. late Y. & L. R.)	1/ 2/41
Varley, A. E.	1/ 2/41
Buckland, F.	1/ 2/41
Coates, A.	1/ 2/41
Copley, W.	1/ 2/41
O'Mara, J.	1/ 2/41
Varey, R. H.	1/ 2/41
Blake, A. C. L.	1/ 2/41
Owen, W. J.	1/ 2/41
Brown, W.	1/ 2/41
Leach, C.	1/ 2/41
Summersgill, H.	1/ 2/41
Todd, H.	1/ 2/41

Adjutant & Quarter-Master

Medical Officer

Agnew, Maj. F., M.B.,	13/ 5/41

YORKSHIRE AREA - contd.

HALLAMSHIRE ZONE - contd.

ROTHERHAM GROUP - contd.

59th WEST RIDING (ROTHERHAM) BATTALION

Lt.-Colonel

Doyle, J. E., M.C. (Capt. late Tank Corps)	1/ 2/41

Majors

Walden, S. J.	1/ 2/41
Jenkinson, E.	1/ 2/41
Prew, A. (Lt. late Y. & L.R.)	1/ 2/41
Jones, H. J.	22/ 7/41

Captains

Venables, A. V. (Capt. late R.W. Fus.)	1/ 2/41
Price, G. J. B.	1/ 2/41
Hampshire, C. H.	1/ 2/41
Duke, C. W.	22/ 7/41

Lieutenants

Turner, T. C. (Lt. late Gordons)	1/ 2/41
Ellis, W., D.C.M.	1/ 2/41
Thomson, A.	1/ 2/41
Roadhouse, G. H., M.M.	1/ 2/41
Morrill, H.	1/ 2/41
Warburton, J. H. B.	1/ 2/41
Musson, C. R.	1/ 2/41
Dyer, G. B.	1/ 2/41
Barlow, R. N.	1/ 2/41
Steel, H., M.M.	1/ 2/41
Busby, C. C.	1/ 2/41
Oxley, W.	7/ 7/41
Hamstead, H.	8/ 7/41
Stoker, S. J.	8/ 7/41

2nd Lieutenants

Russon, W. H.	1/ 2/41
Woodcock, F. H.	1/ 2/41
Goacher, J. A.	1/ 2/41
Fretwell, S.	1/ 2/41
Cooper, C. A.	1/ 2/41
Houghton, E.	1/ 2/41
Mould, H.	1/ 2/41
Marsh, A.	1/ 2/41
Rogers, H.	1/ 2/41
Hardstaff, H.	1/ 2/41
Cooke, S.	1/ 2/41
Holland, F.	1/ 2/41
Ablett, F.	1/ 2/41
Eggleston, R. F.	1/ 2/41
Enzor, W.	1/ 2/41
Robinson, W.	7/ 7/41

Adjutant & Quarter-Master

Medical Officer

Crook, Maj. J.	24/ 6/41

60th WEST RIDING (ROTHERHAM) BATTALION

Lt.-Colonel

Ball, G. C.	1/ 2/41

Majors

Dunn, R. P.	1/ 2/41
Earle, G. F.	1/ 5/41
Wilson, C. W.	1/ 5/41
Bowley, W. H.	1/ 5/41

Captains

Harrop, H. B.	1/ 5/41
Hills, R.	1/ 5/41

Lieutenants

Bowling, A.	1/ 2/41
Rawlinson, S.	1/ 2/41
Layton, E. A.	1/ 2/41
Williams, J.	1/ 2/41
Mills, V.	1/ 2/41
Smith, R. E.	1/ 2/41
Buntin, W.	1/ 2/41
Lord, S. E.	1/ 2/41
Shardlow, A.	1/ 2/41
Perry, H.	1/ 2/41
Selman, H. D.	1/ 2/41
Swift, H.	1/ 2/41

2nd Lieutenants

Sellars, E. A.	1/ 2/41
Whittaker, F.	1/ 2/41
Dean, L. F.	1/ 2/41
Richmond, P.	1/ 2/41
Bowns, R. H.	1/ 2/41
Whitehead, H.	1/ 2/41
Watson, W. J.	1/ 2/41
Murray, A. T.	1/ 2/41
Kettell, C. E.	1/ 2/41
Bairsto, W. H. E.	1/ 2/41
Bocking, R. (2/Lt. late R.A.F.)	19/ 7/41

Adjutant & Quarter-Master

Medical Officer

Griffith, Maj. T. V.	1/ 5/41

YORKSHIRE AREA - contd.

HALLAMSHIRE ZONE - contd.

ROTHERHAM GROUP - contd.

61st WEST RIDING (ROTHERHAM) BATTALION

Lt.-Colonel

Lowe, H. E. (Capt. late Tank Corps) 1/ 2/41

Majors

Turner, H. I. (Lt. late R.A.F.) 1/ 2/41
Johnson, S. 15/ 7/41
Ogley, F. 15/ 7/41
Cooke, R. G. 15/ 7/41
Saul, H. 15/ 7/41

Captains

Dent, W. G. 1/ 2/41
Garnett, G. B. (Lt. late R.G.A.) 1/ 2/41
Wade, R. B. (2/Lt. late R.E.) 1/ 2/41
Russum, R. W. (2/Lt. late W. York R.) 1/ 2/41
Shaw, C. McD. R. 1/ 2/41
Jennings, F. E. 1/ 2/41
Yates, A. 6/ 6/41

Lieutenants

Fitzmaurice, A. M. 1/ 2/41
Parkin, H. 1/ 2/41
Windle, T. H. 1/ 2/41
Veater, H. J. (Lt. late E. York R.) 1/ 2/41
Griffiths, G. 1/ 2/41
Merifield, F. H. 1/ 2/41
Hillerby, A. W. 1/ 2/41
Pickard, J., M.M. 1/ 2/41
Foster, C. 1/ 2/41
Clegg, G. A. 1/ 2/41
Sanderson, J. W. (Lt. late R.E.) 1/ 2/41
Wadsworth, H. 1/ 2/41
Graville, H. G. 1/ 2/41
Franks, H., M.C. (Capt. late M.G. Corps) 1/ 2/41
Lister, G. H. 1/ 2/41
Hinchcliffe, F. P. 1/ 2/41
Johnson, J., D.C.M. 1/ 2/41
Gregg, C. V. 1/ 2/41
Hewitt, G. 1/ 2/41
McClintock, R. le P. (Maj. late Gordons) 1/ 2/41
Waddington, P. 6/ 6/41

Lieutenants - contd.

Childs, S. S. 15/ 7/41

2nd Lieutenants

Greaves, C. D. 1/ 2/41
Wilton, T. A. 1/ 2/41
Taylor, E. A. 1/ 2/41
Allen, W. E. 1/ 2/41
Burns, R. A. 1/ 2/41
Watford, J. E. 1/ 2/41
Pursglove, C. W. 1/ 2/41
Vernon, W. (2/Lt. late R.G.A.) 1/ 2/41
Bisson, R. A. 1/ 2/41
Adey, A. S. 1/ 2/41
Barrett, C. E. 1/ 2/41
Knibbs, G. F. 1/ 2/41
Longworth, F. 1/ 2/41
Brooksbank, D. E. 1/ 2/41
Gilmour, E. W. 1/ 2/41
Fricker, F. J. 1/ 2/41
Holmes, G. F. 1/ 2/41
Wakelin, A. E. 1/ 2/41
Barker, A. 1/ 2/41
Eastwood, F. 1/ 2/41
Atkin, C. H. (Lt. late W. York R.) 1/ 2/41
Richardson, G. B. 1/ 2/41
Fretwell, J. W. 1/ 2/41
Dent, J. E. 1/ 2/41
Sleight, B. 1/ 2/41
Tolley, S., D.C.M., M.M. 1/ 2/41
Sargeantson, J. 1/ 2/41
Morgan, F. L. 1/ 2/41
Johnson, A. D. 17/ 5/41
Athorne, R. D. 17/ 5/41
Booth, C. 17/ 6/41
Lee, G. 17/ 6/41
Wilson, A. R. 16/ 7/41

Adjutant & Quarter-Master

Medical Officer

Pym, Maj. P. E., M.B. (2/Lt. late R.F.A.) 26/ 4/41

YORKSHIRE AREA - contd.

HALLAMSHIRE ZONE - contd.

ROTHERHAM GROUP - contd.

62nd WEST RIDING (ROTHERHAM) BATTALION

Lt.-Colonel

Dick, F. MacK., M.C., T.D. (Bt. Col. T.A. Res.)	1/ 2/41

Majors

Hamilton, D. J. W., M.C. (Capt. late Midd'x R.)	1/ 2/41
Coates, F. P. (Capt. late the King's R.)	1/ 2//1
Carson, S. D. (Lt. late M.G. Corps.)	1/ 2/41
James, E.	1/ 2/41

Captains

Barber, R. S.	1/ 2/41
Pollard, F. B.	1/ 2/41
Smith, C. W. (Lt. late Durham L.I.)	1/ 6/41

Lieutenants

Howlett, S. E., M.M.	1/ 2/41
Hallam, A. E.	1/ 2/41
Cox, W., M.M.	1/ 2/41
Empson, G. L.	1/ 2/41
Bennett, R.	1/ 2/41
Shaw, J. S.	1/ 2/41
Hopewell, B.	1/ 2/41
Hinks, G. A.	1/ 2/41
Beattie, R.	1/ 2/41
Bird, E. F., M.M.	1/ 2/41
Hinchcliffe, R. A.	1/ 2/41
Wright, R.	1/ 2/41
Holland, A. B.	1/ 2/41

Lieutenants - contd.

Bond, J. E. C.	1/ 2/41
Timberlake, H.	1/ 2/41
Jenkins, E. P.	1/ 2/41
Thompson, E.	1/ 2/41

2nd Lieutenants

Stewart, H.	1/ 2/41
Crofts, A. (Lt. late R.C.A.)	1/ 2/41
Naylor, A.	1/ 2/41
Ancliffe, J.	1/ 2/41
Heath, T. H.	1/ 2/41
Barber, P.	1/ 2/41
Beresford, T. W.	1/ 2/41
Haywood, C. R.	1/ 2/41
Foers, W. A.	1/ 2/41
Bishop, W. E.	1/ 2/41
Howson, R. H.	1/ 2/41
Oldham, C. P.	1/ 2/41
Clarke, W. G.	1/ 7/41
Houghton, J.	24/ 7/41

Adjutant & Quarter-Master

Medical Officer

Rawlin, Maj. B. D.	19/ 6/41

YORKSHIRE AREA - contd.

HALLAMSHIRE ZONE - contd.

ROTHERHAM GROUP - contd.

63rd WEST RIDING (ROTHERHAM) BATTALION

Lt.-Colonel

Pickering, B. H. (Capt late T.A.) (Res. of Off.) 1/ 2/41

Majors

Gullick, G. M. (Capt. late The King's R.) 1/ 2/41
Ellis, P. W. (Lt. late R.E.) 1/ 2/41
Scattergood, J. H., M.C. (Lt. late R.F.A.) 1/ 2/41
Bovill, P. J. C. (Lt. late R.A.S.C.) 1/ 2/41

Captains

Higham, J. J. (2/Lt. late Foresters) 1/ 2/41
Robinson, H. (2/Lt. late K.O.Y.L.I.) 1/ 2/41
Bland, F. 1/ 2/41

Lieutenants

Amey, N. F. (Lt. late R.M.) 1/ 2/41
Mills, F. (2/Lt. late Lincoln R.) 1/ 2/41
Carter, B. (Lt. late R.A.O.C.) 1/ 2/41
Hart, F. A. 1/ 2/41
Hossack, G. A 1/ 2/41
Smith, P. J. S. (2/Lt. late Y. & L.R.) 1/ 2/41
Wild, W. 1/ 2/41
Davis, F. A. 1/ 2/41
Ganderton, J. 1/ 2/41
Walker, F. W., M.M. 1/ 2/41
Boyle, J. A. 1/ 2/41

Lieutenants - contd.

Bowdrey, G. W. 1/ 2/41
Lidgett, L., M.M. 1/ 2/41
Milner, W. A. (Lt. late Gen. List) 1/ 2/41
Haynes, S. 1/ 2/41
Ducker, W. 1/ 2/41
Clarkson, H. 19/ 5/41

2nd Lieutenants

Atter, J. T. 1/ 2/41
Wright, C., D.C.M. 1/ 2/41
Crabtree, J. 1/ 2/41
Barber, W. G., M.M. 1/ 2/41
Wild, R. S. 1/ 2/41
Batty, J. C. 1/ 2/41
Wrigley, F. G. 1/ 2/41
Lickorish, J. 1/ 2/41
Powell, J. 1/ 2/41
Wainwright, J. 12/ 5/41
Stones, W. G. 19/ 5/41
Dawson, C. (Lt. late R.A.S.C.) 19/ 7/41

Adjutant & Quarter-Master

Medical Officer

Kemp, Maj. G. S. L. (Capt. late R.A.M.C.) 28/ 5/41

YORKSHIRE AREA - contd.

HALLAMSHIRE ZONE - contd.

SHEFFIELD GROUP

Commander	Branson, Col. D.S., D.S.O., M.C. T.D., A.D.C. (Col. T.A.)	1/ 2/41
Assistant to Commander	Lockwood, Maj. D. E. (Maj. T.A. Res.)	20/ 6/41
Assistant to Commander	Branson, Capt. P. A. (Capt. late Y. & L.R.)	1/ 2/41

64th WEST RIDING (SHEFFIELD) BATTALION

Lt.-Colonel

Smith, W. McK., D.S.O., T.D. (Col. ret. T.A.)	1/ 2/41

Majors

Caufield-Giles, H. R. (Maj. late R.A.)	1/ 2/41
Steel, G. (Capt. late R. Fus.)	1/ 2/41

Captains

Ramsbotham, W. H. (Bt. Col. late Artists Rifles)	1/ 2/41
Howes, S. R. (Lt. late M.G. Corps)	1/ 2/41
Pickering, W. (2/Lt. late T.A. Res.)	1/ 2/41
Barraclough, H. C.	1/ 2/41
Middleton, T. R. (Lt. late R.E.)	1/ 2/41

Lieutenants

Smith, S. (Capt. late R.A.F.)	1/ 2/41
Gorman, M. W. (Lt. late Mon. R.)	1/ 2/41
Hinds, A., M.C. (Capt. late Y. & L.R.)	1/ 2/41
Kenworthy, J. A.	1/ 2/41
Andrew, T. R. (2/Lt. late M.G. Corps)	1/ 2/41
Stewart, J. MacK.	1/ 2/41
Sanderson, H.	1/ 2/41
Banham, G. E.	1/ 2/41
Robertson, D. M.	1/ 2/41
Lewis, H.	1/ 2/41
Place, C. H. (2/Lt. late R.A.F.)	1/ 2/41
Hallas, E.	1/ 2/41
Marshall, T.	1/ 2/41
Hughes, R. E.	1/ 2/41
Brooks, H.	1/ 2/41
Taverner, G. H.	1/ 2/41
Elliott, H. E. (2/Lt. late T.A. Res.)	1/ 2/41
Statham, I. C. F.	1/ 2/41

2nd Lieutenants

Raby, F., M.M. (Lt. late R.F.A.)	1/ 2/41

56455-6 (125)

2nd Lieutenants - contd.

Smith, H.	1/ 2/41
Newbold, J. W.	1/ 2/41
Buxton, C., M.M.	1/ 2/41
Price, T. W.	1/ 2/41
Nutt, W. D.	1/ 2/41
Dixon, W. H.	1/ 2/41
Tucker, R. C.	1/ 2/41
Blanch, N.	1/ 2/41
Harris, F. C. G.	1/ 2/41
Howie, T. W.	1/ 2/41
Bee, L. G.	12/ 6/41
Buckmaster, G. A., M.M.	12/ 6/41
Charles, R. (Lt. late R.F.A.)	12/ 6/41
Darnell, C. T.	12/ 6/41
Gaffney, J. E.	12/ 6/41
Gilham, H. D.	12/ 6/41
Hill, J.	12/ 6/41
Jackson, S. A.	12/ 6/41
Laurence, A., D.C.M.	12/ 6/41
Mason, J. L.	12/ 6/41
Morris, R. G.	12/ 6/41
Priestley, J. E.	12/ 6/41
Quarmby, G. G.	12/ 6/41
Walker, D.	12/ 6/41
Cutler, G. F.	12/ 6/41
Joy, J. D.	12/ 6/41
Aughton. S.	26/ 6/41

Adjutant & Quarter-Master

Medical Officer

Paine, Maj. C. G., M.D.	17/ 5/41

YORKSHIRE AREA - contd.

HALLAMSHIRE ZONE - contd.

SHEFFIELD GROUP - contd.

65th WEST RIDING (SHEFFIELD) BATTALION

Lt.-Colonel

Holmstrom, F. R., (Lt. Comdr. ret. R.N.) 1/ 2/41

Majors

Freeman, H. G. (Capt. Res. of off.) 1/ 2/41
Lee, G. W. (Maj. late R.E.) 1/ 2/41
Deakin, N. (2/Lt. late A. & S.H.) 1/ 2/41
English, G. W. (Maj. late R.A.S.C.) 1/ 2/41
Firth, M. M., (Lt. late T.A.) 1/ 2/41
Newton, S. G., O.B.E., (Maj. late K.O.Y.L.I.) 1/ 2/41
Potts, W. W. (Lt. late R.E.) 1/ 2/41
Wragg, D. 1/ 2/41

Captains

Buckler, H. V. W. 1/ 2/41
Grace, G. L. (2/Lt. late R.A.F.) 1/ 2/41
Hanes, J. P. (Lt. late K.O.Y.L.I.) 1/ 2/41
Hawley, D. D., M.C. (Capt. Y. & L.R.) 1/ 2/41
Hill, C. M., M.C., (Capt. late Y. & L.R.) 1/ 2/41
Myers, C. (Capt. late King's R.) 1/ 2/41
Pye-Smith, B. C. 1/ 2/41
Pryce, W. H., O.B.E. (Maj. ret.) 1/ 2/41
Richards, W. N. (Capt. late Ind. Army) 1/ 2/41
Ruddy, R. H. 1/ 2/41
Russell, H. B. (Lt. late M.G. Corps) 1/ 2/41
Sayers, D. P. 1/ 2/41

Captains - contd.

Squire, J. F. (2/Lt. late R.E.) 1/ 2/41
Staniforth, J. A. R. 1/ 2/41
Starling, F. A. (2/Lt. late R.A.F.) 1/ 2/41
Twivey, H. F. 1/ 2/41
Woodward, W. J. (Lt. late North'd. Fus.) 1/ 2/41
Heathcote, J. W. 1/ 2/41

Lieutenants

Avis, P. S., M.C. (Lt. late R.E.) 1/ 2/41
Askin, H. (2/Lt. late R. Mar.) 1/ 2/41
Baigent, G. G. 1/ 2/41
Bingham, G. A. 1/ 2/41
Board, H. 1/ 2/41
Dalton, W. 1/ 2/41
Dixon, J. B. 1/ 2/41
Dolphin, C. H. 1/ 2/41
Cole, E. S. 1/ 2/41
Flatters, W. G., M.C., D.C.M., (Lt. late R.E.) 1/ 2/41
Gibson, W. J. 1/ 2/41
Giles, G. W. 1/ 2/41
Green, W. L., M.C., M.M. (Capt. late Foresters) 1/ 2/41
Garton, J. W. 1/ 2/41
Hadfield, A. B. 1/ 2/41
Hutcheson, C. R. (2/Lt. late Black Watch) 1/ 2/41
Hurst, G. 1/ 2/41
Jack, D. J., M.C., (Maj. Bt. Lt.-Col. T.A. Res.) 1/ 2/41
Joyce, P. 1/ 2/41
Leet, E. (Maj. late R.F.A.) 1/ 2/41
Lacey, P. W. 1/ 2/41
McWhinnie, J. 1/ 2/41
Nelson, W. V. (Lt. late Welch R.) 1/ 2/41
Parkin, E. H. 1/ 2/41
Powell, J. 1/ 2/41
Procter, J. W. 1/ 2/41
Purse, W. J. 1/ 2/41

YORKSHIRE AREA - contd.

HALLAMSHIRE ZONE - contd.

SHEFFIELD GROUP - contd.

65th West Riding (Sheffield) Battalion - contd.

Lieutenants - contd.

Revitt, C., M.C. (Lt. late Y. & L.R.)	1/ 2/41
Rimmington, H. (Lt. late K.O.Y.L.I.)	1/ 2/41
Smith, S.	1/ 2/41
Young, L. G. (Lt. late Foresters)	1/ 2/41
Wells, C.	1/ 2/41
Wright, W.	1/ 2/41
Woodward, E. A.	1/ 2/41
Williams, H. T. (Lt. late Ind. Army)	1/ 2/41
Wade, T. P.	1/ 2/41
Varley, J. S.	1/ 2/41
Turner, O. M., M.C. (Capt. late R.F.A.)	1/ 2/41
Traviss, G. G., (Lt. late R.A.F.)	1/ 2/41
Stubbs, G. H., M.M.	1/ 2/41
Somerset, B.	1/ 2/41
Holman, L.	1/ 2/41

2nd Lieutenants

Greaves, W. B. (Lt. late K.O.Y.L.I.)	1/ 2/41
Gordon, J. A.	1/ 2/41
Goodwin, J. L.	1/ 2/41
Gegg, C. C.	1/ 2/41
Frost, S. B.	1/ 2/41
Dodson, T. P.	1/ 2/41
Crookes, C. W.	1/ 2/41
Crick, J.	1/ 2/41
Clapperton, J. F.	1/ 2/41
Chambers, J. D.	1/ 2/41
Burrell, J. C. E.	1/ 2/41
Ballington, G. H.	1/ 2/41
Ashforth, E.	1/ 2/41
Archer, J. A.	1/ 2/41
Harris, B. T.	1/ 2/41
Hallam, C.	1/ 2/41

2nd Lieutenants - contd.

Hammond, W.	1/ 2/41
Harrison, T. C.	1/ 2/41
Hayward, P. H., D.C.M.	1/ 2/41
Hiller, A. P.	1/ 2/41
Holt, E.	1/ 2/41
Hobson, H. W.	1/ 2/41
Horner, F.	1/ 2/41
Ingram, P.	1/ 2/41
Johnson, R. H.	1/ 2/41
Jones, F.	1/ 2/41
Ley, W. H.	1/ 2/41
Moody, R.	1/ 2/41
Neale, R. C. W.	1/ 2/41
Phipp, G.	1/ 2/41
Rodgers, A.	1/ 2/41
Roper, W.	1/ 2/41
Rew, L. H.	1/ 2/41
Shaw, S. C.	1/ 2/41
Soar, M.	1/ 2/41
Webster, J. A.	1/ 2/41
Young, W.	1/ 2/41
Hall, E. G.	24/ 3/41
Salmon, F. J.	3/ 5/41
Cusick, V. A., M.M.	3/ 5/41
May, J.	9/ 5/41
Mellor, H. M.	13/ 5/41
Greensmith, D. G.	24/ 5/41

Adjutant & Quarter-Master

Medical Officer

Lees, Maj. G. H., (2/Lt. late Cameronians)	1/ 2/41

YORKSHIRE AREA - contd.
HALLAMSHIRE ZONE - contd.
SHEFFIELD GROUP - contd.

66th WEST RIDING (SHEFFIELD) BATTALION

Lt.-Colonel

Middleton, W., T.D. (Col. ret. T.A.)	1/ 2/41

Majors

Wever, R. O., O.B.E., M.C., T.D. (Col. late T.A.)	1/ 2/41
Pashley, J. (Maj. late R.F.A.)	1/ 2/41
Hargreaves, R. (Lt. late H.A.C.)	1/ 2/41
Tyzack, W. A. (Capt. late Y. & L.R.)	1/ 2/41
Bostock, W.	1/ 2/41

Captains

Grayson, R. B. (Lt. late R.A.)	1/ 2/41
Laver, A. (Flying Offr. late R.A.F.)	1/ 2/41
Mole, H. V. (Lt. late R.G.A.)	1/ 2/41
Rouse, J. (Capt. late Lan. Fus.)	1/ 2/41
Wincott, A. L. (Lt. late Lincoln R.)	1/ 2/41

Lieutenants

Ward, E. A. V., M.C. (Capt. late R.E.)	1/ 2/41
Allport, C. J.	1/ 2/41
Atkinson, A.	1/ 2/41
Brocklehurst, R. W. (2/Lt. late Oxf. &. Bucks L.I.)	1/ 2/41
Brook, A. E. (Maj. late R.E.)	1/ 2/41
Caunt, J.	1/ 2/41
Cavey, G. W.	1/ 2/41
Cotterell, E. G.	1/ 2/41
Daman, C. W. B. (Lt. late R.E.)	1/ 2/41
Forsdike, L. (Lt. late K.O.Y.L.I.)	1/ 2/41
Haigh, M.	1/ 2/41
Hamilton, C. W. (Capt. late R.A.F.)	1/ 2/41
Harrison, J. G. (Lt. late M.G. Corps)	1/ 2/41
Hyde, E.	1/ 2/41
Kirkby, R. A. (Lt. late R.E.)	1/ 2/41
May, R.	1/ 2/41
Murfin, H. S. (Lt. late R.A.)	1/ 2/41
Nicholson, F., M.C. (Capt. late W. York R.)	1/ 2/41
Pochin, G. D. (Capt. late Manch. R.)	1/ 2/41
Pratt, C. R.	1/ 2/41
Ragg, W.	1/ 2/41
Raworth, E. L. (Capt. late R.A.F.)	1/ 2/41
Rhodes, S.	1/ 2/41
Roos, C. B. (Capt. late R.E.)	1/ 2/41

Lieutenants - contd.

Simpkin, A. L., M. C. (Lt. late Y. & L.R.)	1/ 2/41
Stacey, A. D. (Lt. late S. Stafford R.)	1/ 2/41
Teather, G. J. (2/Lt. late R.A.F.)	1/ 2/41
Ward, H. E. (Capt. late The Buffs.)	1/ 2/41
Warren, S. S. (Lt. late Ind. Army)	1/ 2/41
Wildblood, J. W.	1/ 2/41
Wood, G. W.	1/ 2/41

2nd Lieutenants

Gill, F. M.	1/ 2/41
Hinson, J. J.	1/ 2/41
Nicol, R. (Lt. late M.G. Corps.)	1/ 2/41
Angus, T. C. (Lt. late Scots. Rif.)	1/ 2/41
Atha, M.	1/ 2/41
Blagden, A.	1/ 2/41
Cowley, J. C.	1/ 2/41
Driver, H. (Lt. late R.F.A.)	1/ 2/41
Eglen, C. E.	1/ 2/41
Ford, E. A. (Lt. late London R.)	1/ 2/41
Gray, R. W. (Capt. late R. North'd. Fus.)	1/ 2/41
Haughton, C. S.	1/ 2/41
King-Cox R.	1/ 2/41
Laver, J.	1/ 2/41
Macallum, A. H. (Capt. late Ind. Army)	1/ 2/41
MacDougall, A. J.	1/ 2/41
Newton, H. (Lt. late Y. & L.R.)	1/ 2/41
Organ, W. W. (Lt. late R.A.)	1/ 2/41
Oxley, T. A. (Lt. T.A. Res.)	1/ 2/41
Shaw, R. B.	1/ 2/41
Slater, L. (2/Lt. late R.A.F.)	1/ 2/41
Smith, F. B. (Lt. late Lincoln R.)	1/ 2/41
Utley, D. M.	1/ 2/41
Welbourn, H. C. (Lt. late R.A.F.)	1/ 2/41
Wolstenholme, W. H.	1/ 2/41
Wright, A.	1/ 2/41
Jenkins, J. S.	28/ 6/41

Adjutant & Quarter-Master

Medical Officer

Davies, Maj. F., M.D.,	1/ 2/41

YORKSHIRE AREA - contd.

HALLAMSHIRE ZONE - contd.

SHEFFIELD GROUP - contd.

67th WEST RIDING (SHEFFIELD) BATTALION

Lt.-Colonel

Wilkinson, E. W., O.B.E., T.D., (Bt.-Col. T.A. Res.) 1/2/41

Majors

Bibby, J. V., D.S.O., (Maj. late R. North'd. Fus.) 1/2/41
Eardley, H. I. (Capt. late R.A.F.) 1/2/41
Dixon, W. M. (Maj. late Y. & L.R.) 1/2/41
Joyce, E. M. H., M.M. (Lt. late R.A.) 1/2/41
Howard, G. F. (Capt. late K.R.R.C.) 1/2/41

Captains

Hoult, E. (Capt. late Y. & L.R.) 1/2/41
Williams, S. B., (Capt. late R.T.C.) 1/2/41
Thomas, J. M. (Lt. late Cheshire R.) 1/2/41
Goodall, J. A. (Lt. late R.A.O.C.) 1/2/41

Lieutenants

Heron, T. E., M.C., (Capt. late R. North'd. Fus.) 1/2/41
Green, B. B., M.C. (Capt. late Y. & L.R.) 1/2/41
Lee, P. E. (Lt. late T.A.) 1/2/41
Ramsden, J. W., M.M. 1/2/41
Jeffrey, D. C. (Capt. late R.A.) 1/2/41
Everitt, T. A. (Lt. late R.F.A.) 1/2/41
Spafford, A. V., M.C., (Lt. late O.W.R.) 1/2/41

Lieutenants - contd.

Hostombe, E. R. 1/2/41
Powell, E. K. 1/2/41
Styring, E. W., (Capt. late The King's R.) 1/2/41
Winter, L. B., (2/Lt. late R.F.A.) 1/2/41
Wilson, D. L., (Capt. late Ind. Army) 1/2/41
Kirkbride, R. B. 1/2/41

2nd Lieutenants

McLean, G. McI. 1/2/41
Nichols, O. S., M.C. (Lt. late R.F.A.) 1/2/41
Judge, J. W. S., (Lt. late Y. & L.R.) 1/2/41
Inglis, G. B. D., (2/Lt. late A. & S.H.) 1/2/41
Gent, H. S. (Lt. late M.G. Corps). 1/2/41
Cheetham, W. H. 1/2/41
Hebbert, C. O. 1/2/41
Wood, H. O. 1/2/41
Hallett, L. G. 1/2/41
Wilshaw, W. 1/2/41
Atherton, J. 1/2/41
Macbeth, G. 1/2/41
Creswick, W. 1/2/41
Bain, S. 2/7/41
Mill, A. R. 2/7/41
Egan, P. G. 2/7/41

Adjutant & Quarter-Master

Medical Officer

YORKSHIRE AREA - contd.

HALLAMSHIRE ZONE - contd.

SHEFFIELD GROUP - contd.

68th WEST RIDING (SHEFFIELD) BATTALION

Lt.-Colonel

Mackenzie, A. F. (Lt. late T.A.) 1/ 2/41

Majors

Marvin, E. M., M.C. (Maj. late R.E.) 1/ 2/41
Collier, P. P. (Maj. late R.E.) 1/ 2/41
Johnson, D. G. 1/ 2/41
Winch, L. A., (Lt. late R.F.A.) 1/ 2/41
Watson, F. L. (2/Lt. late Hampshire R.) 1/ 2/41

Captains

Young, T. A. 1/ 2/41
Dawes, C. 1/ 2/41
Hopkins, B. F. 1/ 2/41
Abrahams, F., M.C. (Lt. late R.F.A.) 1/ 2/41
Sanders, A. J., (Lt. late H.L.I.) 1/ 2/41

Lieutenants

Browne, D. 1/ 2/41
Jackson, S. F. 1/ 2/41
Bull, E. (Lt. late Y. & L.R.) 1/ 2/41
Hollingworth, J. W. 1/ 2/41
Rigby, A. G. (2/Lt. late Border R.) 1/ 2/41
Bywaters, H. W. 1/ 2/41

2nd Lieuteants

Ibbotson, D. 1/ 2/41
Wrigley, R. 1/ 2/41
Hobson, A. M. 1/ 2/41
McLagan, L. A. J. 1/ 2/41
Wilson, T. E. 1/ 2/41
Ibbotson, W. 1/ 2/41
Quarrell, A. G. 1/ 2/41
Shepherd, M. C. 1/ 2/41
Oscroft, C. 1/ 2/41
Roebuck, J. C. 1/ 2/41
Taylor, J. A. 1/ 2/41
Mears, R. E. 1/ 2/41
Hancock, J. N. 1/ 2/41
Hobson, J. 1/ 2/41
Maxwell, J. H. 1/ 2/41
Thompson, H. (2/Lt. late Y. & L.R.) 1/ 2/41
Graham, A. M. 1/ 2/41
Shirley, H. 1/ 2/41
Reeve, R. A. 1/ 2/41
Stafford, H. 1/ 2/41

Adjutant & Quarter-Master

Medical Officer

Clark, Maj. G. A., V.D. (Surg. Cr. late R.N.V.R.) 1/ 2/41

YORKSHIRE AREA - contd.

HALLAMSHIRE ZONE - contd.

SHEFFIELD GROUP - contd.

69th WEST RIDING (SHEFFIELD) BATTALION

Lt.-Colonel

Howson, W., M.C., T.D. (Bt.Col. ret. T.A.)	1/ 2/41

Majors

Bradley, E. R.	1/ 2/41
Hartmann, B. A. (Lt. late Somerset L.I.)	1/ 2/41
Pearson, N. A., (Lt. late Durham L.I.)	1/ 2/41
Johnston, W. (Capt. late Y. & L.R.)	1/ 2/41
Jones, T. W.	1/ 2/41
Lant, A. (2/Lt. late York R.)	1/ 2/41
Longden, J., M.M. (2/Lt. late Y. & L.R.)	1/ 2/41
Pearson, F.	1/ 2/41

Captains

Barnard, J.	1/ 2/41
Buckle, R.	1/ 2/41
Hall, C. G.	1/ 2/41
Hughes, R. P., (Lt. late R.W. Fus.)	1/ 2/41
Lee, H., (Lt. late Y. & L.R.)	1/ 2/41
Proctor, A. H.	1/ 2/41
Steele, E.	1/ 2/41
Walker, J. W.	1/ 2/41
Wilson, G. A. (Lt. late R.G.A.)	1/ 2/41

Lieutenants

Adams, J. E. C.	1/ 2/41
Allen, G. N.	1/ 2/41

Lieutenants - contd.

Allison, P.	1/ 2/41
Attwood, M. V.	1/ 2/41
Barber, C. E.	1/ 2/41
Brown, S.	1/ 2/41
Burnett, T.	1/ 2/41
Buxton, H. L. (Lt. late R.E.)	1/ 2/41
Dick, W. R.	1/ 2/41
Fretwell, J. F. E.	1/ 2/41
Gooseman, E.	1/ 2/41
Green, M.	1/ 2/41
Hannan, H.	1/ 2/41
Hawley, T. M.	1/ 2/41
Healey, S. H. A.	1/ 2/41
Hill, D.	1/ 2/41
Hitchcock, E.	1/ 2/41
Horlock, C. F.	1/ 2/41
Horsburgh, G. D. L.	1/ 2/41
Horsefield, H.	1/ 2/41
Horner, I. (Lt. late Lan. Fus.)	1/ 2/41
Hunneybell, G. E. H.	1/ 2/41
Lent, A.	1/ 2/41
Mankell, E. H.	1/ 2/41
Morrison, J. (2/Lt. late D.W.R.)	1/ 2/41
Naylor, H.	1/ 2/41
Oliver, F. R.	1/ 2/41
Phillips, E. A.	1/ 2/41
Rhodes, W. G.	1/ 2/41
Ridgway, E. W.	1/ 2/41
Rowley, E. L. (Lt. late R.E.)	1/ 2/41
Rowley, F. E.	1/ 2/41
Sanderson, A. A.	1/ 2/41
Siddall, A.	1/ 2/41
Smeeton, S. E.	1/ 2/41
Soloman, E.	1/ 2/41
Stone, J. W.	1/ 2/41
Summerfield, R.	1/ 2/41
Wilks, H.	1/ 2/41
Williams, R. J.	1/ 2/41
Wolstenholme, A.	1/ 2/41
Smith, J. W.	29/ 3/41

YORKSHIRE AREA - contd.

HALLAMSHIRE ZONE - contd.

SHEFFIELD GROUP - contd.

69th West Riding (Sheffield) Battalion - contd.

2nd Lieutenants

Bateman, A. W.	1/ 2/41
Bloomfield, S. T.	1/ 2/41
Howe, C.	1/ 2/41
Broughton, C. T.	1/ 2/41
Budden, R. W. W.	1/ 2/41
Clarke, F. D.	1/ 2/41
Fisher, G.	1/ 2/41
Hunt, S. G.	1/ 2/41
Kirkman, F.	1/ 2/41
Leggett, W. A.	1/ 2/41
Lewis, L.	1/ 2/41
Marshall, E. A.	1/ 2/41
Mattock, F. S.	1/ 2/41
Middleton, W. H., (2/Lt. late D.C.L.I.)	1/ 2/41
Noakes, E. J.	1/ 2/41
Noble, W.	1/ 2/41
Oakes, F.	1/ 2/41
Pagett, G. A.	1/ 2/41
Palmer, G.	1/ 2/41
Parker, R. M.	1/ 2/41
Pont, H. F.	1/ 2/41
Saxby, S.	1/ 2/41
Turner, H. H.	1/ 2/41
Wainwright, A.	1/ 2/41
Walker, J. B.	1/ 2/41
Woodrow, T. C.	1/ 2/41
Satterfitt, T.	29/ 3/41
Spalding, C. W.	29/ 3/41
Webster, T.	29/ 3/41
Furness, R. F.	11/ 6/41
Burden, H. M.	23/ 6/41
Cowen, A.	23/ 6/41
Hawdin, W.	23/ 6/41
Tomlinson, C.	23/ 6/41
Reilly, G. B.	9/ 7/41

Adjutant & Quarter-Master

Medical Officer

Harding, Maj. H. E., (Maj. T.A. Res.)	1/ 2/41

NORTH MIDLAND AREA

General Staff Officer, 1st grade	Paynter, Col. G. C. B., C.M.G., C.V.O., D.S.O. (Extra Eq. to the King)	1/ 4/41

DERBYSHIRE ZONE

Commander	Walthall, Col. E. C. W. D., C.M.G., D.S.O. (Hon. Brig.-Gen. ret. pay)	1/ 2/41
Assistant to Commander	Thorton, Maj. T., M.C. (Capt. ret. pay)	1/ 2/41
Territorial Army Association administering	The Derbyshire T.A. & A.F. Association, 1, Uttoxeter Rd., Derby.	

N.W. GROUP

Commander	Brooke-Taylor, Col. E. M., M.C., T.D.	1/ 2/41
Assistant to Commander	Parr, Capt. C. J. (Lt. late Cheshire R.)	1/ 2/41

1st DERBYSHIRE (BAKEWELL) BATTALION

Lt.-Colonel

Wales, G. N. (Capt. late T.A.)	1/ 2/41

Majors

Hill, G. B., O.B.E. (Capt. late Y. & L.R.)	1/ 2/41
Douglas, H. (Capt. late Foresters)	1/ 2/41
Baldwin, H. T. (Lt. late Y. & L.R.)	1/ 2/41

Captains

Tait, J. B. (Flt./Cmdr. late R.A.F.)	1/ 2/41
Pryce, J. B. H. (2/Lt. late S. Stafford R.)	1/ 2/41
Britland, H.	9/ 7/41

Lieutenants

Dakin, H. C. (2/Lt. late R.F.C.)	1/ 2/41
Wheatley, J. L.	1/ 2/41
Cradock-Hartopp, L. M. (Maj. ret. pay)	1/ 2/41
Towler, E. W. J. (Sub.-Lt. late R.N.V.R.)	1/ 2/41
Roe, W. E.	1/ 2/41
Stanion, O. B. (Lt. late Can. Mil. Forces)	1/ 2/41
Lymn, C. R. (Capt. late R.A.F.)	1/ 2/41
Wildgoose, H. E. (Lt. late Foresters)	1/ 2/41
Davis, G. G. J.	1/ 2/41
Thompson, R. W. S.	1/ 2/41
Bower, E. (Lt. late R.A.F.)	1/ 2/41
Jago, J. W. (Capt. late Foresters)	1/ 2/41
McKean, R.	1/ 2/41
Fisher, E.	1/ 2/41

NORTH MIDLAND AREA - contd.

DERBYSHIRE ZONE - contd.

N.W. GROUP - contd.

1st Derbyshire (Bakewell) Battalion - contd.

Lieutenants - contd.

Francis, M. H. (Capt. ret. Ind. Army)	1/ 2/41
Irwin, H. J. (Lt. late R. Mar.)	1/ 2/41
Cockerton, R. W. P.	1/ 2/41
Gibbins, G. E.	1/ 2/41
Key, S.	9/ 7/41

2nd Lieutenants

Dakin, W. J.	1/ 2/41
Brierley, A. (Capt. late R.G.A.)	1/ 2/41
Robinson, W. S.	1/ 2/41
Millar, W. A.	1/ 2/41
Plowright, R. (2/Lt. late R.A.S.C.)	1/ 2/41
Sinclair, C. E.	1/ 2/41
Broome, J.	1/ 2/41
Caudwell, E.	1/ 2/41
Fowkes, S.	1/ 2/41
Wildgoose, L. W. (Lt. late Foresters)	1/ 2/41
Keatley, C. F.	1/ 2/41
McElroy, W. E.	1/ 2/41
Mobley, A., D.C.M.	1/ 2/41
Murphy, P. D. N.	1/ 2/41
Gowers, W. B. (Lt. late R.N.V.R.)	1/ 2/41
Bramwell, F., M.C. (Lt. late R.A.)	1/ 2/41
Merrill, S.	1/ 2/41
Gregory, P.	1/ 2/41
Davison, F. H.	1/ 2/41
O'Dowda, B., M.C. (Capt. late R.E.)	1/ 2/41
Hodgson, S.	1/ 2/41
Whitehead, M. J. (Lt. late Y. & L.R.)	1/ 2/41

2nd Lieutenants - contd.

Flather, D. G.	1/ 2/41
How, E. V.	1/ 2/41
Jakeman, R.	1/ 2/41
Hodgson, J. F. M.	1/ 2/41
Osborne, G. T. D.	18/ 6/41
Simcock, J. T.	18/ 6/41
Marsden, G. H.	9/ 7/41

Adjutant & Quarter-Master

Medical Officer

56455-6(134)

NORTH MIDLAND AREA - contd.

DERBYSHIRE ZONE - contd.

N.W. GROUP - contd.

2nd DERBYSHIRE (BUXTON) BATTALION

Lt.-Colonel

Lings, H. C., D.S.O. (Maj. late T.A.) 1/ 2/41

Majors

Peach, L. du G. (Lt. late Manch. R.) 1/ 2/41
Turner, A. P. 1/ 2/41
Boddington, J. E. (Capt. late Manch. R.) 1/ 2/41
Sewell, L. G., M.C. (Capt. late Aust. Imp. Forces) 1/ 2/41
Hoyle, P. N. (Lt. late R.A.F.) 1/ 2/41
Flanders, C. D. 1/ 2/41

Captains

Mycock, F. A. (Lt. late Foresters) 1/ 2/41
Drewry, G. H. (Lt. late R.F.A.) 1/ 2/41
Barker, J. E. (Capt. late Foresters) 1/ 2/41
Riddick, J. D. (Capt. late M.G.A.) 1/ 2/41

Lieutenants

Gregory, G. 1/ 2/41
Mason, A. H. 1/ 2/41
Pemberton, A. S. 1/ 2/41
Rainford, H. (Lt. late Ind. Army) 1/ 2/41
Frater, T. F. 1/ 2/41
Horner, G. S. 1/ 2/41
Davenport, G. R., M.M. 1/ 2/41
Hughes, O. M. 1/ 2/41
Ratcliffe, J. F. 1/ 2/41
Beswick, P. J. 1/ 2/41
Maughan, G. K. K. (Capt. T.A. Res.) 1/ 2/41
Pickworth-Hutchinson, J. (Lt. late Foresters) 1/ 2/41

Lieutenants - contd.

Woodruffe, J. 1/ 2/41
Smalley, E., D.S.O. (Lt.-Col. late Manch. R.) 1/ 2/41
Blood, R. 1/ 2/41
Francopula, J. (2/Lt. late R. Sussex R.) 5/ 4/41
Bowen, B. O. 6/ 4/41
Henriques, G. L. Q. (Lt. late Manch. R.) 8/ 4/41
Thompson, W. E. (Capt. late Foresters) 17/ 7/41

2nd Lieutenants

Harding, W. G. 1/ 2/41
Porter, H. J. (Lt. late The King's R.) 1/ 2/41
Grinshaw, H. C. 1/ 2/41
Cox, S. E. McG. (Lt. T.A. Res.) 1/ 2/41
Stead, M. (Capt. late E. Lan. R.) 1/ 2/41
Keyworth, J. 1/ 2/41
Salt, R. S. (Lt. late R.A.F.) 1/ 2/41
Leete, H. D. 1/ 2/41
Munslow, R. H. 1/ 2/41
Sutcliffe, T. A. 1/ 2/41
Brooks, G. H. 6/ 5/41
Gibbs, A. J. 28/ 6/41

Adjutant & Quarter-Master

McDonald, Capt. (actg. 26/4/41) D. W., Gen. List Inf. 26/ 4/41

Medical Officer

NORTH MIDLAND AREA - contd.

DERBYSHIRE ZONE - contd.

N.W. GROUP - contd.

3rd DERBYSHIRE (CHAPEL-EN-LE-FRITH) BATTALION

Lt.-Colonel

Entwisle, T., M.C. (Capt. late T.A.)	1/ 2/41

Majors

Dodds, W. E. (2/Lt. late K.O.Y.L.I.)	1/ 2/41
McIntosh, A. (2/Lt. late R.E.)	1/ 2/41
Lanceley, T., M.C. (Capt. late The King's R.)	1/ 2/41
Cochrane, J.	1/ 2/41
McArd, L.	1/ 2/41

Captains

Hudson, J. (Lt. late Border R.)	1/ 2/41
Capper, L. A. (Capt. late Cheshire R.)	1/ 2/41
Henry, J. (Maj. late R.S. Fus.)	1/ 2/41
Drinkwater, C.	1/ 2/41

Lieutenants

Harrap, F. L., M.C. (Lt. late Foresters)	1/ 2/41
Clements, L. (2/Lt. late R.E.)	1/ 2/41
Firth, F.	1/ 2/41
Seville, J., D.C.M.	1/ 2/41
Smith, C. C. (Lt. late M.G. Corps)	1/ 2/41
Beever, S. (Flt./Lt. late R.A.F.)	1/ 2/41
McDonnell, F. (Lt. late Foresters)	1/ 2/41
Hesketh, H. R. (Capt. late Manch. R.)	1/ 2/41
Hoyle, F. D., M.C. (Lt. late Foresters)	1/ 2/41
Webster, E. T.	1/ 2/41
Waterhouse, R. B.	1/ 2/41
Fox, W.	1/ 2/41
Flett, M.	1/ 2/41
Harrison, C.	1/ 2/41
Bullough, H. (2/Lt. late R.F.A.)	1/ 2/41
Foden, C.	1/ 2/41
Brindley, W. H., M.C. (Lt. late R.E.)	1/ 2/41
George, R. F.	1/ 2/41

2nd Lieutenants

Gwilliam, V. T.	1/ 2/41
Tallis, T. R.	1/ 2/41
Holmes, H. A.	1/ 2/41
Wood, J.	1/ 2/41
Casey, C. J. (Lt. late I. Rif.)	1/ 2/41
Haigh, J. W.	1/ 2/41
Gerrard, J., D.C.M., M.M. (2/Lt. R.S. Fus.)	1/ 2/41

2nd Lieutenants - contd.

Sewell, B. P.	1/ 2/41
Busby, G.	1/ 2/41
Fergusson, W. C.	1/ 2/41
Cotton, E. J.	1/ 2/41
Radcliffe, H. W.	1/ 2/41
Moring, F. H.	1/ 2/41
Russell, T. M.	1/ 2/41
Hanson, D. M. (Capt. late T.A.)	1/ 2/41
Pontefract, J. E.	1/ 2/41
Hanmer, J.	1/ 2/41
Wildgoose, J.	1/ 2/41
Beever, A.	1/ 2/41
Gaskell, W. (2/Lt. late R.A.)	1/ 2/41
Furniss, G. F.	1/ 2/41
Pearson, W.	1/ 2/41
Schofield, H.	1/ 2/41

Adjutant & Quarter-Master

Medical Officer

15th DERBYSHIRE (TIDESWELL) BATTALION

Lieutenant

Price, G.	24/ 7/41

2nd Lieutenants

Cooke, J. C. (Lt. late R.A.F.)	10/ 7/41
Grace, W.	24/ 7/41

NORTH MIDLAND AREA - contd.

DERBYSHIRE ZONE - contd.

N.E. GROUP

Commander	Tylden-Wright, Col. H. (Lt.-Col. late T.A.)	1/ 2/41
Assistant to Commander	Eyre, Capt. E. (Lt. late Foresters)	1/ 2/41

4th DERBYSHIRE (ECKINGTON) BATTALION

Lt.-Colonel

Archer, H. de B., M.C. (Capt. late T.A.)	1/ 2/41

Majors

Lucas, E., M.C. (Capt. late Y. & L.R.)	1/ 2/41
Walters, L. W. (Lt. late T.A.)	1/ 2/41
Drury, A. (Lt. late Y. & L.R.)	1/ 2/41
Hownsfield, T. D.	1/ 2/41
Marples, G. (Capt. late R.F.A.)	1/ 2/41

Captains

Fricker, N. (Lt. D. L. O. Yeo.)	1/ 2/41
Hartley, F. (Lt. late Green Howards)	1/ 2/41
Dobbs, J.	1/ 2/41
Wesley, A. G.	1/ 2/41

Lieutenants

Vincent, J. S.	1/ 2/41
Calow, C.	1/ 2/41
Glasby, G. W.	1/ 2/41
Fletcher, M. W.	1/ 2/41
Tooke, H. E.	1/ 2/41
Headworth, J. (2/Lt. late Y. & L.R.)	1/ 2/41
Hayes, H. C. (2/Lt. late R.A.F.)	1/ 2/41
Cocker, H.	1/ 2/41
Moore, G.	1/ 2/41
Cownley, A. B.	1/ 2/41
Dye, A. F.	1/ 2/41
Redfern, A. L.	1/ 2/41
Moxon, F. W., M.M.	1/ 2/41
Wilson, W. (Maj. late Derby Yeo.)	1/ 2/41
Cutts, L.	1/ 2/41

Lieutenants - contd.

Young, J. (Lt. late M.G. Corps)	1/ 2/41
Booth, F. G. H.	1/ 2/41
Williams, R. H.	1/ 2/41
Cook, A. (2/Lt. late North'd Fus.)	1/ 2/41
Robinson, C. H.	26/ 4/41

2nd Lieutenants

Heppenstall, A. (Lt. late Foresters)	1/ 2/41
Baron, V.	1/ 2/41
Presswood, R. W.	1/ 2/41
Newstead, W.	1/ 2/41
Copley, H. B.	1/ 2/41
Fells, E.	1/ 2/41
Parkin, G.	1/ 2/41
Stringfellow, J. T.	1/ 2/41
Newton, A.	1/ 2/41
Nettleship, G. D.	1/ 2/41
Robinson, W. S.	1/ 2/41
Oldham, L.	1/ 2/41
Griffith, T. E. A. (Lt. late R.A.F.)	1/ 2/41

Adjutant & Quarter-Master

Medical Officer

NORTH MIDLAND AREA - contd.

DERBYSHIRE ZONE - contd.

N.E. GROUP

5th DERBYSHIRE (BOLSOVER) BATTALION

Lt.-Colonel

North, C., M.C. (Lt. late Tank Corps)	1/ 2/41

Majors

Grice, G. P.	1/ 2/41
Russon, J. H.	
Wharton, H. A. (Lt. late M.G. Corps)	1/ 2/41
Winter, J.	1/ 2/41
Reay, C. H. (Flying Offr. late R.A.F.)	17/ 7/41

Captains

Bishop, D. H. O. (Lt. late T.A.)	1/ 2/41
Elmes, J.	1/ 2/41
Fletcher, R.	1/ 2/41

Lieutenants

Batty, S.	1/ 2/41
Charlesworth, H.	1/ 2/41
Dove, T. N., D.C.M.	1/ 2/41
Evans, J. G.	1/ 2/41
Lambeth, H.	1/ 2/41
Parr, H.	1/ 2/41
Robinson, J.	1/ 2/41
Ward, E.	1/ 2/41
Walker, G.	1/ 2/41
Wells, S. R.	1/ 2/41
Wheeler, W. F. (2/Lt. late R.A.F.)	1/ 2/41
Peach, C. T.	1/ 2/41
Goodman, W.	1/ 2/41
Atkinson, R. E.	1/ 2/41
Twidale, W.	1/ 2/41

2nd Lieutenants

Brown, W. E.	1/ 2/41
Brunton, H.	1/ 2/41
Cockayne, W.	1/ 2/41
Collier, A.	1/ 2/41
Findley, J.	1/ 2/41
Huntington, T. L.	1/ 2/41
Kirkman, W.	1/ 2/41
Noble, A., M.M.	1/ 2/41
Silkstone, G. F. E.	1/ 2/41
Trolley, A.	1/ 2/41
Weaver, J. B., D.C.M.	1/ 2/41
Whitlam, W.	1/ 2/41
Wyllie, R.	1/ 2/41

Adjutant & Quarter-Master

Woodhouse, Capt. (actg. 11/5/41) F. (ret. T.A.)	11/ 5/41

Medical Officer

6th DERBYSHIRE (CHESTERFIELD BOROUGH) BATTALION

Lt.-Colonel

Bird, J. E. (2/Lt. late Serv. Bn. W. Riding R.)	1/ 2/41

Majors

Hindle, G. W., M.C. (Maj. late R.W.K.)	1/ 2/41
Cutts, J. B. (Lt. late Green Howards)	1/ 2/41
Eyre, F. A. (Lt. late R.E.)	1/ 2/41

Captains

Fitzgerald, A. J.	1/ 2/41
Youle, W.	1/ 2/41
Brittlebank, F. S. J.	1/ 2/41
Scrimshaw, R. C.	1/ 2/41

Lieutenants

Waddington, W. F. (Lt. late Notts. Yeo.)	1/ 2/41
Toogood, A. C. G. (Lt. late Hampshire R.)	1/ 2/41
Kirk, G. A.	1/ 2/41
Turner, B., D.C.M.	1/ 2/41
Boulton, D. C.	1/ 2/41
Taylor, F. H.	1/ 2/41
Pates, A. F.	1/ 2/41
Hill, A. E.	1/ 2/41
Eshelby, F.	1/ 2/41
Todd, P.	1/ 2/41
Powell, E. R. L.	1/ 2/41
Slack, A. E.	1/ 2/41
Short, F. S.	1/ 2/41

2nd Lieutenants

Sullivan, J. C. (Lt. late Black Watch)	1/ 2/41
Birch, W.	1/ 2/41
Hubbock, O.	1/ 2/41
Brown, H. A. D.C.M. (2/Lt. late Foresters)	1/ 2/41
Allsopp, E. V.	1/ 2/41
Wing, H.	1/ 2/41
Ogden, F.	1/ 2/41
Harper, C. G.	1/ 2/41
Beeley, A. J.	1/ 2/41
Lipscombe, W. R.	1/ 2/41
Thompson, S. P.	1/ 2/41
Hooton, G. E.	1/ 2/41
Dickson, W.	1/ 2/41
Malson, W. E. C.	1/ 2/41
Bartle, S. J.	1/ 2/41

Adjutant & Quarter-Master

Medical Officer

Furniss, Maj. F. W.	26/ 6/41

NORTH MIDLAND AREA - contd.

DERBYSHIRE ZONE - contd.

N.E. GROUP - contd.

7th DERBYSHIRE (CHESTERFIELD COUNTY) BATTALION

Lt.-Colonel

Orange-Bromehead, J. W., M.C. (Lt.-Col. ret. pay) (Res. of Off.)	1/ 2/41

Majors

Cook, A. J. (Capt. T.A. Res.)	1/ 2/41
Mostyn-Owen, C. H., M.C. (Lt. late Foresters)	1/ 2/41
Hawley, R. J., M.C. (Lt. late Notts. Yeo.)	1/ 2/41
Smith, H. W.	1/ 2/41
Ford, E. L. (Lt. late R. W. Fus.)	1/ 2/41
Smartt, R. B. N. (2/Lt. late Inniskilling Fus.)	8/ 6/41

Captains

Wilcockson, E. K.	1/ 2/41
Rodley, S.	1/ 2/41
Greaves, H., D.S.O., M.C. (Lt. late Foresters)	1/ 2/41
Booth, J. N.	1/ 2/41
Tait, J. G.	1/ 2/41

Lieutenants

Marsh, W.	1/ 2/41
Rouse, W.	1/ 2/41
Brelsford, L.	1/ 2/41
Minchin, J.	1/ 2/41
Baxter, G.	1/ 2/41
Hibbard, H.	1/ 2/41
Mundy, A. W.	1/ 2/41
Meades, M., M.M.	1/ 2/41
Siddall, G.	1/ 2/41
Jeffrey, C. H.	1/ 2/41
Oxley, A. (2/Lt. late R.A.F.)	1/ 2/41
Rayner, J. S.	1/ 2/41
Pick, S. B.	1/ 2/41
Potts, E. W.	1/ 2/41
Naylor, G. R. (2/Lt. late Leicester R.)	1/ 2/41

Lieutenants - contd.

Simmonds, T., D.S.O., M.C., D.C.M. (Lt. late R.N.V.R.)	1/ 2/41
Turnbull, R. A. B.	1/ 2/41
Buxton, S. (Lt. late Leicester R.)	1/ 2/41
Allsop, W.	1/ 2/41
Croote, A.	23/ 7/41

2nd Lieutenants

Oakley, W.	1/ 2/41
Hill, J.	1/ 2/41
Frost, R.	1/ 2/41
Dakin, J.	1/ 2/41
Goodwin, W.	1/ 2/41
Scarborough, C. W.	1/ 2/41
Rooney, S.	1/ 2/41
Wells, H.	1/ 2/41
Naylor, C. H. B.	1/ 2/41
Darley, F.	1/ 2/41
Ashley, F.	1/ 2/41
Mawson, J. C.	1/ 2/41
Withnall, G. P. S.	1/ 2/41
Robinson, R. B.	1/ 2/41
Austin, H. E. D.	23/ 7/41
Westbury, E. A., D.C.M.	23/ 7/41

Adjutant & Quarter-Master

Buckston, Capt. (actg. 21/4/41) R. H. R., R.A.	21/ 4/41

Medical Officer

NORTH MIDLAND AREA - contd.

DERBYSHIRE ZONE - contd.

S.E. GROUP

Commander — Turbutt, Col. R. B. (Maj. ret. pay) 1/ 2/41

Second in Command — Jackson, Lt.-Col. G. R., M.C. 1/ 2/41

8th DERBYSHIRE (ALFRETON) BATTALION

Lt.-Colonel

Wrightson, T. O. (Lt. late R.A.F.)	1/ 2/41

Majors

Wright, E. F.	1/ 2/41
Burditt, F. T. (Lt. late Bedfs. & Herts. R.)	1/ 2/41
Gardner, G. F. (Capt. late Foresters)	1/ 2/41
Hunt, W. A.	1/ 2/41

Captains

Severn, F. D. (2/Lt. late Foresters)	1/ 2/41
Barnes, R. W.	1/ 2/41
Dixon, J. T.	1/ 2/41
Speight, H. F.	1/ 2/41

Lieutenants

Fountain, W. R.	1/ 2/41
Lineham, C. V.	1/ 2/41
Fox, W., M.M.	1/ 2/41
Mein, J. G. (Lt. late S. Lan. R.)	1/ 2/41
Davies, W. T. G. (Lt. late R.N.V.R.)	1/ 2/41
Hughes, A.	1/ 2/41
McNeish, A.	1/ 2/41
Walker, E.	1/ 2/41
Briddon, S. (Lt. late Foresters)	1/ 2/41
Hook, E. C.	1/ 2/41
Atkinson, A.	1/ 2/41
Barlow, J. F.	1/ 2/41
Pinchbeck, A. L.	1/ 2/41
Tristram, G. B.	1/ 2/41
Hallmark, R. L.	1/ 2/41
Riley, G. H.	1/ 2/41
Fletcher, J. S.	1/ 2/41
Holling, W. A.	1/ 2/41
Ashmore, B.	1/ 2/41
Bennett, F. W. C.	1/ 2/41
Dean, A., M.M.	1/ 2/41
Stevenson, F. M.	1/ 2/41
Harry, T.	1/ 2/41
Greaves, S. (Lt. late Foresters)	1/ 2/41
Nicholson, T. L.	1/ 2/41

Lieutenants - contd.

Williams, A. J.	1/ 2/41
Hill, E. J. H.	1/ 2/41
Webber, G. E.	1/ 2/41
Newman, H. R.	1/ 2/41
Marshall, J. R.	1/ 6/41
Watson, L. H.	3/ 7/41

2nd Lieutenants

Swindell, J.	1/ 2/41
Clarke, W. F.	1/ 2/41
Coleman, W.	1/ 2/41
Stooks, C. W.	1/ 2/41
Cope, W. C.	1/ 2/41
Willows, L.	1/ 2/41
Knight, L. A.	1/ 2/41
Smithurst, S. H.	1/ 2/41
Hogg, J. L.	1/ 2/41
Collier, G. H.	1/ 2/41
Marshall, H.	1/ 2/41
Mole, B. S.	1/ 2/41
Green, W. E.	1/ 2/41
Pickering, J.	1/ 2/41
Yeomans, W. F.	1/ 2/41
Brown, W. W.	1/ 2/41
Booth, I.	1/ 2/41
Dean, A.	1/ 2/41
Shardlow, W.	1/ 2/41
Merry, J. L.	1/ 2/41
Booth, E. T. P.	1/ 2/41
Westmoreland, H.	1/ 2/41
Good, F. J. (2/Lt. late Cheshire R.)	1/ 2/41
Beastall, J. W.	1/ 2/41
Wilson, H. F.	1/ 2/41

Adjutant & Quarter-Master

Medical Officer

Heffron, Maj. T., M.B.	3/ 7/41

NORTH MIDLAND AREA - contd.

DERBYSHIRE ZONE - contd.

S.E. GROUP - contd.

9th DERBYSHIRE (ILKESTON) BATTALION

Lt.-Colonel

Robinson, F. G. (Maj. late T.A.)	1/ 2/41

Majors

Thomas, E. L. B., (Lt. late 18th H.)	1/ 2/41
Westwood, J. L.	1/ 2/41
Davie, H. S. (Sub-Lt. late R.N.R.)	1/ 2/41
Hallam, H. V.	1/ 2/41
Wright, F. (Lt. late R. Norfolk R.)	1/ 2/41

Captains

Belfitt, N. P.	1/ 2/41
Burrows, G. K.	1/ 2/41
Travers, G. W.	1/ 2/41
Piper, W. J. F. (Capt. late Ind. Army.)	1/ 2/41
Scott, W.	1/ 2/41
Moll, V. R.	1/ 2/41

Lieutenants

Goodwin, J. W.	1/ 2/41
Hales, N. R.	1/ 2/41
Moore, C. V.	1/ 2/41
Barber, S.	1/ 2/41
Fielden, C. M., (Capt. late K.A.R.)	1/ 2/41
Flint, D. W., M.M. (2/Lt. late R.F.A.)	1/ 2/41
Rimington, J. W.	1/ 2/41
Durance, F. J.	1/ 2/41
Moore, C. A. S.	1/ 2/41
Shakespeare, F. J.	1/ 2/41
West, W.	1/ 2/41
Lane, E. T.	1/ 2/41
Gough, W. E.	1/ 2/41
Gilbert, W.	1/ 2/41
Laing, K.	1/ 2/41
Seaton, F. W. B.	1/ 2/41
Attenborrow, S. A.	1/ 2/41
Belfitt, J. G.	1/ 2/41
Ireland, R. B., M.C., (Capt. late R.E.)	1/ 2/41
Fisher, A.	1/ 2/41

Lieutenants - contd.

Oldham, W.	1/ 2/41
Blasdale, E. A.	1/ 2/41
Wood, S. R. (Lt. late R.G.A.)	1/ 2/41
Booth, A. (2/Lt. late Foresters.)	1/ 2/41
Tillett, J.	1/ 2/41
Collard, C.	1/ 2/41

2nd Lieutenants

Bacon, A. S.	1/ 2/41
Denton, B.	1/ 2/41
Barker, M. H.	1/ 2/41
Lemmon, J. T.	1/ 2/41
Admas, D. V.	1/ 2/41
Bastable, J. A.	1/ 2/41
Gregory, F. E.	1/ 2/41
Wearmouth, J. G.	1/ 2/41
Plackett, B.	1/ 2/41
Waddoups, H. L.	1/ 2/41
Russell, G. W.	1/ 2/41
Evans, A. V.	1/ 2/41
Smith, H.	1/ 2/41
Shelton, F. R.	1/ 2/41
Frew, C. P. W.	1/ 2/41
Granger, C. L.	1/ 2/41
Hosegood, G. F. (Lt. late Devon R.)	1/ 2/41
Watson, A.	1/ 2/41
Buxton, F.	1/ 2/41
Lister, J.	1/ 2/41
Shaw, H.	1/ 2/41
Bremner-Smith, C.	25/ 4/41

Adjutant & Quarter-Master

Medical Officer

Barker, Maj. H. L., M.D., (Capt. late Ind. Med. Serv.)	17/ 5/41

NORTH MIDLAND AREA - contd.

DERBYSHIRE ZONE - contd.

S.W. GROUP

Commander

10th DERBYSHIRE (ASHBOURNE) BATTALION

Lt.-Colonel

Wheatcroft, C. J. (Capt. late T.A.)	1/ 2/41

Majors

Betterton, A H. (Maj. late Derby Yeo.)	1/ 2/41
Ball, C. F. (Maj. late T.A.)	1/ 2/41
Symonds, J. D. B. (Capt. T.A. Res.)	1/ 2/41
Lloyd, N. A. (2/Lt late R.T.C.)	1/ 2/41
Neame, B. (Lt.-Col. ret pay) (Res. of Off.)	23/ 5/41
Vaughan-Williams, R., T.D. (Bt. Col. late T.A.)	2/ 6/41

Captains

Ley, F. D. (Maj. late Derby Yeo.)	1/ 2/41
Round, C.	1/ 2/41
Ivers, W. E.	2// 6/41

Lieutenants

Newton, W. B. (Lt. T.A. Res.)	1/ 2/41
Groocock, G. H. (Lt. late Leicester R.)	1/ 2/41
Robinson, F. (Lt. late Foresters)	1/ 2/41
Walker, I. T.	1/ 2/41
Spurrier, J. M. (Lt. late R.F.A.)	1/ 2/41
Clowes, W. J. (Lt.-Comdr. late R.N.)	1/ 2/41
Coward, H.	1/ 2/41
Mears, H. J.	1/ 2/41
Plowright, R. J. O.	1/ 2/41
Johnson, A.	1/ 2/41
Rush, B.	1/ 2/41
Clark, A. E.	1/ 2/41
Prince, C. H.	1/ 2/41
Jones, J. D. P.	1/ 2/41
Wheatcroft, E. H.	1/ 2/41
Lockton, F. C.	1/ 2/41

Lieutenants - contd.

Lawley, T. H. (Capt. late R. War. R.)	6/ 6/41
Carr, W. J.	6/ 6/41

2nd Lieutenants

Wheatcroft, K. D. (2/Lt. late Foresters)	1/ 2/41
Smith, S.	1/ 2/41
Buckston, G. M. (Capt. late Derby Yeo.)	1/ 2/41
Henson, C. S. (2/Lt. late Leicester Yeo.)	1/ 2/41
Cappendell, T.	1/ 2/41
Doxey, L. A.	1/ 2/41
Shaw, F. C.	1/ 2/41
Barnwell, W. F.	1/ 2/41
Wass, C.	1/ 2/41
Brinkman, L. F.	1/ 2/41
Doxey, J. K.	1/ 2/41
Newton, C. A.	1/ 2/41
Bacon, A.	1/ 2/41
Norris, H. F.	1/ 2/41
Cassells, T.	2/ 6/41
Causer, A. E. B.	2/ 6/41
Clifford, D. A.	2/ 6/41
Clowes, T. W. C.	2/ 6/41
Couldrey, A. R.	2/ 6/41
Dunn, H. E.	2/ 6/41
Foxon, D. L.	2/ 6/41
Hadfield, B. E.	2/ 6/41
Markham, C. R.	2/ 6/41
Pearson, H. T.	2/ 6/41
Wagstaff, M.	2/ 6/41
Woodward, H. S.	2/ 6/41
Hornsby, D. C.	2/ 6/41

Adjutant & Quarter-Master

Medical Officer

56455-6(142)

NORTH MIDLAND AREA - contd.

DERBYSHIRE ZONE - contd.

S.W. GROUP - contd.

11th DERBYSHIRE (REPTON & WOODVILLE) BATTALION

Lt.-Colonel

Morgan-Owen, M.M., T.D., (Lt.-Col. late Serv. Bn.)	1/ 2/41

Majors

Maynard, H. A., M.C., T.D (Maj. Gen. List T.A.).	1/ 2/41
Cattley, L. A., M.C., T.D., (Maj. T.A. Res.)	1/ 2/41
Exham, H., D.S.O., O.B.E., (Lt.-Col. late Ind. Army)	1/ 2/41
Negus, R. E. (Lt.-Col. ret. pay. N. Stafford R.)	1/ 2/41
Paget, J. T. G. (Capt. late R.A.S.C.)	1/ 6/41

Captains

Anson, G. H., M.C., T.D., (Col. late Stafford Yeo.)	1/ 2/41
Blaxland, L. B., (Capt. Gen. List T.A.)	1/ 2/41
Thomas, B. W. (Capt. Gen. List T.A.)	1/ 2/41
Parker, J.	1/ 2/41
Bull, T. (2/Lt. late N. Stafford R.)	1/ 2/41

Lieutenants

Robotham, G. B., D.F.C., (Capt. late Foresters)	1/ 2/41
Davis, T. W.	1/ 2/41
Thompson, F. G. (Lt. late N. Stafford R.)	1/ 2/41
Hulse, A.	1/ 2/41
Talbott, G. M.	1/ 2/41
Lawton, G. O.	1/ 2/41
Stanier, F. (Flying Offr. late R.N.A.S.)	1/ 2/41
Thompson, W.	1/ 2/41

Lieutenants - contd.

Ward, C. T.	6/ 5/41
Eatough, J. O. (2/Lt. late Lan. Fus.)	1/ 7/41
Wallace, W.	8/ 7/41
McBride, F. D.	8/ 7/41

2nd Lieutenants

Stanton, S. G.	1/ 2/41
Timms, H. W.	1/ 2/41
Rose, H. E.	1/ 2/41
Scragg, A.	1/ 2/41
Forrest, C.	1/ 2/41
Wilkinson, B. (Lt. late R.E.)	1/ 2/41
Whitaker, S.	1/ 2/41
Grant, J. A. Mack.	1/ 2/41
McIntyre, G. A.	1/ 2/41
Dicken, C.	1/ 2/41
Spencer, R. J., D.C.M.	1/ 2/41
More, W. H.	1/ 2/41
Parry, F. B. W. (Lt. late M.G. Corps)	1/ 2/41
Raybon, E. J.	5/ 5/41
Baker, A. J. D.	1/ 7/41
Patrick, W. J., D.C.M.	1/ 7/41

Adjutant & Quarter-Master

Medical Officer

NORTH MIDLAND AREA - contd.

DERBYSHIRE ZONE - contd.

DERBY GROUP

Commander	Wright, Col. F. E. F. (Capt. late Bedfds. R.)	1/ 2/41

12th DERBYSHIRE (BELPER) BATTALION

Lt.-Colonel

Marsden, J. H. F., O.B.E., T.D. (Lt.-Col. ret. T.A.)	1/ 2/41

Majors

Johnson, J. G. T., D.S.O. (Maj. late Derby Yeo.)	1/ 2/41
Marshall, W. K., M.C. (Capt. late W. Yorks. R.)	1/ 2/41
Haslam, E. S. (Capt. late R.F.A.)	1/ 2/41
Cokayne, T., M.B.E. (Capt. late Foresters)	1/ 2/41
Clark, J. N. D'A. (Maj. late Derby Yeo.)	1/ 2/41
Hill, E. J. H.	10/ 6/41

Captains

Allen, G. W. (Capt. late Leicester R.)	1/ 2/41
Crowe, N. J.	1/ 2/41
Nutt, G. (Capt. late Foresters)	1/ 2/41
Finlayson, D., M.C. (Lt. late Lovat Scouts)	1/ 2/41

Lieutenants

Fairholme, I. W. F. (Lt. T.A. Res.)	1/ 2/41
Abbot-Anderson, D. G. E.	1/ 2/41
Ball, W. V. (Lt. late Ind. Army)	1/ 2/41
Bates, F. O. (2/Lt. late Foresters)	1/ 2/41
Holmes, H. H.	1/ 2/41
Perks, A. W., M.M.	1/ 2/41
Lincoln, J.	1/ 2/41
Plummer, T. A.	1/ 2/41
Fox, G. N. (Lt. late R.A.F.)	1/ 2/41
Lang, C. S. (Capt. R.T. Corps)	1/ 2/41
Robinson, P. D.	1/ 2/41
Elsom, W. C. (Lt. late Oxfs. & Bucks L.I.)	1/ 2/41
Horne, H. R., M.C. (Capt. late Leicester R.)	1/ 2/41
Cooper, F. S.	1/ 2/41
Hotson, F., M.C. (Lt. late Lincoln R.)	1/ 2/41
Farrington, T. B. (Lt. late Foresters)	1/ 2/41
Hirst, H. D.	1/ 2/41
Eardley-Simpson, L. (Maj. late R.F.A.)	1/ 2/41

Lieutenants - contd.

Piggin, H. A. (Capt. late Remount Serv.)	1/ 2/41
Frayne, C.	1/ 2/41
Wassell, T. E.	1/ 2/41
Laws, W.	1/ 2/41
Roe, W. J.	1/ 7/41
Bourne, E. C.	1/ 7/41
Douglas, A. W.	1/ 7/41
Rudd, S.	1/ 7/41

2nd Lieutenants

Lowry, E. L.	1/ 2/41
Greenwood, C. H.	1/ 2/41
Allen, H. K. W. (Lt. late Foresters)	1/ 2/41
Parkes, S. A. (Lt. late M.G. Corps)	1/ 2/41
Sewell, V. F. U.	1/ 2/41
Cockersole, H.	1/ 2/41
Baines, R. H.	1/ 2/41
Skertchly, E. W.	1/ 2/41
Spencer, W. S. (Lt. late R.F.A.)	1/ 2/41
Jones, J. H.	1/ 2/41
Lowther, J.	1/ 2/41
Bailey, E. P. (Lt. late R.F.A.	1/ 2/41
Wragg, A. S.	1/ 2/41
Robbins, E. S.	1/ 2/41
Gillott, J. C.	1/ 2/41
Cordin, W. E.	1/ 2/41
Thomson, G. M., D.C.M., M.M.	1/ 2/41
Abell, E. E.	1/ 2/41
Starkey, J. G. (Capt. late Foresters)	1/ 2/41
Sanford, D. W. (Capt. late R.E.)	1/ 2/41
Sever, J. (Capt. late E. York. R.)	1/ 2/41
Bestwick, E. E.	25/ 7/41
Longstaffe, J. Q. M.	25/ 7/41
Morley, C. D. (2 /Lt. late M.G. Corps)	25/ 7/41
Oughton, J. S.	25/ 7/41

Adjutant & Quarter-Master

Smith, Capt. (actg. 28/4/41) S. J.. Gen. List Inf.	28/ 4/41

Medical Officer

Hubble, Maj. D. V.	10/ 6/41

NORTH MIDLAND AREA - contd.

DERBYSHIRE ZONE - contd.

DERBY GROUP - contd.

13th DERBYSHIRE (DERBY & BOROUGH) BATTALION

Lt.-Colonel

Nutt, A. V., D.S.O. (Maj. late Y. & L.R.)	1/ 2/41

Majors

Cockram, S. W. (Lt. late R.T.C.)	1/ 2/41
Hands, A. J. G. (Lt. late M.G. Corps)	1/ 2/41
Todd, A. M.	1/ 2/41
Longdon, T. (2/Lt. late R.T.C.)	1/ 7/41

Captains

Rawlings, J. W.	1/ 2/41
Price, J. N.	1/ 2/41
Davis, R. M.	1/ 2/41
Walker, H. (Lt. late Manch. R.)	1/ 2/41
Mann, W. J. B. (Lt. late R.E.)	1/ 7/41

Lieutenants

Barraclough, E. J.	1/ 2/41
Fenn, A. M. (Lt. late R. North'd. Fus.)	1/ 2/41
Grundy, C. S. (Lt. late Foresters)	1/ 2/41
Wooton, J. (2/Lt. late R.H.A.)	1/ 2/41
Middleton, G. E.	1/ 2/41
Shreeve, W. D.	1/ 2/41
Icke, A. R. J. (Lt. late Lan. Fus.)	1/ 2/41
Brooks, F.	1/ 2/41
Goodridge, L.	1/ 2/41
Green, J. G.	1/ 2/41
Revill, A. G. (Capt. late R. Fus.)	1/ 2/41
Harris, G. T.	1/ 2/41
Evans, J.	1/ 2/41
Bryden, J. F. (2/Lt. late R.A.F.)	1/ 2/41
Leech, W. L. (Lt. late R.G.A.)	1/ 2/41
Brownlow, G. H. T.	1/ 2/41
Skinner, G. H.	1/ 2/41
Rumfitt, C. P.	9/ 7/41
Dewick, E. C. (Capt. late R.E.)	28/ 7/41
Glew, Lt. N. H. (Capt. late Foresters)	28/ 7/41

2nd Lieutenants

Pollett, T. S. (Lt. late R.N.V.R.)	1/ 2/41
Jones, C. N., A.F.C. (Capt. late R.A.F.)	1/ 2/41

2nd Lieutenants - contd.

Hughes, B. E.	1/ 2/41
Lackner, K. H.	1/ 2/41
Sturgess, W. J.	1/ 2/41
Campbell, D. (Lt. late Leicester R.)	1/ 2/41
Brown, K. F.	1/ 2/41
Glass, W. M.	1/ 2/41
Lane, W. J.	1/ 2/41
Yorke, J. R.	1/ 2/41
Nunn, G. R.	1/ 2/41
Woolley, C. C.	1/ 2/41
Disney, H. A., M.C., D.C.M. (2/Lt. late M.G. Corps)	1/ 2/41
Bennett, C. J. (Capt. late Derby Yeo.)	1/ 2/41
Speakman, F. W.	1/ 2/41
Bullivant, S. W.	1/ 2/11
Garratt, P. C.	1/ 2/41
Cartwright, L. A.	1/ 2/41
Sage, E. S. (2/Lt. late R.F.C.)	1/ 2/41
Baker, F. W. (Lt. late R.A.S.C.)	1/ 2/41
Walton, R. G. (2/Lt. late R.A.F.)	1/ 2/41
Henstock, F. H.	1/ 2/41
Ness, W., D.C.M.	1/ 2/41
Durnford, E. R.	1/ 2/41
Pepper, F. J.	1/ 2/41
Bell, J. A.	1/ 2/41
Ferguson, M.	1/ 2/41
Broughton, W. S.	1/ 2/41
Fisher, J.	1/ 2/41
Watts, J. E.	1/ 2/41
Buckland, D. E.	1/ 2/41
Cameron, D.	1/ 2/41
Blake, W. J. (Lt. late Lincoln R.)	24/ 4/41
Morley, H. E.	27/ 5/41
Marks, E. (Capt. late Can. Mil. Forces)	11/ 7/41
Wilkins, A. J. F.	25/ 7/41

Adjutant & Quarter-Master

Medical Officer

Revells, Maj. S. (Capt. late R.S. Fus.)	1/ 2/41

NORTH MIDLAND AREA - contd.

DERBYSHIRE ZONE - contd.

DERBY GROUP - contd.

14th DERBYSHIRE (DERBY WORKS) BATTALION

Lt.-Colonel

Bemrose, W. L., O.B.E. (Capt. late T.A.)	1/ 2/41

Majors

Gell, A. F.	1/ 2/41
Land, T. A. C. (Capt. late H.L.I.)	1/ 2/41
Nicholls, S. F.	1/ 2/41
Hunt, R. C. (Capt. late R.A.S.C.)	1/ 2/41
Mattinson, W. H. F. (Capt. late R.A.F.)	1/ 2/41

Captains

Bartlett, S. G.	1/ 2/41
Turner, J. W.	1/ 2/41
Cartmell, N. W. C. (Lt. late R.A.S.C.)	1/ 2/41
Garside, B. H. (Sqdn. Cmdr. late R.N.A.S.)	1/ 2/41
Hudson, W. A.	1/ 2/41
Wheeler, J. W.	1/ 2/41
Broome, T.	28/ 4/41

Lieutenants

Burns, D.	1/ 2/41
Littlewood, S., M.M.	1/ 2/41
Smith, H. H.	1/ 2/41
Hewitt, C.	1/ 2/41
Butt, A. G.	1/ 2/41
Lee-Jones, C. E. (Lt. late R.E.)	1/ 2/41
Roe, W. L.	1/ 2/41
Boaden, G. A.	1/ 2/41
Mozley, C. H.	1/ 2/41
Groutage, H.	1/2/41
Toomer, W. R.	1/ 2/41
Gordon, J. B. (Lt. late K.R.R.C.)	1/ 2/41
Parker, S. T.	1/ 2/41
Bryson, E. R. W. (Lt. late Durham L.I.)	1/ 2/41
Gilmam, D. G.	1/ 2/41
Mooney, R. P.	1/ 2/41
Wozencroft, L. L.	1/ 2/41
Crofts, J. H.	1/ 2/41
McWilliams, A. C.	1/ 2/41

Lieutenants - contd.

Roberts, A. B.	1/ 2/41
Wise, L. B.	1/ 2/41
Wass, S.	1/ 2/41
Cholerton, J. R., M.C. (Capt. late Foresters)	28/ 4/41
Knights, E. J. (Lt. late Foresters)	1/ 5/41
Elliott, F. C. (Lt. late Hampshire R.)	16/ 7/41

2nd Lieutenants

Stephenson, C.	1/ 2/41
Bullivant, F. H.	1/ 2/41
Blackshaw, E., M.M.	1/ 2/41
Riddell, G. D.	1/ 2/41
Coulson, E. A.	1/ 2/41
Warren, W.	1/ 2/41
Fielding, E. W.	1/ 2/41
Shelton, J. H., D.C.M.	1/ 2/41
Dean, J.	1/ 2/41
Slack, W. A.	1/ 2/41
Newton, G.	1/ 2/41
Daniels, D. H.	1/ 2/41
Smith, H.	1/ 2/41
Littlewood, H.	1/ 2/41
Tindall, C.	1/ 2/41
Dean, J. W.	1/ 2/41
Burnett, R.	1/ 2/41
Clark, A. J.	1/ 2/41
Norton, L. G.	1/ 2/41
Jones, R. J. J.	1/ 2/41
Mountford, N. D. G.	1/ 2/41
Markham, R. T.	1/ 2/41
Gilmore, T. W. R.	1/ 2/41
Frost, W. L.	1/ 2/41
Johnson, A. E.	1/ 2/41
Brown, J. K.	16/ 7/41
Short, W. R.	16/ 7/41
Bird, S. A.	16/ 7/41
Dawson, J. N.	2/ 8/41

Adjutant & Quarter-Master

Medical Officer

Hore, Maj. W. G. R.	24/ 4/41

NORTH MIDLAND AREA - contd.

NOTTINGHAMSHIRE ZONE

Commander	Laycock, Col. Sir Joseph F., K.C.M.G., D.S.O., T.D. (Brig.-Gen. ret. T.A.)	1/ 2/41
Second in Command	Kirk, Lt.-Col. F. T., M.C. (Maj. late R.W.K.)	1/ 2/41
Assistant to Commander	Cooper, Maj. L. L., T.D. (Capt. ret. Foresters)	1/ 2/41
Territorial Army Association administering	The Nottingham T.A. & A.F. Association, Derby Road, Nottingham.	

NOTTINGHAM CITY GROUP

Commander	Potter, Col. W. A., D.S.O., D.L. (Lt.-Col. T.A. Res.)	1/ 2/41
Second in Command	Bourner, Lt.-Col. D. (Lt. late K.O.Y.L.I.)	1/ 2/41
Assistant to Commander	Roberts, Capt, A. F. (Capt. T.A. Res.)	1/ 2/41

1st NOTTINGHAMSHIRE (CITY) BATTALION

Lt.-Colonel

Halford, L. R., M.C. (Maj. late Serv. Bn. Foresters). 1/ 2/41

Majors

Bentley, A. O. (2/Lt. Gen. List. T.A.) 1/ 2/41
Wilkinson, R. M., M.C. (Capt. late Y. & L.R.) 1/ 2/41
Staley, H. (2/Lt. late Foresters) 1/ 2/41
Sherwin, W. H. (Capt. late Foresters) 1/ 2/41
Trease, G. E. 1/ 2/41
Bulling, C. L. (Paymr. Lt. late R.N.V.R.) 1/ 2/41
Fox, L. C. (Capt. late London R.) 1/ 2/41
Beesley, F. (Flying Offr. late R.A.F.) 25/ 7/41

Captains

Palmer, R. A. (Capt. Gen. List. T.A.) 1/ 2/41
Hope, J., M.M. 1/ 2/41
Jones, G. W. 1/ 2/41
Procter, W. V. 1/ 2/41
Mitchell, J. D. (Capt. late R.A.S.C.) 1/ 2/41
Hackett, J. (Capt. late North'd Fus.) 25/ 7/41
Verrall, C. W. E. 25/ 7/41

56455-6(147)

NORTH MIDLAND AREA - contd.

NOTTINGHAMSHIRE ZONE - contd.

NOTTINGHAM CITY GROUP - contd.

1st Nottinghamshire (City) Battalion - contd.

Lieutenants

Mee, W., M.M.	1/ 2/41
Mason, T. H.	1/ 2/41
Johnson, H.	1/ 2/41
Draper, G. C.	1/ 2/41
Thomson, G.	1/ 2/41
Murdoch, R. J.	1/ 2/41
Keetch, R. W.	1/ 2/41
Mumford, F. R.	1/ 2/41
Greenwood, J. E. (Capt. late Gren. Gds.)	1/ 2/41
Cleveland, H. A. (Capt. late T.A.)	1/ 2/41
Blackburn, G. S.	1/ 2/41
Parkin, H. C.	1/ 2/41
Taylor, A. E. A.	1/ 2/41
Hook, H. G.	1/ 2/41
Key, A. J. E.	1/ 2/41
Smith, J. W., M.M.	1/ 2/41
Dodd, W. P.	1/ 2/41
Lawton, B. W.	1/ 2/41
Simmons, L.	1/ 2/41
Watson, A. (2/Lt. late Foresters)	1/ 2/41
Bell, W.	1/ 2/41
Baxter, J. H. (2/Lt. late T.A.)	1/ 2/41
Jones, W. A.	1/ 2/41
Morrison, E. W.	1/ 2/41
Loverseed, A. W.	1/ 2/41
Cox, W. H.	1/ 2/41
Minter, E. W.	25/ 7/41
Jones, H. T.	25/ 7/41

2nd Lieutenants

Edwards, J. R.	1/ 2/41
Scofield, G. W.	1/ 2/41
Pare, G. W.	1/ 2/41
Harrison, C. C.	1/ 2/41
Galley, J. A. (Capt. late Wilts R.)	1/ 2/41
Loach, E. L.	1/ 2/41

2nd Lieutenants - contd.

Pyefinch, K. A.	1/ 2/41
Harper, K. H.	1/ 2/41
Foinette, T. W. (Bt. Lt.-Col. late T.A.)	1/ 2/41
Start, H. W.	1/ 2/41
Stoneystreet, L. W.	1/ 2/41
Coffey, C.	1/ 2/41
Porter, J. W., M.M.	1/ 2/41
Keller, F.	1/ 2/41
Dalbell, J. A.	1/ 2/41
Bates, F. C.	1/ 2/41
Rowlands, A. E.	1/ 2/41
Sellars, J. F. F.	1/ 2/41
Taylor, J. E.	1/ 2/41
Botting, A. E.	1/ 2/41
Lattaway, G. W.	1/ 2/41
Clark, G. W.	4/ 6/41
Bentley, B. W.	25/ 7/41
Fudge, F.	25/ 7/41

Adjutant & Quarter-Master

Cave, Capt. (actg. 4/7/41) E. C., Leicester R.	4/ 7/41

Medical Officer

NORTH MIDLAND AREA - contd.

NOTTINGHAMSHIRE ZONE - contd.

NOTTINGHAM CITY GROUP - contd.

2nd NOTTINGHAMSHIRE (WEST BRIDGEFORD) BATTALION

Lt.-Colonel

Hare, A. B., M.C., T.D. (Bt. Col. T.A. Res.) 1/ 2/41

Majors

Dickinson, L. (Lt. late R.A.F.) 1/ 2/41
Speed, H. (Lt. late R.F.C.) 1/ 2/41
Crockford, L. C., M.C., T.D. (Bt. Col. late R. War. R.) 1/ 2/41
Wyles, F. W. 1/ 2/41
Wheater, C., M.M. (Lt. late The King's R.) 1/ 2/41
Bostock, N. S., M.C. (Maj. late S. Stafford R.) 1/ 2/41

Captains

Watson, J. H., M.C. (Lt. late E. Lan. R.) 1/ 2/41
Farr, T. H. 1/ 2/41
Ferreira, P. D. F. (Capt. late A. Cyclist Corps.) 1/ 2/41
Adams, P. T. W. (Lt. late R.A.S.C.) 1/ 2/41

Lieutenants

Payne, C. 1/ 2/41
Stevens, A. C. 1/ 2/41
Wallace, W. D. (2/Lt. late Seaforth.) 1/ 2/41
Price, E. K. 1/ 2/41
Morrell, A. L. (Lt. late R.G.A.) 1/ 2/41
Foley, J. E. (Capt. late M.G. Corps) 1/ 2/41
Perkins, A. B. (2/Lt. late M.G. Corps) 1/ 2/41
Rankin, M. S. (Capt. late H.L.I.) 1/ 2/41
Dabell, C. T. 1/ 2/41
Shaw, R. B. (Lt. late Black Watch) 1/ 2/41

Lieutenants - contd.

Barnett, J. E. 1/ 2/41
Walker, J. D. (2/Lt. late R.E.) 1/ 2/41
Tunbridge, H. S. (Lt. late Y. & L.R.) 1/ 2/41
Ashton, R. T. C. 1/ 2/41
Jones, A. R. (Lt. late Bedfs. & Herts. R.) 1/ 2/41
Rimmer, R., D.C.M. 1/ 2/41
Hodson, G. N. 1/ 2/41
Lambert, A., M.C. (Lt. late North'n R.) 4/ 6/41
Smee, F. U. 4/ 6/41

2nd Lieutenants

Anthony, A. E. 1/ 2/41
Mansell, A. B. (Lt. late Foresters) 1/ 2/41
Stephenson, W. F. A. 1/ 2/41
Wilson, J. C. 1/ 2/41
Carrier, A. L. 1/ 2/41
Norman, C. 1/ 2/41
Spary, H. G., M.C. (Capt. late M.G. Corps) 1/ 2/41
Deppe, H. L. 1/ 2/41
Wootton, J. N. (2/Lt. late R.N.V.R.) 1/ 2/41
Inglis, L. A. (2/Lt. late R.F.A.) 1/ 2/41
Skipworth, R. E. M.B.E., (2/Lt. late R.H. Rif.) 1/ 2/41
Ballachey, J. P. 1/ 2/41
King, C. E. 1/ 2/41
Herbert, T. H. 1/ 2/41
Dominy, J. N. 4/ 6/41
Gilbert, W. 4/ 6/41

Adjutant & Quarter-Master

Bavin, Capt. (actg. 4/5/41) T. E., Gen. List Inf. 4/ 5/41

Medical Officer

Mattock, Maj. S. C. 4/ 6/41

NORTH MIDLAND AREA - contd.

NOTTINGHAMSHIRE ZONE - contd.

NOTTINGHAM CITY GROUP- contd.

3rd NOTTINGHAMSHIRE (BEESTON) BATTALION

Lt.-Colonel

Marshall, J. E. L. (Lt. late Serv. Bn. K.O.Y.L.I.) 1/ 2/41

Majors

Woodward, N. P. (Capt. late R.E.) 1/ 2/41
Hancock, G. A., M.C. (Capt. late Foresters) 1/ 2/41
Pentecost, L. S., M.C. (Capt. late Foresters) 1/ 2/41
Sansom, C. P. (Capt. late Y. & L.R.) 1/ 2/41
Stonehouse, G. (Lt. late R.G.A.) 1/ 2/41
Foster, W. 1/ 2/41
Riddick, S. M. (Capt. late R.A.M.C.) 4/ 6/41

Captains

Fletcher, H. B. (Lt. late E. Yorks. R.) 1/ 2/41
Parker, C. 1/ 2/41
Allen, H. A. 1/ 2/41
Thompson, L. (Lt. late Y. & L.R.) 1/ 2/41
Shaw, F. (Capt. late Manch. R.) 25/ 7/41

Lieutenants

Rowland, A. J. (Capt. late North'n. R.) 1/ 2/41
Broadhead, F. A. (Lt. late R.E.) 1/ 2/41
Willson, L. H., M.C. (Capt. late R. Sigs.) 1/ 2/41
Hobson, S. T. (Lt. late North'n. R.) 1/ 2/41
Eborall, H. L. 1/ 2/41
Sladen, G. (2/Lt. late Foresters.) 1/ 2/41
Whitby, H. S., A.F.C. (Flt. Lt. late R.A.F.) 1/ 2/41

Lieutenantz - C ontd.

Needham, A. C., M.M. (2/Lt. late Lincoln R.) 1/ 2/41
Bailey, J. A. 1/ 2/41
Neville, R. (Lt. late Foresters.) 1/ 2/41
Smith, M. 1/ 2/41
Knight, A. K. (Capt. late R.A.S.C.) 1/ 2/41
Cragg, A. H., M.M. 1/ 2/41
Baker, J. H., 1/ 2/41
Dunn, F. J. 1/ 2/41
Freund, J. J. (Capt. late R.E.) 1/ 2/41

2nd Lieutenants

Brian, C. J. 1/ 2/41
Bayne, C. J. 1/ 2/41
Mitson, L. (Lt. late R.T.C.) 1/ 2/41
Lowe, J. S. 1/ 2/41
Halliday, R. (Lt. late Manch. R.) 1/ 2/41
Griffiths, T. W. 1/ 2/41
Masters, H. 1/ 2/41
Knight, F. E. 1/ 2/41
Hardy, F. 1/ 2/41
Brough, R. A. 1/ 2/41
Renshaw, W. A. (Lt. late North'd Fus.) 1/ 2/41
Chambers, J. F. 1/ 2/41
Pickering, A. McR. (Lt. late Surrey Yeo.) 1/ 2/41
Fernsby, R. 1/ 2/41
March, W. 4/ 6/41
Street, A. E. 4/ 6/41

Adjutant & Quarter-Master

Medical Officer

Riddick, Maj. S. M. (Capt. late R.A.M.C.) 4/ 6/41

56455-6(150)

NORTH MIDLAND AREA - contd.

NOTTINGHAMSHIRE ZONE - contd.

NOTTINGHAM CITY GROUP - contd.

4th NOTTINGHAMSHIRE (BULWELL) BATTALION

Lt.-Colonel

Coy, F., O.B.E. (Capt. late Labour Corps.)	1/ 2/41

Majors

Kaye, A. E. (Lt. late R.E.)	1/ 2/41
Toon, A., M.C. (Lt. late North'd. Fus.)	1/ 2/41
Potts, C. (Capt. late R.E.)	1/ 2/41
Mairs, E. G.	1/ 2/41
Lees, N. S. (Capt. late North'd. Fus.)	1/ 2/41
Brown, S.	1/ 2/41

Captains

Rounds, H. R.	1/ 2/41
Townsend, L. (Lt. late R.A.F.)	1/ 2/41
Slater, J. E. (2/Lt. late R.E.)	1/ 2/41
Thrower, C. R.	1/ 2/41
Gower, T. E.	1/ 2/41

Lieutenants

Brown, R. J.	1/ 2/41
Johnson, H. R.	1/ 2/41
Richards, P. R. (Lt. late North'd. Fus.)	1/ 2/41
Gubbins, H. O.	1/ 2/41
Shepherd, R. T. (Flying Offr. late R.A.F.)	1/ 2/41
Pollard, W. E.	1/ 2/41
Williamson, H. (Maj. late M.G. Corps)	1/ 2/41
Gell, H.	1/ 2/41
Stocker, D. E.	1/ 2/41
Selby, W.	1/ 2/41

Lieutenants - contd.

Storrs, O. T.	1/ 2/41
Rickards, G. M.	1/ 2/41
Shearer, R. G. (Lt. late M.G. Corps)	1/ 2/41
Holmes, G. T. O.	1/ 2/41
Perkins, S.	1/ 2/41
Smith, H.	1/ 2/41
Spooner, J. P.	4/ 6/41
Field, A.	25/ 7/41

2nd Lieutenants

Atkinson, C. W.	1/ 2/41
Dring, J. E.	1/ 2/41
Gibson, T. A.	1/ 2/41
Leivers, H.	1/ 2/41
Godson, G. F.	1/ 2/41
Oldham, J. H.	1/ 2/41
Radford, V. N. (Capt. late R.A.S.C.)	1/ 2/41
Green, L. H. A.	1/ 2/41
Bonser, F.	25/ 7/41
Hollyoak, T. A.	25/ 7/41
King, A.	25/ 7/41
Smith, E. S.	25/ 7/41

Adjutant & Quarter-Master

Medical Officer

NORTH MIDLAND AREA - contd.

NOTTINGHAMSHIRE ZONE - contd.

NOTTINGHAM CITY GROUP - contd.

5th NOTTINGHAMSHIRE (DAYBROOK & BESTWOOD) BATTALION

Lt.-Colonel

Chalmers, G. J. S. (2/Lt. late R.G.A.) 1/ 2/41

Majors

Hill, A. (Lt. late M.G. Corps) 1/ 2/41
Wilson, R. C. (Capt. T.A. Res.) 1/ 2/41
Turner, E., M.C. (Capt. late Foresters) 1/ 2/41
Farr, S., M.C. (Bt.-Col. late T.A.) 1/ 2/41
Francis, B. A. 1/ 2/41
Clough, H. V. (Capt. late R.F.A.) 1/ 2/41
Boot, W. A., M.C. (Lt. late Green Howards.) 1/ 2/41

Captains

Rees, D. M. 1/ 2/41
Spurway, J. E. (Maj. late R.A.S.C.) 1/ 2/41
Haynes, N. P. (Lt. late R.E.) 1/ 2/41
Pearson, G. A. 1/ 2/41
Skevington, R., M.C. (Capt. late M.G. Corps) 1/ 2/41

Lieutenants

Tyler, J. C. (2/Lt. late R.A.F.) 1/ 2/41
Herrod, F. 1/ 2/41
Miller, J. 1/ 2/41
Macadam, L. J. 1/ 2/41
Boden, A. P., M.C. (Capt. late 12th L.) 1/ 2/41
Brace, R. B., M.C. (Capt. late Foresters) 1/ 2/41
Snook, E. N. (Capt. late H.L.I.) 1/ 2/41
Carver, E. L. 1/ 2/41
Penney, G. C. 1/ 2/41
Cheesewright, L. (Capt. late Y. & L.R.) 1/ 2/41
Keywood, S. 1/ 2/41
Parrott, S. C. 1/ 2/41
Stokes, J. C. 1/ 2/41
Sims, A. 1/ 2/41

Lieutenants - contd.

Dent, F. H. (2/Lt. late R.E.) 1/ 2/41
Burbidge, L. 1/ 2/41
Walker, A. E. (Lt. late M.G. Corps) 1/ 2/41
Lewis, W. V. M. 1/ 2/41
Barlow, G. W. 1/ 2/41
Halfnight, N. W. (2/Lt. late R.A.P.C.) 1/ 2/41
Albon, S. G. 1/ 2/41
Wylie, J. D. (Capt. late R. Scots.) 1/ 2/41

2nd Lieutenants

Lee, R. G. 1/ 2/41
Clayton, W. 1/ 2/41
McLean, N. G. (Lt. late R.F.A.) 1/ 2/41
Hampson, H. J., M.C. (Capt. late Manch. R.) 1/ 2/41
Fox, C., M.C. (Lt. late Lincoln R.) 1/ 2/41
King, C. H. 1/ 2/41
Spedding, A. G., M.C. (Lt. late The Kings R.) 1/ 2/41
Kennewell, H. 1/ 2/41
Barter, B. W. 1/ 2/41
Gibson, T. 1/ 2/41
Butcher, O. (Lt. late R.F.A.) 1/ 2/41
Armitage, W. 1/ 2/41
Phillips, J. A. (2/Lt. late R.W. Fus.) 1/ 2/41
Scott, S. H. (Lt. late Gordons) 1/ 2/41
Harrison, O. (2/Lt. late Leicester R.) 1/ 2/41
Fish, A. J. 1/ 2/41
Shouls, E. M. 1/ 2/41

Adjutant & Quarter-Master

Medical Officer

NORTH MIDLAND AREA - contd.

NOTTINGHAMSHIRE ZONE - contd.

MANSFIELD GROUP

Commander	Chadburn, Col. C. W. (Capt. late T.A.)	1/ 2/41
Second in Command	Royce, Lt.-Col. H. (2/Lt. late M.G. Corps)	1/ 2/41

6th NOTTINGHAMSHIRE (MANSFIELD) BATTALION

Lt.-Colonel

Mein, W. H. (Maj. late Y. & L.R.)	1/ 2/41

Majors

Lane, N. M., M.C. (Capt. late R.F.A.)	1/ 2/41
Shooter, J. W. (Lt. late Leicester R.)	1/ 2/41
White, W. R. (Capt. late M.G. Corps.)	1/ 2/41
Martin, T. S.	1/ 2/41
Mee, H. N. (Lt. late Leicester R.)	4/ 6/41

Captains

Moss, G. E. (Lt. late M.G. Corps)	1/ 2/41
Cleland, J. A.	4/ 6/41
King, F. J. (Capt. late Irish R.)	4/ 6/41
List, J. H. (Capt. late R.T.C.)	4/ 6/41
Moss, L. R.	25/ 7/41

Lieutenants

Walton, A. (Lt. late Foresters)	1/ 2/41
Gregory, J. D.	1/ 2/41
Hibbert, E. B. (Lt. late M.G. Corps)	1/ 2/41
Tanner, D. C.	1/ 2/41
Heathcote, C. A.	1/ 2/41
Davies, T. H.	1/ 2/41
Fenwick, E. A. F. (Lt. late R.F.A.)	1/ 2/41
Stevenson, G.	1/ 2/41
Spedding, T.	1/ 2/41
Hutchinson, A. G.	1/ 2/41
Hardy, F. W.	1/ 2/41
Temple, D. W. (Lt. late Middx. R.)	1/ 2/41

Lieutenants - contd.

Large, T. (Lt. late R.A.F.)	1/ 2/41
Machin, H.	1/ 2/41
Hague, J. G., M.M.	1/ 2/41
Bell, E. B.	1/ 2/41
Randall, J. E.	4/ 6/41
Strachan, J. (Capt. late Foresters)	4/ 6/41
Chubb, G. O. (Capt. late R. Norfolk R.)	4/ 6/41
Chatterton, F.	25/ 7/41
Hutchinson, S. D. (Lt. late R.A.F.)	25/ 7/41

2nd Lieutenants

Holmes, C. H.	1/ 2/41
Bradfield, H. (Lt. late Foresters)	1/ 2/41
King, H. F.	1/ 2/41
Billing, W.	1/ 2/41
Pyatt, F. W. (Lt. late R.E.)	1/ 2/41
Holdsworth, F.	1/ 2/41
Machin, T. W. (Capt. late R.E.)	1/ 2/41
Hardy, B. R.	1/ 2/41
Pye, A. J.	1/ 2/41
Heathcote, C. W.	1/ 2/41
Webster, C. B. (Lt. T.A. Res.)	1/ 2/41
Gavaghan, M.	1/ 2/41
Greenwood, H.	1/ 2/41
Banister, R. M.	4/ 6/41
Fisher, A.	25/ 7/41
Green, J.	25/ 7/41

Adjutant & Quarter-Master

Gain, Capt. (actg. 15/7/41) R. S., Gen. List Inf.	15/ 7/41

Medical Officer

Gettleson, Maj. P. M. (Capt. late R.A.M.C.)	25/ 7/41

NORTH MIDLAND AREA - contd.

NOTTINGHAMSHIRE ZONE - contd.

MANSFIELD GROUP - contd.

7th NOTTINGHAMSHIRE (SUTTON-IN-ASHFIELD) BATTALION

Lt.-Colonel

Muschamp, E. P. W. (Capt. late M.G. Corps.)	1/ 2/41

Majors

Edwardes, R. E. S. W. (Lt. late R.E.)	1/ 2/41
Aspinall, F. J. (Capt. late R.E.)	1/ 2/41
Wright, R. C. (Capt. late Foresters)	1/ 2/41
Oates, J. R. (Lt. late R.F.A.)	1/ 2/41
Davis, G.	25/ 7/41

Captains

Blackburn, H. H. (Lt. late Dorset R.)	1/ 2/41
Searson, E.	1/ 2/41
Johnston, J., M.C. (Lt. late R.E.)	25/ 7/41

Lieutenants

Ackroyd, L. F. M. (Lt. late M.G. Corps.)	1/ 2/41
Moulton, T. L. (2/Lt. late Foresters)	1/ 2/41
Coates, H., D.C.M., M.M.	1/ 2/41
Ball, F. M.	1/ 2/41
Sharpe, W.	1/ 2/41
Dallison, A. R.	1/ 2/41
Fisher, W. E.	1/ 2/41
Perkins, E. H.	1/ 2/41
Hitchens, J.	1/ 2/41
Cox, J.	1/ 2/41
Clarke, J. D.	1/ 2/41
Pierpoint, R.	1/ 2/41
Gething, H. (Lt. late R.E.)	1/ 2/41

2nd Lieutenants

Bowing, H. J.	1/ 2/41
Mettam, E. R.	1/ 2/41
Henderson, W. A. D.	1/ 2/41
Waters, T. O.	1/ 2/41
Scothorne, T., D.C.M. (2/Lt. late Lincoln R.)	1/ 2/41
Hanlon, E. G.	1/ 2/41
Elliott, H. M., M.M.	1/ 2/41
Webster, E.	1/ 2/41
Bird, E. B. E.	1/ 2/41
Williamson, F.	1/ 2/41
Wilson, G.	1/ 2/41
Hall, G. W. (Lt. late Foresters)	1/ 2/41
Murray, J. McM.	1/ 2/41
Marsh, W. H.	1/ 2/41
Sheriston, J. A. (2/Lt. late Foresters)	1/ 2/41
Rodgers, W. T.	1/ 2/41
Hunt, E. H.	1/ 2/41
Heathcote, C. M.	1/ 2/41
Guy, T.	1/ 2/41
Woodward, J. E.	1/ 2/41
Barton, H.	4/ 6/41
Blundy, C.	4/ 6/41
Crafts, F. W.	25/ 7/41
Stubley, H. T. J.	25/ 7/41

Adjutant & Quarter-Master

Medical Officer

Donald, Maj. S. J. W. (Maj. late R.A.M.C.)	25/ 7/41

56455-6(154)

NORTH MIDLAND AREA - contd.

NOTTINGHAMSHIRE ZONE - contd.

MANSFIELD GROUP - contd.

8th NOTTINGHAMSHIRE (CLIPSTONE) BATTALION

Lt.-Colonel

Richardson, P. L.	1/ 2/41

Majors

Wilkinson, C. D.	1/ 2/41
Priestley, J.	1/ 2/41
Rice, J. T.	1/ 2/41
Sheppard, W. V.	1/ 2/41
Dilley, A. G.	1/ 2/41

Captains

Carter, R. L.	1/ 2/41
Mace, J.	1/ 2/41
Brown, W., M.M.	1/ 2/41
Smith, G. (Lt. late London R.)	1/ 2/41
Hayes, J. A.	4/ 6/41

Lieutenants

Green, T. A.	1/ 2/41
Bealby, B. R.	1/ 2/41
Davis, T.	1/ 2/41
Holden, H.	1/ 2/41
Lakin, W. B., M.M.	1/ 2/41
Barlow, F. C.	1/ 2/41
Cullen, J. R.	1/ 2/41
Rudge, A. T.	1/ 2/41
Phillips, J. G.	1/ 2/41
Leaper, A.	1/ 2/41

Lieutenants - contd.

Dallman, W.	1/ 2/41
Marriott, A.	1/ 2/41
Philpott, A.	1/ 2/41
Gee, S.	1/ 2/41
Patience, F. E.	1/ 2/41
Goodman, S.	25/ 7/41

2nd Lieutenants

Pearson, J.	1/ 2/41
Tucker, R. A.	1/ 2/41
Clarke, J. F.	1/ 2/41
Weightman, S.	1/ 2/41
Ranby, E. T.	1/ 2/41

Adjutant & Quarter-Master

Bradley, Capt. (actg. 5/5/41) J. G., Gen. List Inf.	5/ 5/41

Medical Officer

Tweedie, Maj. N. L. (Capt. late R.A.M.C.)	25/ 7/41

NORTH MIDLAND AREA - contd.

NOTTINGHAMSHIRE ZONE - contd.

MANSFIELD GROUP - contd.

11th NOTTINGHAMSHIRE (NEWARK) BATTALION

Lt.-Colonel

Shephard, S., M.C. (Lt. late T.A.) 1/ 2/41

Majors

Cherry-Downes, H. A. D. (Lt. late T.A.) 1/ 2/41
Miller- J. D., M.C. (Lt. late Black Watch) 1/ 2/41
Pentecost, E. L. C. 1/ 2/41
Black, T. S. (Capt. late Gen. List) 1/ 2/41
Bowen, A. R. (Lt. late Worc. R.) 1/ 2/41

Captains

Ivens, J. C. (Pilot Offr. late R.A.F.) 1/ 2/41
Lewis, C. L. (Lt. late R.G.A.) 1/ 2/41
Savage, E. G. (Capt. late Ind. Army) 1/ 2/41
Gammage, B. (Lt. late Gen. List) 1/ 2/41
Cohen, V. (Lt. late R. Fus.) 1/ 2/41

Lieutenants

Gaskell, W. R., M.C. (Capt. late M.G.Corps.) 1/ 2/41
Marten, E. R. (Maj. late R.T.C.) 1/ 2/41
Shaw, F. A. (Lt. late Foresters) 1/ 2/41
Dickie, D. H. (Maj. late Can. Militia) 1/ 2/41
Forth, E. (Lt. late R.F.A.) 1/ 2/41
Birch, H. (Lt. late R.A.F.) 1/ 2/41
Cursham, C. (Lt. late Foresters) 1/ 2/41
Wright, F. A. (Lt. late Foresters) 1/ 2/41
Longden, R. W. (2/Lt. late Foresters) 1/ 2/41
Lane, E. W. (Lt. late S. Lan. R.) 1/ 2/41
Carr, E. G. (Capt. late Cheshire R.) 1/ 2/41
Lees, G. M., M.C., D.F.C. (Capt. late R.A.F.) 1/ 2/41
Lane, J. K. (Maj. late Foresters) 1/ 2/41
Jackson, A. H. M. (Lt. late Gren. G'ds.) 1/ 2/41
Dowling, B. V. 1/ 2/41
Carswell, C. L. 1/ 2/41
Steel, C. O. 1/ 2/41
Pell, E. H. (Lt. late 11th H.) 1/ 2/41
Keyworth, W. S. 1/ 2/41
Facer, H. E. 1/ 2/41
Houston, C. D. B. 1/ 2/41
Dickie, R. K. (2/Lt. late R.A.F.) 1/ 2/41
Downman, T. F. C. (Lt. late Foresters) 1/ 2/41
Handbury,, R. (Lt. late Suffolk R.) 4/ 6/41
Brown, E. P. (Pilot Offr. late R.A.F.) 25/ 7/41

2nd Lieutenants

Martin, W. E. 1/ 2/41
Lucas, A. E. 1/ 2/41
Ryland, C. (Lt. late Suffolk R.) 1/ 2/41
Morley, V. L. (2/Lt. late R.A.F.) 1/ 2/41
Mallett, R. W. (Lt. late M.G.Corps) 1/ 2/41
Donald, R. S. (2/Lt. late Gordons) 1/ 2/41
Daubrah, S. (2/Lt. late The Buffs) 1/ 2/41
Hill, T. A. M. (Capt. late R.E.) 1/ 2/41
Lawrence, F. N., M.C. (Lt. late R. War R.) 1/ 2/41
Price, H. H. C. 1/ 2/41
Tomlinson, J. L. (Lt. late M.G.Corps) 1/ 2/41
Hooton, J. T. 1/ 2/41
Waters, J. F. (Capt. late Ind. Army) 1/ 2/41
Tordoff, G. M. (Lt. late E. Riding Yeo.) 1/ 2/41
Lucas, G. R. 1/ 2/41
Rumbell, R. J. 1/ 2/41
Cafferata, B. J. (Capt. late R.A.S.C.) 1/ 2/41
Bradley, R. D. K. 1/ 2/41
Bohling, H. 1/ 2/41
Storer, B. 1/ 2/41
Norcott, H., M.M. 1/ 2/41
Grosse, G. 1/ 2/41
McNamara, J. P. 1/ 2/41
Jones, A. A. 1/ 2/41
Cafferata, G. W. 1/ 2/41
Hurst, R. A. 1/ 2/41
Bayles, J. H. G. (Capt. late York. R.) 1/ 2/41
Allan, A. C. 25/ 7/41
Wigley, N. G. 25/ 7/41
Yeomans, T. G. 25/ 7/41

Adjutant & Quarter-Master

Medical Officer

56455-6 (156)

NORTH MIDLAND AREA - contd.

NOTTINGHAMSHIRE ZONE - contd.

WORKSOP GROUP

Commander	Thompson, Col. R., D.S.O. (Col. ret. T.A.)	1/ 2/41

9th NOTTINGHAMSHIRE (WORKSOP) BATTALION

Lt.-Colonel

Furniss, A. E. (Capt. late T.A.)	1/ 2/41

Majors

Milnes, R. (Maj. late Somerset L.I.)	1/ 2/41
Muirhead, D.	1/ 2/41
Crosse, A. E. S., M.C. (Lt. late R. Fus.)	1/ 2/41
Dunn, G.	1/ 2/41
Wilson, R. J.	1/ 2/41

Captains

Brough, A.	1/ 2/41
Brand, G. W.	1/ 2/41
Dunlop, G. A. (2/Lt. late Cameronians)	1/ 2/41
Bescoby, A. C. (Capt. late T.A.)	1/ 2/41
Atkinson, J. F. V. (Lt. late R.A.F.)	1/ 2/41
Barrass, J. A. (Lt. late Durham L.I.)	1/ 2/41

Lieutenants

Dix, S. A.	1/ 2/41
Ward, J. E.	1/ 2/41
Harrison, F., M.M.	1/ 2/41
Pegg, H. M.	1/ 2/41
Cort, J. R. (Lt. late Seaforth)	1/ 2/41
Dougill, F.	1/ 2/41
Sissons, F. H. R.	1/ 2/41
Knight-Adkin, J. H. (Capt. late T. A.)	1/ 2/41
Clark, V. R.	1/ 2/41
Oldfield, J.	1/ 2/41
Jones, C. F.	1/ 2/41

Lieutenants - contd.

Farnsworth, A.	1/ 2/41
Jackson, W. E.	1/ 2/41
Matthews, A. C., M.M.	1/ 2/41
Clarke, J. F.	1/ 2/41
Shewring, L. B.	1/ 2/41
Newcombe, A. F. (Lt. late Y. & L.R.)	1/ 2/41
Sissons, V. M.	1/ 2/41
Moxon, F. A.	25/ 7/41

2nd Lieutenants

Colls, C. F. D.	1/ 2/41
Clamp, P. V.	1/ 2/41
Leadbeater, H. D.	1/ 2/41
Price, S.	1/ 2/41
Lovely, H. R.	1/ 2/41
Woodhouse, G. F.	1/ 2/41
Cort, A. H. (Lt. late R.A.S.C.)	1/ 2/41
Bickerstaff, W. E.	1/ 2/41
Newman, A.	1/ 2/41
Billam, A.	1/ 2/41
Roberts, J. N.	1/ 2/41
Walker, S. C.	1/ 2/41
Sheppard, J. O.	1/ 2/41
Pennington, W. (Lt. late Labour Corps.)	1/ 2/41

Adjutant & Quarter-Master

Medical Officer

NORTH MIDLAND AREA - contd.

NOTTINGHAMSHIRE ZONE - contd.

WORKSOP GROUP - contd.

10th NOTTINGHAMSHIRE (RETFORD) BATTALION

Lt.-Colonel

Dimock, J. F. D., O.B.E. (Capt. late T.A.) 1/ 2/41

Majors

Clark, A. (2/Lt. R.A.S.C.) 1/ 2/41
Earl, F. C. (Capt. late Y. & L.R.) 1/ 2/41
Mason, B. (Capt. late Worc. H.) 1/ 2/41

Captains

Hollingbery, W. B. (Lt. late R.E.) 1/ 2/41
Neill, W. M. (Capt. late T.A.) 1/ 2/41

Lieutenants

Gascoyne, L. F. 1/ 2/41
Horey, P. G. 1/ 2/41
Yarrow, H. G. 1/ 2/41
Gray, G. C., M.C. (Lt. late W. York R.) 1/ 2/41
Siggs, W. T. 1/ 2/41
Paxton, W. A. (2/Lt. late R.W.K.) 1/ 2/41
Pick, G. W. 1/ 2/41
Minnitt, B. A., M.C. M.M. (Lt. late K.R.R.C.) 1/ 2/41
Jackson, W. S. 1/ 2/41
Moon, T. E. 1/ 2/41
Laban, G. T. 1/ 2/41
Duncan, H. G. 1/ 2/41
Ellis, F. J. (Lt. late R.W.K.) 1/ 2/41
Baker, N. W. 1/ 2/41
Bloore, C. G. 1/ 2/41
Ross, A. S. 4/ 6/41
Vear, W. 25/ 7/41

2nd Lieutenants

Flower, E. 1/ 2/41
Chandler, G. W. F. 1/ 2/41
Bambrook, G. 1/ 2/41
Shearman, F. 1/ 2/41
Rogers, H. 1/ 2/41
Gosling, G. H. 1/ 2/41
Driffill, R. K. 1/ 2/41
Osborne, H. 25/ 7/41
Bilton, G. E. 25/ 7/41
Bowman, A. E., M.M. 25/ 7/41
Bullas, R. W. C. 25/ 7/41
Hawkins, J. 25/ 7/41
Hopkinson, C. W. 25/ 7/41

Adjutant & Quarter-Master

Medical Officer

12th NOTTINGHAMSHIRE (BASSETLAW) BATTALION

Lt.-Colonel

Allen, W. H. (Capt. T.A. Res.) 1/ 2/41

Majors

Sansom, W. H. M.C. (Capt. late R.E.) 1/ 2/41
Patterson, J. F. C., O.B.E. (Rear Admiral ret.) 1/ 2/41
Fowler, C., D.S.O., T.D. (Maj. late R.F.A.) 1/ 2/41
Perry, W. J. H. 1/ 2/41
Fletcher, W. S. 1/ 2/41

Captains

Kennell, J. 1/ 2/41
McTurk, A. G., O.B.E., M.C. (Maj. late Lovat Scouts) 1/ 2/41
Hanna, M. C. (2/Lt. R.A.F.) 1/ 2/41
Warburton, A. V. 1/ 2/41

Lieutenants

Draycott, J. 1/ 2/41
Pitchford, J. H. A. 1/ 2/41
Glover, C. M. H. 1/ 2/41
Walker, E. 1/ 2/41
Doncaster, T. 1/ 2/41
Ferrari, H. 1/ 2/41
Hill, W. G. 1/ 2/41
Dyson, R. A. 1/ 2/41
Swinton, H. 1/ 2/41
Foster, J. T. 1/ 2/41
Murphy, P. J. 1/ 2/41
Morley, J. N. 1/ 2/41
Davis, W. H. T. 1/ 2/41
Beaumont, J. G., D.S.C. (Lt. ret. R.N.) 1/ 2/41
Clough, R. 25/ 7/41
Hall, J. B. 25/ 7/41
Lynham, H. J. 25/ 7/41
Rhodes, G. P. (Lt. late R.A.S.C.) 25/ 7/41

2nd Lieutenants

Hutchinson, F. W. 1/ 2/41
Bowring, C. E. B. S. 25/ 7/41
Wills, C. J. 25/ 7/41

Adjutant & Quarter-Master

Medical Officer

NORTH MIDLAND AREA - contd.

NOTTINGHAMSHIRE ZONE - contd.

INDEPENDENT BATTALIONS

TRENT RIVER PATROL

Lt.-Colonel

Ford, H. W. (Lt. late R.N.) 1/ 2/41

Majors

Burnett, E. 1/ 2/41
Hobson, E., M.C. (Lt. late Oxf. & Bucks. L.I.) 1/ 2/41
Richmond, J. S. 1/ 2/41

Captains

Vamplew, J. W. 1/ 2/41
Bradbury, J. D. G. 1/ 2/41
Reynolds, L. 1/ 2/41
Brock, W. (Lt. late York Dns.) 1/ 2/41
Linkie, T. D. M. 1/ 2/41
Shaw, C. F. (Lt. late Lincoln R.) 1/ 2/41
Sharphouse, J. 1/ 2/41
Fish, H. G. 1/ 2/41
Thirlby, J. F. 1/ 2/41

Lieutenants

Flewitt, G. 1/ 2/41
Fleeman, R. A. 1/ 2/41
Barnes, R. A. G. (2/Lt. late R.F.A.) 1/ 2/41
Dennett, W. C. 1/ 2/41
Woodman, T. J. R. 1/ 2/41
Shadlock, G. E. 1/ 2/41
Wharton, J. 1/ 2/41
Adams, A. N. 1/ 2/41
Gooderidge, W. A. 1/ 2/41
Thurston, H. A. L. 1/ 2/41
Gracie, D. McA., M.B E. (Lt. late R.N.V.R.) 1/ 2/41
Selby, S. G. 1/ 2/41
Davis, W. J. 2/ 5/41
Haile, W. H. 7/ 5/41
Owen, R. D. 15/ 7/41

2nd Lieutenants

Amos, C. F. 1/ 2/41
Norcliffe, C. R. 1/ 2/41
Lawrenson, H. 1/ 2/41
Warburton, A. J. 1/ 2/41
Lowe, R. H. 1/ 2/41
Briggs, D. S. 1/ 2/41
Edwards, B. D. 1/ 2/41
Cotterill, A. J. 1/ 2/41
Randle-Clarke, C. 1/ 2/41
Reynolds, L. J. 1/ 2/41
Witty, J. 1/ 2/41
Hunt, E. A. 1/ 2/41
Derry, A. 1/ 2/41
Pycroft, H. L. 1/ 2/41
Woolley, S. 1/ 2/41
Cragg, F. G. 1/ 2/41
Potter, H. 1/ 2/41
Marshall, W. S. 1/ 2/41
Thompson, W. B. 1/ 2/41
Fordham, J. 1/ 2/41
Jackson, H. V. 1/ 2/41
Beck, F. 1/ 2/41
Mallett, R. G. 1/ 2/41
Brown, A. R. 1/ 2/41
Bramley, R. F. 1/ 2/41
Sims, R. 1/ 2/41
Greasley, P. 22/ 5/41
Forington, J. H. 15/ 7/41

Adjutant & Quarter-Master

Wynne, Capt. (actg. 9/4/41) W. K., Gen. List Inf. 9/ 4/41

Medical Officer

Summers, Maj. G.D., M.B., (Capt. late Seaforth) 5/ 7/41

NORTH MIDLAND AREA - contd.

NOTTINGHAMSHIRE ZONE - contd.

INDEPENDENT BATTALIONS - contd.

13th NOTTINGHAMSHIRE (POST OFFICE) BATTALION

Lt.-Colonel

Wallace, J. N.	1/ 2/41

Majors

Randall, H.	1/ 2/41
Hodge, H. R.	1/ 2/41
Webster, F., D.C.M., M.M.	1/ 2/41

Captain

Stokes, W. G.	1/ 7/41

Lieutenants

Hill, H. H.	1/ 2/41
Clements, J. V.	1/ 2/41
Taylor, H.	1/ 2/41
Matheson, B. H.	1/ 2/41
Harvey, R. V. B.	1/ 2/41
Harding, F.	1/ 2/41
Gamble, J.	1/ 2/41
Humphreys, J. E., D.C.M., M.M.	1/ 2/41
Gladman, J. A.	1/ 2/41
Parkes, P.	1/ 2/41
Larkin, W. H.	1/ 2/41
Owen, F. W.	1/ 2/41

Lieutenants - contd.

Birkby, J.	1/ 2/41
Whitby, F. J.	1/ 2/41
Horsburgh, J.	1/ 2/41
Shaw, E., M.M.	1/ 2/41

2nd Lieutenant

Walker, C.	21/ 7/41

Adjutant & Quarter-Master

Cumberland, Capt. (actg. 21/7/41) C. E., Gen. List Inf.	21/ 7/41

Medical Officer

NORTH MIDLAND AREA - contd.

NORTHAMPTONSHIRE ZONE

Commander	Reid, Col. P. L., O.B.E. (Lt.-Col. ret. pay) (Res. of Off.) 1/ 2/41
Territorial Army Association administering	The Northamptonshire T.A. & A.F. Association, Drill Hall, Clare St., Northampton.

PETERBOROUGH GROUP

Commander

1st NORTHAMPTONSHIRE (CITY OF PETERBOROUGH) BATTALION

Lt.-Colonel

Crowden, R. J. C., M.C. (Capt. late T.A.)	1/ 2/41

Majors

Farrow, H. J. (Lt. late Gloster R.)	1/ 2/41
Bromige, E. W.	1/ 2/41
Hassall, J. E. G. (Flying Offr. late R.A.F.)	1/ 2/41
Hann, G. E.	1/ 2/41
Goodacre, H. A. (Lt. late M.G. Corps.)	1/ 2/41
Bilham, E. A. J., M.C. (Capt. late Res. of Off.)	1/ 2/41

Captains

Heighton, W. A.	1/ 2/41
Neal, E. A. W.	1/ 2/41
Plaistowe, F. H. (Lt. late Oxf. & Bucks. L.I.)	1/ 2/41
Stewart, A. E. (2/Lt. late R.G.A.)	1/ 2/41
Taylor, C., D.C.M.	1/ 2/41
Campbell, J. I. (Lt. late R.E.)	1/ 2/41
Wilson, H. J. (Lt. late North'd. Fus.)	9/ 6/41

Lieutenants

Kettle, H.	1/ 2/41
Thompson, C. J., D.C.M.	1/ 2/41
Adamson, F.	1/ 2/41
Spreckley, T. G., D.C.M.	1/ 2/41
Fuller, F. R. H. (Lt. late A.I.F.)	1/ 2/41
Pailing, W. F.	1/ 2/41
Berridge A. L.	1/ 2/41
Clements, A. W., M.M.	1/ 2/41
Blackman, W. P.	1/ 2/41
Munton, A. C.	1/ 2/41
Larrett, W. D.	1/ 2/41
Howlett, L. T. (Lt. Res. of Off.)	1/ 2/41
Burnett, T. A. (Lt. late R.A.)	1/ 2/41
Bocker, J. H.	1/ 2/41
Banks, D. C. (Lt. late York H.)	1/ 2/41
Wilson, A. W. (Lt. late A. Cyclist Corps)	1/ 2/41
Dawson, H. P. E.	1/ 2/41
Ashling, H.	1/ 2/41
Ruddle, A. W.	1/ 2/41
Errington, F. A.	1/ 2/41
Need, T.	1/ 2/41
Willis, W. F.	1/ 2/41
Hook, R. T.	1/ 2/41

Lieutenants - contd.

Reed, T.	1/ 2/41
Rudge, S. G.	1/ 2/41
Thomson, A. C. A.	1/ 2/41
Knight, H. W.	1/ 2/41
Ruald, F. S., M.M.	1/ 6/41
Shearcroft, W. F. F.	9/ 6/41
Brewer, C.	9/ 7/41
Dent, F.	9/ 7/41

2nd Lieutenants

Collcott, H.	1/ 2/41
Chappell, A.	1/ 2/41
Young, J. H.	1/ 2/41
Allen, A. P.	1/ 2/41
Lawrence, A. C.	1/ 2/41
Twiddy, G. S.	1/ 2/41
Login, W.	1/ 2/41
Bichener, A. L.	1/ 2/41
Rowland, T.	1/ 2/41
Barnes, J. S.	1/ 2/41
Barnard, R. G.	1/ 2/41
German, A. F. E.	1/ 2/41
Smith, J. H.	1/ 2/41
Jones, W. G. M.	1/ 2/41
Milton, A. E.	1/ 2/41
Stroud, W. F.	1/ 2/41
Baylis, C. D.	1/ 2/41
Lawson, J. G.	1/ 2/41
Tebbs, W. H.	1/ 7/41
King, L. N.	9/ 7/41
Saunders, C. H.	9/ 7/41
Coates, N.	9/ 7/41
Allwright, F.	9/ 7/41

Adjutant & Quarter-Master

Medical Officer

Holmes, Maj. E. A. (Surgeon/Lt. late R.N.)	1/ 2/41

NORTH MIDLAND AREA - contd.

NORTHAMPTONSHIRE ZONE - contd.

PETERBOROUGH GROUP - contd.

2nd NORTHAMPTONSHIRE (SOKE OF PETERBOROUGH) BATTALION

Lt.-Colonel

Mellows, A. H., T.D.
(Bt.-Col. late T.A. Res.) 1/ 2/41

Majors

Samson, H. L. 1/ 2/41
Elliot, H. W. A.
(Capt. late Wilts. R.) 1/ 2/41
Peasgood, A., D.C.M. 1/ 2/41
Percival, A. F.
(Lt. late R.G.A.) 12/ 6/41
Warwick, J. G.
(Lt. late The Queen's R.) 12/ 6/41
Goddard, J. W., M.C.
(Maj. late R.F.A.) 12/ 6/41
Avery, J. G. 20/ 6/41

Captains

Dewhurst, H. 1/ 2/41
Everard, C. M. 1/ 2/41
Turnhill, L. G. 1/ 2/41
Allen, A. R., M.M. 12/ 6/41
Canham, E. W. 12/ 6/41
Macro, E. W.
(2/Lt. late R.A.F.) 20/ 6/41
Buckle, W. B.
(Lt. late North'n. R.) 30/ 7/41

Lieutenants

Shorrock, R. W. 1/ 2/41
Ferrier-Kerr, W. G.
(Capt. late Seaforth) 1/ 2/41
Wood, W. R.
(Lt. late M.G. Corps) 1/ 2/41
Perkins, R. 1/ 2/41
Garford, S. G. 1/ 2/41
Bolton, T. C. 1/ 2/41
Hall, G. M. A. 1/ 2/41
Northcott, W. H. E., M.M. 1/ 2/41
Glenn, N. T. 1/ 2/41
Gilby, F. W. 1/ 2/41

Lieutenants - contd.

Little, G. P. 1/ 2/41
Oldfield, T. 1/ 2/41
Conington, J. E. 1/ 2/41
Iliffe, F. 1/ 2/41
Parker, H. P.
(Lt. late Rif. Bde.) 1/ 2/41
Wiseman, C. E. 1/ 2/41
Harridge, C. S. 12/ 6/41
Snushall, G. F.
(Lt. late North'n R.) 27/ 6/41

2nd Lieutenants

Hicks, E. 1/ 2/41
Paten, H. St. J. B. 1/ 2/41
Button, J. W. T. 1/ 2/41
Franks, G. 1/ 2/41
Shelton, A. G. 1/ 2/41
Walker, H. S. 1/ 2/41
Perkins, L. R. 1/ 2/41
Pearson, H. H. 1/ 2/41
Stiggers, R. G. 1/ 2/41
Severn, E. 1/ 2/41
Briers, R. 1/ 2/41
Benstead, C. W. 1/ 2/41
Meeks, F. 1/ 2/41
Burgess, H. G. 1/ 2/41
Pledger, N. A. 1/ 2/41
Teesdale, A. G. 1/ 2/41
de Souza, E. V. 30/ 7/41

Adjutant & Quarter-Master

Carter, Capt. (actg. 4/3/41)
R. P., Gen. List Inf. 4/ 3/41

Medical Officer

Fulton, Maj. D. H., M.D. 1/ 2/41

NORTH MIDLAND AREA - contd.

NORTHAMPTONSHIRE ZONE - contd.

PETERBOROUGH GROUP - contd.

3rd NORTHAMPTONSHIRE (OUNDLE & THRAPSTON) BATTALION

Lt.-Colonel

Berridge, F. R., D.S.O., M.C. (Capt. late T.A.) 1/ 2/41

Majors

Lenton, F. J., M.C. (Lt. late R.E. Signals) 1/ 2/41
Richards, H. L., M.C. (Lt. late 12th L.) 1/ 2/41

Captains

Le Mare, G. 1/ 2/41
Harvey, C. E. (Lt. late Foresters) 1/ 2/41
Allday, E. C. J. (Lt. T.A. Res.) 1/ 2/41
Coombs, P. G. 1/ 2/41
Gainer, E. St. C. (2/Lt. late Seaforth) 1/ 2/41
Priestman, G. (Gen. List T.A.) 1/ 2/41
Spragg, F. F. 1/ 2/41
Weller, F. G. (Capt. late R.E.) 1/ 2/41
Bellville, G. E. (Capt. late 16th L.) 1/ 2/41
Jones, C. R. (2/Lt. late R.A.F.) 1/ 2/41

Lieutenants

Ainsworth, K. 1/ 2/41
Simpson, J. H. (Lt. late W. York R.) 1/ 2/41
Tomkins, J. W. 1/ 2/41
Thorpe, J. 1/ 2/41
Fahie, P. A. 1/ 2/41
White, G. P. 1/ 2/41
Massey, J. K. 1/ 2/41

Lieutenants - contd.

Wild, T. C. 1/ 2/41
Upcott, R. E. 1/ 2/41
Lee, C. M. 1/ 2/41
Micklem, L. O. (Capt. late North'n R.) 1/ 2/41
Ward, R. H. 1/ 2/41
Lascelles, J. E. (Capt. late R.A.F.) 1/ 2/41
Smith, T. W. W. 1/ 2/41
Barnes, E. A. 1/ 2/41
Yeld, R. K., O.B.E. (Maj. late Ind. Army) 1/ 2/41
Blackmore, F. W., M.C. (Lt. late Oxf. & Bucks. L.I.) 1/ 2/41

2nd Lieutenants

Scorer, J. N. 1/ 2/41
Ingrey, H. C. 1/ 2/41
Thorne, W. A. 1/ 2/41
Foster, A. E. 1/ 2/41
Heesom, D. S. 1/ 2/41
Hipwell, W. C. D. 1/ 2/41
Everard, V. 1/ 2/41
Cole, H. 1/ 2/41
Billinghurst, A. R. 1/ 2/41
Sharpe, C. E. 1/ 2/41
Horrell, T. C. 1/ 2/41

Adjutant & Quarter-Master

Sharp, Capt. (actg. 19/5/41) J., R.A. 19/ 5/41

Medical Officer

White, Maj. E. I. H. M.B. (Lt. late R.A.M.C.) 30/ 4/41

NORTH MIDLAND AREA - contd.

NORTHAMPTONSHIRE ZONE - contd.

KETTERING GROUP

4th NORTHAMPTONSHIRE (KETTERING BOROUGH) BATTALION

Lt.-Colonel

Holborow, G.
(Capt. late R.A.S.C.) 1/ 2/41

Majors

Baker, J. (Capt. late R.T.C.) 1/ 2/41
Howard, G. D. 1/ 2/41

Captains

Shepherdson, A. J.
(Capt. late Y. & L.R.) 1/ 2/41
Burns, A.
(2/Lt. late Labour Corps) 1/ 2/41
Russell, A.
(2/Lt. late North'n R.) 1/ 2/41
Johnson, A. 1/ 2/41
Newbould, H. R. 1/ 2/41
Watt, J. W. 1/ 2/41
Westley, F. R. 1/ 2/41
Kay, R. (Capt. late R.E.) 1/ 2/41
Davenport, W. J. F. 1/ 2/41
Culling, P. E. (Lt. late R.E.) 1/ 2/41
Issitt, H. W. 1/ 2/41
Clarke, L. M. 1/ 2/41
Castleton, T. B. 1/ 2/41
Bell, B. W. 14/ 6/41

Lieutenants

Mohun, N. H.
(Lt. late North'n R.) 1/ 2/41
Desborough, E. 1/ 2/41
Chater, J. F. 1/ 2/41
Summerly, F. 1/ 2/41
Toseland, A. 1/ 2/41
Stanley, C. E. 1/ 2/41
Giles, H. A. 1/ 2/41
Brockhurst, C. B. 1/ 2/41
Shepherd, L. A.
(2/Lt. late D.W.R.) 1/ 2/41

Lieutenants - contd.

Marlow, J. A.
(2/Lt. late North'n R.) 1/ 2/41
Smith, H. R. 1/ 2/41
Musgrave, F. 1/ 2/41
Maddocks, R. L. 1/ 2/41
Brodie, J. P.
(Lt. late London R.) 1/ 2/41
Harris, B. M. 1/ 2/41
Wright, W. A. 1/ 2/41
Blunden, A. E. 1/ 2/41
Munton, J. T., M.M. 1/ 2/41
Rowlatt, T. C. 1/ 2/41
Forwood, T. G. 1/ 2/41
Green, C. R. 1/ 2/41
Vickers, R. D. 1/ 2/41
Hicks, T. L. 1/ 2/41
Holmes, E. J. 1/ 2/41
Smith, F., M.M. 14/ 6/41

2nd Lieutenants

Ross, F. W.
(2/Lt. late R. War. R.) 1/ 2/41
Harrod, J. W.
(2/Lt. late North'n R.) 1/ 2/41
Langham, H. C. 1/ 2/41
Bagshaw, F. G. 1/ 2/41
Thurston, H. G. 20/ 6/41

Adjutant & Quarter-Master

Davis, Capt. (actg. 1/4/41)
H., ret. Ind. Army. 1/ 4/41

Medical Officer

Shirkey, Maj. W.
(Lt. late R.A.M.C.) 18/ 4/41

5th NORTHAMPTONSHIRE (KETTERING DISTRICT) BATTALION

Lt.-Colonel

Robinson, Sir Frederick V. L. Bt., M.C. (Maj. late North'n R.) 1/ 2/41

Majors

Colvin, J. C., M.B.E. (Maj. late R.E.) 1/ 2/41
Wright, B., M.C. (Capt. late North'n R.) 1/ 2/41
Saville, P. R. L. (Lt. late A.S.C.) 1/ 2/41
Sargeant, A. E. 29/ 7/41
Oliver, G. C. S. 29/ 7/41

Captains

Wallis, S. (2/Lt. late R. Bucks. H.) 1/ 2/41
Stansfield, J. B. 1/ 2/41
Ginns, R. (Lt. Late Ind. Army) 1/ 2/41
Waterfield, R. W. (2/Lt. late North'n R.) 1/ 2/41
Sanderson, R. M. C. 1/ 2/41
Chapman, W. J. 1/ 8/41

Lieutenants

Lane, A. D. 1/ 2/41
Chawner, J. S. (Capt. late R. War. R.) 1/ 2/41
Snell, E. 1/ 2/41
Hayward, R. F. 1/ 2/41
Hawes, A. J. 1/ 2/41
Barnwell, E. J. 1/ 2/41
Collins, W. A. R. 1/ 2/41
Woolston, C. W. C. 1/ 2/41
Grey, C. R. (Lt. late R.T.C.) 1/ 2/41
Wycherley, F. (Lt. late R.E.) 1/ 2/41
Cooke, A. F. 1/ 2/41
Bull, E. 1/ 2/41
Levett, S. 1/ 2/41
Holt, G. H. (Capt. late Ind. Army) 1/ 2/41

Lieutenants - contd.

Lloyd, N. 1/ 2/41
Watkins-Pitchford, D. J. 1/ 2/41
Pratt, C. J. T. 25/ 6/41
Daniels, A. D. 21/ 7/41
Austin, J. E. 1/ 8/41
Masters, S. S. 1/ 8/41
Freeman, A. 1/ 8/41
Tibbits, T. (2/Lt. late Foresters) 1/ 8/41

2nd Lieutenants

Marks, G. E. (Capt. late North'n Yeo.) 1/ 2/41
Porter, L. V. 1/ 2/41
McClelland, W. V. 1/ 2/41
Patrick, H. W. 1/ 2/41
Sharp, W. 1/ 2/41
Ballard, A. F. 1/ 2/41
Butterworth, J. A. 1/ 2/41
Clements, A. H. 1/ 2/41
Phillips, S. F. 1/ 2/41
Gardiner, S. 1/ 2/41
Barratt, H. 1/ 2/41
York, T. H. 1/ 2/41
Sawford, F. 1/ 2/41
West, F. J. W. 1/ 2/41
Clarke, M. A. 22/ 6/41

Adjutant & Quarter-Master

Butler, Capt. (actg. 28/4/41) F. H., ret. Ind. Army 28/ 4/41

Medical Officer

Gibbons, Maj. G. F. P., O.B.E., M.B. (Maj. late R.A.M.C.) 1/ 2/41

NORTH MIDLAND AREA - contd.

NORTHAMPTONSHIRE ZONE - contd.

KETTERING GROUP - contd.

6th NORTHAMPTONSHIRE (CORBY WORKS) BATTALION

Lt.-Colonel

Menzies-Wilson, J. R., O.B.E. (Capt. late R.E.)	1/ 2/41

Majors

Bell, W. C.	1/ 2/41
Beilby, R. B., M.C. (Lt. late Res. of Off.)	1/ 2/41
Wingate, D., M.C.	1/ 2/41

Captains

Opie, W. L. (Capt. late R.A.)	1/ 2/41
Hendry, D. C.	1/ 2/41
Rutherford, T.	1/ 2/41
Oldale, H. (2/Lt. late Y. & L. R.)	1/ 2/41
Bell, D. J.	1/ 2/41
Houston, W.	1/ 2/41
Hunter, G. A.	1/ 2/41

Lieutenants

Leavers, H. A. (Capt. late R.F.A.)	1/ 2/41
Chadwick, R. M.	1/ 2/41
Anderson, P.	1/ 2/41

2nd Lieutenants

Freeman, H. A.	1/ 2/41
Stimson, W. E. (Lt. late Leicester R.)	1/ 2/41
Yates, A. J. C.	1/ 2/41
Cresswell, J. E. G.	1/ 2/41
Coole, W. H. N.	1/ 2/41
Gray, H. (Lt. late North'd Fus.)	1/ 2/41
Sharp, C. A.	1/ 2/41
MacDougall, M.	1/ 2/41
Caldwell, R.	1/ 2/41
Matthews, A. J.	1/ 2/41
Fraser, D. G.	1/ 2/41
Bell, D.	1/ 2/41
Carlton, J.	1/ 2/41
Montgomery, W. T.	1/ 2/41
Dobie, J. A.	1/ 2/41
Taylor, G. H.	1/ 2/41
Jeavons, C. G.	1/ 2/41
McBride, W. W.	1/ 2/41
Dunn, J.	1/ 2/41
Glen, J.	1/ 2/41
Till, J. W.	1/ 2/41
Alexander, J. C.	17/ 6/41

Adjutant & Quarter-Master

Medical Officer

NORTH MIDLAND AREA - contd.
NORTHAMPTONSHIRE ZONE - contd.
WELLINGBOROUGH GROUP

Commander

7th NORTHAMPTONSHIRE (WELLINGBOROUGH TOWN) BATTALION

Lt.-Colonel

Allsop, H. L.	1/ 2/41

Majors

Higgins, A. H., M.B.E. (Capt. late North'n R.)	1/ 2/41
Curtis, T. R. (2/Lt. late R.T.C.)	1/ 2/41
Bayley, A. E. S., M.C. (Lt. late North'n R.)	1/ 2/41
Young, E., M.C. (Capt. late Gloster R.)	1/ 2/41
Solley, W. S.	1/ 2/41
Bennie, J.	1/ 2/41

Captains

Smillie, T.	1/ 2/41
Fishwick, W.	1/ 2/41
Gammidge, J. R.	1/ 2/41
Jones, G. M.	1/ 2/41
Jones, E. E.	1/ 2/41

Lieutenants

Ambler, E. M.	1/ 2/41
Trulove, W. M.	1/ 2/41
Poole, W.	1/ 2/41
Way, E. H. L	1/ 2/41
Bramham, W.	1/ 2/41
Minney, A. H.	1/ 2/41
Norman, L. F.	1/ 2/41
Hodgson, J. R.	1/ 2/41
Fuller, S. S.	1/ 2/41
Gibson, W. O. (Lt. late W. York. R.)	1/ 2/41
Vickers, C. E., M.M. (Lt. late R. Fus.)	1/ 2/41
Forrester, C. F.	1/ 2/41
Partridge, J. R. M.	1/ 2/41
Holton, W. D.	1/ 2/41
Gilbey, W. G.	1/ 2/41
Mehew, P. T.	1/ 2/41
Darling, R.	1/ 2/41
Bugby, H. D.	1/ 2/41
Dixon, A.	1/ 2/41
Gent, K. J.	1/ 2/41
Saxby, W. E.	1/ 2/41
Linnell, A. J. (Lt. late Manch. R.)	1/ 2/41
Boddington, A. G.	1/ 2/41
Stout, T.	17/ 6/41

2nd Lieutenants

Cooper, H. E. (Capt. late R.F.A.)	1/ 2/41
Sanders, H. J.	1/ 2/41
Ward, V. L.	1/ 2/41
Howlett, H. A.	27/ 5/41
Jones, H. G. C.	17/ 6/41
Pinnock, H. F.	20/ 6/41
Brown, A. G.	28/ 7/41

Adjutant & Quarter-Master

Chouler. Capt. (actg. 1/2/41) C. J., Gen. List Inf.	1/ 2/41

Medical Officer

Arthur, J. (Maj. ret. R.A.M.C.)	1/ 2/41

8th NORTHAMPTONSHIRE (WELLINGBOROUGH DISTRICT) BATTALION

Lt.-Colonel

Sykes, V. H. (Capt. late M.G. Corps)	1/ 2/41

Captains

Freer, A. H.	1/ 2/41
Denton, A. D. (Lt. late R.W.K.)	1/ 2/41
Richardson, J. C. (Lt. late R.W. Fus.)	1/ 2/41
Pettitt, T. F.	1/ 2/41
Allebone, A.	1/ 2/41

Lieutenants

Horrell, W. McC.	1/ 2/41
Sturgess, A. J. (Lt. late R.A.)	1/ 2/41
Deighton, E.	1/ 2/41
Weale, A. F.	1/ 2/41

2nd Lieutenants

Hall, K. W.	1/ 2/41
Warren, S. R.	1/ 2/41
Armitage, R. T.	1/ 2/41
Bletsoe, P. W. (Lt. late North'n Yeo.)	1/ 2/41
Patenall, H. R. (Capt. (Qr.-Mr.) late R.A.M.C.)	1/ 2/41
Jaques, H. F.	1/ 2/41
Fox, S. R.	1/ 2/41
Walpole, J.	1/ 2/41
Bainbridge, R. E.	1/ 2/41
Pyrah, A. C.	1/ 2/41
Streeton, A. V.	1/ 2/41
Gibbard, W. W. S. (2/Lt. late R.F.A.)	1/ 2/41
Rogers, A. G.	1/ 2/41
Reynolds, S. T.	1/ 2/41
Dunmore, E. C.	1/ 2/41
Green, R. K. (Lt. late R.F.A.)	1/ 2/41
Edwards, W.	1/ 2/41
Sargent, A. H.	1/ 2/41
Griggs, W. H.	9/ 6/41

Adjutant & Quarter-Master

Medical Officer

Davies, Maj. R. W., M.B., (Capt. late (R.A.M.C.)	9/ 6/41

NORTH MIDLAND AREA - contd.

NORTHAMPTONSHIRE ZONE - contd.

NORTHAMPTONSHIRE CENTRAL GROUP

Commander

9th NORTHAMPTONSHIRE (BRIXWORTH DISTRICT) BATTALION

Lt.-Colonel

Watson, G. S.
(Capt. late T.A.) 1/ 2/41

Majors

Dickens, R.
(Capt. late M.G. Corps.) 1/ 2/41
Pettit, J. T. H.
(Capt. late Somerset L.I.) 1/ 2/41
Lankester, G. P.
(Maj. late North'n R.) 7/ 6 /41

Captains

Middleton, G. G.
(Lt.-Col. late North'n Yeo.) 1/ 2/41
Howson Craufurd, J. D.
(Lt. late Camerons) 1/ 2/41
Baillon, L. C.
(Lt. late R.A.S C.) 1/ 2/41
Patrick, P. R. 1/ 2/41
Greenish, G. W. I. 1/ 2/41

Lieutenants

Rands, G. St. J.
(Capt. late North'n R.) 1/ 2/41
Merry, T N.
(Lt. late North'n Yeo) 1/ 2/41
Willett, H., M.B.E.
(Lt. late R.E.) 1/ 2/41
Robinson, C. L. 1/ 2/41
Barnard, J. T. 1/ 2/41
Britten, T. H. 1/ 2/41
Day, R. M. 1/ 2/41
Barker, S. 1/ 2/41
Newton, C. M. 1/ 2/41
Hawtin, D. A.
(Lt. late London R.) 1/ 2/41
Allen, S., D.C.M., M.M. 1/ 2/41
Starkie, E. T. W. 1/ 2/41
Sutton, H. J.
(2/Lt. late 3rd H.) 1/ 2/41
Brace, W. 1/ 2/41
Huggins, L. W. 1/ 2/41

Lieutenants - contd.

Skey, R. (Lt. late R. War. R.) 8/ 4/41
Wales, J. A. 16/ 4/41
Flint, C. D. 25/ 4/41
Palmer, H. C. 20/ 5/41
Toulson, F. 12/ 6/41
Jordison, H., O.B.E., D.C.M.
(Maj. (Qr.-Mr.)
late 15/19th H.) 1/ 7/41
Jackson, A. H. 2/ 7/41

2nd Lieutenants

Lee, J. 1/ 2/41
Heygate, L. W.
(Lt. late Bedfs. Yeo.) 1/ 2/41
Chappell, A. 1/ 2/41
Lang, F. W. 1/ 2/41
Spokes, T. H. 1/ 2/41
Smith, F. T. 1/ 2/41
Knight, R. A. 1/ 2/41
Shadlock, J. W., M.M. 1/ 2/41
Bryant, E. R., M.M. 1/ 2/41
Griffiths, P. J. 1/ 2/41
Dunmore, C. 1/ 2/41
Burley, V. R. 1/ 2/41
Rowlatt, T. 1/ 2/41
Elliott, P. T. 1/ 2/41
Burditt, R. E. 27/ 3/41
Ennals, R. W. 10/ 5/41

Adjutant & Quarter-Master

Oakey, Capt. (act. 14/3/41)
G. C., Gen. List Inf. 14/ 3/41

Medical Officer

Cogan, Maj. L. D. B., D.S.O.
(Col. late R.A.M.C.) 16/ 4/41

NORTH MIDLAND AREA - contd.

NORTHAMPTONSHIRE ZONE - contd.

NORTHAMPTONSHIRE CENTRAL GROUP - contd.

10th NORTHAMPTONSHIRE (DAVENTRY DISTRICT) BATTALION

Lt.-Colonel

Lees, G. W. M. (Capt. late T.A.) 1/ 2/41

Majors

Forwood, E. B. (Capt. late R.F.A.) 1/ 2/41
Bishop, A. K. D. 1/ 2/41
Underwood, C. T. (Lt. late North'n. Yeo.) 1/ 2/41

Captains

Coy, T. 1/ 2/41
Ransom, P. L. (Lt. late R.A.) 1/ 2/41
Burges, L. R. 1/ 2/41
Wilkins, N. G. L. 1/ 2/41
Draper, H. M. (Lt. late R.A.) 1/ 2/41
Coleman, J. C. (Lt. late M.G. Corps.) 9/ 6/41

Lieutenants

Mitchison, R. S. 1/ 2/41
Berry, W. C. 1/ 2/41
Smith, C. A. 1/ 2/41
Wykeham, P. H., M.C. (Capt. late R.A.) 1/ 2/41
Davis, T. 1/ 2/41
Gillingham, S. 1/ 2/41
Bean, R. D. J., D.C.M., M.M. 1/ 2/41
Giles, L. R. 1/ 2/41
Henley, Lord (Lt. late R.N.) 30/ 6/41

2nd Lieutenants

Jackson, W. J. 1/ 2/41
Redden, R., M.M. 1/ 2/41
Freeman, H. 1/ 2/41
Goodwin, T. C. 1/ 2/41
Pardo, G. W. 1/ 2/41
King, J. E. 25/ 4/41
Long, D. H. 13/ 6/41
Ashby, G. H. 27/ 7/41
Cooper, F. J. 29/ 7/41

Adjutant & Quarter-Master

Medical Officer

11th NORTHAMPTONSHIRE (HARDINGSTONE DISTRICT) BATTALION

Lt.-Colonel

Fraser, A. J., D.S.O. (Maj. late R.A.S.C.) 1/ 2/41

Majors

Thompson, F. A. (Capt. late Green Howards) 1/ 2/41
Penn, W. J. (Capt. late Welch R.) 1/ 2/41
Knight, J. A. (Maj. late Remount Serv.) 1/ 2/41

Captains

Hawkins, H. 1/ 2/41
Wilson, J. R. 1/ 2/41
Coles, P. E. 1/ 2/41

Lieutenants

Ashby, A. E. 1/ 2/41
Brown, F. 1/ 2/41
Elderton, H. 1/ 2/41
Frost, F. J., M.M. 1/ 2/41
Heygate, J. M. 1/ 2/41
Hill, F. R. 1/ 2/41
Merritt, A. 1/ 2/41
Smith, W. G. 1/ 2/41
Spencer, J. H. 1/ 2/41
Thurley, F. 1/ 2/41
Tomkins, C. R. 1/ 2/41
Marland, H. 1/ 2/41
Wraith, H. D. (Capt. ret. D.W.R.) 1/ 2/41

2nd Lieutenants

Lewis, C. W. 1/ 2/41
Holloway, B. G. 1/ 2/41
Clay, W. H. 16/ 6/41
Highfield, C. 16/ 6/41
Saunders, J. N. 16/ 6/41
Smith, A. C. 16/ 6/41
Smith, P. L. 16/ 6/41
Thomson, W. C. 22/ 7/41
Beardsmore, A. C. 1/ 8/41

Adjutant & Quarter-Master

Dacres-Smith, Capt. (actg. 24/4/41) F., Gen. List Inf. 24/ 4/41

Medical Officer

NORTH MIDLAND AREA - contd.

NORTHAMPTONSHIRE ZONE - contd.

NORTHAMPTONSHIRE CENTRAL GROUP - contd.

12th NORTHAMPTONSHIRE (NORTHAMPTON BOROUGH) BATTALION

Lt.-Colonel

Manning, T. E. (Maj. late T.A.)	1/ 2/41

Majors

Barnes, L. E., M.B.E. (Maj. late North'n. R.)	1/ 2/41
Browne, H. St. J., M.C., T.D. (Maj. late North'n. R.)	1/ 2/41
Manning, R., M.C. (Maj. late R. Bucks. H.)	1/ 2/41
Powell, E. W. H. (Capt. late R.T.C.)	1/ 2/41
Andrews, N. P. (Lt. late Gren. G'ds.)	1/ 2/41
McFarlane, A. (Lt. late M G. Corps.)	1/ 2/41

Captains

Hargrave, O. J. (Lt. late R.F.C.)	1/ 2/41
Patrick, S. B. (Lt. late R.T.C.)	1/ 2/41
Hutton, P. (Lt. late R.G.A.)	1/ 2/41
Baxter, A. S., O.B.E. (Capt. late R.A.S.C.)	1/ 2/41
Marfleet, R. J.	1/ 2/41

Lieutenants

Holder, F. H. (Capt. late M.G. Corps.)	1/ 2/41
Batten, N. C. (Capt. late Mon. R.)	1/ 2/41
Corsby, R. E. (Lt. late K.R.R.C.)	1/ 2/41
Oates, G. H. (Lt. late R.A.)	1/ 2/41
Jones, P. G. (Lt. late M.G. Corps.)	1/ 2/41
Lucas, L. W. (Lt. late Suffolk R.)	1/ 2/41
Harris, C. G. (Lt. late R.T.C.)	1/ 2/41
Thornton, F. K. (2/Lt. late Somerset L.I.)	1/ 2/41
Bennett, S. F. (2/Lt. late Herts. R.)	1/ 2/41
Beeston, E.	1/ 2/41
Mills, J. H.	1/ 2/41
Williams, P. C.	1/ 2/41
Pancoust, W. H.	1/ 2/41
Freestone, F. W.	1/ 2/41
Hasler, S.	1/ 2/41
Barton, A. G. R.	1/ 2/41
Brown, L. H.	1/ 2/41
Nightingale, J.	1/ 2/41
Prentice, E., D.C.M.	1/ 2/41
Wood, W. E.	1/ 2/41
Crask, H. W.	1/ 2/41

Lieutenants - contd.

Amburg, V. H. C.	1/ 2/41
Blason, A. W.	1/ 7/41

2nd Lieutenants

Whiting, F. C. (Capt. late Wilts. R.)	1/ 2/41
Jennings, H. L. C. (Lt. late T.A.)	1/ 2/41
Cole, F. (Lt. late R.A.S.C.)	1/ 2/41
Sheldon, H. S. (2/Lt. late Essex R.)	1/ 2/41
Armitt, R. B.	1/ 2/41
Reynolds, R.	1/ 2/41
Lea, H. E.	1/ 2/41
Vials, G. A. T. (Lt. late D.W.R)	1/ 2/41
Brown, C. H. F.	1/ 2/41
Best, W. H.	1/ 2/41
Rainbow, H. H. T.	1/ 2/41
Gavin, J. S.	1/ 2/41
Marriott, C. W. (Lt. late R. Berks. R.)	1/ 2/41
Evans, W. A. W.	1/ 2/41
Thomson, G.	1/ 2/41
Metcalfe, F. G.	1/ 2/41
Salter, F. H.	1/ 2/41
Bayes, K. G.	1/ 2/41
Bason, A. L.	1/ 2/41
Harris, V. J. H. (Lt. late North'n. R.)	1/ 2/41
Catlow, C. S.	1/ 2/41
Payne, A. C.	1/ 2/41
Pepperell, W. C. (Capt. (Qr.-Mr.) late R.A.V.C.)	1/ 2/41
Turner, E. G.	22/ 4/41
Bird, H. T.	29/ 4/41

Adjutant & Quarter-Master

Gardner, Capt. (actg. 20/5/41) A. W., Gen. List Inf.	20/ 5/41

Medical Officer

Thompson, Maj. G. H. (Capt. late T.A.)	1/ 5/41

NORTH MIDLAND AREA - contd.

NORTHAMPTONSHIRE ZONE - contd.

TOWCESTER & BRACKLEY GROUP

Commander.

13th NORTHAMPTONSHIRE (TOWCESTER) BATTALION

Lt.-Colonel

Atkinson, P. Y., M.C. (Capt. late 5th D.G.) 1/ 2/41

Majors

Beasley, J. N., M.C. (Capt. late North'n. R.) 1/ 2/41
Pebody, H., M.M. (Lt. late M.G. Corps) 14/ 7/41

Captains

Grant-Ives, J. C. (Capt. late Rif. Bde.) 1/ 2/41
Griffin, W. G. T. 1/ 2/41
Davies, F. W. 14/ 7/41

Lieutenants

Millar, J. W. (Lt. late Res. of Off.) 1/ 2/41
Owen, D. H. (Lt. late Welsh Horse) 1/ 2/41
Green, J. G. J. 1/ 2/41
Brader, F. L. 1/ 2/41
Vinning, H. S. 1/ 2/41
Hodges, H. J. (Lt. late R.A.O.C.) 1/ 2/41
Bull, B. 1/ 2/41
Ivens, J. H. 1/ 2/41
Woolacott, W. F. A. 1/ 2/41
Dancer, J. A. 1/ 2/41
Jones, A. L. 1/ 2/41
Sitwell, S. (Lt. late Gren. G'ds.) 1/ 2/41
Cooke, N. A. 1/ 2/41
Edwards, H. F. 1/ 2/41
Prisley, J. G. 1/ 2/41
Seckington, R. M. 1/ 2/41
Collar, T. H., M.M. 1/ 2/41
Rossiter, C. J. 1/ 2/41
Ivens, W. H. 1/ 2/41
Leach, T. H. de B. (Lt. late R.T.C.) 1/ 2/41
Colbourne, E. W. 1/ 2/41
Weston, W. H. 1/ 2/41
Hinton, W. 1/ 2/41
Faux, B. F. 1/ 2/41
Holloway, A. 9/ 6/41
Ratledge, W. H. 9/ 6/41

Adjutant & Quarter-Master

Medical Officer

Reid, Maj. A. E. 15/ 4/41

14th NORTHAMPTONSHIRE (BRACKLEY) BATTALION

Lt.-Colonel

Furlong, N. C. B. (Maj. S. Ir. Horse) 1/ 2/41

Majors

Guinness, G. (Capt. late C. G'ds.) 1/ 6/41
Lassen, E. J. (Capt. late Gen. List) 1/ 6/41
Blakiston, J. F., C.I.E. (Capt. late Ind. Army) 1/ 6/41
Donner, E. L. (Lt. late Ir. G'ds.) 1/ 6/41
Kench, F. C. 1/ 6/41

Captains

Lieutenants

Moore, C. A. St. G., M.B.E. (Capt. late R.E.) 1/ 2/41
Okell, C. E. F. (Lt. late Foresters) 1/ 2/41
Wilks, E. R. (Lt. late Berks. Yeo.) 1/ 2/41
Langdon, E. B. 1/ 2/41
Armstrong, S. G. 1/ 2/41
Law, R. T. I. 1/ 2/41
Garner, R. 1/ 2/41
Mold, H. G. 1/ 2/41
Compton, E. C. 1/ 2/41
King, H. G. 1/ 2/41
Humphris, J. W. 1/ 2/41
Wynne, A. C. 1/ 2/41
Heathorn, N. L. 1/ 2/41
Chittenden, H. F., M.C. (Capt. late R.E.) 28/ 7/41

Adjutant & Quarter-Master

Medical Officer

Soden, Maj. G. E. T. 9/ 6/41

NORTH MIDLAND AREA - contd.

LEICESTERSHIRE ZONE

Commander	Cope, Col. Sir Thomas G., Bt., C.M.G., D.S.O., P.S.C., (Hon. Brig.-Gen. ret. pay) 1/ 2/41
Second in Command	Packe, Lt.-Col. E.C., D.S.O., O.B.E., (Lt.-Col. ret pay) 1/ 2/41
Assistant to Commander	Drummond, Capt. E. R. B., (Capt. Late Rif. Bde.) 1/ 2/41
Territorial Army Association administering	The Leicestershire & Rutland T.A. & A.F. Association, The Magazine, Oxford St., Leicester.

LEICESTER GROUP

Commander	Tyler, Col. H. W. H., M.C., (Bt. Col. T.A. Res.) (Hon. Col. R.E.T.A.) 1/ 2/41
Deputy Commander	Elliott, Lt.-Col. C. A. B., (Maj. late Leicester R.) 1/ 2/41
Assistant to Commander	Boddy, Capt. J. A. V. (Lt. late Durham L.I.) 1/ 2/41

NORTH MIDLAND AREA - contd.
LEICESTERSHIRE ZONE - contd.
LEICESTER GROUP - contd.

1st LEICESTERSHIRE (NORTH LEICESTER) BATTALION

Lt.-Colonel

Hitchings, F. B., M.C. (Maj. late Devon R.)	1/ 2/41

Majors

Jarvis, W. B., O.B.E. (Capt. late Leicester R.)	1/ 2/41
Byford, D. (2/Lt. late R.T.C.)	1/ 2/41
Harding, W. R. (Lt. late M.G. Corps.)	1/ 2/41
Peach, A. N. (Capt. late R.A.S.C.)	1/ 2/41
Rains, F. (Lt. late R. War. R.)	1/ 2/41

Captains

George, A. S.	1/ 2/41
Flint, F. C. (Lt. late Foresters)	1/ 2/41
Kelly, F. H.	1/ 2/41
Russell, P. A. (Lt. late R.A.F.)	1/ 2/41
Grainger, G. C. (Lt. late R. Signals)	1/ 2/41
Evans, J. R.	17/ 6/41

Lieutenants

Fraser, W. M. (2/Lt. late R. Signals)	1/ 2/41
Patrick, F. F.	1/ 2/41
Stewart, D. (Lt. late M.G. Corps.)	1/ 2/41
Vaughan-Harbourne, J. C.	1/ 2/41
Goldsworthy, F. J.	1/ 2/41
Furber, W. J. K.	1/ 2/41
Cayless, F. (Capt. late Y. & L.R.)	1/ 2/41
Godwin, H. W.	1/ 2/41
Rogers, R. G. (Lt. late Manch. R.)	1/ 2/41
Boxall, H. G.	1/ 2/41
Bloore, F. W. (2/Lt. late Res. of Off.)	1/ 2/41
Gardner, J. C.	1/ 2/41
Harrison, F. W. (Lt. late 11th H.)	1/ 2/41
McCrory, H. M. (Lt. ret. R.F.A.)	1/ 2/41
Catlow, N. S. (Lt. late London Rif. Bde.)	1/ 2/41
Voce, A.	4/ 6/41
Whitcher, W. F.	1/ 8/41

2nd Lieutenants

Ward, J. D.	1/ 2/41
Jeyes, H. (2/Lt. ret.)	1/ 2/41
Carr, J. W. L. (Lt. late M.G. Corps.)	1/ 2/41
Chapman, E. O.	1/ 2/41
Padmore, J. K.	1/ 2/41
Heyworth, J. F.	1/ 2/41
Daniels, P. E. (Lt. late A.S.C.)	1/ 2/41
Barrie, S. G.	1/ 2/41
Moore, J. B.	1/ 2/41
Baxter, E. S., M.C. (2/Lt. late R.T.C.)	1/ 2/41
Fillingham, W. (2/Lt. late Manch. R.)	1/ 2/41
Browning, T., D.C.M.	1/ 2/41
Biggs, R. A.	1/ 2/41
Evans, I.	1/ 2/41
Allen, T. W.	1/ 2/41
Sawday, T. T. (Lt. late R.A.F.)	1/ 2/41
Condon, J. C.	1/ 2/41
Glover, E. A.	1/ 2/41
Bown, A. R.	1/ 2/41
Morris, L. M. (2/Lt. late Cheshire R.)	1/ 2/41
Pyne, W. J., D.C.M.	1/ 2/41
Harrison, A. J.	1/ 2/41
Gimson, W.	1/ 2/41
Warden, W. E.	1/ 2/41
Winder, J. A.	1/ 2/41
Rudkin, L. S.	1/ 2/41
Bates, E. B.	1/ 2/41
Roberts, H. S. (Lt. late Leicester R.)	1/ 2/41
Heath, F. S.	1/ 2/41
Carlisle, R.	4/ 6/41
Hallum, W. B. (Lt. late D.L.I.)	4/ 6/41
Smith, D.	18/ 6/41
Judkins, O. V. (Lt. late R.A.F.)	1/ 8/41

Adjutant & Quarter-Master

Medical Officer

Binns, Maj. C. C. H.	1/ 6/41

2nd LEICESTERSHIRE (SOUTH LEICESTER) BATTALION

Lt.-Colonel

Pares, W. T., M.C. (Capt. late Serv. Bn. Bedfs. R.)	1/ 2/41

Majors

Smart, E., M.C. (Lt. late R.H.A.)	1/ 2/41
Davy, A. H. (Maj. late R.A.S.C.)	1/ 2/41
VC Cruickshank, R. E.	1/ 2/41
Hind, A. H., M.C. (Lt. late M.G. Corps.)	1/ 2/41
Browning, L.	1/ 2/41
Richardson, W. N. L. (Lt. late K.S.L.I.)	1/ 2/41

Captains

Day, H. A., M.C. (Capt. late R. Mar.)	1/ 2/41
Kent, M. A., M.B.E., M.C. (Lt. late Foresters)	1/ 2/41
Humphrey, R. S., D.C.M.	1/ 2/41
Ringer, F. J.	1/ 2/41
Hannam, E.	1/ 2/41
Herrick, W. H. (2/Lt. late Leicester R.)	1/ 2/41

Lieutenants

Allen, H. R.	1/ 2/41
Hellicar, G. H. (Capt. late Lan. Fus.)	1/ 2/41
Fox, W. S. (Lt. late R.A.S.C.)	1/ 2/41
Ramsey, F. P.	1/ 2/41
Green, P. A. (Capt. late Ind. Army)	1/ 2/41
Jackson, F.	1/ 2/41
Tuckley, H., M.M. (2/Lt. late R. War. R.)	1/ 2/41
Skeffington, F. (2/Lt. late Leicester R.)	1/ 2/41
Backhouse, J. B.	1/ 2/41
Freer, H. (Lt. late Leicester R.)	1/ 2/41
Watson, A. N.	1/ 2/41
Shepherd, G. H. (2/Lt. late R.G.A.)	1/ 2/41
Kimberley, A.	1/ 2/41
Pickering, W. E.	1/ 2/41
Johnson, F.	1/ 2/41
Williams, C. P. (2/Lt. late R.W. Fus.)	1/ 2/41
Peet, T. A.	1/ 2/41
Loughland, T. H.	1/ 2/41
Jones, R.	1/ 2/41
Wells, G. A.	1/ 2/41

Lieutenants - contd.

Burns, T.	1/ 2/41
Clarkson, A. H.	1/ 2/41
Ramsden, J. W.	1/ 2/41
Miller, W. K. (Lt. late North'n. R.)	20/ 6/41
Blackwell, A. J. S.	1/ 7/41
Slater, J. E.	1/ 8/41
Fox, E. S. (Lt. late A.S.C.)	1/ 8/41
Morgan, W. J. (Capt. late R.A.F.)	1/ 8/41

2nd Lieutenants

Allen, C. R. (2/Lt. late Leicester R.)	1/ 2/41
Cranfield, W. F.	1/ 2/41
Harrison, J. S. (Lt. late R.F.C.	1/ 2/41
Dymock, H. M.	1/ 2/41
Thomson, A. J.	1/ 2/41
Barker, R. G.	1/ 2/41
Barrett, J. A.	1/ 2/41
Crabtree, E. R.	1/ 2/41
Johnson, H. F.	1/ 2/41
Wells, E.	1/ 2/41
Taylor, W. H.	1/ 2/41
Humberstone, F. W.	1/ 2/41
Wale, H.	1/ 2/41
Such, A.	1/ 2/41
Immins, L. T.	1/ 2/41
Orton, C. S.	1/ 2/41
Pick, S. J.	1/ 2/41
Berry, F. A.	1/ 2/41
March, E.	1/ 2/41
Ford, T. E.	1/ 2/41
Hemming, F. W.	1/ 2/41
Meiklejohn, R. (Lt. late Ind. Army)	1/ 2/41
Rawson, R. H.	1/ 2/41
Cottam, E. J.	1/ 6/41
Howe, W. E.	1/ 6/41
Barnett, C. H.	1/ 6/41
Read, F. C., D.C.M., M.M.	1/ 8/41
Wallace, W. E.	1/ 8/41

Adjutant & Quarter-Master

Medical Officer

Barker, Maj. R. S., M.B. (Capt. late R.A.M.C.)	1/ 6/41

NORTH MIDLAND AREA - contd.

LEICESTERSHIRE ZONE - contd.

LEICESTER GROUP - contd.

3rd LEICESTERSHIRE (WEST LEICESTER) BATTALION

Lt.-Colonel

Name	Date
Jones, T. B. (Lt. late Leicester R.)	1/ 2/41

Majors

Name	Date
Palfreyman, G. W., M.C. (Lt. late Leicester R.)	1/ 2/41
Russell, G. (Capt. late Leicester R.)	1/ 2/41
Frears, C. R. (2/Lt. late Foresters)	1/ 2/41
Pope, S. A.	1/ 2/41

Captains

Name	Date
Goadby A. W.	1/ 2/41
Huntrods, R. M. (Capt. late North'd. Fus.)	1/ 2/41
Pochin, H. R. (Capt. late Leicester R.)	1/ 2/41
Ashwell, H. F., M.C. (Capt. late R. Fus.)	1/ 2/41
Kendall, E. C. (Capt. late Cheshire R.)	1/ 2/41

Lieutenants

Name	Date
Smedley, W. H., D.C.M.	1/ 2/41
Harvey, F. W. (Capt. late Cheshire R.)	1/ 2/41
Harris, J. (2/Lt. late Suffolk R.)	1/ 2/41
Hudson, A.	1/ 2/41
Armitage, E. (Lt. late North'd. Fus.)	1/ 2/41
West, R. W.	1/ 2/41
Biggs, A. L., D.C.M.	1/ 2/41
Evison, F. N. (Lt. ret. pay W. York R.)	1/ 2/41
Halford, A. L. (Capt. late Leicester R.)	1/ 2/41
Selkirk, J. G.	1/ 2/41
Kershaw, R. K. W.	1/ 2/41
Lacey, W. (Lt. late Middx. R.)	1/ 2/41
Knight, R. A. (2/Lt. late M.G. Corps)	1/ 2/41
Thomson, F. Y., M.M (2/Lt. late Seaforth)	1/ 2/41
Ward-Willis, G. (Lt. Oxf. & Bucks. L.I.)	1/ 2/41
Allcock, E. S.	1/ 2/41
Horne, J. (Lt. late North'n. R.)	1/ 2/41
Allen, M. G.	1/ 2/41
Warner, W.	1/ 2/41
Fantom, G. (2/Lt. late Manch. R.)	1/ 2/41

Lieutenants - contd.

Name	Date
Pearson, H. R.	1/ 2/41
Hipwell, F.	1/ 2/41
Brown, F.	1/ 2/41
Mills, J. (Lt. late Leicester R.)	1/ 2/41
Wood, S. R.	1/ 2/41

2nd Lieutenants

Name	Date
Laggett, C. M.	1/ 2/41
Smith, J. W. S.	1/ 2/41
Illson, F.	1/ 2/41
Swanson, G. J.	1/ 2/41
Greaves, R. J. L.	1/ 2/41
Sibson, J. W.	1/ 2/41
Jordon, L. T.	1/ 2/41
Burton, T. E.	1/ 2/41
Spiers, E.	1/ 2/41
Alexander, F. A.	1/ 2/41
Hubbard, J. L.	1/ 2/41
Launder, C. L. (Lt. late R.F.A.)	1/ 2/41
Allen, W. R.	1/ 2/41
Russell, H.	1/ 2/41
Lowe, J. W.	1/ 2/41
Hyde, H. C. (Lt. late R.F.C.)	1/ 2/41
Ball, P. H.	1/ 2/41
Hunt, H. W.	1/ 2/41
Davison, L., M.M.	1/ 2/41
Fritchley, A. W.	1/ 2/41
Smith, L. O.	1/ 2/41
Jenkinson, W. E.	1/ 2/41
Fanton, H. J., M.M.	1/ 2/41
Wolstenholme, H. B., O.B.E.	1/ 2/41
Fogerty, V. M.	1/ 2/41
Midgley, H. L. (Capt. late K.O.Y.L.I.)	1/ 2/41
Hardy, L. E.	1/ 7/41
Hill, D. M. J	1/ 7/41
Williams, E. J. (Capt. late W. York R.)	1/ 7/41
Biggs, J. D.	1/ 7/41
Worthing, L. S. (Lt. late R.A.F.)	1/ 8/41

Adjutant & Quarter-Master

Medical Officer

Name	Date
Allen, Maj. T. W. (Capt. late R.A.M.C.)	1/ 5/41

NORTH MIDLAND AREA - contd.

LEICESTERSHIRE ZONE - contd.

LEICESTER GROUP - contd.

4th LEICESTERSHIRE (CENTRAL LEICESTER) BATTALION

Lt.-Colonel

Whitehead, A. S. 1/ 2/41

Majors

Dunn, W. N., (Capt. late Leicester R.) 1/ 2/41
Evans, S. G., M.C. (Maj. late Hampshire R.) 1/ 2/41
Inman, D. S., (Maj. late Cheshire R.) 1/ 2/41
Carn, W. E. B., (Capt. late The Kings R.) 1/ 2/41
Whowell, W., M.C. (Capt. late E. Lan. R.) 1/ 2/41

Captains

Richards, A. C. W. (Flying Offr. late R.A.F.) 1/ 2/41
Stafford, C. H. (Lt. late R.A.F.) 1/ 2/41
Crawford, H. C. (Capt. late R.G.A.) 1/ 2/41
Parson, H. K. 1/ 2/41
Knight, O. B., (Lt. late Leicester R.) 1/ 2/41
Westhead, W. E. 1/ 2/41
Herbert, C. A. 1/ 6/41

Lieutenants

Lincoln, C. D. 1/ 2/41
Lole, E. F. (Lt. late M.G. Corps.) 1/ 2/41
Pickin, H. H. 1/ 2/41
Bowles, F. S. 1/ 2/41
Wilson, H. G. A. R. 1/ 2/41
Duncan, F. A. (Lt. late R.E.) 1/ 2/41
Mills, M. (Lt. late Leicester R.) 1/ 2/41 1/ 2/41
Walker, W. M. 1/ 2/41
Watson, F. 1/ 2/41
Corah, J. H., (Capt. late Leicester R.) 1/ 2/41
Noakes, W. W. 1/ 2/41
Preston, B. W., (Capt. late R.E.) 1/ 2/41
Toone, F. J. 1/ 2/41
Laker, T. T. (2/Lt. late R.A.F.) 1/ 2/41
Murray, G. 1/ 2/41
Pollard, F. 1/ 2/41
Fry, F. E. 1/ 2/41
Flint, H. C. (Lt. late Foresters) 1/ 2/41
Sibson, A. H. 1/ 2/41
Hefford, C. H. 1/ 2/41
Goddard, J. M. 1/ 2/41
Houldsworth, J. 1/ 2/41
Clarke, A. 1/ 2/41
Biggs, R. H. 1/ 2/41
Griffin, T. S. (Lt. late R.G.A.) 1/ 2/41
Fowler, E. G. (Capt. late R.A.S.C.) 1/ 2/41
Benwell, R. B. (Lt. late R.A.) 1/ 2/41
Smith, E. 1/ 6/41
Day, J. 1/ 6/41
Quantrill, G. H., M.C. (Capt. late Lincoln R.) 1/ 7/41
Wood, W. J L. (Lt. late Leicester R.) 1/ 8/41
Love, G. H. 1/ 8/41

NORTH MIDLAND AREA - contd.

LEICESTERSHIRE ZONE - contd.

LEICESTER GROUP - contd.

4th Leicestershire (Central Leicester) Battalion - contd.

2nd Lieutenants

Webster, F. W.	1/ 2/41
Walker, J. (2/Lt. late R.T.C.)	1/ 2/41
Holt, J. A.	1/ 2/41
Whitehead, J. C. H.	1/ 2/41
Tolton, A.	1/ 2/41
Bee, E.	1/ 2/41
York, F. A.	1/ 2/41
Griffin, R.	1/ 2/41
Butler, C. W.	1/ 2/41
Armstrong, R. M.	1/ 2/41
Grimley, H. J.	1/ 2/41
Bentley, W.	1/ 2/41
Seller, G. T.	1/ 2/41
Harris, B. J.	1/ 2/41
Payne, F. W.	1/ 2/41
Cooke, E. A.	1/ 2/41
Tilley, H. W.	1/ 2/41
Barrett, G.	1/ 2/41
Jackson, L. (Sub.-Lt. late R.N.V.R.)	1/ 2/41
Holmes, A. N.	1/ 2/41
Sawyer, F. G.	1/ 2/41
Smith, C. A.	1/ 2/41
Dalkin, T.	1/ 2/41
Barry, J. J.	1/ 2/41
Harrison, R. W.	1/ 2/41
Porter, S. J.	1/ 2/41
Fisher, H. G.	1/ 2/41
West, W.	1/ 2/41
Farthing, A. C., M.M.	1/ 2/41
Billingham, C. H., D.C.M.	1/ 2/41
Broome, A. L.	1/ 2/41
Woolmer, R., D.C.M.	1/ 2/41
Weaving, G. T.	1/ 2/41
Wright, H.	1/ 2/41
Hill, J.	1/ 2/41
Brown, O. J.	1/ 2/41
Silley, B. (Capt. late I.C.)	1/ 2/41
Ingram, E. G. W., D.C.M.	1/ 2/41
Pallett, S. E. (2/Lt. late Leicester R.)	1/ 6/41
Wright, F. R.	1/ 7/41
Lowe, G. H.	1/ 8/41

2nd Lieutenants - contd.

Toon, E.	1/ 8/41
Tubb, F. R.	1/ 8/41

Adjutant & Quarter-Master

Lyall, Capt. (actg. 28/ 4/41) A. E. D., Gen. List Inf.	28/ 4/41

Medical Officer

Cracknell, Maj. D. G.	1/ 6/41

NORTH MIDLAND AREA - contd.

LEICESTERSHIRE ZONE - contd.

LEICESTER GROUP - contd.

5th LEICESTERSHIRE (BELVOIR) BATTALION

Lt.-Colonel

Lockett, W. J., D.S.O. (Col. ret. pay)	1/ 2/41

Majors

Fellowes-Prynne, A. J. (Capt. late Devon R.)	1/ 2/41
Groome, A. W. W., M.B.E., (Capt. late R.A.F.)	1/ 2/41
Marsh, A. P., T.D. (Capt. late Leicester R.)	1/ 2/41
Wilson, W. H. (Maj. late R.A.)	21/ 4/41

Captains

Gates, R. (Capt. late Green Howards)	1/ 2/41
Punchard, W. B.	1/ 2/41
de la Cour, F. R. S. (Lt. late R.A.)	21/ 4/41
Jaggard, H. F.	16/ 5/41

Lieutenants

Black, R. L.	1/ 2/41
Botterill, K. R.	1/ 2/41
Brooks, T.	1/ 2/41
Collier, N. G.	1/ 2/41
Ison, W. A.	1/ 2/41
Platts, A. S.	1/ 2/41
Saunders, C. F. (Lt. late R.T.C.)	1/ 2/41
Smith, C. P. (Capt. late M.G. Corps)	1/ 2/41
Stannage, H. C.	1/ 2/41
Walker, W. G.	1/ 2/41

Lieutenants - contd.

Warner, F. E.	1/ 2/41
Warner, W. E.	1/ 2/41
Warr, G. C.	1/ 2/41
Whitehead, R. W.	1/ 2/41
Wood, K. M.	1/ 2/41
Entwistle, R.	1/ 2/41
Hawley, H.	1/ 2/41
Hempshall, J. A.	1/ 2/41
Cronin, H. D. G.	1/ 6/41

2nd Lieutenants

Coy, C. C.	1/ 2/41
Culpin, E., M.M.	1/ 2/41
Fensome, S. J., (Lt. late R.F.A.)	1/ 2/41
Grasse, F.	1/ 2/41
Ibbotson, G. (Capt. late R.F.A.)	1/ 2/41
Williams, J. F.	1/ 2/41
Brewitt, F. H.	1/ 2/41
Kirk, R. S., M.M.	1/ 7/41
Owen, J. R.	1/ 7/41

Adjutant & Quarter-Master

Medical Officer

Cuddigan, Capt. S. T.	1/ 6/41

NORTH MIDLAND AREA - contd.

LEICESTERSHIRE ZONE - contd.

LEICESTER GROUP - contd.

6th LEICESTERSHIRE (QUORN) BATTALION

Lt.-Colonel

Nutting, Sir Harold S., Bt. (Capt. ret. pay)	1/ 2/41

Majors

Armytage, J. L. (Capt. late K.R.R.C.)	1/ 2/41
Cantrell-Hubbersty, W. P. (Maj. late 14/20th H.)	1/ 2/41
Lorrimer, J. H. (Lt. late R.F.C.)	1/ 2/41
Wilson, J. M. (Capt. late L.G.)	1/ 2/41

Captains

Barnes, H. G.	1/ 2/41
Butteriss, W. G., M.C., M.M. (Lt. late Green Howards)	1/ 2/41
Ewen, N. A. J. (Late R.A.F.)	1/ 2/41
Inglesant, H. E. (Lt. late Leicester R.)	1/ 2/41

Lieutenants

Barrow, G. S. (Capt. late H.A.C.)	1/ 2/41
Buckley, G. R.	1/ 2/41
Cox, C. H. (Lt. late Leicester R.)	1/ 2/41
Ford, T. F. (Lt. late M.G. Corps)	1/ 2/41
Forsell, F. M., M.C., (Capt. late R.F.A.)	1/ 2/41
Frier, W. G., M.C.	1/ 2/41
Gerard-Ligh, J. C. (Capt. late L.G.)	1/ 2/41
Gowling, A.	1/ 2/41
Lea, G. L. (Capt. late Leicester R.)	1/ 2/41

56455-6(179)

Lieutenants - contd.

Mitchell-Smith, C.	1/ 2/41
Morton, H. J.	1/ 2/41
Radford, F. W.	1/ 2/41
Rawlinson, E. H.	1/ 2/41
Riddington, R. A.	1/ 2/41
Swann, A. W., M.M.	1/ 2/41
Thomson, N. K., M.C. (Lt. late R.E.)	1/ 2/41
Brown, F. L.	1/ 2/41
Jaques, F. V. (Late Ref. of Off.)	1/ 2/41
Wholton, G. E.	1/ 2/41
Thompson, H. G.	28/ 3/41
Chandler, A. J.	27/ 5/41
Sharp, A. T., O.B.E. (Capt. late M.G. Corps)	1/ 7/41

2nd Lieutenants

Copeland, W. F. (2/Lt. late A. Cyclist Corps)	1/ 2/41
Boyes, D. E.	1/ 2/41
Foden, S.	1/ 2/41
Smith, W. H.	1/ 2/41
Swain, J. P., M.C., D.C.M. (Maj. late Labour Corps)	1/ 2/41

Adjutant & Quarter-Master

Medical Officer

Fagge, Maj. R. H. (Capt. late R.A.M.C.)	1/ 6/41

NORTH MIDLAND AREA - contd.

LEICESTERSHIRE ZONE - contd.

LOUGHBOROUGH GROUP

Commander

9th LEICESTERSHIRE (LOUGHBOROUGH) BATTALION

Lt.-Colonel

Lewis, S. K.	1/ 2/41

Majors

Ward, J. L., M.C., (Capt. T.A. Res.)	1/ 2/41
Nichol, J., M.C. (Capt. late London R.)	1/ 2/41
Reid, L. G. (Lt. late T.A. Res.)	1/ 2/41
Stamper, H. J. (Lt. late Manch. R.)	1/ 2/41
Tucker, J. P. (Lt. late London R.)	1/ 2/41
Vigden-Jenks, J. C. (Capt. late Ind. Army)	1/ 2/41

Captains

Bell, W. H., M.C. (Capt. late R. War. R.)	1/ 2/41
Ingram, L. P. (Lt. late R.E.)	1/ 2/41
Kidger, J. H. (2/Lt. late 3rd H.)	1/ 2/41
Murray, H. L.	1/ 2/41
Wakefield, P. S. (Lt. late T.A. Res.)	1/ 2/41
Thomas, E. H.	23/ 4/41

Lieutenants

Short, C.	1/ 2/41
Adams, A., D.C.M.	1/ 2/41
Barson, S. (Lt. late E. Lan. R.)	1/ 2/41
Blunt, R. C. L. (Lt. late M.G. Corps)	1/ 2/41
Boon, L.	1/ 2/41
Brears, A. H.	1/ 2/41
Cope, J. S. H. (Lt. late M.G. Corps)	1/ 2/41
Cumberland, A.	1/ 2/41
Flitton, C. E.	1/ 2/41
Fuller, B. (2/Lt. late Leicester R.)	1/ 2/41
Gamble, H.	1/ 2/41
Garner, C. S.	1/ 2/41
Hallam, E. A.	1/ 2/41

Lieutenants - contd.

Hawksworth, T. W., M.M.	1/ 2/41
Mears, B. H.	1/ 2/41
Moorhouse, S.	1/ 2/41
Oliver, A. A.	1/ 2/41
Smith, W. H.	1/ 2/41
Yeates, W. S.	1/ 2/41
Corah, J. H. H.	1/ 2/41
Pattison, C. J.	1/ 2/41
Phipps, J.	1/ 7/41
Bowley, A. A. (2/Lt. late Leicester R.)	1/ 7/41
Fidler, J. P.	1/ 7/41
North, G. L.	1/ 7/41
Wootton, H. E. (Lt. late S. Lan. R.)	1/ 7/41
Turner, A. P.	1/ 7/41
	1/ 7/41

2nd Lieutenants

Choate, J. A.	1/ 2/41
Dickson, J.	1/ 2/41
Clarke, E.	1/ 7/41
Crofts, W. H.	1/ 7/41
Everett, R. H., M.M.	1/ 7/41
Hallam, G.	1/ 7/41
Jones, R. P. (2/Lt. late R.A.F.)	1/ 7/41
Main, B.	1/ 7/41
Pagan, J. H.	1/ 7/41
Parker, F. G.	1/ 7/41
Pennell, H. J.	1/ 7/41
Sears, W. H., M.M.	1/ 7/41
Swift, J. A.	1/ 7/41
Woolley, G. H.	1/ 7/41

Adjutant & Quarter-Master

Saynor, Capt. (actg. 1/5/41) A. E., Res. of Off.	1/ 5/41

Medical Officer

Gray, Maj. A. P., M.B. (Capt. late R.A.M.C.)	1/ 7/41

NORTH MIDLAND AREA - contd.

LEICESTERSHIRE ZONE - contd.

LOUGHBOROUGH GROUP - contd.

10th LEICESTERSHIRE (CHARNWOOD) BATTALION

Lt.-Colonel

Martin, C. H. (Capt. late T.A. Res.) 1/ 2/41

Majors

Toller, W. S. N., D.S.O., T.D. (Bt. Col. ret. T.A. Res.) (Hon. Col. Leicester.R.) 1/ 2/41
Ironside, W. J. 1/ 2/41
Leeson, J. R. (Capt. late Leicester R.) 1/ 2/41
Peshall, S. F., M.C. (Capt. late K.R.R.C.) 1/ 2/41
Spalding, E. H., T.D. (Maj. late Foresters) 1/ 2/41
Swain, H. A., M.C. (Lt. late Leicester Yeo.) 1/ 2/41

Captains

Chorlton, W. D. (Capt. late M.G. Corps) 1/ 2/41
Joels, W. A. (Lt. late E. Surrey R.) 1/ 2/41
Tatham, C. (Capt. late Leicester R.) 1/ 2/41
Winser, E. F., M.C. (Maj. late S. Stafford R.) 1/ 2/41
Wright, A. F. M. (Capt. late R.A.S.C.) 1/ 2/41

Lieutenants

Astle, A. T. 1/ 2/41
Bailey, F. F. (2/Lt. late Foresters) 1/ 2/41
Belton, J. A. 1/ 2/41
Fletcher, R. J. M. 1/ 2/41
Martin, J. B. (2/Lt. late Leicester R.) 1/ 2/41

Lieutenants - contd.

Orton, R. H. (2/Lt. late R.F.A.) 1/ 2/41
Panter, A. W. 1/ 2/41
Staniland, A. F. 1/ 2/41
Stanley, T. H. (Capt. late R.W.K.) 1/ 2/41
Thompson, C. F., M.C. (2/Lt. late N. Stafford R.) 1/ 2/41
Walton, W. H. 1/ 2/41
Dunn, R. 1/ 2/41
Hancock, W. S. 1/ 2/41

2nd Lieutenants

Alexander, G. F. L. 1/ 2/41
Booth, C. (Lt. late Leicester Yeo.) 1/ 2/41
Bates, E. A. 1/ 6/41
Small, A. J. 1/ 6/41
Smith, S. A. 1/ 6/41
Smith, W. A. (Lt. late R.A.F.) 1/ 6/41
Weldon, L. E. 1/ 6/41
Curry, C. N. 1/ 6/41
Godfrey, A. D. (Lt. late Leicester R.) 21/ 6/41
Palfreyman, A. J. 21/ 6/41
Staples, F., M.M. 1/ 8/41
Thornton, C. W. 1/ 8/41

Adjutant & Quarter-Master

Gray, Capt. (actg. 23/4/41) A. E., Gen. List Inf. 23/ 4/41

Medical Officer

Gray, Maj. J. S., M.B. 1/ 6/41

NORTH MIDLAND AREA - contd.

LEICESTERSHIRE ZONE - contd.

MARKET HARBOROUGH GROUP

7th LEICESTERSHIRE (MARKET HARBOROUGH) BATTALION

Lt.-Colonel

Turner, P (Lt. late R. Sussex R.)	1/ 2/41

Majors

Gillilan, E. G., D.S.O. (Maj. late C. G'ds.)	1/ 2/41
Branklin-Frisby, J.	1/ 2/41
Belgrave, H. D., D.S.O. (Col. ret. pay)(Res. of Off.)	1/ 2/41
Lea, C. F.	1/ 2/41
Lee, F. W. (Capt. late The King's R.)	1/ 2/41

Captains

Gandy, W. C.	1/ 2/41
Gibbs, G. M.	1/ 2/41
Hardwicke, J. T.	1/ 2/41
Readman, W. J. G. (Lt. late Somerset L.I.)	1/ 2/41
Gray, A. S.	1/ 8/41

Lieutenants

Attfield, W.	1/ 2/41
Baillie, A.	1/ 2/41
Bray, C. F.	1/ 2/41
Cornes, L. G.	1/ 2/41
Crawford, J. (2/Lt. late Leicester R.)	1/ 2/41
Crittall, [illegible]. N. (Capt. late Midd'x. R.)	1/ 2/41
Garner, S., D.C.M.	1/ 2/41
Gossage, R. W.	1/ 2/41
Harper, C. C. (Lt. late R. War. R.)	1/ 2/41
Inchley, T. A.	1/ 2/41
North, W. N. D.	1/ 2/41
Roberts, A. C.	1/ 2/41
Smith, W. C. L. (2/Lt. late London R.)	1/ 2/41
Stokes, W. E.	1/ 2/41
Tranter, G. (2/Lt. late R.T.C.)	1/ 2/41
Varney, L. B.	1/ 2/41
Woadden, R. W.	1/ 2/41

Lieutenants - contd.

Worth, T. C.	1/ 2/41
Hobbs, J. (Lt. late R. Scots.)	1/ 2/41
Simpson, W. H. (Capt. late M.G. Corps.)	1/ 2/41
Symington, N. H. (Lt. late Leicester R.)	1/ 2/41
Davies, P. V. (Capt. late Lan. Fus.)	1/ 2/41
Berry, J. T. W.	1/ 7/41
Homan, K. K.	1/ 8/41
Blake, E. J.	1/ 8/41

2nd Lieutenants

Campbell, W. G.	1/ 2/41
Newton, R. W. B.	1/ 2/41
Clarke, G. W.	1/ 2/41
Badcock, J. C.	1/ 2/41
Tucker, R. G.	1/ 2/41
Heycock, T. C. H.	1/ 2/41
Brooks, T. J.	1/ 2/41
Tate, A. L. (Maj. late Remount Serv.)	1/ 2/41
Clarke, L. L.	1/ 7/41
Hankinson, G., D.C.M.	1/ 7/41
Marlow, R.	1/ 7/41
Rowlands, J. C. (2/Lt. late Gloster R.)	1/ 7/41
Welton, E. W.	1/ 7/41
Beasley, W. H.	1/ 8/41
Charles, F. D. (Capt. late Ind. Army)	1/ 8/41
Goad, G. M.	1/ 8/41
Hamilton, B. C., D.C.M.	1/ 8/41.

Adjutant & Quarter-Master

Medical Officer

Scott, Maj. C. T.	1/ 6/41

NORTH MIDLAND AREA - contd.

LEICESTERSHIRE ZONE - contd.

MARKET HARBOROUGH GROUP - contd.

8th LEICESTERSHIRE (MARKET BOSWORTH) BATTALION

Lt.-Colonel

Griffiths, J. L., D.S.O., T.D. (Bt. Col. T.A. Res.) 1/ 2/41

Majors

Baxter, J. T. L., M.C. (Lt. late M.G. Corps) 1/ 2/41
Lumb, R. A., M.C. (Maj. late M.G. Corps) 1/ 2/41
Ryley, B. A. (Lt. late R.A.S.C.) 1/ 2/41
Harratt, J. H., M.C. (Lt. late Leicester R.) 1/ 2/41
Wand, A. E., M.C. (Capt. late Leicester R.) 1/ 2/41
Wright, T. K. (Lt.-Col. late R.E.) 18/ 6/41

Captains

Makin, E. St. J. 1/ 2/41
Hawley, A. E., M.C. (Lt. late Leicester R.) 1/ 2/41
Rutherford, H. (2/Lt. late Mon. R.) 1/ 2/41
Wileman, W. A. (Lt. late Leicester R.) 1/ 2/41
Davis, J. E. 1/ 2/41

Lieutenants

Harding, A. 1/ 2/41
Bromley, F. H., M.C. (Lt. late Leicester R.) 1/ 2/41
Cholerton, G. W. (2/Lt. late M.G. Corps) 1/ 2/41
Reeve, J. S. 1/ 2/41
Moore, G. H. M. 1/ 2/41
Smith, I. S. 1/ 2/41
Salmon, F. D. 1/ 2/41
Mayo, J. H. 1/ 2/41
Riley, A. E. 1/ 2/41
Jackson, W. P. 1/ 2/41
Measures, J. V. 1/ 2/41
Hunt, E. L., M.M. 1/ 2/41
Woodcock, A. S. 1/ 2/41
Wright, H. B. 1/ 2/41

Lieutenants - contd.

Harper, I. 1/ 2/41
Brundell, B. B. 1/ 2/41
Pegg, S. (Lt. late Foresters) 1/ 2/41
Harvey, L. W. 1/ 2/41
Livingston, C. D. 1/ 2/41
Cosham, A. E. (Lt. late Norfolk R.) 1/ 2/41
Osborne, S. C. 1/ 2/41
Webber, E. J. 1/ 8/41

2nd Lieutenants

Sleath, G. G. W., M.C. (2/Lt. late Gloster R.) 1/ 2/41
Huckerby, J. H. 1/ 2/41
Flude, M. W. 1/ 2/41
Maltby, S. J. (Lt. late R.F.A.) 1/ 2/41
Couch, J. R. 1/ 2/41
Jones, D. M. 1/ 2/41
Ball, A. E. 1/ 2/41
Spencer, H. 1/ 2/41
Argyle, J. S. (Lt. late Leicester R.) 1/ 2/41
Forman, J. 1/ 2/41
Tomlin, W. G. 1/ 2/41
Moore, F. W. 1/ 2/41
Warner, R. M. 1/ 2/41
Butterley, A. D. 1/ 6/41
Johnston, H. 1/ 6/41
Nethercot, G. 1/ 6/41
Bates, C. 1/ 8/41
Gilbert, C. T. 1/ 8/41
Peters, W. W. 1/ 8/41
Ridgway, B. 1/ 8/41
Tyack, S. A. 1/ 8/41

Adjutant & Quarter-Master

Medical Officer

Cook, Maj. J., M.B. (Maj. late R.A.M.C.) 1/ 8/41

NORTH MIDLAND AREA - contd.

LEICESTERSHIRE ZONE - contd.

INDEPENDENT BATTALIONS

11TH LEICESTERSHIRE (ASHBY-DE-LA-ZOUCH) BATTALION

Lt.-Colonel

Sowter, W. H. (Maj. late Leicester R.) 1/ 2/41

Majors

Statham, L. A. (Lt. late Leicester R.) 1/ 2/41
Woodcock, T. A. (Lt. late D.W.R.) 1/ 2/41
Sheilds, J. (Capt. late R.A.F.) 1/ 2/41
Surman, J. (Flight Lt. late R.A.F.) 1/ 2/41
Lowe, G. D. 1/ 2/41
Perry, S. E. (Lt. late M.G. Corps.) 1/ 2/41

Captains

Turner, J. S. (Lt. late R.F.A.) 1/ 2/41
Parsons, C. M. K. (2/Lt. late R.A.F.) 1/ 2/41
Wilson, M. J. 1/ 2/41
Lewis-Jones, D. E. (Lt. late M.G. Corps.) 1/ 2/41
Dalby, R. O. 1/ 2/41
Jones, J. L. 1/ 8/41

Lieutenants

Harvey, C. R. 1/ 2/41
Dowthwaite, S. 1/ 2/41
Tagg, L. 1/ 2/41
Foulstone, S. H. 1/ 2/41
Lane, C. V. 1/ 2/41
Wootton, T. 1/ 2/41
Veasey, F. H. 1/ 2/41
Roberts, G. C. 1/ 2/41
White, A. W. 1/ 2/41
Platts, C. 1/ 2/41
Ford, J. E. 1/ 2/41
Walker, G. A. 1/ 2/41
Hodges, F. 1/ 2/41
Leddra, H. R. 1/ 2/41
Ketchley, H. 1/ 2/41
Dronfield, H. 1/ 2/41
Lunge, G. H. 1/ 2/41
Freckelton, S. T. 1/ 2/41

Lieutenants - contd.

Bruce, W. (Lt. late R.E.) 1/ 2/41
Booth, C. W., M.M. 1/ 2/41
Woods, P. R. 1/ 2/41
Wortley, T. H. 1/ 2/41
Perkins, W. C. 1/ 2/41
Glithero, J. 1/ 2/41
Hughes, E. A. 1/ 2/41
Sutton, J. A. H. 1/ 2/41
Eckersley, G. 1/ 8/41
Kay, S. 1/ 8/41
Beadsmoore, W. 1/ 8/41

2nd Lieutenants

Brown, F. A., M.M. 1/ 2/41
Devereux, P. G. 1/ 2/41
Samson, A. A. 1/ 2/41
Goodwin, R. G. 1/ 2/41
Rowley, G. E. 1/ 2/41
Danvers, G. H. 1/ 2/41
Riley, G. P. 1/ 2/41
Luther, R. 1/ 2/41
Moyens, G. W. 1/ 2/41
Atkins, A. G. 1/ 2/41
Johnson, B. H. 1/ 2/41
Jackson, W. 1/ 2/41
Bollard, S. 1/ 2/41
Denholm, G., M.M. 1/ 2/41
Caunt, G. C. 1/ 2/41
Wileman, D. E. 1/ 2/41
Atkins, J. W. 1/ 2/41
Smith, W. 1/ 2/41
Blake, T. W. 1/ 2/41
Hill, W. 1/ 2/41
Alletson, W. H. 1/ 2/41
Botterill, R. G. 1/ 2/41
Farmer, S. W. 1/ 2/41
Armson, A. E. 1/ 2/41
Ward, J. W. 1/ 2/41
Smith, A. 1/ 2/41

Adjutant & Quarter-Master

Medical Officer

Prys-Jones, Maj. H. T. (Flight-Lt. late R.A.F.) 1/ 7/41

NORTH MIDLAND AREA - contd.

LEICESTERSHIRE ZONE - contd.

INDEPENDENT BATTALIONS - contd.

12th LEICESTERSHIRE (MOTOR RECONNAISSANCE) BATTALION

Lt.-Colonel

VC Symons, W. J. (Capt. late A.I.F.) 1/ 2/41

Majors

Russell, P. W. G. (Lt. late M.G. Corps.) 1/ 2/41
Horley, H. H. (Capt. late R.T.C.) 1/ 2/41

Captains

Bray, A. L. 1/ 2/41
Robertson, J. G. 1/ 2/41
Wale, F. 1/ 2/41
Taylor, R. 1/ 2/41

Lieutenants

Coltman, F. T. (Lt. late Camb. R.) 1/ 2/41
Bastock, S., M.M. (Lt. late W. York R.) 1/ 2/41
Whitehouse, B. H. 1/ 2/41
Crace, S. H. 1/ 2/41
O'Callaghan, T. J. 1/ 2/41
Wilson, J. W. 1/ 2/41
Bee, E. J. 1/ 2/41
Stimpson, P. T. 1/ 2/41
Pepper, C. W. 1/ 6/41

2nd Lieutenants

Howkins, H. P. 1/ 2/41
Warner, R. F. 1/ 2/41
Lofthouse, K. W. 1/ 2/41
Garner, T. L. 1/ 2/41
Wigley, E. B. B. 1/ 2/41
Thompson, J. L. 1/ 2/41
Osborne, R. W. 1/ 2/41
Eyre, F. G. 1/ 2/41
Oldham, W. A. 1/ 2/41

Adjutant & Quarter-Master

Medical Officer

Gill, Maj. G. B., T.D. (Maj. late R.A.M.C.) 10/ 5/41

13th LEICESTERSHIRE (POST OFFICE) BATTALION

Lt.-Colonel

Newcombe, W. H. 1/ 2/41

Majors

Blakey, C. 15/ 5/41
Whitehead, W. C. 14/ 7/41

Captains

Wells, A. H. 1/ 2/41
Brealey, E. C. 15/ 5/41
Trethewy, A. W. 20/ 5/41
Johnson, H. E. (Capt. (Qr.-Mr.) late Midd'x. R.) 14/ 7/41

Lieutenants

Noton, J. 1/ 2/41
Moore, J. A. 1/ 2/41
Roberts, W. V. 1/ 2/41
Clewer, R. W. H. 1/ 2/41
Robinson, F. S. P. 1/ 2/41
Hullott, F., M.M. 1/ 2/41
Butcher, O. E. 1/ 2/41
Hemington, H. 1/ 2/41
Penman, G. 1/ 2/41
Bull, A. J. 20/ 5/41
Jenkins, H. J. 20/ 5/41
Wilford, H. A. 14/ 7/41
Watson, W. A. (Lt. late R. Signals) 14/ 7/41
Surman, W. L. 14/ 7/41

2nd Lieutenants

Grimes, S. M. 1/ 2/41
Davis, A. W. 1/ 2/41
Glover, H. R. 1/ 2/41
Lane, W. J. 1/ 2/41
Perry, H. A. 1/ 2/41
Taborn, F. G. 1/ 2/41
Bass, J. T. 14/ 7/41

Adjutant & Quarter-Master

Geipel, Capt. L. H. H., T.A. Res. 5/ 8/41

Medical Officer

NORTH MIDLAND AREA - contd.

RUTLAND ZONE

Commander	Ogilvy-Dalgleish, Col. J. W., O.B.E. (Wing Cmdr. late R.A.F.	1/ 2/41
Assistant to Commander	Cartwright, Capt. H.	1/ 2/41
Territorial Army Association administering	The Leicestershire & Rutland T.A. & A.F. Association, The Magazine, Oxford St., Leicester.	

1st RUTLANDSHIRE BATTALION

Colonel

Ogilvy-Dalgleish, J. W., O.B.E. (Wing Cmdr. late R.A.F.)	1/ 2/41

Majors

Cahusac, C. F., D.S.O. (Lt.-Col. ret. Ind. Army)	1/ 2/41
Chaplin, V. (Lt. late R.H.G.)	1/ 2/41
Newton, C. N., M.C. (Capt. late Gren. G'ds.)	1/ 2/41
Saunders, V. T. (Capt. late R.A.)	1/ 2/41
Whaley, H. E. (Maj. late C. G'ds.)	1/ 2/41

Captains

Bolton, E. G.	1/ 2/41
Johnson, C. S. (Lt. late E. York R.)	1/ 2/41
Wilson, R. W. (Lt. late R.H.G.)	1/ 2/41

Lieutenants

Ball, C. (Lt. late 3rd H.)	1/ 2/41
Bell, J. C. (Lt. late R.A.F.)	1/ 2/41
Cook, W.	1/ 2/41

Lieutenants - contd.

Evans, D. J. J.	1/ 2/41
Hornsby, J. A., (Capt. ret.) pay)	1/ 2/41
Leatherbarrow, W. (Capt. late R.A.M.C.)	1/ 2/41
Lovell, H. T. (Lt. late Bedfs. & Herts. R.)	1/ 2/41
Palmer, E.	1/ 2/41
Turner, A., M.M. (Capt. K.A. Rif.)	1/ 2/41
Varty, R. B. (Lt. late Loyal R.)	1/ 2/41
Wakefield, W. A. W.	1/ 2/41
Wakefield, W. G., M.C. (Lt. late Leicester Yeo.)	1/ 2/41
Watson, S. S.	1/ 2/41
Trump, R. W., M.C. (Lt. late R.E.)	14/ 5/41
Patrick, H. I. (2/Lt. late London R.)	10/ 7/41

Adjutant & Quarter-Master

Abell, Capt. (actg. 9/5/41) J. G., Gen. List Inf.	9/ 5/41

Medical Officer

Wallace, Maj. F. H. (Capt. late R.A.F.)	10/ 4/41

LINCOLNSHIRE DIVISION

General Staff Officer, 1st Grade	Sutton-Nelthorpe, Col. O., D.S.O., M.C., T.A. (Lt.-Col. Res. of Off.) t.a. 24/ 2/41

LINDSEY ZONE

Commander	Winteringham, Col. J. W., M.C. (Maj. late T.A.)	1/ 2/41
Assistant to Commander	Blakeborough, Maj. G. W. A. (Lt. late R.A.)	1/ 2/41
Territorial Army Association adminstering	The Lincolnshire T.A. & A.F. Association, The Old Barracks, Burton Rd., Lincoln.	

SCUNTHORPE GROUP

Commander	Eccles, Col. J. G. T. (Lt. late Ind. Army)	1/ 2/41
Assistant to Commander	Edwards, Capt. C. E.	1/ 2/41

1st LINDSEY (SCUNTHORPE & DISTRICT) BATTALION

Lt.-Colonel

Hunting, N. R., M.C. (Capt. late Serv. Bn. North'n. R.)	1/ 2/41

Majors

Wrigley, B. F. (2/Lt. late Wilts. R.)	1/ 2/41
Bell, W.	1/ 2/41
Gibson, N. (Capt. late Lincoln R.)	1/ 2/41

Captains

Slawson, A. C. (2/Lt. late D.W.R.)	1/ 2/41
Kirman, H. (2/Lt. late Lincoln R.)	1/ 2/41

Lieutenants

Rees, J. D.	1/ 2/41
Taylor, R.	1/ 2/41
Jones, A. A. (Lt. late R.E.)	1/ 2/41
Bowen-Colthurst, C. P. R.	1/ 2/41
Sheffield, J. V.	1/ 2/41
Hudson, W. A.	1/ 2/41
Bawden, W. T. C.	1/ 2/41
Smith, N.	1/ 2/41
Hanley, P.	1/ 2/41
Pinder, T.	1/ 2/41
Hippisley, R.	1/ 2/41
Proctor, W. S.	1/ 2/41
Driffill, R.	1/ 2/41
Roberts, J. W.	1/ 2/41
Pool, J. R.	1/ 2/41

56455-6 (187)

Lieutenants - contd.

Cowie, B.	1/ 2/41
Shaw, G. E.	1/ 2/41

2nd Lieutenants

Shearsmith, A. E.	1/ 2/41
Barnes, W. H.	1/ 2/41
Drinkall, A., M.M.	1/ 2/41
Mellor, G. J. B.	1/ 2/41
Clegg, A. W.	1/ 2/41
Blyth, H.	1/ 2/41
Howram, J. H.	1/ 2/41
White, H.	1/ 2/41
Stanley, H.	1/ 2/41
Fowler, W. E.	1/ 2/41
Mole, P. A.	1/ 2/41
Brayshaw, H. W.	1/ 2/41
Brown, W. W.	1/ 2/41
Richardson, W. J.	1/ 2/41
Dodd, J.	1/ 2/41
Bolton, F. D.	1/ 2/41
Fawcett, G. (Lt. late W. York. R.)	14/ 7/41

Adjutant & Quarter-Master

Medical Officer

Paterson, Maj. G. W. M., M.B., F.R.C.S. (Lt. late R.Scots.)	1/ 2/41

LINCOLNSHIRE DIVISION - contd.

LINDSEY ZONE - contd.

SCUNTHORPE GROUP - contd.

2nd LINDSEY (SCUNTHORPE WORKS) BATTALION

Lt.-Colonel

Hett, E. J. R. (Capt. late T.A.)	1/ 2/41

Majors

Hall, W. P. (Lt. late Lincoln R.)	1/ 2/41
Percival, A. V. (Capt. late M.G. Corps)	1/ 2/41
Branston, W. P. (2/Lt. late Leicester R.)	1/ 2/41
Wragg, F.	1/ 2/41

Captains

Walshaw, J. H. (2/Lt. late R.A.)	1/ 2/41
Goodland, E.A. (Lt. R. Signals T.A.)	1/ 2/41
Dring, C. F. (Capt. late Lincoln R.)	1/ 2/41

Lieutenants

Scott, M.	1/ 2/41
Osgerby, R. A. (2/Lt. late Lincoln R.)	1/ 2/41
Mart, G. E.	1/ 2/41
Nisbet, J. N.	1/ 2/41
Smith, W. E.	1/ 2/41
Elliot, G. D.	1/ 2/41
Chapman, H. S. (2/Lt. late R.A.F.)	1/ 2/41
Bond, J. A.	1/ 2/41
Stephenson, H. P. (2/Lt. late R.T.C.)	1/ 2/41
Rudkin, J.	1/ 2/41
Norris, A. H.	1/ 2/41
Bates, J.	1/ 2/41
Riddle, T. W.	1/ 2/41
Brooke, W. J.	1/ 2/41
Eland, W.	1/ 2/41
Halahan, G. E. D.	1/ 2/41
Tow, F. W., M.M.	1/ 2/41
Mills, B. R.	1/ 2/41
Mann, A. A.	1/ 2/41

2nd Lieutenants

Bowskill, H. F.	1/ 2/41
Moore, G.	1/ 2/41
Wilson, J., D.C.M.	1/ 2/41
Crooke, W. G.	1/ 2/41
Griffin, H.	1/ 2/41
Towndrow, R. P.	1/ 2/41
Shaw, A. E.	1/ 2/41
Windsor, G. E.	1/ 2/41
Martin, J. H.	1/ 2/41
Radford, W. H.	1/ 2/41
Eley, R. H.	1/ 2/41
Fielding, A. L.	1/ 2/41
Mason, C. A.	1/ 2/41
Hunt, J. H.	1/ 2/41
Johnson, G. W.	1/ 2/41
Davis, W. H.	1/ 2/41

Adjutant & Quarter-Master

Medical Officer

Stanford, Maj. R. A. J.	1/ 2/41

3rd LINDSEY (EPWORTH) BATTALION

Lt.-Colonel

Reynolds, C. L. (Capt. late T.A.)	1/ 2/41

Majors

Marrison, A. W.	1/ 2/41

Captains

Cranidge, A. W.	1/ 2/41
Taylor, P. D.	1/ 2/41
Newborn, G. W. (Lt. T.A. Res.)	20/ 5/41

Lieutenants

Dixon, F. T.	1/ 2/41
Bellamy, J. H.	1/ 2/41
Tarbet, W. S. (2/Lt. late R.F.A.)	1/ 2/41
Syvret, C. R.	1/ 2/41
Robinson, F., D.C.M.	1/ 2/41
Lockwood, T. J.	1/ 2/41
Grice, R. K.	1/ 2/41
Balding, T. C.	1/ 2/41
Maw, H.	1/ 2/41
Wall, H.	1/ 2/41
Calvert, J. B.	1/ 2/41
Cooper, J. J.	1/ 6/41

2nd Lieutenants

Lithgow, H.	1/ 2/41
Cousin, F.	1/ 2/41
Dimbleby, D.	1/ 2/41
Fawcett, H.	1/ 2/41
Stones, C. W.	1/ 2/41
Troop, T.	1/ 2/41
Tarbet, C. H.	21/ 7/41

Adjutant & Quarter-Master

Medical Officer

Strachan, Maj. H. S., M.B.	1/ 2/41

LINCOLNSHIRE DIVISION - contd.

LINDSEY ZONE - contd.

GRIMSBY GROUP

Commander

5th LINDSEY (GRIMSBY TOWN) BATTALION

Lt.-Colonel

Hinton, J. H. (Lt.-Col. late T.A.) 1/ 2/41

Majors

Gower, W. F., M.C. (Maj. T.A. Res.) 1/ 2/41
Falconer, H., M.C. (Capt. late Manch. R.) 1/ 2/41
Surfleet, C. L. (Capt. late Lincoln R.) 1/ 2/41

Captains

Mason, P. R., M.C. (Capt. late R.F.A.) 1/ 2/41
Bloomfield, W. H. 1/ 2/41
Watson, H. (Lt. late W. York. R.) 1/ 2/41

Lieutenants

Smith, G. R. 1/ 2/41
Bantock, H. J. 1/ 2/41
Porter, C. J. 1/ 2/41
Haylett, R. S. 1/ 2/41
Cullen, H. F. 1/ 2/41
Gage, F. G. 1/ 2/41
Mastin, H. 1/ 2/41
David, R. F., M.C. (Maj. late R.F.A.) 5/ 5/41

2nd Lieutenants

Farrow, J. 1/ 2/41
Anderson, H. S. 1/ 2/41
Spendelow, C. W. 1/ 2/41
Debnam, J. H. 1/ 2/41
Heald, L. 1/ 2/41
Frayne, G. H. 1/ 2/41
Wressell, E. 1/ 2/41
Fox, J. L. 1/ 2/41
Marfleet, R. W. 1/ 2/41
Peckett, K. A. 1/ 2/41
Green, R. E. 12/ 5/41
Stather, F. E. H. 11/ 6/41

Adjutant & Quarter-Master

Medical Officer

Fawssett, Maj. F. W. (Capt. late R.A.M.C.) 1/ 5/41

6th LINDSEY (CLEETHORPES TOWN) BATTALION

Lt.-Colonel

Thomas, S. F., D.S.O. (Lt.-Col. late K.S.L.I.) 1/ 2/41

Majors

Will, J. V. (Lt. late R.F.C.) 1/ 2/41
Brown, T. S. (Capt. late R.G.A.) 1/ 2/41

Captains

Osborne, A. (2/Lt. late Lan. Fus.) 1/ 2/41
Hirst, R. T. (Lt. late R.G.A.) 1/ 2/41
Cullum, M. (2/Lt. late R.E.) 1/ 2/41

Lieutenants

Beel, C. W. 1/ 2/41
Robson, J. H. 1/ 2/41
Cox, J. W. P. 1/ 2/41
Stokle, R. (2/Lt. late R.T.C.) 1/ 2/41
Scoffin, V. E. 1/ 2/41
Towle, R. B. 1/ 2/41

2nd Lieutenant

Hall, G., M.M. 16/ 7/41

Adjutant & Quarter-Master

Medical Officer

Smith, Maj. N. J. W. 4/ 7/41

LINCOLNSHIRE DIVISION - contd.

LINDSEY ZONE - contd.

GRIMSBY GROUP - contd.

7th LINDSEY (GRIMSBY RURAL) BATTALION

Lt.-Colonel

Mountain, H., T.D. (Lt. Col. T.A.) 1/ 2/41

Majors

Bloomer, H. S., M.C. (Maj. late Manch. R.) 1/ 2/41
Spilman, H., M.C. (Capt. late R.F.A.) 1/ 2/41
Marshall, D. O. (Capt. late R.A.) 1/ 2/41
Taylor, C. (Capt. late R.G.A.) 1/ 2/41
Butt, W. W. W. 1/ 2/41
Brears, C. (Flying Offr. late R.A.F.) 28/ 5/41

Captains

Harrison, T. J. 1/ 2/41
Taylor, L. R. (Lt. late Lincoln R.) 1/ 2/41
Cartwright, F. H. 1/ 2/41
Burt, D. N. 1/ 2/41

Lieutenants

Barraclough, E. (Lt. late R.T.C.) 1/ 2/41
Vickers, C. 1/ 2/41
Barker, J. (Lt. late R.A.F.) 1/ 2/41
White, A. E. 1/ 2/41
Lyons, P. S. 1/ 2/41
Chapman, H. 1/ 2/41
Adlard, H., D.C.M., M.M. 1/ 2/41
Casswell, J. S. 1/ 2/41
Fenner, A. R. (2/Lt. late Rif. Bde.) 1/ 2/41
Borrill, E. G. 1/ 2/41
Rashbrook, G. 1/ 2/41
Stark, P. E. 1/ 2/41
Lee, A. L. 1/ 2/41
Bramley, W. B. 1/ 2/41
Harrington, L. F. (Late R.A.F.) 1/ 2/41

2nd Lieutenants

Bannister, A. (Lt. late Lincoln R.) 1/ 2/41
Taylor, T. 1/ 2/41
Morgan-Smith, G. O. 1/ 2/41
Robinson, H. F. (Lt. late Lincoln R.) 1/ 2/41

Adjutant & Quarter-Master

Medical Officer

Chidlow, Maj. W. J. B., M.B., F.R.C.S. 1/ 2/41

8th LINDSEY (CAISTER) BATTALION

Lt.-Colonel

Lucas, J. de B. T. (Maj. ret. T.A.) 1/ 2/41

Majors

Gash, B. (Lt. late Border R.) 1/ 2/41
Meakin, H. M., M.C. (Capt. late Ind. Army) 1/ 2/41
Broughton, E. B. (Capt. late R.A.F.) 1/ 2/41
Bradford, R. F. (Lt. late Devon R.) 1/ 2/41
Weston, E. H. 1/ 2/41

Captains

Jackson, A. J. (Capt late Lincoln R.) 1/ 2/41
Wilkinson, W. B. 1/ 2/41
Waddington, G. E. (late R.T.C.) 18/ 6/41
Heneage, A. P., D.S. (Lt.-Col. ret. pay) 24/ 6/41

Lieutenants

Workman, C. F. M., C.B.E. 1/ 2/41
Bayles, W. 1/ 2/41
Simpson, C. 1/ 2/41
Wressell, J. E. 1/ 2/41
Franks, P. C. 1/ 2/41
Beckerleg, V. C., M.C. (2/Lt. late D.C.L.I.) 1/ 2/41
Greenfield, S. H. 1/ 2/41
Shegog, F. W. 1/ 2/41
Clayton, J. (Lt. late Manch. R.) 1/ 2/41
Copping, C. 1/ 2/41
Loveday, H. W. 1/ 2/41
Greenwood, W. E. 1/ 2/41
Neale, V. 1/ 2/41
Parker, D. S. 1/ 2/41
Spink, B. E. 1/ 2/41

2nd Lieutenants

Smith, W. A. 1/ 2/41
Wynn, P. 1/ 2/41
Barron, P. W. 1/ 2/41
Dunnill, S. B. 1/ 2/41
Chambers, C. H. 1/ 2/41
Milligan-Manby, R. A. S. 1/ 2/41
Carter, A. P. 24/ 6/41

Adjutant & Quarter-Master

Medical Officer

LINCOLNSHIRE DIVISION - contd.

LINDSEY ZONE - contd.

LOUTH GROUP

Commander

9th LINDSEY (LOUTH) BATTALION

Lt.-Colonel

Hall, A. K. D. (Maj. ret. pay) 1/ 2/41

Majors

Hotchkin, S. V., M.C., T.D., (Maj. late T.A. Res.) (Hon. Col. R.A.) 1/ 2/41
Colley, W. W. J., M.C. (Maj. late Bedfs. & Herts. R.) 1/ 2/41
Boland S., M.B.E. (Capt. ret. pay) 1/ 2/41
Walker, L. W. 1/ 2/41
McCulloch, L. F. (Capt. late Foresters) 1/ 2/41
Dixon, O. (Capt. late Lincoln R.) 1/ 2/41
Payne, J. R. (Capt. late R.A.) 1/ 2/41

Captains

Slade, M. G. 1/ 2/41
Morrison, B. C. (Lt. late R.A.S.C.) 1/ 2/41
Dove, A. B. 1/ 2/41
Macphail, D. C. 1/ 2/41
Boswell, F. K. 1/ 2/41
Helmer, R. H., M.C. (Capt. late R. Signals) 1/ 2/41

Lieutenants

Jacklin, W. (2/Lt. late Lan. Fus.) 1/ 2/41
Merrikin, J. G. 1/ 2/41
Sandys, A. F. 1/ 2/41
Charlton, G. H. 1/ 2/41
Taylor, C. H. 1/ 2/41
Nicholl, E. McK., O.B.E. (Maj. late R.A.V.C.) 1/ 2/41
Forman, A. W. 1/ 2/41
Read, F. E. 1/ 2/41
Grant, J. I. 1/ 2/41
Ward, R. H. 1/ 2/41
Price, F. 1/ 2/41
Robinson, A. K. (Lt. late R.E.) 1/ 2/41
Swift, W. R. 1/ 2/41

Lieutenants - contd.

Turner, F. F. 1/ 2/41
Hall, B. C., T.D. (Capt. late Lincoln R.) 1/ 2/41
Butt, A. W. (Lt. late R.G.A.) 1/ 2/41
Odlin, J. E., D.C.M. 1/ 2/41
Dixon, H. 1/ 2/41
Francis, R. W. 1/ 2/41
Wilson, H. 1/ 2/41
Lambert, L. 1/ 2/41
Musgrave, G. P. 10/ 5/41
Cowling, R. (Lt. late Manch. R.) 19/ 7/41

2nd Lieutenants

Musson, F. 1/ 2/41
Pacey, A. J. 1/ 2/41
Marfleet, C. B. 1/ 2/41
Appleby, R. W. 1/ 2/41
Hall, J. 1/ 2/41
Vamplew, H. 1/ 2/41
Tweed, H. R. (Capt. Lincoln R.) 1/ 2/41
Drakes, J. B. (Lt. late Warwick Yeo.) 1/ 2/41
Keep, A. H. (Lt. late M.G. Corps.) 1/ 2/41
Bullwinkle, H. J. 1/ 2/41
Adams, S. C. 1/ 2/41
Enderby, L. A. 1/ 2/41
Mumby, A. W. 1/ 2/41
Kenyon, J. L. H. 1/ 2/41
Goulsbra, W. T., M.M. 1/ 2/41
Shepherd, F. W. N. 1/ 2/41
White, A. W. 1/ 2/41
Dobbs, G. 1/ 2/41
Jackson, J. W. 1/ 2/41
Mawer, R. R. 1/ 2/41
Wood, J. H. 1/ 2/41
Davey, F. H. 1/ 2/41
Clarke, J. R. 20/ 5/41

Adjutant & Quarter-Master

Hoare, Capt. E. J., M.C., ret. pay 21/ 5/41

Medical Officer

LINCOLNSHIRE DIVISION - contd.

LINDSEY ZONE - contd.

LOUTH GROUP - contd.

10th LINSDEY (SKEGNESS) BATTALION

Lt.-Colonel

Jay, C. E. (Capt. late Ind. Army)	1/ 2/41

Majors

Searby, H. R. ([illegible] late Oxf. & Bucks. L.I.)	1/ 2/41
Straw, P. W., M.C. (Capt. late Seaforth)	1/ 2/41
Matthews, R. R. H.	1/ 2/41
Ward, T. J. (Lt. late Lincoln R.)	1/ 2/41

Captains

Swaby, G. F. (Lt. late D.W.R.)	1/ 2/41
Wallis, E. S., M.M.	28/ 6/41

Lieutenants

Draper, J. E.	1/ 2/41
Palethorpe, H. N. (Lt. late Herts. Yeo.)	1/ 2/41
Nesbitt, A. W. (Lt. late Durham L.I.)	1/ 2/41
Balderston, T. H., M.M.	1/ 2/41
Smith, G. F., (Lt. late Remount Serv.)	1/ 2/41
Overton, C. S. R.	1/ 2/41
Chapman, T., D.C.M. (2/Lt. late Lincoln R.)	1/ 2/41
Owen, H. L. H., A.F.C. (Maj. late R.A.F.)	1/ 2/41
Cantwell, F. S. (Lt. late R.F.A.)	1/ 2/41
Church, E. A.	1/ 2/41
Coppin, A., M.M. (2/Lt. late Lincoln R.)	1/ 2/41
West, B. T.	1/ 2/41
Gale, H. A.	1/ 2/41
Bucknall, F.	1/ 2/41
Manning, J. G.	1/ 2/41
Burnett, H.	1/ 2/41

Lieutenants - contd.

Burton, G. A. J.	1/ 2/41
Major, W. H., (Lt. late R. Norfolk R.)	1/ 2/41
Smith, A. H.	1/ 2/41
Brewer, H. (2/Lt. late Lincoln R.)	1/ 2/41
Close, R. M. (Lt. late The King's R.)	1/ 2/41
Taylor, J., M.M.	1/ 2/41
Richings, M. W.	1/ 2/41
South, G. T.	1/ 2/41
Twelvetrees, S. H.	1/ 2/41
Belton, H.	8/ 7/41
Carter, T. S., D.C.M.	8/ 7/41

2nd Lieutenants

Hudson, R. S.	1/ 2/41
Riggall, B. W.	1/ 2/41
Parkinson, G. H., D.C.M.	1/ 2/41
Dolan, W. R.	1/ 2/41
Birkitt, F. W.	1/ 2/41
Shaw, J. D. F.	1/ 2/41
Heane, G. F. H.	8/ 7/41
Hoyles, S. G.	8/ 7/41
Mountain, C.	8/ 7/41
Tuplin, W. R. H.	8/ 7/41
Mawer, H. H. (Lt. late R.F.C.)	11/ 7/41

Adjutant & Quarter-Master

Medical Officer

LINCOLNSHIRE DIVISION – contd.

LINDSEY ZONE – contd.

BRIGG GROUP

Commander	Wilson, Col. H. G., D.S.O., T.D. (Col. ret. T.A.)	1/ 2/41

4th LINDSEY (BRIGG) BATTALION

Lt.-Colonel

Haynes, A. R. (Lt. late R.E.)	1/ 2/41

Majors

Keay, W. G. (Capt. late A. Cyclist Corps.)	1/ 2/41
Stevenson, J. C.	1/ 2/41

Captains

Spring, R. M.	1/ 2/41
Riggall, C. B., M.C., (Capt. late R.F.A.)	1/ 2/41

Lieutenants

Briggs, A. G.	1/ 2/41
Green, C. E.	1/ 2/41
Lammiman, C. S. (Lt. late R.A.F.)	1/ 2/41
Cowie, J. A., M.C. (Lt. late R.E.)	1/ 2/41
Temple, S., M.C. (2/Lt. late E. York R.)	1/ 2/41
Ford, H. C., M.C. (Capt. late R.W. Fus.)	1/ 2/41
Uppleby, P. (Lt. late Lincoln R.)	1/ 2/41
Maxby, A. (2/Lt. late Lincoln Yeo.)	1/ 2/41
Davey, J. H.	1/ 2/41
Smith, J. N.	1/ 2/41
Farrow, W. H.	1/ 2/41
Roberts, F. J.	1/ 2/41
Johnson, J. W.	1/ 2/41
Fisk, S.	5/ 4/41
Marshall, H. A.	5/ 4/41

2nd Lieutenants

Strange, C. H.	1/ 2/41
Cladingbowl, C., M.M. (Lt. late Manch. R.)	1/ 2/41
Wild, G.	1/ 2/41
Cabourne, G. W. (2/Lt. late Lincoln R.)	1/ 2/41
Archer, J.	1/ 2/41
Sawyer, W.	1/ 2/41
Brown, T. C.	1/ 2/41
Wheeler, E. G.	1/ 2/41
Spilman, G.	1/ 2/41
Leaning, J. W.	1/ 2/41
Gouldthorp, H., D.C.M.	1/ 2/41
Sinclair, A. L.	1/ 2/41
Dawson, E. W.	1/ 2/41
Tinley, G. (2/Lt. late R.A.)	1/ 2/41
Frank, C.	1/ 2/41
Ellis, R. H.	1/ 2/41
Denby, T. A.	1/ 2/41
Hutchinson, G. H.	1/ 2/41
Thompson, T.	1/ 2/41
Kirby, L.	1/ 2/41
Gray, G. W.	1/ 2/41
Darbyshire, D. H.	20/ 5/41

Adjutant & Quarter-Master

Medical Officer

Tippet, Maj. J. A., M.C. (Capt. late R.A.M.C.)	1/ 2/41

LINCOLNSHIRE DIVISION - contd.

LINDSEY ZONE - contd.

BRIGG GROUP - contd.

11th LINDSEY (GAINSBOROUGH) BATTALION

Lt.-Colonel

Jarvis, C. F. C. O.B.E., (Maj. late Lincoln R.) 1/ 2/41

Majors

Henson, H. D., T.D. (Maj. late Lincoln R.) 1/ 2/41
Jones, A. W. (Lt. late R.F.A.) 1/ 2/41
Barham, J. A. 1/ 2/41
Wilson, C. (Maj. late Notts. Yeo.) 1/ 2/41

Captains

Wright, H. W. (Lt. late Lincoln R.) 1/ 2/41
Playford, G. E. (Flight late R.A.F.) 1/ 2/41
Clark, F. H. (Lt. late Foresters) 1/ 2/41
Pinder, C. 21/ 5/41

Lieutenants

Bayes, J. A. 1/ 2/41
Atkins, H. H. 1/ 2/41
Harper, J. T. 1/ 2/41
Lawson, G. W. 1/ 2/41
Stennett, F. G. M. (2/Lt. late R.F.C.) 1/ 2/41
Gibbons, A. T., D.C.M. 1/ 2/41
Keightley, C. H. (2/Lt. late R.G.A.) 1/ 2/41
Brett, A. 1/ 2/41
Lilley, W. 1/ 2/41
Taylor, A. L. (Lt. late R.E.) 1/ 2/41
Smith, J. H. 1/ 2/41
Ingall, H. 1/ 2/41
Arnold, H. J. F. (Late Chaplain to the Forces 4th Class) 1/ 2/41
Hackman, H. E. C. 17/ 5/41
Fieldsend, R. 26/ 5/41
Lockwood, F. W. 9/ 6/41

Lieutenants - contd.

Cartlidge, F. T. 11/ 6/41
Jenkinson, W. 20/ 6/41

2nd Lieutenants

Powell, H. G. 1/ 2/41
Wright, H. 1/ 2/41
Lane, H. J. 1/ 2/41
Plant, A. D. 1/ 2/41
Eyres, J. 1/ 2/41
Curtis, W. M. (Lt. late Lincoln R.) 1/ 2/41
Frost, C. W. (Lt. late Manch. R.) 1/ 2/41
Gray, F. G. 1/ 2/41
Hyslop, H. 1/ 2/41
Emerson, J. P. 1/ 2/41
Sweet, J. M. 1/ 2/41
Bowling, T. C. (Lt. late R.A.S.C.) 1/ 2/41
Stevenson, C. 1/ 2/41
Burgess, E. 1/ 2/41
Levack, K. J. 1/ 2/41
Knott, W. B. C. 1/ 2/41
Thornton, R., M.M. 1/ 2/41
Lewis, G. 1/ 2/41
Hawley, H. R. 20/ 6/41

Adjutant & Quarter-Master

Medical Officer

Wray, Maj. S. 15/ 7/41

LINCOLNSHIRE DIVISION - contd.

HOLLAND ZONE

Commander	Luker, Col. R., C.M.G., M.C. (Col. ret pay)	1/ 2/41
Territorial Army Association administering	The Lincolnshire T.A. & A.F. Association, The Old Barracks, Burton Rd., Lincoln.	

1st HOLLAND (BOSTON) BATTALION

Lt.-Colonel

Giles, O. B. (Capt. late T.A.)	1/ 2/41

Majors

Bettison, H. (Lt. late E. York R.)	1/ 2/41
Rysdale, A. C. (Capt. late R.G.A.)	1/ 2/41
Cheer, W. (Capt. late Lincoln R.)	1/ 2/41
Greenfield, A. (Capt. late R.F.A.)	1/ 2/41
Valentine, J. G., D.C.M. (Lt. late Fife & Forfar Yeo.)	7/ 7/41

Captains

Russell, E.	1/ 2/41
Porcher, E. H. (Capt. late R.A.S.C.)	1/ 2/41
Chandler, T. H. (Lt. late Wilts. R.)	1/ 2/41
Kerrick, E.	1/ 2/41
Saville, S. O. (Lt. late R.A.F.)	1/ 2/41
Dodsworth, H. M.	23/ 7/41

Lieutenants

Casswell, L. S.	1/ 2/41
Clark, G. V.	1/ 2/41
Spinks, W. P.	1/ 2/41
Barber, W.	1/ 2/41
Barnes, G. S.	1/ 2/41
Randall, A. A.	1/ 2/41
Holland, R. C.	1/ 2/41
Mobbs, H. A.	1/ 2/41
Towell, J. L.	1/ 2/41
Clarke, R.	1/ 2/41
Dennis, P. K.	1/ 2/41
Pocklington, Richard	1/ 2/41
Munks, A.	1/ 2/41

Lieutenants - contd.

Pocklington, Ralph	1/ 2/41
Forman, S. M.	1/ 2/41
Lee, T. K.	1/ 2/41
Oliver, A.	1/ 2/41
Callaghan, R. D.	1/ 2/41
Clark, L. I.	1/ 5/41
Bloom, M.	10/ 5/41

2nd Lieutenants

Smith, W. M.	1/ 2/41
Leafe, A.	1/ 2/41
Clark, C. W.	1/ 2/41
Clements, C.	1/ 2/41
Bird, H. J. R.	1/ 2/41
Ward, J., M.M.	1/ 2/41
Allatt, F.	1/ 2/41
Fleet, C. B.	1/ 2/41
Lauder, L. S.	1/ 2/41
Johnson, H.	1/ 2/41
Luesby, H.	1/ 2/41
Taylor, A. H.	1/ 2/41
Leggott, W.	1/ 2/41
Lealand, A.	29/ 5/41
West, H. (Lt. late R.A.F.)	29/ 5/41
Buchner, G. E. E.	26/ 6/41
Smith, O.	26/ 6/41
Wing, V. A.	26/ 6/41
Fawcett, R. H.	7/ 7/41
Borgonon, R. V.	23/ 7/41
Cooper, N. F.	23/ 7/41
Holmes, J. S.	23/ 7/41

Adjutant & Quarter-Master

Gething, Capt. F. F., T.A. Res.	21/ 7/41

Medical Officer

Darlow, Lt. J. E.	14/ 5/41

LINCOLNSHIRE DIVISION - contd.

HOLLAND ZONE - contd.

2nd HOLLAND (SPALDING) BATTALION

Lt.-Colonel

Cooke, R., M.C. (Lt. late T.A.) 1/ 2/41

Majors

Burrows, C. A. E. (Lt. late R.A.S.C.) 1/ 2/41
King, J. M. (Lt. late Lincoln R.) 1/ 2/41
Allen, G. T. 1/ 2/41
Casswell, T. R. (2/Lt. late M.G. Corps) 1/ 2/41
Wright, A. K. 1/ 2/41
Scotney, C. C. (2/Lt. late M.G. Corps) 1/ 2/41

Captains

Shinner, C. R., M.C. (Capt. late R.E.) 1/ 2/41
Mawby, T. L. (Lt. late Lincoln R.) 1/ 2/41
Gooch, E. H. (Capt. late Lincoln R.) 1/ 2/41
Seymour, E. H. (Lt. late Foresters) 1/ 2/41
Pick, T. A. 1/ 2/41

Lieutenants

Gonyou, H. H., D.F.C. (Capt. late R.A.F.) 1/ 2/41
Woodman, G. A. 1/ 2/41
Gostick, W. H. K. (Lt. late M.G. Corps) 1/ 2/41
Eastwood, G. 1/ 2/41
Blackburn, S. 1/ 2/41
Goodacre, A. E. 1/ 2/41
Ross, D. H. G. 1/ 2/41
Smith, C. E. 1/ 2/41
Kingston, G. S. (Capt. late Lincoln R.) 1/ 2/41

Lieutenants - contd.

Harty, M., M.M. (2/Lt. late Aust. Imp. Force) 1/ 2/41
Turner, C. F. 1/ 2/41
Guyton, E. 1/ 2/41
Hammond, W. G. 1/ 2/41
Blood, W. A. 1/ 2/41
Clark, R., D.C.M. M.M. 1/ 2/41
White, G. H. 1/ 2/41
Lane-Sansam, J. 1/ 2/41
Buck, J. 1/ 2/41
Heath, R. G. M. 1/ 2/41
Thompson, R. 1/ 2/41
Ground, W. J. 1/ 2/41
Garrett, E. O. 15/ 7/41

2nd Lieutenants

Woodcock, L. F. (Lt. late Labour Corps) 1/ 2/41
Hallifax, J. M. 1/ 2/41
Smith, S. H. B. 1/ 2/41
Wright, F. 1/ 2/41
Johnson, H. C. 1/ 2/41
Ward, A. R. 1/ 2/41
Myers, G. H. 1/ 2/41
Needs, E. W. 1/ 2/41
Bearcock, R. 1/ 2/41
Mulley, A. 1/ 2/41
Parkin, J. C. G. 1/ 2/41

Adjutant & Quarter-Master

Medical Officer

Martyn, Maj. F. de R. (Capt. late R.A.M.C.) 1/ 2/41

LINCOLNSHIRE DIVISION - contd.

HOLLAND ZONE - contd.

3rd HOLLAND (EAST ELLOE) BATTALION

Lt.-Colonel

Reeves, A. E. (Maj. late T.A. Res.)	1/ 2/41

Majors

Holte, L. S. (Maj. late R.E.)	1/ 2/41
Thompson, G. (2/Lt. late Gren. G'ds.)	1/ 2/41
Johnson, E. F.	1/ 2/41
Hailey, V. (Capt. late R.F.A.)	1/ 2/41
Hickman, E. H. (Capt. late Lincoln R.)	1/ 2/41

Captains

Coates, A. S. (Capt. late London R.)	1/ 2/41
Bullin, J. L.	1/ 2/41
Mawby, J. D.	1/ 2/41
Weston, R.	1/ 2/41

Lieutenants

Buttery, F. (Lt. late London R.)	1/ 2/41
Marlow, W. E.	1/ 2/41
Todd, W. B. (Lt. late Lincoln Yeo.)	1/ 2/41
Barnes, H. W.	1/ 2/41
Campbell, H., M.M.	1/ 2/41
Subley, F.	1/ 2/41
Crockatt, R. E.	1/ 2/41
Kinder, J. D.	1/ 2/41
Dicker, W. S.	1/ 2/41
Green, H. J.	1/ 2/41
Daniels, D. V.	1/ 2/41
Hesketh, C.	1/ 2/41
Worth, W. P.	1/ 2/41

Lieutenants - contd.

Ashton, J.	1/ 2/41
Proctor, R. E.	1/ 2/41
Barton, A. L.	1/ 2/41
Malt, A. E.	1/ 5/41

2nd Lieutenants

Hubbard, G. H.	1/ 2/41
Welcher, H. S.	1/ 2/41
Rose, F.	1/ 2/41
Housham, A.	1/ 2/41
Bacon, C. R.	1/ 2/41
Pratt, R.	1/ 2/41
Chennery, A. E.	1/ 2/41
Crouch, S.	1/ 2/41
Hay, A.	1/ 2/41
Clifton, A. A.	1/ 2/41
Cliff, A., M.M.	1/ 2/41
Tinsley, P. C.	1/ 2/41
Tubbs, A.	26/ 5/41

Adjutant & Quarter-Master

Medical Officer

Hunter, Capt. J. C. A., M.B.	20/ 5/41

LINCOLNSHIRE DIVISION – contd.

KESTEVEN ZONE

Commander	Brace, Col. H. F., D.S.O., M.C. (Col. ret. pay. Res. of Off.)	1/ 2/41
Assistants to Commander	Welby, Maj. H. R. E. E., C.M.G. (Capt. late African Forces)	1/ 2/41
	Huggins, Capt. W. J.	1/ 2/41
Territorial Army Association administering	The Lincolnshire T.A. & A.F. Association, The Old Barracks, Burton Rd., Lincoln.	

NORTH GROUP

Commander	Henderson, Col. Rt. Hon. Sir Neville M., G.C.M.G.	1/ 2/41

1st KESTEVEN (NORTH) BATTALION

Lt.-Colonel

Lambert, R. C. K., D.S.O. (Rear-Admiral ret.)	1/ 2/41

Majors

Milnes, H. R. (Maj. late Lincoln R.)	1/ 2/41
Battle, T. H. N., M.C. (Lt. late R.G.A.)	1/ 2/41
Barker, E. W. (Lt. late Lincoln R.)	1/ 2/41
Scorer, C. E. (Capt. late Lincoln R.)	1/ 2/41
Brown, F., D.C.M. (Lt. late R.E.)	1/ 2/41
Burtt, E. B.	1/ 2/41
Dodds, R. W.	1/ 2/41
Lewins, J.	1/ 2/41

Captains

Harris, C. V. (Lt. late Hampshire R.)	1/ 2/41
Robinson, H. J. B.	1/ 2/41
Pratt, C. (Lt. Res. of Off.)	25/ 7/41
Gilliat, C. B. S. (Lt. late R.A.F.)	25/ 7/41

Lieutenants

Laws, J., M.C. (Capt. late London R.)	1/ 2/41
Garfoot, A. A.	1/ 2/41

56455-6(198)

Lieutenants – contd.

Birkett, H., M.C. (Lt. late M.G. Corps)	1/ 2/41
Griffen, D. E.	1/ 2/41
Meanwell, F.	1/ 2/41
Stewart, W. L.	5/ 7/41

2nd Lieutenants

Patchett, T.	1/ 2/41
Smedley, B. R.	1/ 2/41
Brown, F. W.	1/ 2/41
Towl, E.	1/ 2/41
Cheer, A. B.	1/ 2/41
Hatliff, A. C.	1/ 2/41
Butler, T. W.	1/ 2/41
Bingham, R. F.	1/ 2/41
Smith, A.	1/ 2/41
Lunn, G. A.	1/ 2/41
Wilkinson, P. J.	1/ 2/41
Humberstone, T.	1/ 2/41

Adjutant & Quarter-Master

Medical Officer

Harrison, Maj. W. P. (Surgeon Lt. Cmdr. late R.N.V.R.)	25/ 6/41

LINCOLNSHIRE DIVISION - contd.

KESTEVEN ZONE - contd.

NORTH GROUP - contd.

2nd KESTEVEN (EAST) BATTALION

Lt.-Colonel

Aldercron, R. L., C.M.G., D.S.O. (Hon. Brig.-Gen. ret. pay) 1/ 2/41

Majors

Cox, W. C. C. (Lt. late Lincoln R.) 1/ 2/41
Fisher, J. T., D.S.O. (Lt.-Col. ret. pay) 1/ 2/41
Chambers, M. T., M.C. (Capt. late Lincoln R.) 1/ 2/41
Simpson, R. G. (Lt. late R.G.A.) 1/ 2/41
Davies, E. H. 1/ 2/41

Captains

Thornton, R. E. 1/ 2/41
Baines, F. W. (Lt. late R.F.A.) 1/ 2/41
Robson, F. (Capt. late North'd. Fus.) 1/ 2/41
Money, D. G. 1/ 2/41

Lieutenants

Jeudwine, J. G. (2/Lt. late R.A.) 1/ 2/41
Whitley, J. R. G. 1/ 2/41
Moore, G. A. 1/ 2/41
Ison, A. J. (Capt. late T.A.) 1/ 2/41
Dwane, P. H., M.C. 1/ 2/41
Tomlinson, B. 1/ 2/41
Parker, E. 1/ 2/41
Wright, J. N. 1/ 2/41

Lieutenants - contd.

Blyth, R. B. 1/ 2/41
Lucas, A. S. 1/ 2/41
Smith, A. 1/ 2/41
Neal, H. C. 1/ 2/41
Shelley, F. 1/ 2/41
Taylor, J. E. 1/ 2/41
Owen, W. H. 1/ 2/41
Baker, A. 1/ 2/41
Roberts, H. 1/ 2/41
Pearce, P. G. 1/ 2/41
Harcourt, C. J. 1/ 2/41
Callow, C. E. 1/ 2/41

2nd Lieutenants

Wright, T. 1/ 2/41
Farmer, J. C., D.C.M. (Lt. late Leicester R.) 1/ 2/41
Burtt, J. B. 1/ 2/41
Holmes, A. S. 1/ 2/41
Amos, F. C. 1/ 2/41
Gilbert, G. H. 1/ 2/41
Watson, J. 1/ 2/41
Pogson, F. L. S. 1/ 2/41

Adjutant & Quarter-Master

Medical Officer

LINCOLNSHIRE DIVISION - contd.

KESTEVEN ZONE - contd.

SOUTH GROUP

Commander	Grinling, Col. E. J., D.S.O., M.C., T.D. (Col. T.A.) 1/ 2/41

3rd KESTEVEN (GRANTHAM & SPITALGATE) BATTALION

Lt.-Colonel

Peacock, C. M. (Maj. late T.A. Res.)	1/ 2/41

Majors

Tatchell, E., D.S.O. (Lt.-Col. late Lincoln R.)	1/ 2/41
Raymond, M. H. (Bt. Maj. T.A. Gen. List)	1/ 2/41
Jaques, G. P. R. (Lt.-Col. late Ind. Army)	1/ 2/41
Thornton, C. S.	1/ 2/41
Widdowson, J. A. (Lt. late K.R.R.C.)	1/ 2/41
Salaman, G. H. (Maj. late R.A.F.)	1/ 2/41
Macdonell, A., O.B.E. (Maj. late E. Surrey R.)	1/ 2/41

Captains

Moye, B. J.	1/ 2/41
Skinner, F. W.	1/ 2/41
Oliver, E., M.C. (Capt. late M.G. Corps)	1/ 2/41
Edwards, E. J.	1/ 2/41
Tinn, J. S. (Lt. late R.A.F.)	1/ 2/41
Ashworth, F. R.	1/ 2/41

Lieutenants

Lee, S. (Capt. late Lincoln R.)	1/ 2/41
Gibson, W. (Capt. late T.A.)	1/ 2/41
Sutton, G. E. J. (2/Lt. late R.G.A.)	1/ 2/41
Hinckley, W. H.	1/ 2/41
Bromley, R. T.	1/ 2/41
Broadbent, J. G. M.	1/ 2/41
Swallow, F. H. W.	1/ 2/41
Stroud, B. E. B.	1/ 2/41
Lovell, S. E.	1/ 2/41
Marsh, N. F.	1/ 2/41
Clewes, G. W.	1/ 2/41
Pailing, G.	1/ 2/41

56455-6(200)

Lieutenants - contd.

Pilkington, S. P.	1/ 2/41
Purchase, W. S. E.	1/ 2/41
Galloway, J. A.	1/ 2/41
Kendall, J. K.	1/ 2/41
Todd, W. T.	1/ 2/41
Berry, J. L.	1/ 2/41
Tooke, G. D.	1/ 2/41
Wright, W. H.	9/ 5/41
Hempton, H. J.	19/ 5/41
Harfield, W. H.	9/ 7/41
Dixie, R. J. H.	26/ 7/41
Coffin, R.	6/ 8/41

2nd Lieutenants

Statham, C. W., M.C. (Lt. late M.G. Corps.)	1/ 2/41
Rowell, W.	1/ 2/41
Barrell, G. F.	1/ 2/41
Hardy, W. H.	1/ 2/41
Ogley, F. C.	1/ 2/41
Penn, O. S., M.M. (Capt. late R.T.C.)	1/ 2/41
Fisher, J. (Lt. late M.G. Corps)	1/ 2/41
Tyson, C. O.	1/ 2/41
Pretty, G. W.	1/ 2/41
Turner, T. W.	1/ 2/41
Young, J. E.	19/ 5/41
Pacey, R. A.	24/ 5/41
Field, S. L. F.	20/ 6/41
Dale, W. H.	28/ 6/41
Cameron, A. E. (2/Lt. late Foresters)	16/ 7/41
Lowe, C. G.	28/ 7/41

Adjutant & Quarter-Master

Medical Officer

Dodson, Maj. C. S. (Maj. late R.A.M.C.)	9/ 5/41

LINCOLNSHIRE DIVISION - contd.

KESTEVEN ZONE - contd.

SOUTH GROUP - contd.

4th KESTEVEN (BOURNE & STAMFORD) BATTALION

Lt.-Colonel

Stanton, H. M. A.
(Lt. late R.F.A.) 1/ 2/41

Majors

Lyall, T. R.
(Lt. late M.G. Corps) 1/ 2/41
Hoare, C. G., M.C.
(Lt. late R.H.G.) 1/ 2/41
Wade, F. R.
(Sub-Lt. late R.N.V.R.) 1/ 2/41

Captains

Wright, A. M. 1/ 2/41
Tinsley, S. L. 1/ 2/41
Tinsley, H. C. 1/ 2/41

Lieutenants

Palmer, F. J. 1/ 2/41
Whatton, C. D. 1/ 2/41
Courton, W. J. 1/ 2/41
Medwell, P. G. 1/ 2/41
Watts, R. P. 1/ 2/41
Castley, D. E. 1/ 2/41
Baldwin, T. C. 26/ 5/41
Rickard, C. E. 24/ 7/41

2nd Lieutenants

Andrews, W. E. 1/ 2/41
Wallis, G. W. 1/ 2/41
Smith, B. N. 1/ 2/41
North, F. 1/ 2/41
Fairchild, H. 1/ 2/41
Dorrington, J. B. 20/ 5/41

Adjutant & Quarter-Master

Medical Officer

5th KESTEVEN (SOUTH) BATTALION

Lt.-Colonel

Myers, W. R., T.D.
(Capt. ret. T.A.) 1/ 2/41

Majors

Holderness, H., D.S.O.
(Col. ret. Ind. Army) 1/ 2/41
Mann, R.
(Lt. late M.G. Corps) 1/ 2/41

Captains

Mann, G. R.
(Lt. late Lincoln R.) 1/ 2/41
Bates, C. F. 1/ 2/41
Appleby, S. E. 1/ 2/41
Lythell, H., O.B.E.
(Lt. late E. York R.) 23/ 6/41

Lieutenants

Smith, F. G. 1/ 2/41
Chessum, S. G. 1/ 2/41
Cooper, R. J.
(2/Lt. late Lincoln R.) 1/ 2/41
Forster, J. T. 1/ 2/41
Atkinson, J. E. 1/ 2/41
Sharman, R. 1/ 2/41
Kettle, E. C. 1/ 2/41
Walton, G. E., D.C.M. 1/ 2/41
Whotten, T. 27/ 6/41
Richards, J. N. P.
(Lt. late Lincoln R.) 29/ 7/41

2nd Lieutenants

Miller, H. L. 1/ 2/41
Rivett, M. 1/ 2/41
Turner, J. 1/ 2/41
Roberts, J., M.M. 1/ 2/41

Adjutant & Quarter-Master

Medical Officer

Morris, Maj. G. C. 23/ 6/41

LINCOLNSHIRE DIVISION - contd.

KESTEVEN ZONE - contd.

LINCOLN CITY GROUP

Commander — Phillips, Col. W. M. (Maj. late King's Own R.) 5/ 6/41

Assistant to Commander — Manderson, Maj. A. J. 14/ 7/41

1st CITY OF LINCOLN BATTALION

Lt.-Colonel

Hobbs, H. F., D.S.O., M.C. 5/ 6/41

Majors

North Coates, W., M.C. (Maj. late R.A.) 1/ 2/41
Smalley, G. E. (Capt. late Lincoln R.) 1/ 2/41
Rogers, J. A. (Lt. late Lincoln R.) 14/ 7/41
Walker, J. A. (Lt. late Lincoln R.) 14/ 7/41
Payne, D. G. 14/ 7/41
Newsum, H. N., M.C. 14/ 7/41

Captains

Turner, C. G., M.C. (Capt. late R.E.) 1/ 2/41
Sanderson, J. R. 1/ 2/41
Baggley, J., M.M. 1/ 2/41
Sansome, F., M.M. (Lt. late Gloster R.) 14/ 7/41
Chapman, V. G D. (Lt. late Middx. R.) 21/ 7/41

Lieutenants

Hill, A. R. 1/ 2/41
Wood, W G. 1/ 2/41
Metcalfe, L. W. (Lt. late W. York R.) 1/ 2/41
Hobson, J. E. (Lt. late D.W R.) 1/ 2/41
Smalley, H. 1/ 2/41
Meadows, W. A. (2/Lt. late R. War. R.) 1/ 2/41
Hall, F. 1/ 2/41
Letts, F. J. 1/ 2/41

Lieutenants - contd.

Otter, F. J. 1/ 2/41
Attale, W. M. E. (Lt. late M.G. Corps) 1/ 2/41
Milan, F. E. 1/ 2/41
Neeves, F. 1/ 2/41
Dobbs, W. 1/ 2/41
Webb, C. H. (Capt. late K.O.Y.L.I.) 14/ 7/41
Steel, H. H. (2/Lt. late K.O.S.B.) 14/ 7/41
Withers, V. J. 14/ 7/41

2nd Lieutenants

Bridge, H. 1/ 2/41
Steele, W. E. 1/ 2/41
Gibson, H. P. 1/ 2/41
Woodward, R. C. 1/ 2/41
Footit, A. E. 1/ 2/41
Spiers, J., M.C. (Lt. late North'd. Fus.) 1/ 2/41
Chambers, J. H. 1/ 2/41
Leigh, A., M.M. 1/ 2/41
Parsons, T. 1/ 2/41
Roberts, S. J. 1/ 2/41
Whitton, R., M.B.E. (Capt. late Foresters) 21/ 5/41
Moon, W. J. E. 16/ 7/41
Holmes, F. L. 17/ 7/41

Adjutant & Quarter-Master

Medical Officer

Vaughan, Maj. H. W. 2/ 7/41

LINCOLNSHIRE DIVISION - contd.

KESTEVEN ZONE - contd.

LINCOLN CITY GROUP - contd.

2nd CITY OF LINCOLN BATTALION

Lt.-Colonel

Riggall, H. (Maj. late T.A.) 1/ 2/41

Majors

Temple, W. H., M.C. (Lt. late S. Wales Bord.) 1/ 2/41
Hockney, R. 1/ 2/41
Grimshaw, J. E. (Lt. late E. Lan. R.) 1/ 2/41
Iles, G. H. 1/ 2/41
Bergne-Coupland, J. R. (Lt. late R.N.V.R.) 1/ 2/41

Captains

Clarke, F. 1/ 2/41
Barnes, J. F. 1/ 2/41
Walker, J. E. (Lt. late Lincoln Yeo.) 20/ 5/41

Lieutenants

Joyce, S. K. D. (Lt. late A.S.C.) 1/ 2/41
Gott, J. W. 1/ 2/41
Pacy, R. T. (Lt. late M.G. Corps.) 1/ 2/41
Schofield, R., M.M. 1/ 2/41
Howard, W. 1/ 2/41
Morris, G. A. 1/ 2/41
Martin, J. H. 1/ 2/41
Brammer, E. 1/ 2/41
Thomson, A. 1/ 2/41
Chapman, P. D. 1/ 2/41
Richardson, F. W. 1/ 2/41
Ivatt, J. F., M.M. 1/ 2/41
Ward, G. 1/ 2/41
Brown, F. J. 1/ 2/41

2nd Lieutenants

Copland, F. E. 1/ 2/41
Shepherd, R. C. 1/ 2/41
Fox, H. M. H. 1/ 2/41
Poore, G. 16/ 6/41
Swain, A. 17/ 6/41
Hogan, T. P. 26/ 7/41
Howley, T. 26/ 7/41
Underwood, C. B. 26/ 7/41

Adjutant & Quarter-Master

Medical Officer

Semple, Maj. W. V., M.B., F.R.C.S. 2/ 7/41

3rd CITY OF LINCOLN BATTALION

Lt.-Colonel

Whiteley, D. 1/ 2/41

Majors

Cook, G. H. (2/Lt. late M.G. Corps.) 1/ 2/41
Andrews, F. C. (Lt. late Foresters) 1/ 2/41
Curtis, A. C. (Lt. late N. Stafford R.) 1/ 2/41
Hunter, G. (Lt. late R.E.) 1/ 2/41
Heck, W. C. 1/ 2/41

Captains

Walker, J. C. 1/ 2/41
Taylor, T. F. 26/ 6/41

Lieutenants

Harrison, F. C. S. (Late T.A. Res.) 1/ 2/41
Cosyns, P. J. 1/ 2/41
Butters, G. 1/ 2/41
Timms, T. H. 1/ 2/41
Codling, F. 1/ 2/41
Balshaw, G. H. 1/ 2/41
Kennett, L. W. J. 1/ 2/41
Kirk, W. 1/ 2/41
Chiplen, L. R. 27/ 6/41
Leachman, F. 27/ 6/41

2nd Lieutenants

Knight, E. P. 1/ 2/41
Leachman, H. H. 1/ 2/41

Adjutant & Quarter-Master

Medical Officer

Summers, Maj. G. D. (Lt. late Norfolk R.) 2/ 7/41

DEATHS

INDEX

56455-6(212)

C

G

56455-6(226)

L

M

N

56455-6(254)

56455-6(257)

U

56455-6(259)

56455-6(263)

D 56455-6(266) 475 10/41 P R P

www.ingramcontent.com/pod-product-compliance
Ingram Content Group UK Ltd.
Pitfield, Milton Keynes, MK11 3LW, UK
UKHW021052270726
13967UKWH00012B/580